PURSUING CROWNS

A Study of First Samuel

by
CHRISTY VOELKEL

Copyright © 2023 by Christy Voelkel

Scripture taken from the New King James Version®. Copyright © 1982 by Thomas Nelson. Used by permission. All rights reserved. Unless otherwise noted, all Scripture cited in this study is from the NKJV.

Scriptures passages have been copied from the online Bible reference source, Blue Letter Bible (www.blueletterbible.org) using its copy feature.

Strong's Hebrew Lexicon definitions from Blue Letter Bible. Web. Septmber 2021.

Table of Contents

Introduction — 3

The Brides and Priests

    Lesson 1: Crown of Rubies, Crown of Grace — 23

    Lesson 2: Loss of the Crown of Glory — 35

    Lesson 3: The Exiled King — 65

    Lesson 4: The Rejected King — 81

The Kings: Saul and David — 101

    Lesson 5: Behold, Your King! — 105

    Lesson 6: Defeat of the Serpent King — 127

    Lesson 7: The Endurance Test of Kingship — 143

    Lesson 8: Fighting a Good Fight — 163

    Lesson 9: The Cost of Disobedience — 187

    Lesson 10: Defeat of a Giant (and a Critic) — 215

    Lesson 11: My Worst Enemy — 239

    Lesson 12: A Choice Between Crowns — 261

The Exile Years — 277

    Lesson 13: My Hiding Place — 281

    Lesson 14: The Importance of Inquiring of God — 297

    Lesson 15: Out of Enemy Hands — 313

    Lesson 16: My Enemy in My Hands — 329

    Lesson 17: Into Enemy Hands — 393

    Lesson 18: The King's Reward — 417

Conclusion — 451

Introduction

Welcome to our study of First Samuel! In this study we will be working through the book in an expository manner with a particular theme in mind, that is, pursuing crowns. I use the term crowns loosely because this isn't just about a king pursuing a physical crown, although that example will consume much of the book. In a more general sense, a crown describes the concept of a reward or inheritance—any kind of a lasting legacy that carries with it a heaviness of honor, blessing, and dignity, even the preeminence of royalty. The ideas of "crown," "reward," and "inheritance" are blended together in the pictures presented in First Samuel, just as they are in the New Testament texts, so perhaps we should begin by examining this theme of pursuing crowns from the New Testament perspective to give us a foundation for our study.

Pursuing Crowns

When we talk about pursuing crowns from a New Testament standpoint, what are we talking about?

In its New Testament usage, a crown is defined as a reward or inheritance that we will receive as part of our glorification, and it is described in various ways. There is a crown of rejoicing (First Thessalonians 2:19), a crown of righteousness (Second Timothy 4:8), a crown of life (James 1:12), and a crown of glory (First Peter 5:4). Paul counts his brethren in the faith as being his joy and crown, meaning his legacy (Philippians 4:1). Paul describes it as being similar to a prize that competitors seek, only of an imperishable quality rather than a perishable one (First Corinthians 9:25).

But what does attaining a crown represent, doctrinally speaking? Is it equated with salvation and being given a place in the kingdom[1] or does a crown represent a fuller honor granted apart from salvation? There is a tremendous amount of doctrinal division over these questions, and, depending on which stance you take, you will interpret the pictures in

---

[1] "The kingdom" can be either the spiritual kingdom of heaven, Christ's physical millennial kingdom, or both, depending on your theology. My own personal belief is in a physical millennial kingdom which then transcends to the spiritual kingdom.

First Samuel in different ways. For the sake of clarity, let me present my stance on these issues, so that you will understand in which direction I am taking the lessons.

To begin, the New Testament exhortations to pursue the crown stem from the belief that we will be co-heirs with Christ as part of our glorification in the kingdom. The LORD has promised to extend the glory of royalty to us if we endure even as Christ endured, as Paul writes:

> "The Spirit Himself bears witness with our spirit that we are children of God, and if children, then heirs—heirs of God and joint heirs with Christ, if indeed we suffer with Him, that we may also be glorified together."
> —Romans 8:16-17

Isaiah 55 also alludes to this concept of the democratization of kingship:

> "Incline your ear, and come to Me. Hear, and your soul shall live; And I will make an everlasting covenant with you—the sure mercies of David. Indeed I have given him as a witness to the people, a leader and commander for the people. Surely you shall call a nation you do not know, and nations who do not know you shall run to you, because of the LORD your God, and the Holy One of Israel; for He has glorified you."
> —Isaiah 55:3-5

Notice the change in pronouns through the Isaiah verses. David remains leader and commander, but the everlasting covenant of David is extended to "you." "You" shall command nations, because the LORD has glorified "you." You will be granted the honor, blessing, and responsibility equated with royalty as co-heirs with the coming Messianic king—*if you endure without losing faith*. That is not specifically stated in the text, but it is the greater context of Isaiah. This prophetic promise is given as an assurance to those who are suffering through the Babylonian captivity, that if they remain faithful and endure, they will be glorified and receive the reward.

So we have two steps being described: enduring or persevering through trial, which is called the process of sanctification, and then glorification. But there is another aspect which must be accomplished, and that is salvation. How do you define salvation? Is salvation the reward—the outworking of the sanctification process that isn't determined until the end—or is it a separate step that is accomplished apart from the endurance test of sanctification?

I believe it is a separate act that must be accomplished first, based on its character as it is defined in Ephesians 2:8-9:

> "For by grace you have been saved through faith, and that not of yourselves; it is the gift of God, not of works, lest anyone should boast."
> —Ephesians 2:8-9

Our salvation is accomplished at the moment of belief and is based on faith in Christ alone by grace alone and not by works. The "not by works" part is what makes the difference between salvation and sanctification, because sanctification *is* based on works. If salvation is not earned by works, then it cannot be lost by works either. The moment we confess our faith in Christ, we are granted a permanent citizenship in the kingdom *on Christ's merit*, not our own; and the only way we could lose that citizenship is if Christ Himself loses His citizenship in the kingdom, which will never happen. The price for sin was paid at the cross once and for all. Salvation is not a reward for having passed the endurance test. It is not the crown awarded us for having achieved something by our own will or works. Salvation is its own step in the process, and once it is granted, it is guaranteed so long as Christ is King on the throne.

Crowns fall into the category of rewards for works that are determined at the end of the sanctification process, apart from citizenship—something earned by persevering through trials and enduring tests of faith. They can be won and lost, but the winning or losing does not affect our citizenship in the kingdom. It does, however, affect our glorification, which includes the right to claim the status and benefits of royalty, as Paul writes in Second Timothy 2:11-13:

> "This is a faithful saying: For if we died with Him, we shall also live with Him. If we endure, we shall also reign with Him. If we deny Him, He also will deny us. If we are faithless, He remains faithful; He cannot deny Himself." —Second Timothy 2:11-13

Notice that living with Him is separate from reigning with Him. The first is the act of faith and identification that gives us salvation and citizenship. The second is an act of endurance through trials that is rewarded with the crown and the right to reign. Attaining the crown involves more than simply believing in Christ. It requires action over time. You don't just step into the position of royalty without having learned how to discern and judge issues by right values, how to submit to authority and wield authority correctly, and how to be a leader and example, even in a limited capacity. Peter writes this to church leaders:

> "Shepherd the flock of God which is among you, serving as overseers, not by compulsion but willingly, not for dishonest gain but eagerly; nor as being lords over those entrusted to you, but being examples to the flock; and when the Chief Shepherd appears, you will receive the crown of glory that does not fade away." —First Peter 5:2-4

There is an endurance test that must be passed to attain the crown, and that endurance test is what we encounter during the sanctification process. Here are some other verses I believe support this:

> "Blessed is the man who endures temptation; for when he has been approved, he will receive the crown of life which the LORD has promised to those who love Him." —James 1:12

> "I have fought the good fight, I have finished the race, I have kept the faith. Finally, there is laid up for me the crown of righteousness, which the LORD, the righteous Judge, will give to me on that Day, and not to me only but also to all who have loved His appearing."
> —Second Timothy 4:7-8

> "Do not fear any of those things which you are about to suffer . . . Be faithful until death, and I will give you the crown of life." —Revelation 2:10

The awarding of crowns or rewards comes at the end of the sanctification process, and they are based on works:

> "For the Son of Man will come in the glory of His Father with His angels, and then He will reward each according to his works." —Matthew 16:27

> "And behold, I am coming quickly, and My reward is with Me, to give to every one according to his work." —Revelation 22:12 (cf. Isaiah 40:10, 62:11)

Crowns can be earned but also lost in the course of the process:

> "Because you have kept My command to persevere, I also will keep you from the hour of trial which shall come upon the whole world, to test those who dwell on the earth. Behold, I am coming quickly! Hold fast

what you have, that <u>no one may take your crown</u>." —Revelation 3:10-11 (emphasis added)

"And everyone who competes for the prize is temperate in all things. Now they do it to obtain a perishable crown, but we for an imperishable crown. Therefore I run thus: not with uncertainty. Thus I fight: not as one who beats the air. But I discipline my body and bring it into subjection, lest, when I have preached to others, <u>I myself should become disqualified</u>." —First Corinthians 9:25-27 (emphasis added)

This is where church doctrine divides:

- If you do *not* believe that your salvation is based on Christ's merit alone and is therefore permanent and guaranteed at the point of belief, then you can interpret these verses to mean that you can lose that salvation and citizenry in the kingdom.

- If you *do* believe that salvation is based on Christ's merit alone and is therefore permanent, then losing the crown or being disqualified doesn't mean that you have lost your citizenry. It only means that you have lost the added glorification of royalty.

As we work through the pictures in First Samuel, we will see crowns and rewards being won and lost. I am not going to interpret these gains or losses in terms of salvation. I don't believe that the author's intent in chronicling Eli's or Saul's loss of the crown was to create a discussion over whether or not they were ever saved and if they went to hell. We are not going there with this study. The purpose of chronicling these lives is so that we can examine <u>the process</u> by which crowns are attained and lost, and what issues crop up in the process. That will be the focus of this study: how to pursue a crown.

How to Pursue the Crown

So, what is involved with the pursuit of a crown? It sounds epic, doesn't it? I imagine some sweeping saga involving a long journey through deep forests and barren wastelands, fierce battles against giants, all manner of intrigue and alliances, radical reversals of fortune—all in pursuit of the inestimable rewards of power, prestige, and wealth. I imagine the valiant hero conquering his enemies against all odds and riding into his kingdom to claim his crown, then calling his loyal servants forward to grant them their knighthood.

We tend to focus on the king, but what do these loyal servants look like? What did they do that was so great that they should be granted a knighthood? Maybe one gave the king good advice. Maybe one took a message for him. Maybe one made him dinner or simply held his horse while he mounted. Does that make them worthy to be treated as royalty by the rest of the citizenry? Yes, it does. The point is not *what* they did through the journey; it is the fact that they endured the ordeal side-by-side with the king to the end. They stuck with him when his strategies ended in victories. They suffered with him when his errors in judgment put them in jeopardy. But more than that, they embraced the vision of the reward that he was pursuing to the hilt—even to death.

Are you a servant of the King? If you are, you should know that the moment you placed your faith in Christ, you were catapulted into this epic endeavor of pursuing a crown. Whatever you were pursuing before, you are no longer pursuing. Whatever your values and goals have been, they have changed. You are under new leadership with a new mission and vision, and there is a magnificent reward waiting for you if you endure to the end. So what if there's a giant to battle? There's a reward, right? Right!

But . . . is the reward that the King is pursuing one that you want for yourself? That is the question. This is not about pursuing a reward that *you* desire. It's about embracing *the King's* pursuit of a *crown*, the glory and blessing of which He intends to extend to you. Like it or not, you have become royalty-elect, and whether you embrace the calling or not, your works are being evaluated toward that end.

How do you feel about being royalty?

Sounds daunting, doesn't it? Royalty involves a lot of responsibility—having to make decisions, judge between people, and manage a kingdom. Who wants to spend eternity shouldering that headache? Maybe you think it's not for you. Maybe you think it will be enough just to be a citizen—a greeter at the kingdom's gate, shaking the saints' hands as they come marching in. How is an average person with average abilities even qualified to step into that level of leadership and carry out that duty with any kind of skill or understanding anyway? Do you think it's not for you?

Actually, it is for you, and you will not be unqualified by the time you get through this trial by fire. The process of pursuing a crown teaches you all the skills you will need, as we will see in the course of this study.

Sometimes we shy away from daunting tasks because we 1) don't have a right understanding of what it is we are pursuing; 2) don't know what is involved with the task; or 3) don't have an example to go by. All three of these points will be remedied with this study. As we work through First Samuel, we will be examining the lives of two brides, two priests, and two kings in pursuit of a legacy—a crown of sorts. The crown or reward is defined a little differently in each case, but taken collectively, we will find a picture of what we should be pursuing—and also what we should *not* be pursuing. Each pair presents us with a contrasting picture of how the legacy is defined, what motivates its pursuit, the methods used to attain that legacy, and the reasons why it is either kept or lost. So, we have some models to go by.

As we begin to draw application from the Old Testament models and apply it to our own sanctification journey, we are going to keep these four basic guidelines in mind:

1) **There are right and wrong <u>kings</u> with whom to align yourself when pursuing a crown**. God never, ever, relinquishes His kingship over His people, even when they decamp from Him, and there is always a reckoning for unfaithfulness. Israel will pursue a crown, and in doing so, they will throw off God as King and turn their allegiance to the lesser human king with disastrous consequences. Eli the high priest and King Saul will deny the LORD's headship over them and so become disqualified. When we pursue a crown, we, too, must consider whom we acknowledge as having headship over us. Christ is our King-to-be in a future kingdom, and yet in this current earthly kingdom there reigns another king who offers a facsimile of the glorification and reward we are pursuing. We will lose the reward when we align ourselves under the wrong king.

2) **There are right and wrong <u>crowns</u> to pursue.** How you define the crown is important. Paul uses the example of what he calls a perishable crown—a prize of temporal, earthly value in the eyes of men—then challenges us to pursue an imperishable crown of everlasting, heavenly value in the eyes of God. We understand the

tangible qualities of the perishable crown fairly well, but the heavenly qualities of the imperishable one often lack luster because they are more intangible. The value in the imperishable crown is this: should you attain it, then you will attain not just the heavenly blessings but all the benefits of the perishable one as well, as it says:

> *"But seek first the kingdom of God and His righteousness, and all these things shall be added to you."* —Matthew 6:33

It's like getting a two-for-one deal. The other option is a none-for-one. If you seek only the temporal, earthly crown, then even if you gain it in this life, you shall lose it in the next. The earthly crown has no eternal value. You can't take it with you when you die. There really is only one crown worth pursuing, but we must learn to see the value in it or it will be lost to us.

3) **There are right and wrong <u>reasons</u> for pursuing a crown.** Why pursue a crown at all? What motivates such a pursuit? A desire for glory? Power? Validation? Vindication? Some people pursue the crown for their own glory and the building of their own kingdom while others pursue it for God's glory and the building of God's kingdom. We will see how that works out for Saul and David.

4) **There are right and wrong <u>ways</u> to pursue crowns.** As Paul said, you cannot flail about aimlessly, without vision or restraint. It takes self-control and discipline to achieve the crown and claim the full reward in the kingdom. It requires bringing your carnal nature into submission even as you push back the influence of the ungodly world around you. As we work through the narrative, we will be focusing on how the crowns are pursued and what issues arise from doing it the right and wrong way.

As we work through the narrative, we will find these New Testament principles working themselves out in very practical, relatable ways through the lives of the main characters in First Samuel. We will keep these guidelines in mind and learn from Israel's examples how to discern between the right and wrong models. This study will be an exercise in learning what it takes to be not just a citizen in the kingdom, but royalty.

So, we have our overall theme of rewards for this study. Now let's talk a bit about the books of Samuel in general.

About the Books of Samuel

While we will only be covering First Samuel in this particular study, the books of First and Second Samuel were originally one continuous narrative in the Hebrew Bible. Together, they narrate Israel's transition from the age of the judges into the age of the kings and span the reign of David. The Septuagint authors divided the book into two, breaking the narrative at the turning point of King Saul's death and David's ascent to the throne. It may seem somewhat of an arbitrary break, but the break serves a thematic purpose in bringing us to a summary conclusion of our theme of rewards at the end of First Samuel.

According to Jewish scholars, the narrative of First Samuel was written by Samuel himself, up to the point of his death in chapter 25. After Samuel's death, the historical narrative was taken over by the prophets Gad and Nathan, who are mentioned in First Chronicles 29:29 as being co-authors with Samuel in recording the history of David. While the books of Samuel are technically historical narratives, Jewish Bibles place them among the writings of the prophets by reason of their authorship by prophets.

Continuity between the Books of Judges and First Samuel

In addition to First Samuel, the book of Judges is also attributed to the prophet Samuel, and there is tremendous continuity between the two books in terms of structure, theme, and writing style. The book of Judges does much to set the scene and tone for First Samuel. Before we get into the book of First Samuel, I would like to begin with a brief recap of the book of Judges, just to get a sense of the continuity between the two books and the narrative flow.

The book of Judges isn't arranged in chronological order. If we were to follow the chronology, then Eli, the high priest and judge at the beginning of First Samuel, would follow Samson. Samson is the twelfth judge; Eli, the thirteenth; and Samuel, the fourteenth and final judge. The last five chapters of the book of Judges actually happen at the beginning of the age of the judges, not the end, but they are purposely placed at the end of the book to set us up for the narrative of First Samuel.

These last chapters in Judges are bookended with this critical comment:

> *"In those days there was no king in Israel; everyone did what was right in his own eyes."* —Judges 17:6, 21:25

The statement implies that the people's ability to govern themselves had failed, and the only solution to their condition would be found in a king, which is a bit ironic because they already had a king. They just didn't recognize Him as King.

When Israel came into the Land, the nation was established originally as a theocracy with God as King and the priesthood as the ruling class, but something went very wrong with this arrangement almost immediately. With the exception of Phinehas, the son of Eleazar, who presided at the Tabernacle in the early days of the judges, there is no mention in the book of Judges of any legitimate member of the high priesthood, and the few Levites mentioned are not exemplary. The priesthood is notably missing.

In place of the priesthood, God raised up the *shofetim*—the judges—who delivered Israel from oppressors, judged Israel, and served as chieftains with a limited ruling capacity. But the judges were never national leaders who unified the people as a whole.

The age of the judges bleeds over into the narrative of First Samuel. Twelve judges are mentioned in the book of Judges, and they come from various tribes with the notable exception of Levi. By contrast, First Samuel opens with two final judges who are both from the tribe of Levi. (We should note that while Samuel is a priest, he does not replace Eli as a high priest, only as a judge.)

In addition to the critical comment, the ending chapters of the book of Judges anticipate the time of the kings in subtle ways. In Judges 17, there is a contrasting picture between Bethlehem and Gibeah. The man from Bethlehem is exceedingly hospitable and yet not so good at dealing with sin in his house, while the men of Gibeah are inhospitable, brutal, and debased. This is a curious pairing when you consider the kings that come from these places. King David is from Bethlehem and pictured as most exemplary in the First Samuel text, although he is not so good at dealing with sin in his own house as we see at the end of Second Samuel. King Saul of Gibeah is presented as David's inferior and is of a more brutal, base character.

In the book of Judges, a Levite calls Israel to gather at Mizpah as a nation to deal with the crime of Gibeah. Ironically, Samuel will gather the nation back to Mizpah to crown a man of Gibeah as king over the nation. The offensiveness and inappropriateness of Gibeah in the book of Judges underscores the poor choice of a king in Saul.

Judges 19-21 are outlined in a chiastic structure that pivots around the moment when Israel is unified as nation. Judges 20:1 notes:

> *"So all the children of Israel came out, from Dan to Beersheba, as well as from the land of Gilead, and the congregation gathered together as one man before the LORD at Mizpah." —Judges 20:1*

This is the first time in the entire book of Judges that Israel is presented as a unified people, as yet without a king, and makes a natural segue into Israel's demand for a king in First Samuel.

The totality of the land of Israel is reckoned "from Dan to Beersheba" in the days of the judges and throughout First and Second Samuel in the days of David's reign. The phrase "from Dan to Beersheba" is unique to these books and suggests the limits of the kingdom proper under David before its expansion under Solomon.

And so we see that the events in the book of Judges set not only the scene but also the tone for First Samuel. In the book of Judges, the author focused on the consequences of Israel not pursuing the full inheritance. We saw the internal and external warfare that arose when Israel stopped seeking that relationship with God, embraced the carnal world around them, and did what was right in their own eyes. The book of Judges provided an example of carnal Christianity and its out-workings. The pursuit of a crown only appeared in the negative example of Gideon's son, Abimelech, who went about it the wrong way and for the wrong reason, and, so, was disqualified. Here in First Samuel, as the kingdom is coming into view, the focus now shifts to the process of pursuing an inheritance in the form of a crown or reward and the consequences of not pursuing it correctly.

Samuel's Writing Style

Samuel writes with tremendous flair. His narrative is rich in detail and drama, and he gives his characters a certain transparency in describing their emotions and even their inner thoughts at times. He does not mince words over his own reaction to being replaced with Saul. But the narrative is not without structure. Samuel structures his writings with a very deliberate sense of order and progression, and makes breaks between chapters to focus on specific contrasts between characters and events.

It is typical for Samuel's writing style to begin with models at the individual level first, then expand the dynamic to the family level, community level, and finally the national level. In the book of Judges, the last five chapters are arranged in a chiastic structure beginning with the focus on an individual and building to the apex view of Israel united as a whole, then resolving back through the progression to a comment on the individual. Here in First Samuel, he works from least to greatest with models of three contrasting sets of characters. He begins with two wives within a family setting, contending for an individual legacy, then telescopes out to the priesthood at community level with the contrast between Samuel and the House of Eli, and finally to the national level with the contrasting kings, Saul and David.

Chiastic Structures

Chiastic structures are a specific way of structuring a narrative or argument. A chiasm will open with an initial statement of the conflict or a premise. The argument or narrative will then build, statement by statement, to a point that is the main focus. Having come to the point, the statements that follow begin to work their way back through the premises, statement by statement, presenting either a resolution to the conflict or a reversal. So, there is a mirroring effect across a body of text.

Samuel's penchant for using chiastic structures extends into First Samuel where he knits the narrative together with extensive use of chiastic structures within chapters and across chapters. The chiasms help us pinpoint the crucial element in the given structure and establish the sub-themes within the text.

The narratives within chapters 1, 3, 12, 20, 23, 25, 28, and 31 are built with chiastic structures. On a higher plane, Chapters 2–8 form a chiastic structure that revolves around the theme of ascents and descents of the brides, priests, and the Ark of God (which is treated like a character).

    Chapter 2: Ascent of Samuel over sons of Eli
      Chapter 3: Ascent of Samuel to prophet; Descent of Eli
        Chapter 4: Death of the House of Eli/Descent of the Ark
          Chapter 5: Descent of the Ark of God into enemy hands
        Chapter 6: Ascent of the Ark of God out of enemy hands
      Chapter 7: Ascent of Samuel to judge/priest; Israel restored
    Chapter 8: Ascent (?) of the king

Chapter 8 brings the narrative to the turning point where Israel demands a king and challenges us to consider if this next step is an ascent or descent for Israel.

The theme of ascents and descents continues into the narrative of the kings in chapters 9–31 as Saul ascends to the throne but then loses it, while David ascends to honor, then descends into exile, only to ascend to the throne at the end. The ascent and descent pattern in David's journey echoes the Ark's journey in chapters 4–7. Samuel uses the theme of ascents and descents to emphasize the right and wrong ways to pursue a reward or crown and the consequences of pursuing it in the wrong way. The priests in chapters 2–8 form one block of ascents and descents focusing on the spiritual side of Israel's leadership; chapters 9–31 carry the same theme into the civic side of Israel's leadership with the kings.

David's exile in Chapters 21–29 is presented in a grand chiastic structure that pivots around Chapter 25, as follows:

    Chapter 21: David rejected by the Philistines
      Chapter 22: Saul kills the priesthood
        Chapter 23: David gets out of a trap through God's wisdom
          Chapter 24: Saul at David's mercy (David cuts his cloak)
            Chapter 25: David, Nabal, and Abigail
          Chapter 26: Saul at David's mercy (David cuts his spear and jug)
        Chapter 27: David gets into a trap by his own wisdom
      Chapter 28: Saul seeks a medium
    Chapter 29: David rejected by the Philistines

Chapter 25 itself is arranged in a tight chiastic structure, the apex of which is Abigail's dialogue. We will consider the centrality of Abigail's model to the greater theme of rewards.

Picture Comparisons

In addition to using chiastic structures, Samuel relies very heavily on the use of picture comparisons and progressions, particularly in presenting the kings in Chapters 9–31. The comparison of the kings is very complex, and so he breaks their narratives into comparative picture sections.

It is an important part of Old Testament study to be able to recognize and draw application from picture comparisons, and so, in addition to teaching you the text itself, I want to teach you this study technique. I will explain the technique here, and then I will show you how it works as we work through the text.

How to Study the Old Testament Pictures

Picture comparison is one technique that Jewish scholars have used to study the Old Testament from time immemorial, and if the apostle Paul drives you nuts with his comparison/contrasts, you can thank Gamaliel and his teachers for training his mind this way.

The method was actually established by God Himself in Genesis 1:3-5:

> *"Then God said, 'Let there be light'; and there was light. And God saw the light, that it was good; and God divided the light from the darkness. God called the light Day, and the darkness He called Night. So the evening and the morning were the first day."* —Genesis 1:3-5

In the beginning, God created the light and made a determination about it. The light was good. He then separated it from the darkness. Why did He leave the darkness? Because the character of the light could only be understood by its contrast to the character of darkness, and vice versa. We needed to see light in relationship to darkness to understand the difference.

God then labeled them Day and Night and placed them in an order. The order established another level of relationship between them. Evening comes before morning; man would begin his days in darkness and then proceed toward the light and enlightenment.

God then gathered these picture elements into one day—the first day. First is a relative term. The first day become the start of the next level order—it is the first day relative to seven days. Thus, we now have days to compare to days, each with their own grouping of picture elements. Thus, picture builds on picture in a relational model such that everything works toward a final grand picture.

An understanding of the Old Testament Scriptures is achieved by a continuous comparison of pictures for the purpose of separating what is good from what is bad, what is right from what is wrong. Enlightenment comes from putting two things side by side and considering what they tell you about each other. The comparisons or contrasts can be between physical things, actions people take, or two passages that picture similar or contrasting events. The application is often found not in how they are similar but at points where they differ—in the elements that one narrative records but another doesn't.

This approach to Old Testament study is similar and yet different from New Testament study. The New Testament studies pictures on a more theoretical, doctrinal plane (topics like salvation and rewards) and typology mostly as it pertains to Christ. The New Testament will tell you "this is right and that is wrong and this is why," whereas the Old Testament presents you with two pictures and asks you to decide what is right and what is wrong and why. The New Testament explains and clarifies, but in the Old Testament, you don't have any explanations given. You have to exercise your mind to discern the correct relationship for yourself. For this reason, the Old Testament requires a very intent examination of the physical pictures in order to establish the relationships, then make the analogies, and finally distill the doctrinal teachings. When I show you that process from beginning to end, you will appreciate the challenge that the writers of the New Testament faced when using the Old Testament texts to build doctrinal teachings.

Old Testament study requires a different approach from New Testament study because the use of picture comparisons can create a seeming discontinuity in the flow of the narrative texts that is not found in the New Testament. In New Testament study, you begin with a verse. The interpretation of that verse hinges on it how it fits with the verses immediately before it and after it, and then how that passage fits with the passages immediately before and after it, the chapters before and after, and then within the greater context of the book. Everything flows from point to point in a continuous, progressive building of doctrine and is knit together. But this is a very Greek method of building an argument. It is the correct approach to studying the Greek New Testament, but when you apply the Greek method to the Old Testament, you will run up against places where the narratives don't knit together from passage to passage, as they do not in First Samuel 16-17, for instance. Chapter 16 is about the Spirit entering David at his anointing and subsequently departing from Saul. Chapter 17 is about David's battle with Goliath, but as the narrative progresses, we find that the timeline is out of sequence. Saul doesn't even know David, and all the details about David's family are repeated a second time. So there is this seeming inconsistency and redundancy in the text. The Greek-oriented mind often tries to reconcile the lack of continuous knitting in the Old Testament by using the argument "another author must have written that part" instead of considering that it is the same author writing the "conflicting" passage. The writers of the Septuagint actually deleted the parts in the David and Goliath narrative that contained the "inconsistencies" and "redundancies" in order to force the sequence into a timeline.

In reality, the author was deliberately writing his narrative that way to create specific picture segments that aren't necessarily meant to be arranged in immediate order to one another. That is a departure from the Greek method, and yet its validity proves out in passages like First Samuel 16-17. David's anointing at the beginning of Chapter 16 is compared to Saul's anointing in Chapter 9 and includes the transferring of the Spirit from one to the other. But that is where the picture comparison ends. A different picture comparison begins with Chapter 17, and it was necessary to include redundant information from Chapter 16 to make the new picture parallel. In Chapter 17, David's battle with Goliath is written with parallel elements to Saul's battle with Nahash in Chapter 11, and the redundant details in Chapter 17 are the clues the author uses to prompt us toward the comparison of Chapters 17 and 11. When Chapter 17 is compared to Chapter 16, those details appear discordant, unless you understand that each chapter is a self-contained picture and the picture comparisons don't always follow one another in an orderly timeline sequence.

So, if the pictures don't butt up to one another in the text, how do you know which pictures to compare to each other? Here are some guidelines for matching pictures:

- **Consider what elements are being compared in the immediate verse.** For example, Exodus 23:19: *". . . You shall not boil a young goat in its mother's milk."* Two physical things are presented in relationship to one another within one verse. So consider what is the right and wrong relationship between a young goat and mother's milk, and how the right relationship is achieved. A mother's milk is supposed to bring life, but if you break the commandment, what should have brought life then facilitates death for the young animal. I have just taught you the premise for Romans 7:10: *"And the commandment, which was to bring life, I found to bring death."* Why? Because of sin. The commandment had been broken and sin had entered in the picture. Paul then goes on to unpack the "why" of it.

- **Consider what is being compared within a passage.** If the passage is about a battle, compare and contrast the shepherd boy and Philistine giant who face one another in that battle. Another example is the previously noted First Samuel 16, which is divided into two parts. In the first part the Spirit enters David; in the second, the Spirit departs from Saul.

- **Consider the comparisons between groupings of passages in the greater context.** In First Samuel, we are studying the comparison between kings. That is the overall picture, but there are multiple aspects within each narrative to be compared. Each king has an anointing sequence, followed by a battle sequence, and a victory celebration—Saul in Chapters 9-11; David in Chapters 16-18. Compare the anointing with the anointing, the battle with the battle, and the celebration with the celebration. The anointing sequences have elements in common, as do the battles—but the pictures don't necessarily follow one another immediately. There is the intervening picture of the Spirit departing Saul in Chapter 16 which completes the comparison but was also needed to set us up for future picture comparisons. Events flow together generally in a timeline, but the picture comparisons are really what drive the narrative and its structure.

- **Look for repeated verses, phrases, or words that pull different passages into context with one another.** In First Samuel, the author will deliberately phrase verses in a way to point us to specific comparisons. For instance, First Samuel 23:19 says: *"Then the Ziphites came up to Saul at Gibeah, saying, 'Is David not hiding with us in strongholds in the woods, in the hill of Hachilah, which is on the south of Jeshimon?'"* The author uses almost the same phrasing three chapters later in First Samuel 26:1: *"Now the Ziphites came to Saul at Gibeah, saying, 'Is David not hiding in the hill of Hachilah, opposite Jeshimon?'"* That is a clue for us to compare those two passages. David had a reaction to the news in both cases, but his second reaction was opposite the first and led to a different outcome. Did he react correctly or incorrectly the second time? Why? There is an application in the comparison.

  Repeated phrases or words aren't necessarily confined to one book. They can bring together picture elements from Genesis to Malachi under one picture grouping such as "the third day" or "sons of Belial." This is how patterns begin to appear and establish typology.

- **Look for picture order, progression, and series.** Order is supremely important, but a picture sequence might include intervening pictures that aren't part of the sequence. David's anointing, battle, and celebration follow the same order as Saul's in the narrative and in relative timeline order. There is a theme of ascents and descents throughout the text that is communicated through physical movement from place to place, actions taken, and changes in status. The author often arranges pictures in series of threes that have a common theme. We will see all of these in play throughout First Samuel.

The goal of picture comparison is to:

1) **Understand the character of something by comparing it with something else.** Sometimes the Scripture compares things of similar kind—firstborn son to firstborn son, a barren woman to a barren woman, priests to priests, kings to kings, etc. Picture elements of like kind establish patterns that carry forward. Sometimes they set up opposites, like a lowly shepherd boy and an exalted giant. Sometimes pictures will have all the same elements in common, but one will have

an added element. The added element becomes a point of particular emphasis that leads to application.

2) **Identify the relationship between the compared elements.** The Old Testament is ultimately a study of relationships. The relationships are like ratios. They remain the same whether they are applied in a limited context or a large context, and the physical is often a reflection of the spiritual. The relationships become the basis for making analogies: A is to B as C is to D. Husband is to wife as Christ is to the Church. The relationship often transcends the physical into the spiritual, and bridges the gap between the Old Testament picture and New Testament doctrine.

So that is a brief overview of how to study the Old Testament pictures. Now let's apply it.

First Samuel specifically focuses on the pictures of wives (brides), priests, and kings—all terms that equally describe believers in the Church age. We are the bride of Christ and also the royal priesthood and royalty-elect, so the comparisons we are given in the narrative will have parallels to our own experience. The brides of First Samuel pursue an inheritance through children. The priesthood and judges wear crowns of different sorts and are challenged to keep them. The kings pursue kingdoms and crowns. These are comparisons at the highest level.

We will begin working through the picture sequences of First Samuel, beginning in Chapter 1 with the wives of Elkanah. As we move from lesson to lesson, I will give you the verses we are covering, a breakdown of the narrative structure Samuel is using (if any), and then we will begin to identify the picture. Once we have grasped the literal picture, we will consider what profile or type is being modeled for us and what New Testament teachings derive from it. Finally, where applicable, I will cast the typology into the model of Christ. First Samuel is, after all, a prophetic book. So, let's begin!

LESSON 1: FIRST SAMUEL 1-2

Crown of Rubies, Crown of Grace

READ

First Samuel 1:1–2:11

NARRATIVE STRUCTURE

The book of First Samuel begins with a comparison of two brides, Hannah and Peninnah, in Chapter 1. After an introduction that sets the scene and characters for us, the narrative is broken into three main parts—according to where they happen—and are arranged in a chiastic structure (A-B-A):

1) Introduction (1:1–7)
2) The Wives of Elkanah
    A) The scene at Shiloh (1:8–18)
    B) The scene at Ramah (1:19–23)
    A) The return to Shiloh (1:24–28)
3) Hannah's Prayer (2:1–11)

The story is capped off with Hannah's song in Chapter 2 which provides a narrative break between the pictures of the brides and priests.

BUILD THE PICTURE

The Wives of Elkanah

1. Where did Elkanah live?

Elkanah lived in Ramathaim Zophim. This name is later shortened to Ramah, but it is interesting that it is introduced by this long name. We should look at the meaning of the name.

Ramah means "a high place" or "a height," usually in the context of a high place used for idolatrous worship. **Ramathaim** is the plural of Ramah, suggesting a double or exceeding height—a high, high place. **Zophim** means "watchmen."

So, Ramathaim Zophim means "the high, high hill of the watchmen." You get a mental picture of a place that is like a promontory lookout where watchmen might keep vigil because they could see a distance. That seems an appropriate birthplace for Samuel, a far-seeing and foreseeing prophet.

2. **What is Elkanah's lineage? (See Levite Family Tree chart)**

    He is the son of Jeroham, the son of Elihu, the son of Tohu, the son of Zuph, an Ephraimite. Except he was not an Ephraimite, which we discover from the book of First Chronicles.

    In First Chronicles 6, we find a retelling of Elkanah's lineage, except that it doesn't trace back to the tribe of Ephraim but the tribe of Levi. For the sake of clarification, I have provided you with a family tree chart of the house of Levi in First Chronicles 6 (see the lineage chart). On the chart, we will begin with Elkanah's lineage on the bottom right in black and then work our way up the family tree.

    In First Chronicles 6:33-38, we see that the renowned singer in David's administration, Heman, was the son of Joel, the son of Samuel, the son of Elkanah, the son of Jeroham, the son of Eliel (aka Elihu), the son of Toah (aka Tohu), the son of Zuph. Despite the variation in a few names, this is clearly the house of Elkanah described in First Samuel 1:1. But First Chronicles doesn't stop at Zuph. It extends the length of Elkanah's ancestry back to Levi.

    Notice the patriarchal names. Levi's son, Kohath, had four sons. Amram was the first, and through him came the high priestly line of Aaron described in First Chronicles 6:1-15 (gray). Izhar is the second son and the father of Korah. Remember Korah from the book of Numbers? He is the one who staged a rebellion against Aaron and Moses along with Dathan and Abiram in the middle of Israel's wilderness wanderings. The second census in Numbers 26:9-11 tells us that the children of Korah did not die. In fact, it is from Korah's line that Samuel springs.

LEVITE FAMILY TREE

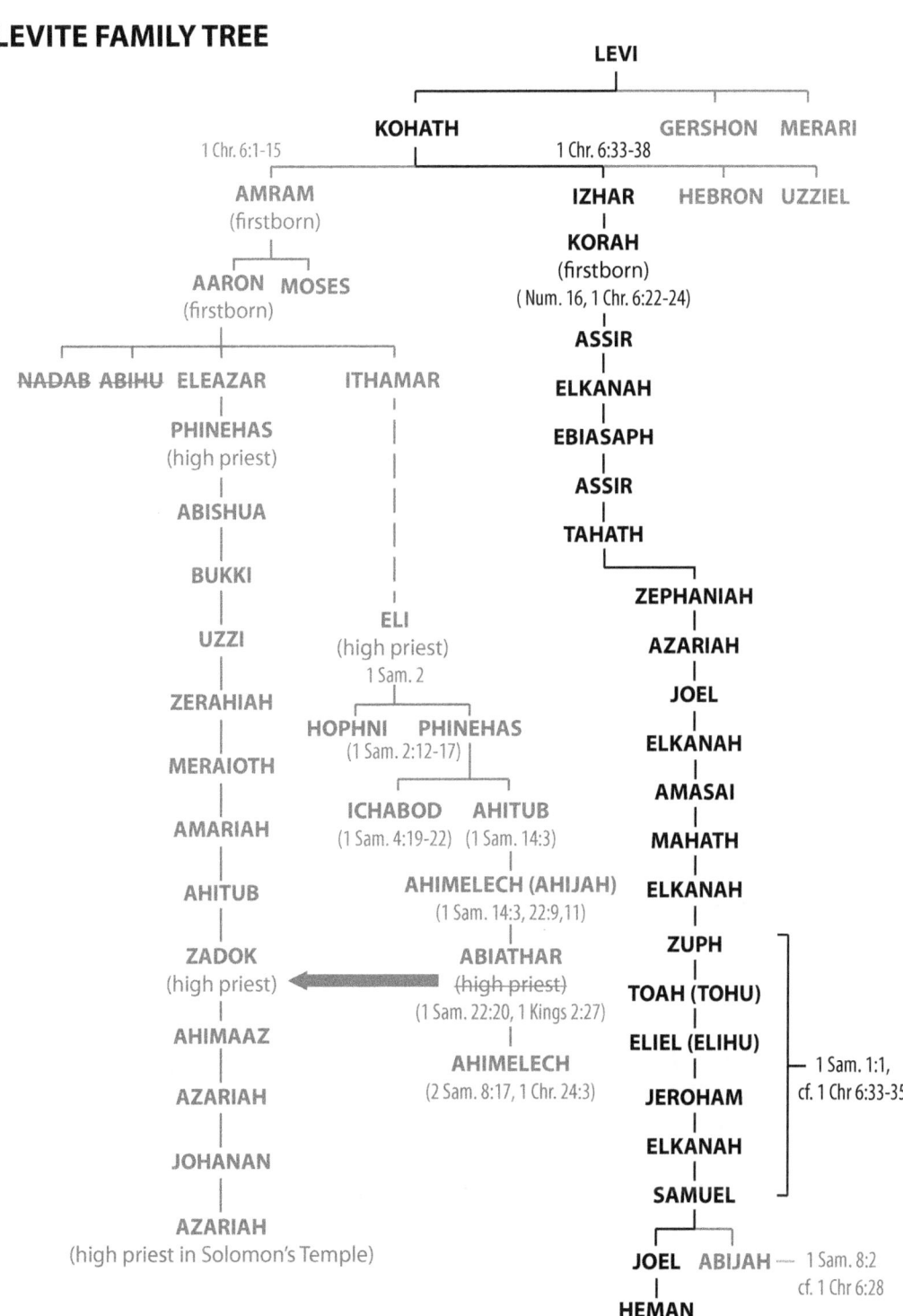

If Elkanah is a Levite, why is he called an Ephraimite? I don't know. Since Levites do not own land, they are usually claimed by the tribe to which they are assigned. In Elkanah's case, his family is assigned to Ramah, but that city is within the tribal land of Benjamin, not Ephraim.

3. **What do we know about Elkanah's wives?**

    Hannah is named first, possibly because she was the first wife, but she is barren, which might explain why Elkanah took a second wife who would bear him sons. It was a sign of the LORD's favor that a woman would be able to have children. Barrenness in a wife was considered a judgment from God, because it meant the end of a man's lineage if he could not have children. For this reason, barrenness was considered a legitimate ground for divorce, and yet we see that Elkanah does not put Hannah away. Quite the contrary. He loves her and honors her by giving her a double portion.

    Peninnah is the second wife, who gave Elkanah many sons and daughters, and was Hannah's antagonist. Peninnah should have been favored by Elkanah, and yet she doesn't have his love nor does she receive an extra portion. When he gives her a portion at the time of offerings, she gets a single portion for herself and her children as is her due.

4. **Why does Peninnah torment Hannah?**

    Because 1) Hannah has no children, 2) Hannah is loved more, and 3) Hannah receives a greater portion. (Notice that Peninnah's harassment steps up at the time of the yearly offering.)

5. **If Hannah is so loved and provided for, why does she still weep?**

    Even if they aren't true, hateful words can wreck a person. The torment and oppression she is experiencing in her family is not something she can get away from, and it grieves her.

6. **How does Hannah respond to Peninnah's harassment?**

    It is a tribute to Hannah's humility that she doesn't retaliate with hateful words or rub in the fact that Elkanah loves her more than Peninnah. Even so, she goes to the LORD and asks for what she thinks will relieve the oppression—one son. She doesn't even ask to keep him. She promises he will be devoted to the LORD's service all his days, and he will be a Nazirite (no razor shall come on his head).

What she is really asking for is the LORD's validation. She has her husband's validation, but it isn't enough to overcome Peninnah's torment. Only validation from the LORD will stop it.

7. **How does Hannah respond to Eli's rebuke for being drunk?**

   Where she did not answer Peninnah, this time she answers back in her own defense. It is clear from her spirited address that she is most certainly not drunk. Eli, who is both a high priest and a judge, misjudges Hannah because of what he sees—or imagines he sees—and not by the truth. She stands up to her accuser and pleads her case. Having misjudged her, Eli then blesses her.

8. **What is the reward for Hannah's faith?**

   God blesses her with a son, Samuel, whom she devotes to the LORD's service; but then in Chapter 2, we find that He also blesses her with more children to make up for her gifting of Samuel to His service. She has three sons and two daughters. And so she is blessed exceedingly.

APPLY THE PICTURE

Before we move on to Hannah's prayer, I want to consider the author's purpose in focusing so heavily on Hannah and Peninnah as an opening picture. Of course, it is a way of introducing Samuel into the narrative, but the build-up seems to have more purpose than that. The conflict between the two women is driven by Hannah's barrenness. Let's sketch a profile of each woman in regards to the reward or inheritance they are pursuing.

What Peninnah and Hannah Model

The name **Peninnah** means "rubies." She is blessed with an earthly abundance of children for which she labors, literally, and for her effort, she is rewarded with what is due her for her labor. The reward or inheritance that she pursues is of an earthly nature to build an earthly kingdom for her own glory. Her abundance of children gives her personal value, status, and validation.

The topic of rubies introduces a sub-picture to Peninnah's picture—an underlying element that expands the application. In Scripture, rubies form a comparison to wisdom:

> *"... For the price of wisdom is above rubies."* —Job 28:18b

> *"For wisdom is better than rubies, and all the things one may desire cannot be compared with her."* —Proverbs 8:11

> *"There is gold and a multitude of rubies, but the lips of knowledge are a precious jewel."* —Proverbs 20:15

> *"Who can find a virtuous wife? For her worth is far above rubies."* —Proverbs 31:10

The comparison of rubies to wisdom then carries into the comparison of Peninnah and Hannah, and we are left with a clue as to which is the wiser.

The name **Hannah** means "grace." Lacking the earthly abundance of physical children, she has the love of her husband and a double portion. These things are gifted, not earned, and therefore scorned by Peninnah as being unmerited.

Like Peninnah, Hannah also pursues the legacy of children, but she seeks it in a different way. She seeks validation from God in asking for one child—a child who she willingly gives back to the LORD. Even as she attains that crown, she casts it before the LORD's throne for His glory and for the building up of His spiritual kingdom instead of her earthly kingdom. For this He grants her an additional abundance of children as a rebuke to Peninnah.

Interestingly, Peninnah's children are not mentioned in any of the great lineages, but Hannah's descendants will be among those who sing praises to God in His court.

Crown of Rubies, Crown of Grace

Set the Hebrew names aside for a moment and consider the comparison between rubies (riches) and grace. In these two women, we see two ways of pursuing a particular reward or inheritance, which in this case is embodied in children. Children are a sort of crown for a mother. They are her legacy.

The **crown of rubies** is a temporal, earthly reward gained by human works. Its value is weighed by size or quantity—the more you have, the more valuable you are. A person pursuing a crown of rubies seeks glory and validation for his/herself from men only and not God.

The **crown of grace** is a heavenly blessing gifted by God according to a promise[1]. Grace's crown is not reckoned by earthly standards, and yet the honor it receives is comparable. While those pursuing the crown of grace seek glory and validation for themselves, they seek to glorify God first and be glorified by God and not man. In attaining this crown, they also receive an additional blessing of the crown of rubies.

Why would this contrast between Hannah and Peninnah, the legacy of grace versus the legacy of riches, be the first picture Samuel presents in developing this theme of pursuing crowns? Because defining the crown is foundational. This picture has to be established first. You can pursue a crown for right reasons and right ways, but if the crown you are pursuing is the wrong crown, your effort is to no avail.

There are right and wrong crowns to pursue.

There are right and wrong ways to pursue a crown. One way is by works validated by men, the other is by works validated by God. Hannah stands out not just as a model of grace, but also as a model of wisdom in how she pursues the reward.

There are right and wrong reasons to pursue a crown. One is for personal glory; the other, for God's glory. Hannah pursued hers to God's glory and was rewarded.

---

[1] When we speak of grace in a dispensational New Testament context, it is often in regards to salvation. Salvation is by grace but it is *not* the reward. On the point of salvation and that granting of grace, the LORD sets aside a crown for us which we then pursue as a reward. That crown, the crown of grace, is offered to those who believe in Christ and pursue that relationship through their sanctification journey.

The Barren Woman Typology

The conflict that surrounds Hannah provides a picture of the contrast between an inheritance pursued by works versus grace, but she is not alone in illustrating this picture. Hannah is only one in the pantheon of barren women who have this picture in common and form an Old Testament type. Let's compare them.

All barren women mentioned in Scripture are gifted by God with firstborn sons who became men of renown and a legacy to the mothers. These women include Sarah, Rebekah, Rachel, Samson's mother, Hannah, and Elizabeth in the Gospels. Consider the honor their sons attained:

- Sarah had Isaac, the son of the promise and type of Christ.
- Hannah, Samson's mother, and Elizabeth all had Nazirite sons with special callings.
- Hannah and Samson's mother had sons who were judges.
- Hannah and Elizabeth had sons who were priests and prophets.
- Rachel and Samson's mother had sons who were deliverers.

These women and their sons give us some rich typology in regards to crowns or legacies that are pursued. Just as Hannah and her crown of grace are contrasted to Peninnah and her crown of rubies, so Sarah is contrasted similarly to Hagar. Paul uses Sarah and Hagar as an analogy of two covenants: one of bondage and flesh, and the other of freedom and the Spirit through the promise.

Rebekah gave birth to Jacob and Esau, two sons who were opposite one another by nature. One valued and pursued an inheritance (at his mother's prompting) while the other despised it and gave it up (though he was his father's favorite). The writer of the book of Hebrews uses Esau as the example of one who sought a blessing and inheritance only after he had lost it (Hebrews 12:14-17). Paul also uses the example of Jacob and Esau to explain God's election based on grace as opposed to works in Romans 9:10-13.

Isaiah 54 also addresses the barren woman in regards to pursuing a reward and an inheritance. She becomes a projection of Israel in a future kingdom, as it says:

> *"'Sing, O barren, you who have not borne! Break forth into singing, and cry aloud, you who have not labored with child! For more are the children of the desolate than the children of the married woman,' says the LORD. 'Enlarge the place of your tent, and let them stretch out the curtains of your dwellings; Do not spare; lengthen your cords, and strengthen your stakes. For you shall expand to the right and to the left, and your descendants will inherit the nations, and make the desolate cities inhabited.*
>
> *"'Do not fear, for you will not be ashamed; neither be disgraced, for you will not be put to shame; for you will forget the shame of your youth, and will not remember the reproach of your widowhood anymore. For your Maker is your husband, the LORD of hosts is His name; and your Redeemer is the Holy One of Israel; He is called the God of the whole earth. For the LORD has called you like a woman forsaken and grieved in spirit, like a youthful wife when you were refused,' says your God . . .*
>
> *"'O you afflicted one, tossed with tempest, and not comforted, behold, I will lay your stones with colorful gems, and lay your foundations with sapphires. I will make your pinnacles of rubies, your gates of crystal, and all your walls of precious stones. All your children shall be taught by the LORD, and great shall be the peace of your children. In righteousness you shall be established; you shall be far from oppression, for you shall not fear; and from terror, for it shall not come near you.'"* —Isaiah 54:1-6, 11-14

This is the promise given to the barren woman, that the barrenness she once suffered would be turned into abundant fruitfulness, her reproach would be taken away, and she would be granted a perpetual covenant of peace by the LORD, who is both her Husband and Redeemer. Her abundance comes in the form of children, but notice that she is also granted a kingdom built of jewels—sapphires, *rubies*, crystal, and all manner of precious stones. This is the wealth that the world covets and tries to attain by its own effort, but such blessing comes by grace and faith and not by works.

So, the picture of the barren woman begins with the literal lives of Old Testament women like Hannah who pursue an inheritance, then blossoms into the figurative picture of Israel's hope in a future king, kingdom, and reward, and finally leads into the doctrinal teachings on a spiritual kingdom inherited by grace and faith instead of works.

Like the barren woman in Isaiah 54, Hannah sings out a prayer of exultation and worship to the LORD for the grace granted to her. Hannah's song seems uncharacteristic for a woman of her place and circumstance. It has the strength of the prophetess about it. It begins and ends with much the same theme of the Song of Moses in describing God as Israel's rock of salvation and His power in avenging His people and judging their adversaries.

BUILD THE PICTURE

Hannah's Prayer

9. What understanding of God has Hannah gained through this episode in her life?

Let's work through the verses of her prayer and consider the picture she paints of God as she sees Him:

(2:1-2) Hannah opens with her praise of God. His honoring of her has given her reason to smile at her enemies as she rejoices in her salvation. (Salvation here is the Hebrew word *yeshua*, which is alternately translated as deliverance or help.) I love that phrasing—to smile at one's enemies. She had no need to say anything. God had said everything for her.

(2:3) *"Talk no more so very proudly; Let no arrogance come from your mouth, For the LORD is the God of knowledge; And by Him actions are weighed."* This is a direct rebuke of her critics, certainly to Peninnah but also perhaps to Eli, God's priest and judge, who presumed to know something about her yet judged her wrongly. The comparisons within the body of her prayer demonstrate not only God's power but also His righteous judgment.

Verses 4-8 of Hannah's song present a series of reversals that are comparable to those found throughout Isaiah 40-62. The verses are arranged roughly in a chiastic structure. Verses 4-5 open with a statement. Verses 6-7 introduce God as the pivotal figure upon Whom the reversals hinge. Verses 8-10a mirror verses 4-5 but attribute the reversal to God. Consider the attributes of God presented in the reversal comparisons:

(2:4) *"The bows of the mighty men are broken, and those who stumbled are girded with strength."* This is the first reversal and focuses on strength.

(2:5) *"Those who were full have hired themselves out for bread, and the hungry have ceased to hunger. Even the barren has borne seven, and she who has many children has become feeble."* The last part of that phrasing is echoed in Isaiah 54:1. It focuses on those who are hungry for food but figuratively for children (another kind of provision).

(2:6-7) *"The LORD kills and makes alive; He brings down to the grave and brings up. The LORD makes poor and makes rich; He brings low and lifts up."* Verse 6 is almost a direct quote from the Song of Moses (Deuteronomy 32:39) and one of the proof texts used to support the doctrine of resurrection based on the word order (God kills, then makes alive). These verses together form the core statement that it is the LORD around Whom all reversals of fortune hinge.

(2:8) *"He raises the poor from the dust and lifts the beggar from the ash heap, to set them among princes and make them inherit the throne of glory. For the pillars of the earth are the LORD's, and He has set the world upon them."* This is the resolution to verse 5. It is the LORD who accomplishes this. Hannah testifies to the LORD's sovereignty.

(2:9-10a) *"He will guard the feet of His saints, but the wicked shall be silent in darkness. For by strength no man shall prevail. The adversaries of the LORD shall be broken in pieces; from heaven He will thunder against them . . ."* This is the resolution to verse 4. It is the LORD who breaks those who stand by their own strength, but preserves the humble.

(2:10b) *"The LORD will judge the ends of the earth. He will give strength to His king, and exalt the horn of His anointed."* This statement returns to the opening statement in verse 3. The last part of verse 10 is prophetic.

It speaks of a king at a time when there is no king, and anticipates the kingdom to come.

Hannah's paean of praise to the LORD rings with the triumph of a woman who has realized her reward by aligning herself with the right king, the right way, and for the right reasons.

> ## Questions for Reflection
>
> - What are you pursuing as your legacy in life?
> - What are you pursuing for your validation, and to whom are you looking for that validation?
> - Can you speak of God's work in your life as Hannah did?
> - What are some ways God has blessed you that the Peninnahs of this world might not value?

LESSON 2: FIRST SAMUEL 2-4

Loss of the Crown of Glory

SERIES STRUCTURE

This lesson will follow the descent of the House of Eli to its demise in First Samuel 2–4. The series opens with a comparison of the House of Eli to the House of Elkanah, and then begins the interplay of ascents and descents: the ascent of Samuel and the descent of the house of Eli.

1) The house of Eli vs. the house of Elkanah (2:12–26)
2) The man of God's prophecy against Eli (2:27–36)
3) Samuel's prophecy against Eli (3:1–21)
4) Death of the House of Eli and the Ark's capture (4:1–22)

First we will work through comparison pictures of the priests in Chapter 2 and discuss the models being presented. Then we will discuss the structure and narrative of Chapter 3 as Samuel ascends to the role of prophet. We will end with the death of the House of Eli in Chapter 4.

The House of Eli vs. the House of Elkanah

READ

First Samuel 2:12–26

BUILD THE PICTURE

The contrast between Elkanah's wives segues to the contrast between priests—Samuel, the son of the House of Elkanah, and Hophni and Phinehas, sons of the House of Eli. Let's look at the House of Eli first.

1. **What do we know about Eli himself?**

   In First Samuel 1, Eli cropped up unexpectedly in the narrative without introduction, except to say that he was sitting by the door post of the Tabernacle watching Hannah as she prayed. He made an error in rebuking Hannah for being drunk, which he then retracted by giving a blessing. The initial presentation of Eli is one of a priest who lacks judgment. In actuality, Eli is a high priest and a judge (we don't know he is a judge until First Samuel 4:18). He also has two very degenerate sons whom he has failed to restrain.

   For a man who wore the crowns of a high priest and a judge, you would think that Eli would be something of an exalted character, but all the usual details are missing. Eli's ancestral lineage isn't even noted. Like kings, a high priest is usually given the honor of having his fathers' names mentioned. That is a significant omission. Let's consider that.

2. **What is Eli's lineage? (See Levite Family Tree chart)**

   Eli's ancestral lineage is not mentioned anywhere in Scripture; however, there are some clues we can glean from the books of Samuel and First Chronicles 6.

   Let's begin with the fact that Eli is a high priest, which means he must come from the tribe of Levi. First Chronicles 6:1-15 give us the family tree of Levi. The high priestly line traces down from Amram to Aaron to Eleazar to Phinehas who was high priest at the start of the judges' era. This is the Phinehas with whom God made the covenant of an eternal priesthood. Seven named generations pass before we come to Zadok, the eighth, who Solomon made high priest instead of Abiathar in First Kings 2:27.

   Abiathar is a descendant of Eli, not Eleazar. None of Eli's line are found in the lineage of the first sons descended from Aaron who would have been the high priests, and yet he is clearly officiating as the high priest at the opening of First Samuel, and his great-great-grandson Abiathar is high priest at the start of First Kings. So clearly we are looking at two separate arms of the family.

   That begs the question: Where does Eli fit into the Levitical family tree then? I have gleaned Eli's family out of the books of Samuel and charted

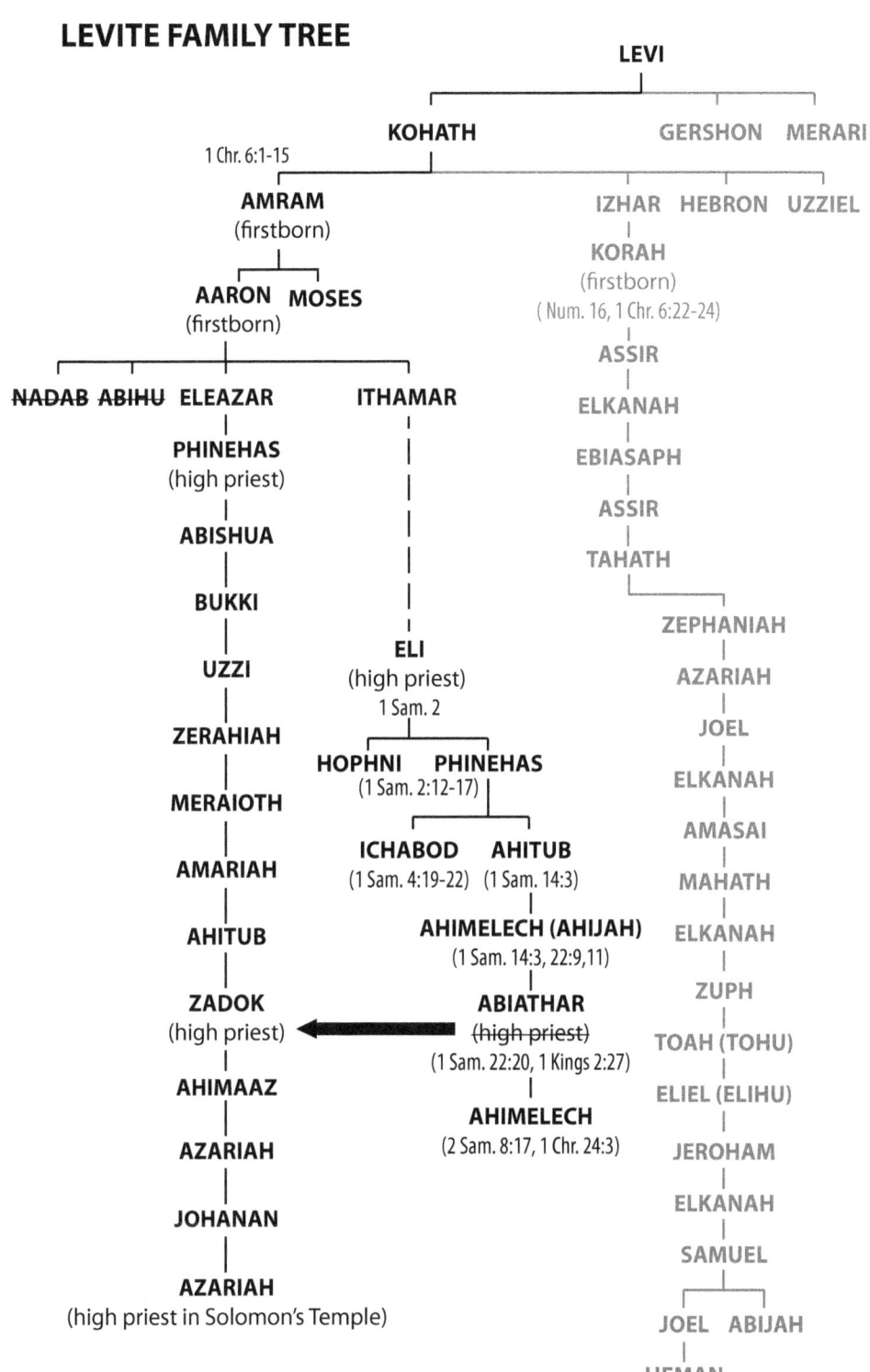

Eli's descendants along with the verses where they are referenced. In First Samuel 14:3, we find this reciting of Ahijah's lineage:

> "Ahijah the son of Ahitub, Ichabod's brother, the son of Phinehas, the son of Eli, the LORD's priest in Shiloh, was wearing an ephod..."
> —First Samuel 14:3a

Here, Ahijah is mentioned as the acting high priest going back to Eli. The relationship between Ahijah and Ahimelech in First Samuel 22:9 is bit murky. Either he is Ahimelech by another name, or he is brother to Ahimelech. It's not clear. Ahimelech is the priest that David seeks when he is fleeing from Saul—the priest who gives him the show-bread to eat along with Goliath's sword. Ahimelech and his family lose their lives for that act, except for one son, Abiathar, who escapes.

Abiathar figures heavily in the life of David and eventually becomes high priest. His son Ahimelech (named for his grandfather) becomes part of David's priestly administration, as noted in Second Samuel 8:17. This Ahimelech in the sixth generation is our clue. First Chronicles 24:3-6 gives us a second account of David placing this young man in priestly service, only this time Ahimelech is not called the son of Abiathar but the son of Ithamar.

> "So David reigned over all Israel... Zadok the son of Ahitub and Ahimelech the son of Abiathar were the priests..."
> —Second Samuel 8:15a,17a

> "Then David with Zadok of the sons of Eleazar, and Ahimelech of the sons of Ithamar, divided them according to the schedule of their service." —First Chronicles 24:3

In the Second Samuel passage, Zadok and Ahimelech are identified relative to their immediate fathers; but in First Chronicles, they are identified relative to their patriarchal fathers.

Who is Ithamar? He is the fourth son of Aaron, the original high priest, and brother to the high priest Eleazar. Ithamar is technically a member of the Aaronic priesthood, just not in the designated line for the high priesthood.

In the days of the judges, we know that something went horribly wrong with the priesthood after Phinehas, the son of Eleazar—so much so that no high priest is mentioned in the book of Judges except for Phinehas. It might be that the high priestly line shifted away from the line of Eleazar and into the line of Ithamar for this reason. There will be a second reason for the shift, which we will see when we get to the prophecy of the man of God against the house of Eli.

3. **What do we know about the sons of Eli?**

In First Samuel 1:3, there is a mention of Eli's sons, Hophni and Phinehas, being at the Tabernacle in Shiloh when Elkanah went up to the yearly offering, but, like their father, they are a mere byline. Now, in First Samuel 2:12-17, we get more details.

Hophni and Phineas were corrupt and degenerate priests who scorned the portion of the sacrifice allotted to them in God's Law. According to Leviticus 7 and 8, the priests were allowed the breast and right thigh of the sin, trespass, and peace offerings, and the meat was to be boiled and the fat removed before they took their portion. Hophni and Phinehas made the boiling pot a grab bag and demanded raw meat for roasting instead of boiling. If the people did not give it, it would be taken by force. In addition to this sin, they also lay with the women who assembled at the door of the Tabernacle.

The name **Hophni** means "two-fisted" as a boxer, but he is really more of a thug. The name **Phinehas** means "mouth of brass" or "mouth of a serpent," which speaks for itself.

4. **Did Eli make any effort to restrain his sons?**

He gave them a good talking-to, but it was completely ineffectual. They didn't heed the voice of their father, because the LORD desired to kill them (2:25).

5. **Compare the house of Elkanah and the house of Eli.**

The author contrasts the house of Eli's descent into degradation with the blessing on the house of Elkanah and Samuel's ascent to honor in an alternating pattern. After the description of Hophni and Phinehas' wickedness in verses 12-17, Samuel is presented in verses 18-21 as a priest ministering before the LORD and wearing an ephod even in his youth, and Elkanah's house is blessed. After the description of Eli's rebuke of his sons in verses 22-25, Samuel is commended in verse 26.

The house of Eli enjoys the blessings of God but is presented as a degenerate house lacking good judgment, mercy, and conscience. We see this in Eli's lack of judgment with Hannah. Eli's sons, Hophni and Phinehas, also ministered before the LORD, and yet they do not grow. They are, in fact, going to die.

By contrast, the house of Elkanah is presented as a gracious, God-fearing family that has the blessings of God from year to year and an increase in his kingdom. Their son, Samuel, ministered and grew before the LORD.

APPLY THE PICTURE

Hophni's and Phinehas' Model

Hophni and Phinehas are perfect models for those who have attained crowns but become disqualified and lose them.

> *"... Thus I fight: not as one who beats the air. But I discipline my body and bring it into subjection, lest, when I have preached to others, I myself should become disqualified."*—First Corinthians 9:26-27

Paul's analogy of a fighter who beats the air is appropriate for "two-fisted" Hophni. A boxer can flail about and hope to win, or he can discipline himself, take aim, and land an effective punch. Hophni flailed about his duties with a complete lack of restraint or self-reflection. Both he and Phinehas were men who had failed to discipline their bodies and bring them under submission. They focused on the earthly gratifications instead of their spiritual responsibilities and gave themselves over to the pursuit of their lusts. As priests charged with being examples and teaching God's people, they disqualified themselves. They are good examples of the bad shepherds that Peter warns against:

> *"Shepherd the flock of God which is among you, serving as overseers, not by compulsion but willingly, not for dishonest gain but eagerly; nor as*

being lords over those entrusted to you, but being examples to the flock; and when the Chief Shepherd appears, you will receive the crown of glory that does not fade away." —First Peter 5:2-4

They were men who sinned deliberately, and so the LORD gave them over to their uncleanness and lusts and hardened their heart so that their sinfulness becomes exceedingly sinful, as Paul says in Romans 1:

"And even as they did not like to retain God in their knowledge, God gave them over to a debased mind, to do those things which are not fitting; being filled with all unrighteousness, sexual immorality, wickedness, covetousness, maliciousness; full of envy, murder, strife, deceit, evil-mindedness . . ." —Romans 1:28–29a

There are a number of New Testament teachings that address the issue of abusing the station God has given us in our worldly ministry. Peter warns us about using our liberty as a cloak for vice (First Peter 2:16) but let's look at the greater context in which he houses that statement:

"You also, as living stones, are being built up a spiritual house, a holy priesthood, to offer up spiritual sacrifices acceptable to God through Jesus Christ . . . you are a chosen generation, a royal priesthood, a holy nation, His own special people, that you may proclaim the praises of Him who called you out of darkness into His marvelous light . . . Beloved, I beg you as sojourners and pilgrims, abstain from fleshly lusts which war against the soul, having your conduct honorable among the Gentiles, that when they speak against you as evildoers, they may, by your good works which they observe, glorify God in the day of visitation." —First Peter 2:5, 9-12

There are ways to maintain the crown. Abstain from fleshly lusts. Discipline yourself.

There are reasons to discipline yourself—that God might be glorified.

There are kings under which we must align ourselves for God's glory, because our submission to the authorities He ordained on the earth are a reflection of our submission to Him as an authority. So Peter segues into the issues of submission:

"Therefore submit yourselves to every ordinance of man for the Lord's sake, whether to the king as supreme, or to governors, as to those who

are sent by him for the punishment of evildoers and for the praise of those who do good. For this is the will of God, that by doing good you may put to silence the ignorance of foolish men—as free, yet not using liberty as a cloak for vice, but as bondservants of God. Honor all people. Love the brotherhood. Fear God. Honor the king." —First Peter 2:13–17

Respect for authority is a lesson that will crop up again and again throughout First Samuel. A person who has no respect for authority, particularly God's authority, loses the right to wield authority. That is one way a crown is lost. We will come back to this in some future lessons.

Apostate leaders and false teachers also follow the model of Hophni and Phinehas (Jude 1, Second Peter 2) in that they present themselves among God's children, but the reason they pursue that crown of priesthood is for the gratification of their own lusts. There are right and wrong reasons for pursuing a crown.

Samuel's Model

Samuel is the foil of Hophni and Phinehas, but we don't know much about him at this point. We will go into what Samuel models in a bit, but I want to draw your attention to a couple of verses that describe him in the passage we just read.

> *"Meanwhile the child Samuel grew before the LORD . . . And the child Samuel grew in stature, and in favor both with the LORD and men."*
> —First Samuel 2:21, 26

Does the phrasing of that verse remind you of other people in the Bible? It reminds me of the descriptions of Samson, John the Baptist, and Jesus. Let's compare the verses:

> *"So the woman bore a son and called his name Samson; and the child grew, and the LORD blessed him."* —Judges 13:24, speaking of Samson

> *"So the child grew and became strong in spirit, and was in the deserts till the day of his manifestation to Israel."* —Luke 1:80, speaking of John the Baptist

> *"And the Child grew and became strong in spirit, filled with wisdom; and the grace of God was upon Him."* —Luke 2:40, speaking of Jesus

"And Jesus increased in wisdom and stature, and in favor with God and men" —Luke 2:52. This statement in Luke's account follows the picture of Jesus in His youth, sitting in the Temple with the priests and teachers, listening and teaching. That is a very close picture comparison with Samuel. Just as Samuel stood in contrast to the degenerate priesthood of his day, so Jesus stood in contrast to the chief priests and Pharisees of His day.

Interesting, how the phrasing draws together this set of men. Three of them—Samson, Samuel, and John the Baptist—were born to barren women and were Nazirites from birth. Samson and Samuel were both judges. John the Baptist and Samuel were both Levites and prophets.

While Jesus is not born of a barren woman like the rest, He has this typology in common with them: that they were all born by divine gifting and grace. While He was not a Nazirite like the rest, nevertheless, He was *nazir* (separated) from His brethren—called out for a specific purpose to serve the LORD.

So we have a very interesting comparison between the pictures of Samson, Samuel, John the Baptist, and Christ, but particularly between Samuel and Christ based on the particular repeated phrasing, *"...grew in stature, and in favor both with the LORD and men."* We will have to see how that picture comparison develops in the on-going narrative.

Summary

The theme of pursuing crowns that began with the contrast at the individual level between barren Hannah and abundant Peninnah, now telescopes out to the family and community levels. We have the greater comparison of the houses of Elkanah and Eli represented by their sons. Elkanah's house ascends to blessing through his son Samuel, while Eli's house descends into curse because of his sons Hophni and Phinehas. The contrasting pictures that we have so far fall along these lines:

- There are those who value earthly rewards—the lust of the eyes, lust of the flesh, pride of life—and pursue immediate gratification and an earthly abundance by their own effort or works. These are contrasted to those who pursue an eternal reward gifted by grace from God and hold to the promise of a future blessing and inheritance.

- There are those who seek validation and glory from men, and they are contrasted with those who seek validation from God and give glory to God in their pursuit of a legacy.

- There are those who walk by sight, contrasted with those who walk by faith. Despite being a high priest and judge, Eli is a man of poor vision that will grow even dimmer in the narrative to come.

The Prophecy of the Man of God

READ

First Samuel 2:27-36

BUILD THE PICTURE

An unnamed man of God delivers the LORD's judgment against Eli. In verses 27-28, he begins with reminding Eli of God's calling of the sons of Aaron to be a priesthood when He brought them out of Egypt and how the Lord gave them a portion of the offerings made to Him.

6. **What are the charges that the man of God brings against Eli?**

   It seems that even though Eli rebuked his sons for what they were doing, he nevertheless reaped the benefits of their sin. The LORD charges Eli and his sons with making themselves fat with the best of the offerings. Eli dishonored the offering that the Lord had set aside for His priesthood and honored his sons instead.

7. **What is the curse that the LORD institutes with Eli's house?**

   - He will cut off the "arm" of Eli's house and his father's house.

     The Hebrew word for arm is *zeroah*, which means a literal arm; or figuratively, a family line or a division of something, like an arm of government or military. It carries with it the sense of strength—physical, political, or military strength.

     But more importantly, the *zeroah* is the arm of the sacrificed animal that was apportioned to the priesthood. It is the LORD's *zeroah* that Eli and his sons had despised; therefore, God despises Eli's *zeroah*. This is an eye-for-an-eye type of judgment.

- There will not be an old man in their house forever.

  Eli's descendants will die in the flower of their age. This curse is reiterated three times (2:31-33) and begins with the prophesied death of Hophni and Phinehas. Those of Eli's house who are not cut off from the altar will bring his house to grief.

- *"You will see an enemy in My dwelling place."* I will discuss this in the next lesson when I talk about why the Ark of God returned to Kirjath Jearim and not Shiloh in 1 Samuel 7:1.

- God will raise up a faithful priest for Himself, one who will do according to the LORD's heart and mind, and will build up his house. This priest will walk before God's anointed—His *mashiach*—forever. *Mashiach* can either refer to a king of Israel, specifically the Messianic king, or a high priest.

The man of God begins by reminding Eli of the covenant God made with his father's house, and he was clearly referring to Aaron, Eli's ancestor, and not his immediate father. So, when God says he is going to cut off the arm of Eli's father's house, that would seem to conflict with the previous covenants God made.

8. **What previous covenants might the curse negate?**

There was a covenant made with the tribe of Levi and then with the house of Aaron, that they would be a priesthood before God forever; but God also made another covenant specifically with Phinehas, the son of Eleazar, the son of Aaron, along the same lines.

> *"Therefore say, 'Behold, I give to him [Phinehas] My covenant of peace; and it shall be to him and his descendants after him a covenant of an everlasting priesthood, because he was zealous for his God, and made atonement for the children of Israel.' "* —Numbers 25:12-13

Since this new curse falls not just on Eli's house but on his father's house as well, who is his father? The word "father" is a little vague in the Hebrew. It can refer to an immediate father or an ancestral father such as Phinehas or Aaron.

Is the LORD bringing the curse on the priesthood in its entirety? This would negate the covenants He made with Aaron and Phinehas. Once God makes a covenant with a people, does He go back on His word? No. Can the LORD bring a curse on an arm of the family without affecting the previous covenants? Yes, He can. We know He did just such a thing with the kings of Israel when Solomon's line incurred a curse. The Davidic covenant was preserved because the Messiah came through a different family line from Solomon's.

Then perhaps the curse is limited to Eli's specific family "arm." This means that the house of Eli would have to be disconnected from the house of Phinehas, which it is as we saw in the family tree. This is the second reason for the shift out of the line of Eleazar and into the line of Ithamar, as we discussed earlier.

9. **Who then is the faithful priest that God raises up for Himself?**

   It is tempting to say Samuel, because the narrative is making a comparison between Samuel and the House of Eli, but I am pretty sure it isn't Samuel. Samuel was a priest, but not from the priestly line that qualified to replace the high priest. We need to look for a new high priest to reclaim that role. I think it is Zadok for these reasons.

   The high priesthood will remain in Eli's line until Abiathar. Then it will shift back along covenantal lines when Solomon takes the high priesthood away from Abiathar and gives it to Phinehas' descendant Zadok in First Kings 2:27:

   > "So Solomon removed Abiathar from being priest to the LORD, that he might fulfill the word of the LORD which He spoke concerning the house of Eli at Shiloh." —First Kings 2:27

   Therefore, the faithful priest mentioned in First Samuel 2:35 might be a reference to Zadok, as it says:

   > "Then I will raise up for Myself a faithful priest who shall do according to what is in My heart and in My mind. I will build him a sure house, and he shall walk before My anointed forever."
   > —First Samuel 2:35

This covenant is reiterated in Ezekiel 48:11, where Ezekiel writes that the sons of Zadok will be given a place in the new Jerusalem and the new Temple to minister as priests.

So, we can see that while Eli's house is an offshoot of the high priestly line, it does not affect the previous covenants when it falls under judgment.

The prophecy of the man of God ends abruptly without any narration over Eli's reaction or what happened after that. Instead the narrative immediately moves to the episode with young Samuel and Eli in the Tabernacle. We will finish building the picture through Chapter 3, then apply it.

Ascent of Samuel, Descent of Eli

READ

First Samuel 3:1–21

NARRATIVE STRUCTURE

First Samuel 3 is arranged in a tight chiastic structure (ABCDEDCBA) which underscores the importance of the events. Here is the breakdown:

- (A) The word of the LORD was rare in those days (3:1a)
- (B) There was no widespread revelation (3:1b)
- (C) The scene between Eli and Samuel (Samuel goes to Eli) (3:2-9)
- (D) God speaks to Samuel—the announcement of judgment (3:10-11)
- **(E) God speaks to Samuel—what the judgment is (3:12-13)**
- (D) God speaks to Samuel—the affirmation of judgment (3:14-15)
- (C) The scene between Samuel and Eli (Eli goes to Samuel) (3:16-18)
- (B) There was widespread revelation (3:19-20)
- (A) Then the LORD appeared again at Shiloh (3:21)

"A" and "B" represent the opening and closing pictures of Israel's overall condition. Note the end reversal and resolution.

"C" includes the scenes between Eli and Samuel. Verses 2-9 build the tension in the narrative as Samuel keeps running to Eli every time the LORD speaks to him. There is a resolution at the end in verses 16-18 where Eli comes to Samuel this time and asks for the prophecy. Samuel went to Eli in the beginning. Now Eli comes to Samuel. So, there is a reversal and a resolution.

"D" and "E" are part of the prophecy where God speaks to Samuel. He begins with the announcement, followed by a description of the judgment and the reason for it, and finishes with the resolution that the judgment is final and there will be no atonement.

"E" is the apex of the chiasm. The chiasm brings us to a pointed focus on God's judgment of Eli, which is the confirmation of the man of God's prophecy, and points to the resolution of events in the next chapter.

Now let's flesh out the narrative and get into some details. We will begin by identifying the particulars of the picture (who, what, when, where).

BUILD THE PICTURE

10. Who are the key characters?

The chapter focuses exclusively on Samuel, Eli, and the LORD.

11. What is happening?

The LORD calls to Samuel and gives him his first prophecy.

12. When do the events take place?

At night, near morning. It is the high priest's duty to keep the light in the lamp stand burning overnight, so it would have been close to morning when the oil needed replenishing.

13. Where do the events take place?

In verse 3, it says that the lamp stand stood in the *hekal* of the LORD. The NKJV translates *hekal* as tabernacle, but that is not a good translation. The Hebrew word *hekal* actually means "palace" or "temple"—a permanent structure with walls and doors and doorposts. It is the word used when the Scriptures speak of Solomon's

Temple and the king's palace. This is odd because there is no record of such a structure being built for the LORD's dwelling, at least not yet.

In Joshua's day, the Tabernacle was still an *ohel*, a tent. Joshua 18:1 tells us that the people set up the *ohel* of meeting at Shiloh, and nothing more is mentioned of it throughout the book of Judges. But now there is this deviation from the original tent to a semi-permanent structure here in First Samuel. While it anticipates the transition to a permanent Temple, this *hekal* seems rather inglorious for the lack of description, compared to the amount of detail given for the Tabernacle and Temple.

Eli and Samuel were both sleeping in the house of God. There were no sleeping quarters mentioned in the original Tabernacle arrangement, and yet it seems that this *hekal* has accommodations not just for Eli, but Samuel as well, and they clearly weren't sleeping in the same chamber. The original Hebrew word order indicates that Samuel was actually sleeping in the same chamber as the Ark of the Covenant. Technically this would have been the holy of holies into which no man was allowed except the high priest once a year, and yet here in the *hekal*, there doesn't seem to be a separation of the holy of holies from the rest of the sanctuary.

This also explains the fine wording in First Samuel 3:10, where it says that the LORD came and took His place and called to Samuel. The place from which the LORD speaks is the Ark of the Covenant. It appears that Samuel was indeed sleeping in the sanctuary, while Eli was in an adjoining chamber somewhere.

So, a little child stands close to the LORD while the aging priest sleeps in another room. The physical arrangement provides a comment on the spiritual relationships as well.

14. There is a theme of light and dark that runs through Chapter 3. How does it play out in the narrative?

First Samuel 3:1-3: The scene opens with a picture of physical and spiritual darkness. It begins with a critical comment that the word of the LORD was rare in those days. A spiritual darkness had settled over the nation in the days of Eli and his sons, and there is a distance between God and His high priest.

Eli is in bed at night, but his sleepiness—the heaviness of his eyes—is amplified by the fact that his eyes have grown dim so that he cannot see. His blindness is physical, but it reflects his spiritual state as well. We have already seen in Hannah's case that Eli judges by what he sees, but he doesn't see well and doesn't judge rightly.

This event happens just before the lamp of God went out. The phrase adds a sense of dimness and darkness to the scene. Just as God's light is about to die, God calls Samuel.

First Samuel 3:7: The LORD calls three times, and each time, Samuel runs to Eli's side with the response "Here I am, for you called me." There is a parenthetical note in verse 7 that although Samuel served in the house of the LORD, he did not know the LORD nor had the Word of God been revealed to him. This speaks to the LORD's on-going silence and His ministers' lack of enlightenment in these days.

First Samuel 3:8: It isn't until Samuel comes to Eli a third time and insists that Eli had called him that Eli perceives it is the LORD speaking to the boy. Eli is dull of understanding.

First Samuel 3:11-15: The theme of darkness then gives way first to a dawning of enlightenment and then physical light. The narrative reaches a climax as the LORD gives Samuel his first prophecy—an enlightenment. The scene ends with Samuel rising in the morning and opening the doors of the house of the LORD to the morning light.

First Samuel 3:18-19: Then his prophecy is revealed to Eli, and from there his status as a prophet spreads to the rest of Israel. The spreading of the light continues.

First Samuel 3:21: The LORD appears again in Shiloh, and it is like the dawning of a new day.

15. What reason does God give for judging Eli?

Verse 13 says that God is judging Eli "because his sons made themselves vile, and he did not restrain them." The word translated as vile means to be slight or fleeting—of little account, lightly esteemed, and so diminished. Hophni and Phinehas treated the LORD and His service with disregard, but in taking glory away from God, they diminished themselves.

APPLY THE PICTURE

Eli's Model

Eli wore the crown of a high priest and a judge. The LORD brings judgment on Eli's sons for what they have done, but He also brings judgment on Eli for not having restrained them and even joining them in benefiting from their sin. Eli is going to lose both crowns because he failed to lead as both a priest and judge.

Where Hophni and Phinehas were examples of what Paul talks about in Romans 1:28-32, Eli is the picture of what Paul talks about in Romans 2. (Note: We are tracking through Romans with these illustrations.)

Read Romans 2:1-11.

In this part of his argument, Paul is not necessarily speaking to believers. Paul is building a case against all kinds of sinners, and he will conclude that all have sinned and therefore need grace gifted to them through Christ's death on the cross.

Paul's words are addressing the moral sinner who points the finger at others' sin but doesn't judge himself—the one who knows the Law, as Eli certainly knew the Law, and yet is only a hearer of the Law and not a doer of it. And we see the judgment come upon him.

- **Do we have a role in restraining/rebuking one another?**
  Yes, we do. Eli and his sons are good examples of the apostates of whom Jude speaks when he exhorts us to have compassion on some, making a distinction, but some we save with fear, pulling them from the fire (Jude 1:22-23). Throughout the New Testament there are various teachings exhorting us to rebuke a sinning brother, but the reasons we do it and the way we do it must be considered.

- **What are right or wrong reasons or ways to do this?**
  There are many New Testament verses I could point to, but I prefer a verse from the Law that encompasses most of them:

  "You shall not hate your brother in your heart. You shall surely rebuke your neighbor, and not bear sin because of him." —Leviticus 19:17

The order in which information is related is important in Old Testament pictures. Why is the act of rebuking prefaced by the command not to hate your brother? Because rebuking someone without loving him or her first is the wrong way to go about it and speaks to a wrong reason for doing it. The Pharisees rebuked people, not because they loved them but because they didn't want to be guilty of breaking this law. That is a self-focused reason for rebuking someone. Rebuke should be delivered out of a love for a brother, a desire to keep him from sinning, and to turn him back to God. It should be more concerned with the well-being of your brother than receiving a divine pat on the head. The Pharisees sought God's blessing the wrong way and for the wrong reason, and we can, too.

- **Do we earn a rebuke from God for not rebuking a sinning brother?**

    Yes, I think we do, but, again, avoiding rebuke should not be the reason we rebuke. Loving our brother should be the motivating factor.

If you are pursuing the crown, you are training to be a leader. The role of leader will require you to bear the responsibility for others. Leadership begins with having an others-focused mindset. You are responsible for the well-being of those under you. You must demand accountability from them even as you hold yourself accountable, and warn them when they are sinning.

Hophni's and Phinehas' Model (3:13)

First Samuel 3:13 adds an additional detail in the LORD's summary of Eli's sons. He says they made themselves vile—lightly esteemed, dishonorable. They had been given a glorious calling and place in the LORD's kingdom and yet they abused their position and scorned what the LORD had given them. They have disqualified themselves and will lose their crowns.

Hophni and Phinehas are bad role models, and yet we cannot judge them without looking at ourselves through the same lens. We are holy vessels and a royal priesthood. We have a priestly role in our handling of not just the ministry but each other.

> Questions for Reflection
>
> - Can we take glory from God in our handling of one another or in our mishandling of the ministry with which we have been entrusted?
>
> - How do we diminish ourselves in the process?
>
> Another example of this is in the husband and wife dynamic. Paul says in Ephesians 5:28 that husbands ought to love their own wives as their own bodies, that he who loves his wife loves himself. So, when a man diminishes his wife's value and treats her with contempt, he diminishes his own value and becomes contemptible. Likewise, when a woman does not respect her husband, she loses respect for herself in the process. As it is with husband and wife, so it is with Christ and the Church. When we take glory from Him, we take glory from ourselves. This is not a difficult concept to understand. This is the model that Hophni and Phinehas are modeling for us.
>
> > *"For the time has come for judgment to begin at the house of God; and if it begins with us first, what will be the end of those who do not obey the gospel of God?"* —First Peter 4:17

The Glory Departs

READ

First Samuel 4:1–22

BUILD THE PICTURE

16. Who are the Philistines?

The Philistines were descendants of Noah's son, Ham, through the line of Mizraim, who is also the patriarch of the Egyptians. Mizraim is an ancient name for Egypt. So, the Philistines have ancient ties to Egypt.

They have been living in the Promised Land long before Abraham arrived. Since the days of Abraham, the Philistines had been localized to the coastal lands in Judah's territory, but they began to gain power and territory in the days of the judges and were just reaching their height in the days of the kings.

Samson, the twelfth judge, partially delivered Israel from the Philistines but not completely. He takes down the temple of Dagon at Gaza but dies in the process. Nothing has been done about the Philistines since Samson.

17. Where are we on the timeline and what is Israel's condition?

There aren't any time markers given at the beginning of the chapter, but in verse 18, we see a note that Eli, the judge who followed Samson, had judged Israel for forty years at his death.

Forty years is a long time. Forty years is a generation of people. Think of the changes that take place in a nation when a new generation rises to take over the old way. Even with good judges who provided a restraining presence for Israel and its enemies, Israel immediately fell into idolatry again once the judge died. Restraint is not exactly Eli's forte as judge or priest. He wouldn't restrain himself and his own sons, let alone the nation. We can see from the narrative what the condition of Israel is like now that an entire generation has been raised with a lack of restraint and reverence for God. When a nation has lost its values, vision, and its national identity as a people of God, what happens when a foreign enemy strikes it? We should look at Israel's experience.

18. Where does the battle set up?

Just when Israel hits this spiritual low point, the physical enemy begins an expansion into the land. The Philistines have swarmed over the coastal lands of Judah and Dan and made it as far as this place called Aphek deep in Ephraim's territory. The name Aphek means "fortress." It was a well-situated and reinforced encampment.

According to the commentary in the Satellite Bible Atlas[1], Aphek

---

[1] Schlegel, William. *Satellite Bible Atlas, Historical Geography of the Bible,* 2nd ed., (Jerusalem: SkyLand Publishing, 2016), pg 64.

was a strategic choke-point on the coastal highway that was ideally positioned for a strike into Israel's interior as well as an expansion upward through the Plain of Sharon and into the Jezreel Valley. The Philistines were preparing to springboard themselves across Israel.

Israel's armies assembled against the Philistine forces on the high ground above Aphek, at a place called Ebenezer. The name Ebenezer means "stone of help."

19. How does the battle play out?

The Philistines engage Israel in battle and defeat them. Israel loses four thousand men of their field army.

20. What is the leadership's response?

"Why has the LORD defeated us today before the Philistines?" Notice that they don't ask why the Philistines defeated Israel. They ask why the LORD defeated them. Any time Israel goes into battle and loses, it is because they have done something to anger the LORD.

21. When this kind of defeat occurred in the past, what did the leadership do then?

After the victory of Jericho, Joshua was defeated at Ai. Joshua and the elders threw themselves down before the LORD and mourned until evening, and then set to the task of dealing with the sin of Achan, who had taken forbidden spoil from Jericho (Joshua 7).

In the days of the judges when Israel went against Benjamin and was defeated twice, all the people came before the LORD weeping and fasting and offering burnt offerings and peace offerings. Once they changed their attitude toward their brethren, the LORD then gave them victory (Judges 20).

22. Is this what the leadership does here?

No. They send for the Ark of the Covenant.

23. What was the purpose of the Ark of the Covenant?

It was the place where God dwelt among His people, from where He spoke to them, and the place where intercession was made for Israel as a nation. It held the covenant agreement between God and His people.

That agreement promised blessings but also curses. Victory over the enemy was only guaranteed if the people upheld the covenant, which they hadn't. So, the only thing standing between the people and judgment at this point was the mercy seat. Without the blood of the sacrifice placed on the mercy seat, and the mercy seat covering the covenant, there would be no forgiveness for sins and God's judgment would fall on His people. That mercy seat had to be guarded jealously. If the mercy seat were put in jeopardy, then the nation wouldn't just be in physical jeopardy but spiritual jeopardy as well.

Of all the things to bring to the battlefield, the Ark of the Covenant was a really bad choice. The high priesthood was already compromised. And now Hophni and Phinehas had removed the Ark with its mercy seat from the house of God.

24. When was the last time the Ark left the Tabernacle and was carried into battle?

With the exception of the Jericho campaign, never. The Ark was never meant to be carried into battle. This was an unprecedented action.

25. What did the elders think would happen when they brought the Ark out to the battlefield?

They thought if the Ark of the Covenant was with them, then they would prevail against the Philistines. They thought they could manipulate God into acting by forcibly bringing the Ark out to the battlefield—as if the power of the LORD could be summoned like a foot soldier. The Israelites had sunk so far into idolatry that they had begun to treat the Ark of the LORD as an idol—attributing power to the article itself as if it were a good luck charm. They put God in a box and thought that if they just carried that box around with them without having an actual relationship with God, then they would automatically have victory over their enemies.

There isn't even a pricking of conscience when the Ark arrives. Instead of falling on their faces and inquiring of the LORD about why they had been defeated, the people gave an earth-shaking roar of victory.

26. How do the Philistines react?

They are afraid. They, too, recognize that this is an unprecedented event (4:7). It is interesting that they recognize God as coming into camp, but then He isn't just one God that they are up against but many gods. They think that these many gods are going to visit the plagues of Egypt on them (curious, that the Philistines would retain some knowledge of Israel's history with Egypt after 300-plus years). Nevertheless, they encouraged themselves and went to war.

27. What is the outcome?

It is a massacre for Israel. The Philistines cut down 30,000 foot soldiers, routed the rest, captured the Ark, and killed Hophni and Phinehas.

Think about how demoralizing it must have been for Israel to have counted the victory as already won for having the Ark with them, only to realize in the midst of battle that the Ark was not going to save them. The power was never in the Ark. It was in the God who dwelt between the cherubim and in their covenant relationship with Him.

Think of the glory that God lost in this battle. His enemies have seemingly triumphed over Him by defeating His people. The Philistines are now thoroughly convinced that their god Dagon is stronger than Israel's God. God's rival has prevailed and will get the glory for this coup. He doesn't even have the distinction of being one God in the Philistines' mind. Yahweh is just one of a group of gods that they had beaten.

God Himself will correct the Philistines' thinking in the next lesson, but at this point, Israel's treatment of the holy things of God and even God Himself has diminished God in the eyes of the enemy. In diminishing God, they have followed Hophni and Phinehas' example and diminished themselves as His people.

APPLY THE PICTURE

Israel's Model

So far, in this chapter, we are presented with a people who claim the name of God but haven't maintained a relationship with Him. They are faced with a battle they cannot win by their own strength and so they carry with them the Ark—that symbol of God's presence—to help them in the battle. They think that just because they have the Ark with them, the victory is assured.

Israel had already given herself over spiritually to the dark side, so it is no wonder that when the actual Philistines attacked, she was unable to withstand the assault. Even though she has the Ark with her, there is no relationship with God. She goes about the battle the wrong way, and so she loses the battle at that point. It is not a permanent loss, but for a time, God's dwelling place gets overrun and taken captive by the Philistines.

- **Do we put God in a box like this?**

    Do we tell God "Thanks, but I've got this. If I need you, I'll let you know," and then put the relationship into a box and put Him aside? Do you realize how demeaning it is for the Creator of the universe to be relegated to a corner of our lives and only trotted out when we get into trouble?

- **Where is God's dwelling place among us now?**

    Like Israel, we have God's dwelling place within us. It is not a physical Ark that we carry around. It is an indwelling Holy Spirit that we carry inside us, who is God within us, and also our intercessor. And yet we still must contend with that carnal Philistine side of our human nature.

- **Just because we have the Holy Spirit within us, does that mean we have conquered our Philistine side?**

    No. The Spirit is there. He prods us toward holy living and conscience before God, and yet the battle remains to us to conquer our inner Philistine. Conquering our carnal side is part of pursuing the crown. Remember what Paul said:

    > "And everyone who competes for the prize is temperate in all things. Now they do it to obtain a perishable crown, but we for an imperishable crown. Therefore I run thus: not with uncertainty. Thus I fight: not as one who beats the air. But I discipline my body and bring it into subjection, lest, when I have preached to others, I myself should become disqualified." —First Corinthians 9:25-27

Christians who give themselves over to carnality lose the battle on the internal front and allow that holy dwelling place to be overrun with Philistines. As a result, the power and glory depart from them until the relationship with God is remedied.

Just because we carry that indwelling Spirit with us into battle does not mean we are assured victory. Victory only happens when:

- We are aligned with the God and pursuing a relationship with Him.
- We are aligned with His goals and pursuing the reward the right way and in a way that glorifies Him.
- We are pursuing the reward for the right reason.

When we lose the internal battle and let our carnal side rule our bodies, then when the ungodly world attacks, we should not be surprised if we lose the battle on that front as well.

BUILD THE PICTURE

28. How did Eli react?

Verse 13 says that Eli sat on a seat by the gate, watching the road, and his heart trembled for the Ark of God. Not for his sons, but for the Ark. It seems as if he had given up any concern for his sons, but then he knew the prophecy against them. His only anxiety was for the Ark. Out of all the details that Eli hears about Israel's defeat, the capture of the Ark is what kills him.

The passage gives us a number of details about Eli. Eli was 98-years old, heavy, unable to see; and he died from a broken neck after falling off backward from his seat. It is a most inglorious kind of death.

29. How did Phinehas' widow react?

When she hears the news of the Ark's capture and the death of her husband and father-in-law, her labor pains come upon her, and she dies giving birth to Ichabod.

Labor Pains (Hebrew: *Tsiyr*)

The Hebrew word for labor pains is a curious one. It is the word *tsiyr* (pronounced like tsar, but with an "e"—tseer). It doesn't mean labor pains specifically. It is a word used to describe a pivoting or writhing action, but also a messenger that goes back and forth to deliver a message. Here are some of its usages:

- A hinge (Proverbs 26:14)

    *"As a door turns on its hinges **[tsiyr]**, so does the lazy man on his bed."* —Proverbs 26:14. It is something that goes back and forth in a literal sense.

- A person in the throes of pain or distress (First Samuel 4:19; Isaiah 13:8, 21:3; Daniel 10:16).

    *"And they will be afraid. Pangs **[tsiyr]** and sorrows will take hold of them; They will be in pain as a woman in childbirth; They will be amazed at one another; Their faces will be like flames."* —Isaiah 13:8

    *"Therefore my loins are filled with pain; Pangs **[tsiyr]** have taken hold of me, like the pangs **[tsiyr]** of a woman in labor. I was distressed when I heard it; I was dismayed when I saw it."* —Isaiah 21:3

    But what is causing the *tsiyr* in Isaiah's case? The visions that the LORD is giving him concerning Israel's defeat and impending captivity.

- A messenger or envoy who relays messages back and forth (Isaiah 18:2, Obadiah 1:1, Jeremiah 49:14, 57:9, Proverbs 13:17). The arrival of this messenger is never a good sign, though. These are the kind of messengers who precede an invading army. They are the sign that God's judgment is assured and imminent, and the terror they inspire is likened to labor pains, as the prophets describe:

    *"The vision of Obadiah. Thus says the Lord GOD concerning Edom (We have heard a report from the LORD, and a messenger **[tsiyr]** has been sent among the nations, saying, 'Arise, and let us rise up against her for battle')"* —Obadiah 1:1

> *"I have heard a message from the LORD, and an ambassador [tsiyr] has been sent to the nations: 'Gather together, come against her, and rise up to battle!'"* —Jeremiah 49:14
>
> *"Woe to the land shadowed with buzzing wings, which is beyond the rivers of Ethiopia, which sends ambassadors [tsiyr] by sea, even in vessels of reed on the waters, saying, 'Go, swift messengers, to a nation tall and smooth of skin, to a people terrible from their beginning onward, a nation powerful and treading down, whose land the rivers divide.'"* —Isaiah 18:1-2
>
> *"A wicked messenger falls into trouble, but a faithful ambassador [tsiyr] brings health."* —Proverbs 13:17. Note: This ambassador who brings health is not a good-will ambassador. This ambassador heralds the beginning of labor pains in your life which will bring health in the end, but you will have to go through this ordeal first before the health is returned.

The *tsiyr* that Phinehas' wife experiences pairs the pains of an impending birth with Israel's impending defeat by the Philistines as a judgment from God. Even as the first messenger came with the news, now this second messenger, the *tsiyr*, in the form of labor pains, confirms it. The child that came from that birth embodied the message: "The glory has departed from Israel, for the Ark of God has been captured." The name Ichabod means "no glory."

This is not the last time the birth of a child would herald the impending defeat by an enemy. In Isaiah 8, the birth of Maher-Shalal-Hash-Baz heralded the Assyrian invasion that took the northern kingdom of Israel into captivity.

Tsyir in the Hebrew is the same as the word *odeen* in the Greek.

> *"And you will hear of wars and rumors of wars. See that you are not troubled; for all these things must come to pass, but the end is not yet. For nation will rise against nation, and kingdom against kingdom. And there will be famines, pestilences, and earthquakes in various places. All these are the beginning of sorrows [odeen]."* —Matthew 24:6-8

"For when they say, 'Peace and safety!' then sudden destruction comes upon them, as labor pains [odeen] upon a pregnant woman. And they shall not escape." —First Thessalonians 5:3

30. The chapter ends with the widow's dying cry: *"The glory has departed from Israel, for the Ark of God has been captured."* What glory is she talking about?

When you see the word "glory" in your Bibles, it can be any one of ten Hebrew words, each with a slightly different picture and context. Here, the Hebrew word for glory is *chabod*. It is the word that is used when the glory of the LORD appears to men—when it appeared on Mount Sinai, when it passed before Moses in the cleft of the rock, when the glory filled the Tabernacle and the Temple. This is the glory that Hannah spoke of when she said that the LORD lifts up the beggar and makes him inherit the throne of glory. This is what Israel has lost.

Chabod embodies a quality or condition of gloriousness. It means weighty in the sense of being heavy in honor, abundance, dignity, and reputation. This is important to grasp. We tend to shy away from the idea of reigning as royalty with Christ, but the phrasing is meant to convey this granting of heaviness upon us—heaviness of honor and dignity and abundance, like the heaviness of a woman with child. Even as the *chabod* of a child, its weightiness, is granted Hannah, the same heaviness now leaves the body of Phinehas' wife, and she cries out that the *chabod* has departed from Israel.

As we close the chapter on Eli's house and Israel's loss of the Ark and its glory, I will remind you of Peter's exhortation:

"Shepherd the flock of God which is among you, serving as overseers, not by compulsion but willingly, not for dishonest gain but eagerly; nor as being lords over those entrusted to you, but being examples to the flock; and when the Chief Shepherd appears, you will receive the crown of glory that does not fade away." —First Peter 5:2-4

Questions for Reflection

- Have you put God in a box like Israel did?

- Have you ever had a *tsiyr* show up in your life—someone who brought life-changing bad news? What were some of the long-term results of that?

LESSON 3: FIRST SAMUEL 5-6

The Exiled King

NARRATIVE STRUCTURE

This lesson will cover the Ark of God's descent and ascent in First Samuel 5-6. In Chapter 5, the narrative detours away from Samuel and Israel and gives us a picture of God dealing with the Philistines as the Ark of God descends into enemy hands. In Chapter 6, He will bring the Philistines under subjection, and then return to deal with Israel's spiritual condition.

The narrative of the Ark's journey interrupts Samuel's storyline, and yet remains in keeping with the ascent and descent rhythm of the narrative.

Chapter	Event	Status change
4	Ark leaves the House of God at Shiloh and is taken down to the battlefield at Ebenezer	**Descent** of Eli's house into death; descent of the Ark into defilement
5	Ark in Philistine lands—moves from Aphek to Ashdod to Gath to Ekron	**Descent** of the Ark into defilement (lowest point)
6:1-19	Ark taken returned to Beth Shemesh	**Ascent** of the Ark—increasing toward holiness
6:20	Ark taken from Beth Shemesh to Kirjath Jearim	**Ascent** of the Ark—increasing toward holiness
7:1	Ark at Abinadab's House	**The Ark restored**—rests in state of holiness

The Ark Among Philistines

READ

First Samuel 5:1–12

BUILD THE PICTURE

1. **Who are the key characters?**

   The chapter focuses exclusively on the Philistines, their god Dagon, and the Ark of the God of Israel. The narrative treats the Ark almost as a character.

   Dagon was the Philistine fertility god. The Hebrew word *dagon* means "fish." For this reason the idol of Dagon is represented as half man, half fish. He has the head and arms of a man, but the body of a fish. The name is also very close to the Hebrew word *dagan* which means "wheat or corn." So he is also considered the god of grain or crops.

2. **Where do the events take place?**

   The Philistines take the Ark first from Ebenezer to the temple of Dagon at Ashdod, then to Gath, then to Ekron. We should note that Ashdod, Gath, and Gaza, were the only places where the Anakim—the giants—remained after Joshua took the Land (Joshua 11:22). Samson dealt with Gaza in his day. Now God takes on the giants of Ashdod and Gath.

3. **What happens when the Philistines take the Ark to Ashdod?**

   First, God takes down their god, Dagon. Next, God ravages the crops with an infestation of rats. Then, God ravages the people with tumors.

4. **How does God deal with Dagon?**

   The Philistines set the Ark of God beside Dagon as a trophy, and the next morning, they find Dagon face down before the Ark of God in the attitude of worship. It happens again the next day, only this time God doesn't just tip Dagon over. He defaces him. The head of Dagon and both palms are broken off, leaving the rest of him looking like a gutted fish.

In verse 5, the note about the people not treading on the threshold where Dagon fell refers to an ancient superstition that you shouldn't walk where a god has lain. Even though this image of Dagon has been rendered powerless, the people still attribute power and godship to his smashed remains, which is a little absurd; but then idolatry is absurd.

5. **How does God deal with the people?**

   Having rendered their god powerless, God begins to ravage both the land and the people of Ashdod. Most Bible translations say He struck them with tumors, but the Septuagint (Greek) and Vulgate (Latin) versions add this information to verse 6:

   > *"But the hand of the LORD was heavy on the people of Ashdod, and He ravaged them and struck them with tumors and in the midst of their land rats sprang up, and there was a great death panic in the city, both Ashdod and its territory."* —First Samuel 5:6

   Scholars generally agree that the combination of tumors and sores point to a sudden infestation of rats carrying the bubonic plague, which is spread by the fleas on rats and causes tumorous sores. This addition is surmised from the verse in First Samuel 6:5 that says that rats ravaged the land.

   The plague of vermin that attacked the Philistines' grain was also another manifestation of God's supremacy over Dagon, who was the god of crops. So, we have something akin to the plagues of Egypt being visited on the Philistines until they let the Ark go.

6. **How do the Philistines decide to deal with the Ark?**

   The five lords of the Philistines convened to decide what to do with the Ark. The consensus was to send it deeper into Philistine territory, to Gath. But why?

7. **If the Ark was causing this devastation in Ashdod, why not send it back to Israel?**

   The Philistines had captured the Glory of Israel and were loath to give up their trophy. The issue of taking trophies will crop up again in the narrative of the kings. It is never good to use God's things to glorify yourself. He doesn't react well when you do that.

8. **What happens when they take the Ark of God to Gath?**

    The same thing that happened in Ashdod. The name Gath means "winepress," and you can imagine the devastation of the people of Gath being likened to God treading out a winepress. First He puts His sickle to the wheat fields of Ashdod and reaps the souls there; then He treads out the winepress of Gath. A bit apocalyptic. The citizens of Gath quickly move it on to Ekron.

9. **What happens when the Ark arrives at Ekron?**

    The people cry, "We don't want it!"

Return of the Ark of the LORD

READ

First Samuel 6:1–7:1

BUILD THE PICTURE

10. **What do the Philistines decide to do with the Ark?**

    They call the priests and diviners, who say: Return the Ark of the LORD back to God in Israel. This is a fine point, but notice the switch in pronouns here:

    > The Philistines say *"Tell us how we should send it to its place."*
    > The diviners reply *"Return it to Him with a trespass offering."*

    The Philistines are still focused on the Ark as if it is the entity that is causing their grief. God is still in the box. The priests and diviners bring Him out of the box. The Ark was not a god like Dagon to be carried somewhere and set up by the hands of man. The Ark belonged to the LORD God who is a living God. He had not been defeated at all, but was still very much King over His kingdom and able to visit His wrath on His enemies for stealing something that belonged to Him. So now the Philistines realize they are dealing with a living God.

11. What is a trespass offering?

A trespass offering is for unintentional sin against a holy thing or a commandment. Restitution of an additional one-fifth is required for any harm done to the holy thing. A sin can be committed in ignorance, but once the offense is known, it becomes a sin for which atonement must be made. Once the atonement is made, the sin is forgiven. (See Leviticus 5.)

The Philistines have been made aware that they have committed a sin against God—now that they recognize that God is God and not just some idolized box. The box was a holy thing that belonged to God, and they had mishandled it out of ignorance.

12. What was the Philistines' trespass offering?

In addition to the cows and cart that would be used for the burnt offering, they added an additional "one-fifth" offering for restitution. The diviners and priests said to include five golden tumors and five golden rats—one each for the five lords of the Philistines who were representatives of their afflicted people and their afflicted land. But when we get to verses 17-18, we see that the Philistines actually sent more. They sent the five golden tumors, but many more golden rats—according to the number of cities, both fortified and country villages, over an extensive area. These were symbols of the peoples' suffering that they laid before the LORD as an acknowledgement of His sovereignty over His creation and the heaviness of His hand upon them.

13. What did they think this would accomplish?

They would be healed, and they would understand why God had sent the plague. By giving glory (*chabod*, heaviness) to the LORD in the form of this heavy gifting, they hoped He would lighten the heaviness of His hand against:

    1) Their land that had been ravaged (represented by the rats)
    2) The people who were afflicted (represented by the tumors)
    3) Their gods who had been overthrown

All has been brought into submission to the God of Israel.

14. **How would heathen Gentiles know anything about offering a trespass offering?**

    By all rights they shouldn't have known how to do this unless they learned the Law of God from Israel, which was unlikely given the debauchery of the House of Eli. It would seem that the understanding was given the priests and diviners by divine inspiration.

15. **What warning are the Philistines given?**

    It is time to let go of the trophy. Don't harden your hearts and resist the God of Israel like Egypt did. Remember, the Philistines have ancient family ties to Egypt, so the plagues that fell on Egypt when God took His children out of there would have been something of legend. They knew what happened when Egypt hardened its heart against letting God's children go, and so it would be wise to sue for peace at this point rather than resist further. They are forced to let go of the Ark as surely as Egypt was forced to send Israel away.

16. **What was the test that proved it was God's hand on them and not just some freak coincidence?**

    They put the offering on a cart drawn by two milk cows and turned it loose. Instead of going after their calves back at home, the cows set off in the opposite direction toward Beth Shemesh, though not without protest, it seems.

17. **When do the events take place?**

    In this chapter, we are given a time marker for these events, so let's look at that. First Samuel 6:1 tells us that the Ark was in the Philistines' hands for seven months. First Samuel 6:13 says it was returned at the time of the wheat harvest, which would have been in the third Hebrew month of Sivan. If we count back seven months from Sivan, this puts the battle back in the eighth month of Heshvan.

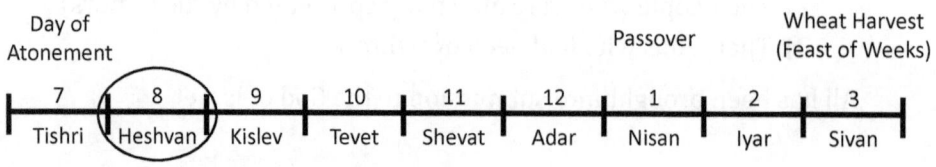

Heshvan is just one month after the all-important seventh month, when Israel is called before the LORD on the Day of Atonement. If they failed to repent and turn from their wicked ways on that day, God said He would render judgment on them in the following year. And so we have this battle in which unrepentant Israel led by a wicked priesthood suffers a devastating loss of the Ark to their enemies in the days after the Day of Atonement. At the same time, God's judgment is rendered against the House of Eli.

It seems appropriate that the Day of Atonement should hang in the background of these events. The warnings of judgment were given. Eli gave his sons a very Day-of-Atonement-like warning in First Samuel 2:

> *"If one man sins against another, God will judge him. But if a man sins against the LORD, who will intercede for him?"* —First Samuel 2:25a

The LORD also tells Samuel that the sin of the house of Eli would not be atoned for by sacrifice or offering (First Samuel 3:14). Eli and his sons would die before the year was over. And now that the judgment is rendered, we have this seven-month span of God hiding His face from Israel and going instead to make Himself known to a heathen nation. The number seven denotes a time of fullness and completion.

In addition to the judgment day imagery, there is also an echo of the Exodus imagery. The Philistines remembered the stories of God's judgment on Egypt and the plagues that took that land when God brought His children out of that bondage. The Philistines made servants of Israel even as Pharoah had, and have good reason to be afraid. The Passover is another feast that crops up during these seven months when God is dealing with the Philistines, and may coincide with the diviner's warning against resisting God as Egypt had.

18. What is the reaction of the men of Beth Shemesh?

They rejoice to see the Ark return, and then proceed to do something very right and very wrong. The Levites came to collect the Ark, and they offered the burnt offerings and made sacrifices. So that was a good start toward repairing the relationship with God. But then they decided to look into the Ark. That was bad.

19. Immediately God strikes them just as He had the Philistines. Why?

Just because God's Ark had returned to His people didn't mean that they could treat His holy things familiarly. He is Almighty Holy God, and He demands respect from all people for His person and His things. What applied to the Philistines applied to Israel. There is no partiality with God. You cannot approach the Ark without being properly consecrated.

The NKJV reads that 50,070 men died, but that far exceeds the population of Beth Shemesh. Alternate versions suggest only seventy men.

20. How do the men of Beth Shemesh react to the LORD's judgment?

They act a lot like the Philistines. They lament over the loss of their kinsmen and send the Ark on to the next place, which is Kirjath Jearim.

They are God's people, and yet they are still in ignorance and carnality. The Ark would have brought them a blessing if they had treated it correctly, but they would rather put it away from them than learn from the experience. A lot of Christians are like that. When they let their relationship with God lapse and return to that carnal mentality, it is often more effort than they care to take to change their behavior and don't pursue it.

21. Why take the Ark to Abinadab's house in Kirjath Jearim?

Let's consider the terrain we are covering, as well as names. While Beth Shemesh stood in the foothills at 800 feet above sea level, Kirjath Jearim rests in the high hills at 2,500 feet above sea level. That is a steep climb of roughly 1,700 feet.

The name Kirjath Jearim means "city of forests," and suggests a hilltop city set in the lush verdure of a thick forest. Abinadab means "noble father" from a root that means "one whose heart is impelled to give willingly"—which is fitting, since Abinadab willingly offers his house for the LORD's dwelling place.

So we have this picture of the LORD's glorious Ark—His throne—ascending with stately heaviness to the heights of a lush hilltop stronghold and the house of a nobleman. There is a tremendous amount of pomp and grandeur suggested in this, as appropriate for a victorious King—a noble father—returning from battle.

Apart from this picture made by the names, there is little other description of the Ark's new resting place in Abinadab's house or his son Eleazar. It appears that a formal Tabernacle was never set up in Kirjath Jearim. Nothing is mentioned about the lampstand, the table of showbread, and all the rest of the Tabernacle furnishings. We don't even know if Abinadab and Eleazar were Levites and therefore qualified to tend to the holy things of God. All we know is that Eleazar was consecrated and given the job.

22. How long does the Ark stay in Kirjath Jearim?

Twenty years. For twenty years, there is no proper Tabernacle or priesthood serving the LORD's house. The LORD is with them, and yet things are not right. Israel's spiritual life remains in this limbo, and it is a time of lament.

23. Why not take it back to Shiloh?

The question we should ask is: Is there still a Shiloh standing to which the Ark could return?

In First Samuel 2, we listed all the elements of God's judgment prophesied against Eli, but we skipped over a discussion of the clause that said: *"You will see an enemy in My dwelling place, despite all the good which God does for Israel."* If Shiloh is God's dwelling place, which it was when this prophecy is given, then when was the enemy seen in that place? Did it happen with this attack of the Philistines, when the Ark is captured and Eli's sons killed, or is this an event that a descendant of Eli would see? That remains in debate.

At some point in Israel's history, Shiloh is destroyed by enemies. We know that from a number of Scriptural references. But the actual destruction is not mentioned in the Scriptures anywhere, and some commentaries suggest that it might have happened here after the Philistine's defeat of Israel because of the fact that the Ark never returns to Shiloh. It is argued that it could not return because there was no place to which it could return. But this is a supposition only. There is no hard evidence to confirm it.

Regardless of when it is destroyed, Shiloh was rejected as God's dwelling place and became an object lesson. Jeremiah pointed to the destruction of Shiloh as a picture of what will happen to a future Temple in Jerusalem:

> "'But go now to My place which was in Shiloh, where I set My name at the first, and see what I did to it because of the wickedness of My people Israel. And now, because you have done all these works,' says the LORD, 'and I spoke to you, rising up early and speaking, but you did not hear, and I called you, but you did not answer, therefore I will do to the house which is called by My name, in which you trust, and to this place which I gave to you and your fathers, as I have done to Shiloh. And I will cast you out of My sight, as I have cast out all your brethren—the whole posterity of Ephraim.'"
> —Jeremiah 7:12-15

APPLY THE PICTURE

The Philistine's Model

We have been tracking with the book of Romans, first with Hophni and Phinehas (Romans 1:28-32), then with Eli (Romans 2:1-11). Now the Philistines are modeling something Paul says in Romans 2:11-15:

> "For there is no partiality with God. For as many as have sinned without law will also perish without law, and as many as have sinned in the law will be judged by the law (for not the hearers of the law are just in the sight of God, but the doers of the law will be justified; for when Gentiles, who do not have the law, by nature do the things in the law, these, although not having the law, are a law to themselves, who show the work of the law written in their hearts, their conscience also bearing witness, and between themselves their thoughts accusing or else excusing them)" —Romans 2:11-15

It's hard to imagine the Philistines modeling something good, but then the Jews who Paul addressed in Romans probably felt the same way about the Gentiles. It is a testament to God's impartiality that He brings judgment on all but also offers grace to all. Even so, it is not those who merely hear the warning who are justified. It is those who heed the warning and act accordingly in good conscience toward God.

The Taking of Trophies

The Philistines are also modeling a variation of the theme of pursuing crowns that has to do with taking trophies.

Trophies represent a measure of success, and we like to have that tangible evidence of our success because it is validating and gives us a sense of status and personal worth. It communicates to everyone that we have won the prize. It can also become a stumbling block for pride.

Trophies can be things that we grip onto in life because of what they represent to us. They may be earthly things such as wealth, or physical things that embody intangible qualities like power, status, security, pleasure, or independence. They can even take the form of people. Peninnah's children were her trophies. They were the tangible fruits of her effort that represented her success over Hannah, and while she had a lot of them, they fell short of bringing her the glory she sought. Hannah, on the other hand, was granted a *chabod* glory that reflected her relationship with God—that heaviness of abundance and riches and glory and reputation and dignity. Peninnah saw herself in competition with Hannah for that glory as if it was an earthly kingdom and earthly rewards that she could take by her own hand, and yet she could not obtain it.

Like crowns, there are right and wrong trophies to pursue, and there are right and wrong reasons for taking a trophy.

The Philistines took the Ark of the LORD thinking that trophy would bring with it the heaviness of reputation and glory that they sought over Israel, but it brought a different kind of heaviness—a heaviness of judgment. They didn't understand that the glory was God's and without the relationship with God, that glory could not be attained. In the end, it was a trophy they wished they had not pursued, nor were they allowed to keep.

Have you ever battled for something, only to discover that the prize was not worth the battle? Trophies can become an embarrassment and a millstone around our necks, but if we are too heavily engaged in that pursuit, we will cling to them just to save face—even if it kills us. If we cling to those trophies to any degree, they can become a sickness in us because of the fear they generate—a fear of losing the material things, losing face or status, or losing security and self-determination.

There is a Philistine side in all of us—our carnal side that comes with living in a body that craves things. The Philistine side of us rises up at times and goes to war with other people in pursuit of some desire. We see this happen in all kinds of battles between people—children fighting over toys, spouses fighting each other in divorce battles, or heirs fighting over inheritances.

Our Philistine side will fight for the reward, even to the death of the relationship with the other party. This is where the understanding of right values becomes vital, because you must decide which is more important: the trophy or the relationship? Paul admonishes:

> *"But brother goes to law against brother, and that before unbelievers! Now therefore, it is already an utter failure for you that you go to law against one another. Why do you not rather accept wrong? Why do you not rather let yourselves be cheated?"* —First Corinthians 6:6-7

What goal is Paul proposing when he exhorts us to accept wrong or let ourselves be cheated? What are the physical things of this world to us that we should grasp them to the point of ruining one another like Philistines?

The Philistines went to war with Israel, and they took a trophy and became sick. James 4:1-4 says:

> *"Where do wars and fights come from among you? Do they not come from your desires for pleasure that war in your members? You lust and do not have. You murder and covet and cannot obtain. You fight and war. Yet you do not have because you do not ask. You ask and do not receive, because you ask amiss [Greek: kakos], that you may spend it on your pleasures."* —James 4:1-4

The Greek word *kakos* is translated as "amiss" (NKJV) or "having wrong motives." But this is an atypical use of the word. *Kakos* is used most heavily in the Gospels, where it means to have a sickness or be diseased. People brought to Jesus all that were *kakos*—sick or diseased—and He healed them. James is saying that there is a sickness or disease inside us—a craving or a lust—that drives our Philistine wars with one another, and the Philistine is a sick man.

> Questions for Reflection
>
> Our Philistine pursuits can bring us into wars with each other.
>
> - Have you been battling anyone lately? If so, for what were you battling?
>
> - Are you pursuing that trophy as a way of building up yourself or God? Who gets the glory if you win?
>
> - If you won the trophy, what did it cost you (financially, emotionally, mentally, physically)? What did it cost you in terms of your relationship with family, friends, coworkers, or other believers?
>
> - If you won the trophy, did having that trophy cause new problems, distress, or anxieties?
>
> - Are you hanging onto the trophy as a matter of pride, just to save face?
>
> - What would you be losing if you let go of the trophy to which you are clinging and pursued God instead?
>
> - Are the fears that are making you sick brought on by something you need to lay down before the LORD?
>
> - Is the trophy something you need to lay down before God and admit that it was a Philistine pursuit, or will you harden your heart and refuse to let go? (God has ways of making you let go!)

Acknowledging God

Throughtout this series, there has been a subtle progression of how the Ark has been addressed which contributes to Samuel's theme of ascents and descents. Let's review the changes in the name up to this point, beginning in Chapter 4.

In the opening scene, the Ark is called **"the Ark of the Covenant of the LORD (Jehovah) of hosts, who dwells between the cherubim"** (4:4a). This is the most formal and weightiest name given to the Ark while it rests in state in the House of God at Shiloh. Once Hophni and Phinehas take it from its honored place, the name is truncated and becomes **"the Ark of the**

Covenant of God (Elohim)" (4:4b). Notice how the wording shifts from LORD (Jehovah) to God (Elohim). Where Jehovah is the most proper and formal name for the LORD, Elohim is a more generic term that can apply to rulers, judges, and gods, as well as God Himself. The Ark loses some of its grandeur. This is a small detail that is easily overlooked, except that it is the beginning of a trend.

When the Ark comes into camp, it is greeted by Israel as **"The Ark of the Covenant of the LORD."** There is an up-tick from Elohim to Jehovah in the name as God's people give God praise in verse 5, but then the Philistines call it **"the Ark of the LORD"** in verse 6. What is missing between the names? The "covenant"—but then the Philistines have no covenant with the God of Israel. Even so, the omission is significant. This is the last time the Ark will be called the Ark of the Covenant throughout the narratives of First and Second Samuel. The name will crop up one very singular time in Second Samuel 15:24, but after that, it is never referred to as the Ark of the Covenant of the LORD again until it is installed in Solomon's Temple.

Once it is captured by the Philistines in First Samuel 4:11, the Ark becomes simply **the Ark of God (Elohim)**. The Ark has lost more of its titular glory in its descent into the hands of the Philistines, which the author communicates with this shortened addressed. It will remain the Ark of God through the end of Chapter 4.

Now, in Chapter 5, there are some new developments as the Ark begins to gain a reputation in Philistine lands. It begins as **the Ark of God (Elohim)** in 5:1-2, but then alters to **the Ark of the LORD (Jehovah)** in 5:5-6. Why does it change? Because, in these verses, the Ark representing Israel's God stands in the presence of the Philistine god Dagon. The name is elevated from the generic Elohim to the proper name of Jehovah to indicate superiority.

It undergoes another upgrade in 5:7-11. There it is **the Ark of the God of Israel**. This is a curious hybridization. The Philistines don't recognize God as being God over them, but they recognize He is God over Israel and He is more powerful than Dagon, as noted in verse 5:7: *"His hand is harsh toward us and Dagon our god."*

When the Ark returns to Israel in First Samuel 6, it transitions back to the name, **the Ark of the LORD (Jehovah)**, and yet the covenant aspect remains missing. The Ark will not be referred to as the Ark of the Covenant again until Second Samuel 15:24.

LESSON 4: FIRST SAMUEL 7–8

The Rejected King

In First Samuel 4, God's people lost their spiritual relationship with Him, and then they lost the battle with the Philistines who assumed control as well. God's dwelling place was captured, and His Ark taken deep into enemy territory. In Chapters 5 and 6, He began the process of return by dealing with the Philistines. He dealt with the spiritual enemy first by putting Dagon under His feet. Then He dealt with the human adversaries and brought all things under His feet (god, people, and land).

Having established His sovereignty over the heathen nation, the LORD returned to deal with His own people. The men of Beth Shemesh were little better than Philistines in how they handled the Ark and how they sent it away instead of regarding it as a blessing. The men of Kirjath Jearim gave the LORD the elevation due Him (literally), but the Ark remained isolated and removed from God's people.

Now, in Chapter 7, it is time to set God's people in order. Instead of reinstating the high priesthood in a Tabernacle, God sets Samuel as a judge over Israel, and Samuel accomplishes the restoration. But Israel is not content to have God as their King and Samuel as their judge. They want a human king to judge them, and God decides to humor them. First Samuel 7–8 mark the pivotal transition from the age of the judges to the age of the kings.

Samuel Becomes Judge

READ

First Samuel 7:1-17

NARRATIVE STRUCTURE

Chapter 7 presents a series of ascents. The ascents are not necessarily physical ascents but ascents in status as Israel is restored. The narrative of Chapter 7 is broken down into these elements:

1) The Ark ascends to Kirjath Jearim (7:1-2)
2) Samuel restores Israel spiritually (7:3-6)
3) Samuel restores Israel physically (7:7-17)
4) Samuel's on-going ministry (7:15-17)

BUILD THE PICTURE

The Ark Ascends to Kirjath Jearim

1. **If the Ark had returned, why was Israel lamenting over the LORD?**

   Just because the Ark had been returned didn't meant that God was speaking to His people. The Ark is isolated at Kirjath Jearim, separated from the Tabernacle and the priesthood (what remained of it now that the high priest and his sons were killed). The Ark will not be reunited with the Tabernacle until David brings it to Jerusalem in 2 Samuel 6, so the Ark with its mercy seat for atonement is out of the picture for the rest of First Samuel.

2. **When did we last see Samuel in the narrative?**

   Samuel hasn't been mentioned since Chapter 4, before the previous battle with the Philistines. Instead, the Ark of the LORD has been the focus. But now there is this abrupt shift away from the Ark and back to Samuel.

3. **When do the events take place?**

   When Samuel comes back on the scene, twenty or so years have passed. Assuming he was in his teens when we last saw him with Eli, this places him somewhere in his thirties. According to Mosaic Law, thirty is the age when priestly service officially begins. It is also the age when kingly service begins (in David's case).

4. **What is Samuel's role this time?**

   Samuel has already been established as prophet, but now he takes on two other roles, those of priest and judge. We should note that he replaces Eli as a judge, but not as *high* priest. He makes offerings and intercession for Israel as a Levitical priest would, but not the atonement as the high priest would through the Ark and mercy seat.

   The high priesthood and Tabernacle system are dysfunctional at this point, just as they were in the book of Judges. So the picture deliberately shifts away from the priesthood and onto the judgeship. Samuel is called to be the fourteenth and final *shofet* or judge. The *shofet* is not just a judicial judge like the *dayan* or *paleel*. He carries an added distinction of being a civic authority along the lines of chieftain—not a king, but not just a judge.

Samuel Restores Israel Spiritually

5. **How does Samuel begin to restore Israel spiritually?**

   He tells Israel to put away their idolatry, and they do, apparently, on a national scale. Having put away their idolatry, what should follow is a formal act of atonement for Israel's reconciliation with God to be complete. At this point, Samuel calls them to Mizpah.

6. **Why not call them to Kirjath Jearim where the Ark is?**

   The Ark of the LORD is at Kirjath Jearim but without the Tabernacle and its altar for offerings. The LORD has not given direction as to where to put His name and administer the offerings now that Shiloh is abandoned. The formal trappings needed for the ritual atonement practices according to the letter of the Law are missing. What remains is the practice of faith according to the spirit of the Law (just as it is for us in the Church age).

7. **Why Mizpah? What do we know about Mizpah?**

   Samuel is a priest but it is his role as a judge that takes the forefront now. And where does a judge preside? In a court of law. Mizpah is not a religious center but a place where the judges brought people for judgment and sorting out congregational matters (see Genesis 31:49, Judges 10:17, 11:11, 11:34, 20:1-3).

   The original Mizpah east of the Jordan was the place where Jacob and Laban came together to set boundaries for family relations. In Genesis 31:51, we see Jacob and Laban establish this place where a heap of stones (a *galeed*) and a pillar (a *mizpah*) stood as testament to their covenant agreement. Mizpah means "watchtower," and the mizpah pillar was a reminder that God, the great Judge, was watching the proceedings. Mizpah became the line in the sand that Laban the Syrian could not cross to do harm to Israel. This Mizpah was the same place that Jephthah took his oath to be judge over his brethren and also to deal with Israel's enemies.

   The Mizpah to which Samuel calls the people is on the west side of the Jordan between Ramah and Bethel, but it is used for the same function as a place of judgment. In the book of Judges, it was the place to which the Levite called Israel to render judgment for Gibeah's crime against his concubine. It was likely the place where the prophetess Deborah sat to judge Israel (between Ramah and Bethel).

   Mizpah is the place of judgment, but also the proverbial line in the sand that the enemy is not allowed to cross to do Israel harm. Hold that thought.

8. **What does Israel do at Mizpah?**

   Initially there are no offerings made. The children of Israel humble themselves before the LORD with pouring out water, fasting, and confession. Jewish sources will note that drawing water and pouring it out is not an actual religious practice associated with repentance and atonement. The only time something like this is practiced is with the later traditions of the Feast of Tabernacles where the people pour out water in conjunction with a prayer for rain. So why are they doing this?

The act of pouring out can be symbolic of groanings of distress, pouring out one's heart when seeking refuge, or a blessing being poured out as a reward for repentance.

> *"For my sighing comes before my bread, and my groanings pour out like water. For the thing I greatly feared has come upon me, and what I dreaded has happened to me. I am not at ease, nor am I quiet; I have no rest, for trouble comes."* —Job 3:24-26

> *"Trust in Him at all times, you people; Pour out your heart before Him; God is a refuge for us."* —Psalm 62:8

> *"Turn at my rebuke; Surely I will pour out my spirit on you; I will make my words known to you."* —Proverbs 1:22

We find an example of all three playing out in what happens next in the narrative.

In the middle of this national turning, the Philistine enemy rises up against Israel again. The events here will be an echo of Chapter 4, so we should put the pictures side by side and compare Israel's reaction this time to their reaction last time and how the result differed.

9. **Why do the Philistines attack now?**

It says that they saw Israel gathered at Mizpah. Perhaps they assumed that Israel was gathering an army. You would think that they had learned a lesson after their experience with the Ark, but that had happened twenty years ago. How complacent do a people become over a period of twenty years when they have no one to challenge them? It has been twenty years since the 9/11 attack on American soil. How complacent is America now (I write this in 2023) in regards to those enemies?

10. **How did Israel react last time?**

When the Philistines attacked back in Chapter 4, Israel marshaled an army at Ebenezer, went into battle, and lost 4,000 men. Then they brought out the Ark, went into battle, and lost 30,000 men, the Ark, and the priests.

Lesson 4: The Rejected King

Last time, they lifted themselves up and tried to deal with the enemy on their own but were defeated. Then they brought the Ark to them, but not for the purpose of consulting God. They never once addressed the LORD in the last battle. They went at the enemy with arrogant bravado and lost.

11. How is Israel's reaction to the Philistines different this time?

This time, they hear the Philistines coming and are afraid just like before. Instead of sending for the Ark, they humbly turn to Samuel to make intercession for them and ask God to save them. Samuel makes a whole burnt offering for the people and intercedes for them, and God answers with deliverance.

So that is a gigantic change of attitude on Israel's part. They poured out their hearts in groanings because of their fear, put their trust in God as their refuge, and, in return, God poured out His grace on them. Mizpah is the line in the sand. It is the place where the enemy is not allowed to cross to do harm to Israel. The LORD goes into battle before Israel with loud thunderings, and the people join the battle and push the enemy back to Beth Car.

Samuel Restores Israel Physically

12. How does Samuel restore Israel physically?

The physical restoration of Israel only comes after the spiritual restoration and as a blessing of the spiritual restoration.

The text says that the hand of the LORD was with them all the days of Samuel. Not only were the Philistines subdued, they withdrew from Israel's territory. They retook the cities of the Philistines (from Ekron to Gath), and they had peace with the Amorites.

Samuel is following the pattern of the judges in the book of Judges in restraining Israel's enemies as well as being a restraining influence over Israel themselves—unlike Eli, whose lack of restraint gave Israel a semblance of peace when there was no peace. The Philistines would not have gained so much land from Israel in Eli's day if Eli had been a godly judge and priest.

13. Why did Samuel set up the Ebenezer stone?

Ebenezer means "stone of help." The original Ebenezer was the site of Israel's first defeat at the hands of the Philistines. The stone had been no help to them then. But now God, who is the true rock of help, gives them victory because of their turning to faith, and Samuel reinforces the lesson by setting up another Ebenezer stone. This Ebenezer is in a different place from the last, and perhaps that was part of the lesson. The location is not important so much as the relationship it represented.

Samuel's On-going Ministry

14. Why did Samuel travel a circuit of Bethel, Gilgal, and Mizpah?

First let's consider the significance of those places.

Mizpah was the place of Israel's judgment and repentance here in the narrative. We fleshed out that picture of that place earlier.

Bethel means the house of God. It was the place where God promised Abraham to give the land to his descendants (Genesis 12). It is the same place where Jacob saw the vision of the ladder ascending to heaven as the promise of the Land was renewed (Genesis 28). At Bethel, Jacob vowed to give back to the LORD a tenth portion of the increase with which the LORD provided him.

Gilgal was the place where Joshua set up the memorial stones taken from the Jordan River during their crossing into the Land to remind Israel of their deliverance from Egypt. (Joshua 4:18-20) It was also the place where Israel renewed her covenant with God by circumcision and celebrating the Passover (Joshua 5). The LORD is the one who named Gilgal.

> *"Then the LORD said to Joshua, 'This day I have rolled away [galal] the reproach of Egypt from you.' Therefore the name of the place is called Gilgal to this day."* —Joshua 5:9

The name Gilgal means "the rolling" or "wheel" in the sense of something that is whirled away. The word *galal* means "to roll away" and is often in reference to rolling back a stone that blocks a well or a cave. Think of the rolling back of the stone from Christ's grave that marked the rolling away of our own reproach. That was our Gilgal. It was a symbolic act based on this Old Testament picture.

Samuel makes a yearly circuit of Bethel, Mizpah, and Gilgal—from the house of God, to the place of judgment and repentance, to the place where Israel's reproach was rolled away. These places are the reminders of battles won, lost, and won again when Israel returns to God. They are also reminders of the covenant between God and Israel to preserve them in the Land if they are faithful to Him. It is part of Samuel's role as intercessor to help keep the lessons and promises embodied in these places alive in their minds as they pursued a relationship with God.

The text says Samuel also went home to Ramah and built an altar there. Ramah is a discordant picture, because it means high hill. High hills with altars on them were usually associated with illicit idolatrous practices, but here Samuel reclaims the high place and uses it for worship of God.

So, everything is good in the kingdom. Why would they want to change it?

Israel Demands a King

READ

First Samuel 8:1–22

BUILD THE PICTURE

15. What was Samuel's family like?

He had two sons. The first he named Joel, which means "Jehovah is God," and the second he named Abiah, which means "God is my father"—two names that reflect a father's vision and desire for his sons to follow in his footsteps in that relationship with God. But they didn't. They went the way of Hophni and Phinehas, which just goes to show that even good parents and godly leaders can have rebellious, wicked children the same as ungodly parents. While Samuel is a contrast to Eli overall, he has this in common with Eli in regards to his children.

16. How did Samuel's sons become judges?

Samuel appoints them, and therein lies the problem, I think. Unlike the priesthood and kingship in which the son is expected to assume the father's mantle, the judges' sons are not. God is the one who raises up His judges when and where they are needed and not one judge in the history of the judges has ever had a son step into his shoes by default. God reserves the right as King to appoint His cabinet of ministers.

I don't know why Samuel took the initiative in doing this instead of waiting for God's direction. Maybe it seemed natural to the father to pass this position onto his sons. Maybe it was because he didn't want to leave the ministry with this leadership vacuum to fill. But it is notable that Samuel is the one who does the choosing instead of God, and it doesn't end so well.

Samuel made his sons judges, but it wasn't their calling. Joel would be the father of Heman, who became a notable singer and worship leader in David's court along with Asaph. All of Heman's family became singers and psalmist and musicians. I'll venture to say that might have been Joel's gift and calling, too, and yet he is put into a position that is not his gifting and performs poorly.

At any rate, Israel's elders come to Samuel at Ramah to tell him they don't want his sons to be judges over them. They want a king to judge them just like the other nations.

17. Was it just the corruption of Samuel's sons that made Israel ask for a king, or would they have asked for a king anyway?

I think Israel would have asked for a king anyway, because it was actually anticipated in the writings of the Law. God gives the people instruction over this very request in Deuteronomy 17:14-20.

18. Why is Samuel displeased with Israel's demand for a king?

The people's rejection is two-fold: Samuel is old, and his sons don't walk in his ways. There is a personal element in their summation of

Samuel. They aren't just replacing him, but they are doing away with his job title. But then there is the rejection of Samuel's sons.

In spite of an exemplary life and all the good that Samuel did for Israel, Samuel feels the people's rejection, and he takes it personally. The word "displeased" (Hebrew: *yara*) is a shortened translation of "displeasing in his eyes," but it carries the sense of being broken up, grieved, or trembling.

Like Hannah who was also grieved (*yara*), Samuel doesn't rebuke his critics but pours out his heart before the LORD. The LORD responds:

> "... they have not rejected you, but they have rejected Me, that I should not reign over them."—First Samuel 8:7

Samuel is feeling rejected as a *shofet*, a chieftain-judge, because the people have asked for a king to judge them, but God points out that he isn't seeing this rightly. What they are really asking for isn't a judge to replace a judge. They are looking for a king to replace the King.

Note: Even though Samuel's sons have gone the way of Eli's sons, Samuel himself does not receive the condemnation from the LORD for being equally guilty of their sins as Eli had been condemned. Instead the LORD comforts him. Why?

Because Samuel has not upheld and joined his sons in their sin as Eli did but entered into the LORD's suffering with Him, as the LORD acknowledges:

> "According to all the works which they have done since the day that I brought them up out of Egypt, even to this day—with which they have forsaken Me and served other gods—so they are doing to you also." —First Samuel 8:8

APPLY THE PICTURE

This is the core lesson of pursuing crowns. If we are going to be worthy of reigning and sharing Christ's glory in the Kingdom, we must experience suffering as God suffers and as Christ suffered as King. And we must endure it, even as the Father and Son endured it and continue to endure it.

This means taking unfair criticism, enduring rejection, condemnation, and persecution in spite of living a godly life, and being bearers of God's Word to the people.

It is glorifying to God when we identify with His suffering, and God extends His glory to those who suffer for His name. Peter addresses this aspect of pursuing a crown in depth in First Peter:

> "Coming to Him as to a living stone, rejected indeed by men, but chosen by God and precious, you also, as living stones, are being built up a spiritual house, a holy priesthood, to offer up spiritual sacrifices acceptable to God through Jesus Christ." —First Peter 2:4-5

> "If you are reproached for the name of Christ, blessed are you, for the Spirit of glory and of God rests upon you. On their part He is blasphemed, but on your part He is glorified. But let none of you suffer as a murderer, a thief, an evildoer, or as a busybody in other people's matters. Yet if anyone suffers as a Christian, let him not be ashamed, but let him glorify God in this matter." —First Peter 4:14-16

> "Shepherd the flock of God which is among you, serving as overseers, not by compulsion but willingly, not for dishonest gain but eagerly; nor as being lords over those entrusted to you, but being examples to the flock; and when the Chief Shepherd appears, you will receive the crown of glory that does not fade away." —First Peter 5:2-4

BUILD THE PICTURE

19. What is the difference between a chieftain-judge and a king?

God lays that out in verses 9-22. A king will:

- Take your sons for his army, to work his fields, and to make his weapons for war
- Take your daughters to be perfumers, cooks, and bakers
- Take the best of your fields, vineyards, and olive groves
- Take a tithe of your grain and wine (like a priest)

- Take your servants, man and beast, to work for him
- Take you as his servants

The king will take and take and take and take until you cry out in distress. And in that day, God the King will not hear you.

Even after all this is explained and the people know what a king will cost them, they still want a king. They want to be like all the other Canaanite nations around them.

20. What has life been like under Samuel?

It seems pretty good. Israel had an extended period of peace all around and the relief that comes when oppression is lifted. Their spiritual relationship with God started out well back at Mizpah. We don't know how old Samuel was, but that he was old implies that a goodly amount of time has passed.

21. Had Israel served Samuel the way they will serve a king?

No. The chieftain-judge was not the ruler of the kingdom to demand this level of servitude from them. Samuel never had an army. Samuel never lived like a king with a king's administration to support. It was just Samuel, who travelled a circuit year after year serving Israel's needs for instruction and intercession and making sacrifices.

APPLY THE PICTURE

Is the pursuit of kingship a bad thing? No—unless you already have a King and you are trying to supplant Him with a king of your own choosing. There are right and wrong kings to pursue in this life, and Israel is preparing to make a very bad choice.

So, what kind of king is a good choice? Let's look for a moment at the Deuteronomy 17:14-20 passage and consider what the core requirements are for royalty in God's kingdom according to the Law.

> *"When you come to the land which the LORD your God is giving you, and possess it and dwell in it, and say, 'I will set a king over me like all the nations that are around me,' you shall surely set a king over you <u>whom the LORD your God chooses; one from among your brethren</u> you*

shall set as king over you; you may not set a foreigner over you, who is not your brother. But <u>he shall not multiply horses for himself, nor cause the people to return to Egypt to multiply horses,</u> for the LORD has said to you, 'You shall not return that way again.' <u>Neither shall he multiply wives for himself,</u> lest his heart turn away; <u>nor shall he greatly multiply silver and gold for himself.</u> Also it shall be, when he sits on the throne of his kingdom, that <u>he shall write for himself a copy of this law in a book,</u> from the one before the priests, the Levites. And it shall be with him, and he shall read it all the days of his life, <u>that he may learn to fear the LORD his God</u> and be careful to observe all the words of this law and these statutes, <u>that his heart may not be lifted above his brethren,</u> that he may <u>not turn aside from the commandment to the right hand or to the left,</u> and <u>that he may prolong his days in his kingdom,</u> he and his children in the midst of Israel." —Deuteronomy 17:14-20 (emphasis added)

In summary, the king:

#1 Must be a man whom God chooses from among the brethren of Israel and not a foreigner

#2 Shall not multiply horses for himself

#3 Shall not multiply wives for himself

#4 Shall not multiply riches for himself

#5 Shall know and keep the Law, so that . . .
   a. He will fear the LORD
   b. His heart shall not be lifted up above his brothers
   c. He might not turn aside to the right or left
   d. He might prolong his days in the kingdom

Peter tells us we are a royal priesthood (First Peter 2:9). Paul tells Timothy, if we endure, we will reign with Christ (Second Timothy 2:12b). So do these requirements for royalty extend to or translate for us as Church-age believers? I think they do, in a sense.

We begin by being a citizen of the kingdom (#1). We cannot attain the crown without that first step. Those of us who are Gentiles would not have qualified as physical heirs under the Mosaic Law, but we are co-heirs with Christ according to the promise given Abraham and our faith in Christ, in contrast to unbelievers who are of the "foreigner" class. Having gained our

Lesson 4: The Rejected King | 93

citizenry in the kingdom by association with the King, we then live out our lives in a way that reflects our understanding of the crown we wear (#2–5).

The crown we pursue is a spiritual crown, not an earthly one. It is not for those who are concerned with amassing earthly wealth (#2 and #4). Horses and riches fall into this category, although the amassing of horses also speaks to power and the ability to marshal an army. A man in pursuit of a crown can return to Egypt—sell himself into bondage—in pursuit of earthly power and alliances that bolster his security in his earthly kingdom. We, too, can become focused on pursuing power and security through our own effort and not with God's help.

The instruction not to amass wives (#3) speaks to more intimate relationships that can turn our hearts away from God by bringing us into bondage to our own desires or to other people and their pursuits. A pursuit of physical lusts and inappropriate sexual relations (which include harlotry and adultery) places this in the same category as pursuing wealth and power. How we handle our bodies and restrain our pursuit of these forms of lust affects our relationship with God, because our bodies are the Spirit's dwelling place. For those of us who are married, we are called to be content with the spouse we have and not seek after others.

Points #2–4 can be summed up in seeking the kingdom of God and righteousness, and not being driven by the lusts of the eyes and flesh or the pride of life. Remember that your body is the dwelling place of God's spirit and keep it holy.

The last qualification (#5) is about keeping the Law, and we need to clarify that with a New Covenant understanding.

In regards to our salvation, that is, our being given a place in God's kingdom, we understand that there is no return to the Law now that Christ has fulfilled its requirements on our behalf and covered us with His blood as payment for our sins. Our place in the kingdom is by faith alone in Christ alone, apart from works. We are created for good works according to the Lord's purpose but not justified by them (Ephesians 2:8-10).

In regards to our sanctification, we pursue godly living according to the spirit of the Law and not the letter. I think it is significant that this discussion of kingship crops up here in the First Samuel narrative when Israel can keep the Law in spirit only and not the letter because of a lack of priesthood and functioning Tabernacle. I have heard an argument from some Messianic Jewish factions declaring that it is possible to keep the Law perfectly because we now have an indwelling Holy Spirit, but I will argue that. We most certainly could not keep the Law before we had an indwelling spirit, but neither can we keep it with an indwelling Spirit because we must still contend with a Philistine world and our internal Philistine nature with its lusts. The only reason we have any assurance of our status before God is because our failings are covered by Christ's blood. Having begun in the Spirit, we are not now perfected by the flesh (Galatians 3:3).

Keep in mind that the Law can only be kept in its perfection when not just the individual but the entire kingdom adheres to it, from the king to the slave. If the king does not uphold the Law (for instance, keeping the Sabbath), he forces his subjects into breaking the Law as well. It all flows downhill from the king, which is why you must choose the right king with whom to align yourself. Jesus said *"If you love Me, keep My commandments,"* (John 14:15), and *"If you keep My commandments, you will abide in My love, just as I have kept My Father's commandments and abide in His love."* (John 15:10) It all flows from the King.

We are called to keep His commandments, but according to the New Covenant. In Romans 7:4-6, Paul explains the nature of the change in command between the Mosaic Covenant and New Covenant:

> *"Therefore, my brethren, you also have become dead to the law through the body of Christ, that you may be married to another—to Him who was raised from the dead, that we should bear fruit to God. For when we were in the flesh, the sinful passions which were aroused by the law were at work in our members to bear fruit to death. But now we have been delivered from the law, having died to what we were held by, so that we should serve in the newness of the Spirit and not in the oldness of the letter."* —Romans 7:4-6

So let's put aside the Law itself and consider the reasons why the king is called to keep the Law in Deuteronomy 17. What is the heart goal shared by both the Mosaic Law and the New Covenant commandments?

The purpose of keeping the commandments is, first, so that the one who seeks a crown will fear the LORD. It sets the correct relationship between those who would be royalty and the King Himself. Even as Christ the King put Himself below the Father's headship, so we put ourselves under Christ's headship and maintain the chain of command. There is always a King above you, even if you are a king.

Secondly, keeping the commandments should keep us from lifting ourselves above our brothers. It sets the correct relationship between fellow believers and accords with the command to abide in love toward one another. There are right ways and wrong reasons to pursue a crown. How are we to be lifted up? Do we lift ourselves up or does God do this to us?

Thirdly, keeping the commandments gives wisdom and discernment needed to rule with justice and righteousness, turning neither to the left or right. There is a right way to pursue the crown, and it promotes a singleness of purpose that keeps you from being drawn off in wrong directions. This is a warning to would-be kings who drift through life pursuing one thing and then another as their lusts take them. It can also speak to those who are double-minded and driven to and fro by other people's direction instead of following God's direction. James 1:5-8 is a good pairing for this because it talks about the double-minded man—the man who asks God for wisdom but then seeks other opinions.

Finally, like the proverbs, keeping the commandments leads to wise living and prolongs our days in the kingdom—but then there are right and wrong kingdoms to pursue. We seek a long life in an eternal kingdom, not a fleeting life in an earthly one. A long life is one of the hallmarks of Messiah's kingdom (Isaiah 65:20). And yet, even in this life, we are taught to live wisely and skillfully so that our days may be prolonged.

When considered in light of the end goals, I don't see any conflict between the Deuteronomy passage and the New Testament teachings. But as we will see in the lessons to come, the Law is not sufficient to produce a godly king, even one to whom the Spirit is given. There is food for thought in that.

Questions for Reflection

As we move into the next series of comparisons, we will see two kings in pursuit of crowns. Each king will view his relationship to the great King differently, define the kingdom differently, and pursue his goals in

> different ways and for different reasons. Before we begin our study of these kings, perhaps we should evaluate ourselves, because like it or not, the moment we accepted Christ as our Savior, we entered into the pursuit of a crown. So ask yourself:
>
> - Am I king material?
> - Do I value that role or scorn it?
> - Do I even know what the pursuit of a crown entails?

Review: The Ascents and Descents of First Samuel 1-8

Chapter 8 marks the end of the time of the judges with Israel's rejection of Samuel's sons and their demand for a king. So let's take a moment for a quick review and discuss the overall structure of Chapters 1-8. (See the chart on the next page.)

Samuel structures his writings with a very deliberate sense of order and progression. He makes breaks between chapters to focus on specific contrasts between characters and events, and arranges the information to reflect a series of ascents and descents. This is where a minute study of physical people moving through physical places reveals the author's theme. As I summarize the chapters in the chart, consider who is the focus of the chapter, what is the setting, which physical direction the action takes (if stated), and how that direction reflects a spiritual status.

The interruption of Samuel's narrative with a focus on the Ark's journey is thought provoking. The Ark is treated almost like a narrative character. On one side of the Ark's narrative, we see Samuel as a prophet. On the other side, his role of judge is emphasized.

In my study of the book of Judges[2], I explained how the judges were a picture type of the Holy Spirit. They dwelt among the people and provided a restraint for Israel's enemies but also a restraint for Israel's Canaanite tendencies—something the priesthood failed to do.

---

[2] Voelkel, Christy, *Walking a Winding Road, A Study of the Book of Judges* (Ingram-Spark, 2021), pgs 36-40.

Chapter	Setting	Status change
1:1-28	Family of Elkanah at Ramah Hannah goes up to Shiloh Hannah returns to Ramah Hannah goes up to Shiloh to present Samuel	**Ascent** of Hannah over Peninnah (in status)
Break in the narrative: Hannah's Song 2:1-11		
2:12-36	Family of Eli at the House of God at Shiloh	**Ascent** of Samuel in favor **Descent** of the House of Eli
3	Eli and Samuel at the House of God at Shiloh	**Ascent** of Samuel as prophet **Descent** of Eli's house confirmed
Break in Samuel's narrative—no mention of him again until Chapter 7. Focus shifts to the Ark of God.		
4	Ark leaves the House of God at Shiloh and is taken down to the battlefield	**The Glory departs** **Descent** of the High Priest into death **Descent** of the Ark into defilement
5	Ark in Philistine lands—moves from Aphek to Ashdod to Gath to Ekron	**Descent** of the Ark into defilement (lowest point)
6:1-19	Ark taken back up to Beth Shemesh	**Ascent** of the Ark—returns to Israel
6:20	Ark taken up from Beth Shemesh to Kirjath Jearim	**Ascent** of the Ark—ascends to the heights
7:1	Ark at Abinadab's House	**The Ark restored**—rests in state of holiness but removed from the people
Samuel's narrative resumes		
7:2-6	Israel removes idols; Samuel judges Israel at Mizpah	**Ascent** of Samuel as judge/priest **Ascent** of Israel—increasing toward holiness
7:7-17	Israel reclaims the Land and has peace under Samuel's administration	**Israel restored spiritually** **Israel restored physically** to her land
8	Israel goes up to Samuel at Ramah and demands a king	Ascent or descent?

Judges 2:18-19 describes the judges' role:

> *"And when the LORD raised up judges for them, the LORD was with the judge and delivered them out of the hand of their enemies all the days of the judge; for the LORD was moved to pity by their groaning because of those who oppressed them and harassed them. And it came to pass, when the judge was dead, that they reverted and behaved more corruptly than their fathers, by following other gods, to serve them and bow down to them. They did not cease from their own doings nor from their stubborn way."* —Judges 2:18-19

So, Samuel is a picture of the Holy Spirit at work among the people at a time when the Ark itself is out of the picture. The Ark is still present in Israel, but its role is suspended while the picture of the judge comes to the forefront as an intercessor.

On the one side of the Ark's narrative, we have the words of the prophet foretelling the demise of the old priesthood—an event which is fulfilled with the departing of the Glory into enemy lands. On the other side of the Ark's narrative, we have the rise of a new intercessor likened to the Holy Spirit in a time when Israel lives more by the spirit of the Law than the letter of it. So, of what character, then, is the Ark figurative? I think it is figurative of Christ.

Christ, the Glory, left the heavenly place to come to an earthly battlefield and a defiled Philistine world. He was badly mishandled by the religious leaders of His day and subjected to defilement and even death. Having gone down into the depths of the Enemy's territory at His death, He was then delivered back to Israel and finally lifted again to the heights to sit at the right hand of the Father. And there He remains in state until He comes as King. He is still present and at work among His people, but His work is through the Holy Spirit who dwells among the people in His stead.

A view of the Church age is skipped as the picture moves from Christ's first advent to the anticipation of His second advent, but then the Church age was a mystery in these days. The Ark of God had to make its journey first before the restoration of the people could be accomplished.

And now we move into a picture of the kings.

INTRODUCTION

The Kings: Saul and David

We have studied the brides and the priests in First Samuel 1–8, and now we are transitioning from the judges into the kings. First Samuel covers the reign of Saul until his death at the end of the book, and as much of David's story that overlaps it.

Both Saul and David are in pursuit of a crown, but they define their goal differently and pursue it in different ways and for different reasons. God takes greater pains to train David for the kingship than He does with Saul. That is the purpose of David's time in exile in Chapters 21–29, which is a major narrative element not found in Saul's narrative and a point of application. Times of exile are rich training grounds for kingship.

As I wrote in the opening introduction, the picture comparison of the two kings is a complex one, and the author uses a number of devices to help us connect the pictures he wants us to compare.

The Narrative Structure

There is a baseline structure to the way the narrative flows, and deviations from the baseline help establish thematic series and pivotal moments.

Most pictures begin and end with a narrator comment. The opening narrator comment establishes the scene location and characters; the closing comment notes a departure, e.g. *"And Saul went home, but David and his men went up to the stronghold."* (First Samuel 22)

Select pictures open with dialogue instead of a narrator comment. In Chapter 14, Jonathan challenges the Philistines but ends up in conflict with his father Saul. In Chapters 23, 24, and 26, there are four pictures where David and Saul come into conflict and these open with dialogue where one or the other man is told something by a third party. Chapters 14, 23, 24, and 26 have significant comparisons to each other.

In Chapter 27, the picture opens with dialogue detailing David's inner conflict over Saul. This is a turning point in the narrative.

Chapters 15 and 16 notably open with the LORD making a command. These two chapters are pivotal because they mark the transfer of the kingship from Saul to David.

If the pictures don't end in a narrator comment, it is often because the picture connects thematically to the next picture. First Samuel 21-22 have three pictures that form a series marking David's descent, as do Chapters 27, 28, and 29. Likewise, the narrative of David and Goliath in Chapter 17 ends with dialogue instead of a narrator's note, prompting us to incorporate the first part of Chapter 18 into the picture. Chapter 17 and 18 together form one picture that parallels Saul's battle with Nahash and his coronation in Chapter 11. Thus, the narrator comments mark the breaks between pictures, and they aren't always at the end of the chapter.

Chapter 12 is unique in that it both begins and ends with Samuel's dialogue. This is the indictment against Israel for having rejected God as King and chosen a human king instead, and introduces the series detailing Saul's three failures by which he loses the kingdom.

Occasionally you will find **oddly placed narrator comments** that seem incongruent with their immediate context—like random notes inserted into the narrative (e.g., First Samuel 21:7, 23:6, 25:1). Any time a verse seems out of place, it isn't. These verses mark pivot points in a picture or provide a theme for contrasting the pictures before and after. In addition to the narrator comments, the author uses **inclusios, chiastic structures, and parallels** to emphasize particular themes or key contrasts.

These are a few ways the author directs our attention to specific comparisons and lessons. As we work through the text, we will be examining each picture by itself first and then in comparison to other pictures. For the sake of this study, I have identified the main picture blocks and numbered them for easy reference as we work through the text. I have listed these on the next pages.

Pictures for Comparison

Saul, First Samuel 9–15

1	Saul's Anointing	First Samuel 9:1–10:16
2	Saul Proclaimed King	First Samuel 10:17-27
3	Saul's First Battle/Coronation	First Samuel 11:1-15
4	The Indictment Against Israel	First Samuel 12:1–25
5	Saul's First Failure *Saul Loses the Eternal Kingship*	First Samuel 13:1-3-15
6	No Weapons for the Army	First Samuel 13:16-23
7	Saul's Second Failure	First Samuel 14:1-46
8	Saul Establishes His Kingdom	First Samuel 14:47-52
9	Saul's Third Failure *Saul Loses the Temporal Kingdom*	First Samuel 15:1-35

David, First Samuel 16–20

10	David's Anointing	First Samuel 16:1-23
11	David's First Battle/David Honored	First Samuel 17:1–18:9
12	Saul Fears David (3 Ascents/Descents)	First Samuel 18:10-30
13	Saul Persecutes David (3 Interventions)	First Samuel 19:1-24
14	Jonathan Sends David Away *David Loses the Temporal Kingdom (Temporarily)*	First Samuel 20:1-42

David in Exile, First Samuel 21–31

15	David Flees to the Tabernacle	First Samuel 21:1-9
16	David Flees to Gath	First Samuel 21:10-15
17	David Flees to the Cave of Adullam	First Samuel 22:1-2
18	David in the Stronghold	First Samuel 22:3-5
19	Saul Murders the Priests of Nob	First Samuel 22:6-23
20	The Battle at Keilah	First Samuel 23:1-13
21	In the Wilderness: The Statement	First Samuel 23:14-15
22	In the Wilderness: The Comforter	First Samuel 23:16-18
23	The Rock of Escape: The Experience	First Samuel 23:19-29
24	David at the Rock of Wild Goats	First Samuel 24:1-22
25	Death of Samuel/David and Nabal	First Samuel 25:1-44
26	David at the Hill of Hachilah	First Samuel 26:1-25
27	David Returns to the Philistines	First Samuel 27:1-12
28	David's Dilemma	First Samuel 28:1-2
29	Saul Seeks the Medium	First Samuel 28:3-25
30	Philistines Reject David	First Samuel 29:1-11
31	David's Final Battle (Reward)	First Samuel 30:1-31
32	Saul's Final Battle (Loss)	First Samuel 31:1-12

LESSON 5: FIRST SAMUEL 9–10

Behold, Your King!

SERIES STRUCTURE

Picture #1 (9:1–10:16) is the choosing and anointing of Saul.

Picture #2 (10:17-27) is the presentation of Saul to the people.

I put both pictures into one lesson because together, these two will compare with one picture that is David's anointing in Chapter 16. They will also create a prophetic picture of Christ, although we will not see it fully until after Saul's coronation as king in Chapter 11.

I admit I was a little surprised to find a prophetic picture of Christ in Saul. In David, yes, we would expect to find this, but not in Saul. And yet, the picture is definitely here, as I will show you. I think it has been short-sighted of Christian scholars to look for pictures of Christ only in the more laudable examples such as Joseph, David, and Solomon. When Jesus Christ died on the cross, He became all that was vile and cursed, and the prophetic pictures of this image and understanding of Him often present in the less noble characters such as Abimelech in Judges 9 and Saul here in First Samuel. The villains in Scripture have their use as well.

1 Saul's Anointing

READ

First Samuel 9:1–10:16

NARRATIVE STRUCTURE

In **Picture #1**, the theme of ascents and descents continues. I have charted out the narrative to show you the symmetry of its structure and how the author creates this rhythm of walking and talking in seven conversations.

9:3	**Discussion** between Saul and his father about the donkeys	
9:4-5a	Three-day journey with four stops: 1) Land of Shalisha, 2) Land of Shaalim, 3) Land of Benjamin, 4) Land of Zuph	
9:5b-10	**Turning point: Conversation 1** (Saul and his servant)	
9:11-13	Go up the hill halfway	Ascent
	Conversation 2 (Saul with the women)	
9:14-21	Go up to the city to the gate	Ascent
	Conversation 3 at the gate (God and Samuel); **Conversation 4** at the gate (Samuel and Saul)	
9:22-24	Go up to the high place to the banquet table	Ascent
	Conversation 5 at the table (Samuel and Saul)	
9:25	Down from the high place into the city	Descent
	Conversation 6 on the rooftop (Samuel and Saul)	
9:26-27	Down from the roof and out of the house Down to the outskirts of the town	Descent/ Descent
10:1-8	**Turning point: Conversation 7** (Samuel anoints Saul)	
10:9-12	One-day journey with four stops: 1) Rachel's tomb at Zelzah, 2) The terebinth tree at Tabor, 3) The hill, 4) Gilgal[1]	
10:13-16	**Discussion** between Saul and his uncle about the donkeys	

---

1 Samuel tells Saul to go to Gilgal, but that event isn't recorded until Chapter 13. In the immediate context, Saul goes up to the high place at Gibeah after prophesying.

Picture #1 begins with the narrator's introduction of Saul and account of his journey, which is marked by conversations. It ends with a dialogue between Saul and his uncle instead of a narrator's note of departure, which indicates that this picture continues on to the next. I have broken it down into sections according to conversations:

1) Saul's Journey (9:1-5)
2) Conversation #1 (9:5-10)
3) Conversation #2 (9:11-13)
4) Conversation #3 (9:14-17)
5) Conversation #4 (9:18-21)
6) Conversation #5 (9:22-24)
7) Conversation #6 (9:25-26)
8) Conversation #7 (9:27–10:8)
9) Saul's Turning (10:9-16)

BUILD THE PICTURE

Saul's Journey (9:1-5)

1. **What do we know about Saul?**

   Saul is the son of Kish, "son of Abiel, the son of Zeror, the son of Bechorath, the son of Aphiah, a Benjamite, a mighty man of power." It is always good to look up the names.

Saul	"desired"
Kish	"one who is bent, like a trap being set over a lure"
Abiel	"God is my father"
Zeror	"one bound in a sack, compressed and distressed"
Bechorath	"first-born"
Aphiah	"I will make breathe"
Benjamin	"son of my right hand"

   That is a curious string of descriptors. Let's consider the picture they paint for us. Saul is going to be the king, the one whom Israel desires. That is understood. Kish implies that he is a trap being set for Israel, perhaps a trap that God will use to teach them the consequence

Lesson 5: Behold Your King | 107

of pursuing the wrong crown. The picture then segues to that of a firstborn son still in the womb, in the throes of labor pains as he is being born—a son whose father is God, whom God makes to breathe, the son of His right hand.

This isn't just the birth of a son portrayed here. It is the birth of a nation.

Saul comes from a wealthy family in Gibeah of Benjamin. His father Kish is described as a mighty man of power or *chayil*—having strength, might, wealth, or military strength. He is a man of many resources, and he has a son who is exemplary, at least in appearance. Saul himself is described as a choice and exceedingly handsome young man, and very tall—a giant among his people.

As the narrative introduction, Saul is sent out with a servant on the menial task of finding some donkeys that have wandered off.

2. **Where does the narrative begin and what are our time markers?**

The chapter begins with a focus on the opening journey. There is a divine purpose driving Saul's meanderings, but if we were to follow in Saul's shoes, the journey seems a little aimless. Saul is wandering around the countryside, looking for some elusive donkeys, getting farther and farther afield, and running out of supplies.

The places in which Saul searches for the donkeys are rather vague. Not even the meanings of the names give us much of a clue. The mountains of Ephraim represent a vast area that stretches across the territory of Benjamin, Ephraim, and into Manasseh. Shalisha means "thirds" or "three parts," but does not give us a clue as to what the three parts are. Shaalim means "foxes" which also has little context with the narrative. The land of Benjamin is also vague. The land of Zuph is interesting. You will remember the name Zuph from Samuel's lineage. Saul may have stumbled into the ancestral lands of Samuel's family, or there may be no connection at all. Nevertheless, it puts Samuel in mind.

What is important is not so much where he went, but how long it took him. The span of time is a three-day journey. We find this little detail tucked into Samuel's words in First Samuel 9:20.

3. **What is significant about a three-day's journey?**

   Three-day journeys are significant in the Scripture because they represent a space of time or distance for the purpose of sanctification or separation. Here are some examples:

   - After a three days' journey, Abraham and Isaac came to Mount Moriah (Genesis 22:4)
   - Moses tells Pharoah that Israel must go three days' journey into the wilderness in order to sacrifice to the Lord. (Exodus 3:18, 5:3, 8:27)
   - Men must keep themselves from women for three days in order to be sanctified to meet the Lord (Exodus 19, First Samuel 21:5)

   The third day is often a day of verdict and decision that brings about a turning point or a change of life direction. Here are some examples:

   - On the third day, Abraham determined to sacrifice Isaac, but Isaac was spared—major turning point in Israel's history.
   - On the third day, Simeon and Levi delivered judgment on Shechem for the rape of their sister, Dinah (Genesis 34:25)—a vindication of Dinah but also the cause for a future judgment and loss of blessing for Simeon and Levi.
   - On the third day, the verdict was pronounced upon Pharoah's baker and butler according to the prophecy of Joseph (Genesis 40:20)—the butler facilitates Joseph's eventual release from prison.
   - Joseph held his brothers captive for three days and on the third day announced his decision concerning them (Genesis 42:17-18)—led to the salvation and revival of Israel.
   - On the third day, when the people had been separated and sanctified, the Lord descended on Mount Sinai to give the Law (Exodus 19 & 20).
   - David delayed three days before coming to Saul's feast, to determine if Saul wished to harm him (First Samuel 20)—a turning point in David's life as he goes into exile.
   - Saul's death was made known to David three days after the fact (Second Samuel 1:2)—a turning point in David's life.

- Rehoboam delayed three days before delivering his verdict concerning the taxes levied on the children of Israel which caused Israel's rebellion against the house of David. (First Kings 12:12; Second Chronicles 10:12). The dividing of the nation is a major turning point in Israel's history.
- Jesus' three days in the grave and resurrection on the third day.

In Saul's case the three-day journey will be an act of separation and sanctification necessary for what happens when he finally meets up with Samuel. That third day marks a significant decision that will change the course of Saul's life.

Conversation #1 (9:5-10)

4. **What decision marks the turning point on the third day?**

   On the third day, when their supplies have run out, Saul and his servant come to a crossroads over which direction to take. Saul wants to go home, but the servant suggests going to the nearby city to ask advice from the man of God. A lengthy discussion ends with the decision to go to the city. This is a turning point in the narrative.

5. **In the conversation between Saul and his servant, we get a feel for Saul's character. What does it tell us about him?**

   Saul is the master's choice son and the servant is the servant, and yet the servant speaks to him almost as an equal. When Saul makes a decision, the servant disagrees and suggests something else. When Saul points out that they have nothing to offer as a gift to the man of God, the servant produces money, where Saul has none. The servant is more dominating of the two personalities, and Saul gives way to the servant's advice.

   We know that the LORD is actually leading Saul to Samuel for a purpose, so the servant naturally prevails. Even so, this penchant for following other people's urging is something that is characteristic of Saul. He is a bit of a people-pleaser and allows himself to be convinced.

Conversation #2 (9:11-13)

On their way up the hill to the city, Saul and his servant meet women going down to draw water. They ask the women direction, and the women offer a description of where to find the man of God. The women could have just said "go up to the city and ask someone there," but they don't. Instead, they offer a lot of inconsequential details about the sacrifice ceremony on the high place. They even make it a point to say that only those who are invited will eat with the man of God. Saul and his servant were not invited, obviously, so perhaps they should hurry to catch the man of God before he goes into the banquet hall and the doors are shut against them.

6. **Why include this conversation?**

    Because it builds tension and urgency in the narrative. You feel like something big is getting ready to happen, which it is.

Conversation #3 (9:14-17)

When they get to the gate, Saul and his servant meet Samuel coming out of the city on his way up to the high place. There are two conversations that happen at the gate: one between God and Samuel, and one between Samuel and Saul. Let's look at the one between God and Samuel first.

7. **What does God tell Samuel about Saul?**

    God had told Samuel the day before to look for Saul and to anoint him as commander over Israel to save His people from the Philistines. That is a very specific anointing and not necessarily one with the title of king as the people had requested. They had requested a *melech,* but the word king or *melech* is not used. Instead, Saul is made a *nageed,* which is a commander, ruler, or prince but can also be an honorary title for a prefect or governor—royalty of a slightly lesser status to the king but above Samuel's chieftain-judge status.

    God tells Samuel that Saul's particular purpose is to save the people from the Philistines. So, apparently, the Philistines are beginning to make a resurgence in the land, even though Israel had recovered its territory many years before. The verb for "save" is *yasa,* from which we get the noun, *moshia* or *mashiach*, that is, messiah, deliverer, or savior. This is the same designation given to the judges who were also deliverers. Israel asked for a king to judge them, and Saul's calling is on par with Samuel and the judges, except he has the added honor of royalty.

Samuel knew Saul was coming. When Saul arrives, the LORD points him out to Samuel. "There is the one who will reign over my people!" We should note the word the LORD uses for "reign." It is the Hebrew verb *atsair* which doesn't mean to reign like a king per se (which would be the word *sarair*), but to restrain or shut up his people. Only the ESV translates the word as restrain, but it is the more correct translation. That seems like an odd purpose for a king, but then that is what the king will do as Samuel explained to the people. He will make servants of the people and bring them into bondage to serve his own desires. Remember the meaning of the names? Saul the son of Kish is the one desired, who will be like the lure that snares God's people in their own desires.

Conversation #4 (9:18-21)

8. **How does Samuel address Saul?**

    Samuel greets Saul as if he knows him, which he does. He introduces himself, invites Saul to go to the banquet with him, and promises to answer all the questions in his heart—and oh, by the way, don't worry about the donkeys. They have been found. And then he makes this rather cryptic statement:

    > "And on whom is all the desire of Israel? Is it not on you and on all your father's house?" (9:20)

    The one desired is a pun on Saul's name, and I think Samuel says it a bit tongue-in-cheek. Saul will be the one who fits the bill in regards to Israel's desire for a king, but he fits the bill for the LORD's purposes as well, and so is equally desired by the LORD. Saul is the man.

9. **Imagine this from Saul's eyes. What is his response?**

    This man who Saul has never seen before knows all about the donkeys, so that fits with the man being a seer. But then the seer starts punning off his name and promises to tell him all that is in his heart. All he really wanted to know about was the donkeys, so to what exactly is the seer referring, and why is he addressing him in such exalted terms?

Saul's response is self-effacing.

> "Am I not a Benjamite, of the smallest of the tribes of Israel, and my family the least of all the families of the tribe of Benjamin? Why then do you speak like this to me?" (9:21)

There are two ways to look at this statement. First is from the perspective of what is polite in Middle Eastern conversation. Saul is the choice son of a wealthy family. They are not the least of all the families in the tribe of Benjamin, and yet he downplays his family's status, which is a typical Middle Eastern nicety.

But the part about Benjamin being the smallest of the tribes has some truth about it. How did Benjamin end up the smallest of the tribes? Because of a crime perpetrated by the men of Gibeah who killed a Levite's concubine and so sparked off a war that almost wiped out the entire tribe (Judges 20-21). The only reason Saul's family exists is because wives were found for the remnant of the men of Benjamin among the people of Jabesh Gilead (in addition to the wives they stole from the vineyards of Shiloh). So, there is this stigma about Benjamin, and Gibeah in particular, because of this ancient crime, and so they are diminutive not just in physical size but also in status among the tribes.

Saul must be wondering why a man who is clearly a Levite priest would address him in this manner. Is the guy playing with him or is he serious?

Conversation #5 (9:22-24)

Samuel doesn't answer him, but instead hustles Saul up to the banquet hall, seats him in a place of honor, and calls for the reserved portion to be brought to Saul.

10. What is the significance of the portion Samuel orders for Saul?

The portion turns out to be the thigh—Samuel's own portion. The thigh is allotted to the priest who performs sacrifice for the peace offering (Leviticus 7:33). While the thigh is reserved for the priest, the rest of the meat from the peace offering could be shared with worshippers, the poor, and the hungry as a fellowship meal. Saul was undoubtedly hungry, seeing as their supplies had run out just that day, but Samuel belabors the point that this portion had been reserved for Saul as a particular honor.

Proverb 23:1-3 warns us that when we sit down at the King's table, we do not treat it like some common dinner.

> *"When you sit down to eat with a ruler, consider carefully what is before you; and put a knife to your throat if you are a man given to appetite. Do not desire his delicacies, for they are deceptive food."*
> —Proverbs 23:1-3

Saul sits at the LORD's table at Samuel's urging without even the least amount of reflection or circumspection and eats the priestly portion without even questioning it. He gave in to his appetite without an inkling that God was setting him up. That food was deceptive.

Just because someone urges or even commands you to do something, you should think about what your actions are communicating and how they will reflect on God and your understanding of who you are before God. When you sit down to the LORD's table, do you consider the manner in which you eat or even pause to consider if you should eat? What judgment might you be incurring if you partake in an unworthy manner or when you have not taken time to sanctify yourself? Do you take the plate that is urged on you, or do you let it pass?

It would have shown a reverence for God and respect for His priest if Saul had refused the portion God had specifically reserved for Samuel.

Perhaps it was okay for Saul to eat the priestly portion. We can make a number of rationales for Saul doing what Samuel urged him to do, and yet I wish there had been some indication in the text that Saul had even paused to think and consider his actions. This won't be the last time that Saul treats God's sacrifice as a light thing.

Conversation #6 (9:25-26)

When they leave the feast, Samuel takes Saul down to a house in the city and arranges for him to sleep on the rooftop—a choice place because it is cool. In the Masoretic Hebrew, it says that Samuel *dabar*-ed (conversed, spoke with) Saul there, although the conversation itself is not included. Most Bible translations follow the Masoretic text, but the ESV follows the Septuagint and Vulgate versions in omitting a reference to this conversation. Since there is no actual conversation recorded, it seems a trifling detail to make, but that detail is part of the rhythm being established of walking and talking.

Samuel rouses Saul the next morning with the command "Get up, it's time to go!" as if Saul needed prompting like a son. Then Saul arises and goes down from the roof into the city with Samuel, and then down to the outskirts of the city.

Conversation #7 (9:27–10:8)

As they come to the outskirts of the city, Samuel instructs Saul to send the servant ahead so he can speak with Saul privately.

There is a curious break at this point. The conversation is introduced at the end of Chapter 9, but the content of the conversation begins in Chapter 10. I think this is done purposely to indicate the end of a sequence in Chapter 9's narrative structure.

11. What did Samuel do?

> He took out a flask of oil, anointed Saul, and kissed him in the manner of anointing royalty. This practice of kissing royalty is reflected in Psalm 2:10-12: *"Now therefore, be wise, O kings; Be instructed, you judges of the earth. Serve the LORD with fear, and rejoice with trembling. Kiss the Son, lest He be angry, and you perish in the way, when His wrath is kindled but a little. Blessed are all those who put their trust in Him."*
>
> Kiss the son means to pay homage due the king. These are not just instructions for lay people. These are instructions for kings and judges concerning the King. When pursuing a crown, receiving instruction from the LORD and giving homage to the King play a big part in achieving that end.
>
> As Samuel anoints Saul, he explains why he is doing this: The LORD has anointed Saul as commander (*nageed*) over His inheritance. There

is a subtle reminder in those words that this kingship is contingent on the relationship with God who retains the ultimate Kingship over His people and Saul must also answer to Samuel who is the one giving him God's instructions.

12. What were the signs Samuel told Saul to look for?

Samuel gives Saul three very specific signs to look for on his return trip home that will confirm his anointing. The signs involve places, people he will meet coming and going, and certain actions they take.

First sign:

> **Where:** Rachel's tomb in the territory of Benjamin at Zelzah. According to Genesis 35:19, Rachel's tomb is just outside of Bethlehem which would have been Judah's territory, but here it is located more within the vicinity of Ramah and Bethel. (In Jeremiah 31:15, Rachel is associated with Ramah.) The exact location is not certain, but the name of the place, Zelzah, is unique to this verse. Zelzah is a compound word meaning shadow and sun, or shade in the heat of the sun. In context with the prophecy, it implies that something hidden in shadow—figuratively, a question—will be brought to light—answered.
>
> **Who will he meet:** Two men.
>
> **What will they do:** They will speak to him and tell him the donkeys have been found. What had been dark was made light. Mystery solved. In this case, Saul *hears* something.

Second sign:

> **Where:** The terebinth tree of Tabor.
>
> **Who will he meet:** Three men going up to God at Bethel, one carrying three goats, one carrying three loaves of bread, and one carrying a skin of wine.
>
> **What will they do:** Give Saul two loaves of bread. In this case, Saul *receives* something.

Third sign:

> **Where:** The hill of God (the *gibeah* of God), that is, the city on the hill where the Philistine garrison is stationed (perhaps Gibeah, Saul's hometown).
>
> **Who will he meet:** A group of prophets coming down from the high place in procession with a stringed instrument, a tambourine, a flute, and a harp before them.
>
> **What will they be doing:** They will be prophesying. In this case, Saul will *do* something. The Spirit of the LORD will come upon him, he will prophesy with them, and he will be turned into another man.

Three signs will be given, each with a growing involvement. First Saul will hear something, next he will receive something, and then he will act. Samuel instructs him to do what the occasion demands in each case. The signs were meant to be proofs that God was with him.

Finally, Samuel gives Saul a last set of instructions to go down to Gilgal before him. There Saul is to wait seven days until Samuel joins him to officiate the sacrifices and tell Saul what he is to do next. Even though he is king, Saul still has to take instructions from Samuel, not because Samuel is the judge, but because he is the prophet through whom God gives instruction.

This journey with four named stops (the tomb at Zelzah, the tree of Tabor, the hill of God, and Gilgal) creates a mirroring of the four stops named at the outset of the journey (Shalisha, Shaalim, Benjamin's territory, and Zuph). What is not clear at this point is that the command to go to Gilgal doesn't happen immediately. In fact, this event isn't recorded until First Samuel 13. Instead, Saul makes a final stop at the high place in Gibeah.

Saul's Turning (10:9-16)

13. What is Saul's reaction to all this?

He doesn't question it. He simply goes, and in going, he becomes a new man.

In First Samuel 10:6, Samuel prophesies that when Saul meets the prophets at the third stop, he will be turned into another man, but here in 10:9, the text indicates that the change actually happens when Saul turns his back to go from Samuel. I don't know if these are two separate acts or if verse 9 is simply a summary note.

The word for "turning" used here is the Hebrew word *haphak*, which has several different applications. Let's look at the word *haphak*.

Haphak

A) *Haphak* can mean to turn and go in another direction:

"And the LORD turned *[haphak]* a very strong west wind, which took the locusts away and blew them into the Red Sea..." —Exodus 10:19

"And when the men of Israel turned back *[haphak]*, the men of Benjamin panicked, for they saw that disaster had come upon them." —Judges 20:41

"So David's young men turned *[haphak]* on their heels and went back; and they came and told him all these words." —First Samuel 25:12

B) *Haphak* can also mean to have a change of body, character, or condition:

"Go to Pharaoh in the morning, when he goes out to the water, and you shall stand by the river's bank to meet him; and the rod which was turned *[haphak]* to a serpent you shall take in your hand... 'Thus says the LORD: "By this you shall know that I am the LORD. Behold, I will strike the waters which are in the river with the rod that is in my hand, and they shall be turned *[haphak]* to blood."'" —Exodus 7:15, 17

"He turned *[haphak]* the sea into dry land..." —Psalm 66:6

"You have turned *[haphak]* for me my mourning into dancing; you have put off my sackcloth and clothed me with gladness," —Psalm 30:11

C) *Haphak* can mean to have a change of heart:

"Now it was told the king of Egypt that the people had fled, and the heart of Pharaoh and his servants was turned *[haphak]* against the people; and they said, 'Why have we done this, that we have let Israel go from serving us?'" —Exodus 14:5

*"See, O LORD, that I am in distress; my soul is troubled; my heart is overturned **[haphak]** within me, for I have been very rebellious..."*
—Lamentations 1:20

*"All my close friends abhor me, and those whom I love have turned **[haphak]** against me."*—Job 19:19

*"He turned **[haphak]** their heart to hate His people, to deal craftily with His servants."* —Psalm 105:25

D) *Haphak* can describe a people or nation being physically overthrown and brought to an end:

*"And he said to him, 'See, I have favored you concerning this thing also, in that I will not overthrow **[haphak]** this city for which you have spoken.' ... So He overthrew **[haphak]** those cities, all the plain, all the inhabitants of the cities, and what grew on the ground. ... And it came to pass, when God destroyed the cities of the plain, that God remembered Abraham, and sent Lot out of the midst of the overthrow, when He overthrew **[haphak]** the cities in which Lot had dwelt."*
—Genesis 19:21, 25, 29

14. In which sense was Saul *haphak*-ed?

   A. Turned and went in another direction
   B. Was physically changed into a different person
   C. Was given an internal change of heart
   D. Overthrown

I would say "A" and "C" definitely. "B" might be considered in light of Saul having a distinct personality change as noted by the people. I will tell you that "D" will also apply when we get to Chapter 31.

15. Why would the people who knew Saul be so surprised at his prophesying?

Even the people who knew him recognized the bizarre shift in personality. Saul was clearly not himself, and it raised comment. Notice they say, "What has happened to the son of Kish," emphasizing his identification with his father.

"Is Saul among the prophets? . . . But who is their father?" Their words are disdainful and rhetorical. Prophets were not known to be from prominent, well-heeled families like the son of Kish. They were from a different social caste and role. This was definitely out of character for Saul to be associating with them.

This is kind of like Jesus saying, "I am the bread which came down from heaven," and then all of His people sneering at Him, saying, "Is not this Jesus, the son of Joseph, whose father and mother we know?"

16. Why didn't Saul tell his uncle all that Samuel said?

Apparently he is back home at Gibeah at this point. So this makes the fourth and final stop on his journey, which forms a parallel structure with his initial journey to find the donkeys.

According to Samuel, there is a Philistine garrison stationed at Gibeah. How would the Philistines react to hearing that the newly anointed king of Israel was right in their midst? They'd probably come after Saul before he could be made king and marshal an army against them.

APPLY THE PICTURE

Saul's Model

What was driving Saul's journey initially and how does it evolve into a different kind of journey?

Initially, Saul is a man driven by the cares of the world—the cares of his father for the donkeys, his father's care for him, his own need for food. He was sent out one day on the mundane errand to find some lost donkeys, and he went farther and farther down the road until he comes to the end of his own resources and has to make a decision to continue pursuing the cares of his father or seek a different direction.

He seeks a different direction from the man of God, and that decision changes his path in life. Suddenly he is greeted and ushered into a banquet hall and treated like a king. Then the next morning, he finds himself anointed as king and given a very different set of tasks from the ones with which he started, and he is sent on a very different journey. He must no longer live life in pursuit of donkeys, but in pursuit of a crown. What does that entail? Maybe we should look at it from our own standpoint.

We, as believers, should understand what Saul is going through. We, too, have spent much of our early life being driven by the cares of this world and chasing donkeys aimlessly in a wilderness. We, like Saul, were brought to that crossroad in life where we had to make a decision to let the cares of this world continue to drive us or to seek another path.

When we made that decision to pursue a different path and it led us to this new relationship with God through Christ, did we realize that we were in the process of becoming not just a new creation, but kings? It was a *haphak*-ing moment when the Spirit came to indwell us. We were told it would happen, and it did happen. We are still the same person, and yet not the same person at all. It's all very confusing, wouldn't you agree? And now we find ourselves suddenly thrust into this new life with its new goals and expectations. We are on a parallel journey of sorts, but of an entirely different nature with a different set of tasks. We are no longer chasing donkeys, but instead we are pursuing a crown.

So where do we go from here?

Questions for Reflection

- Apart from becoming a believer, have you ever had a *haphak*-ing moment in your life—maybe a change of heart, maybe a decision that changed the course of your life, maybe a reversal of fortune or a complete overthrow of some aspect in your life?

- How do Saul's hearing, receiving, and acting experiences mimic our own entrance into faith and a pursuit of the crown?

- How does this tie into Paul's teachings on becoming a new man? What is involved with that change? (Ephesians 4, Colossians 3)

- When the Spirit came upon Saul, the change inside him began to manifest itself outwardly to the point that it drew comment from family and friends. Has the Spirit ever manifested itself through you in such a way that your behavior raised comment from the people who know you? (Consider Peter's words in 1 Peter 4:3-4.)

- We, too, are supposed to be pursuing crowns toward a future kingdom. Why wouldn't we want the crown? Isn't the crown an honor? On the upside, think of all the perks that come with being royalty. Is there a downside?

 ## Saul Proclaimed King

READ

First Samuel 10:17-27

NARRATIVE STRUCTURE

Picture #2 is broken into three sections with a chiastic structure (A-B-A):

(A) Opening action: The people reject God as king (10:17-19)
(B) The presentation of Saul (10:20-26)
(A) Closing action: The rebels reject Saul as king (10:27)

The chiastic structure reaches a climax at Saul's presentation where the narrator comments that he stands head and shoulders above the rest.

BUILD THE PICTURE

You might recognize the words in this sutitle from the passage in John 19. It is the passage where Pilate brings Christ the Lord out to the judgment seat before the people, and cries "Behold, your King!" But the people reject Christ, saying, "We have no king but Caesar!" This is a perfect parallel to what is happening in First Samuel 10. Here at Mizpah, the judgment seat, the children of Israel reject God as King over them and hail a human king in His place. It's a poignant moment of failing on Israel's part and a prophetic picture of Christ to come. We will talk about the big picture of Christ in the next lesson.

17. Why does Samuel call Israel back to Mizpah?

The last time he called them to Mizpah, he judged them. Now Samuel calls them to announce the king, and yet he prefaces the proceedings with an indictment against them, for having rejected God as their King. And so, he sets about this process of determining the new king by calling them out by tribe, by clan (or thousands), then by family. Samuel already knows whom God has chosen, but he goes through this process purely as the facilitator between God and the people, so that they understand that their man is also God's choice.

The Hebrew word for "family" being used here is a curious one. The word is *mishpaha*. *Mishpaha* means "family" in the immediate context, but its root verb *sapa* means "to sweep bare or to scrape away." What does laying something bare have to do with families?

Sometimes we get words like this in the Hebrew where the study word seems to have an unrelated meaning to its root. When that happens, we have to consider the combined picture that is formed and how it fits with the context of the passage. So let's flesh out the picture of the root verb *sapa* first and then see how it fits with what Samuel is chronicling here.

Sapa means "to sweep bare or pare away" until something that was hidden is revealed. It is used twice in the Scriptures—once to describe a man's bones that begin to stick out because of a wasting sickness. Bones were never meant to be seen, but they can *sapa*, stick out in an unsightly manner. The second example is a high, wind-swept hill that sticks up baldly above the others and becomes a place easily seen—so easily seen that it becomes a rallying point where a banner is planted.

Samuel is calling the people family by family, *mishpaha* by *mishpaha*, looking for the one among them that sticks out—one who is like a high hill standing head and shoulders above the rest on whom Israel will plant that banner. Who does that description fit better than Saul of Gibeah (Saul of the Hill)? But where is he?

18. Why didn't Saul present himself when called?

The LORD has to point out that Saul has hidden himself among the equipment. He didn't want to stick out, so he was keeping a low profile. He knew what was going to happen. Saul's actions reveal something about his feelings, or perhaps misgivings, over being king. Did he want to be king?

I don't think he did. I think he had a good life as the choice and handsome son of his father and was satisfied with the inheritance he would get in terms of an earthly kingdom. He was happy just pursuing wayward donkeys. And he is probably wondering how he got into this mess.

I almost feel a little sorry for Saul. What was happening wasn't a good thing. The people were throwing off God's kingship and pursuing the wrong man for the crown. He didn't want the kingship, it was not the right thing, and yet he was powerless to prevent it. But then we could ask, why wouldn't Saul want to be king, seeing as how it has been handed to him? Isn't it a good thing to want to pursue a crown?

As soon as Saul stood up, the people's eyes fastened on him. He was perfect! He was young, handsome, and wealthy—a man among men—and they embraced him as their king. Then Samuel stands Saul up before them and reminds the nation of what this king will do, writes it before the LORD, and sends everyone home again.

Does it seem anticlimactic that Samuel makes the big announcement proclaiming Saul is king, and then everyone just goes home? Even Saul goes home, like nothing has happened.

19. What were the two reactions people had toward Saul?

Overall, everyone embraced him. A group of valiant men went with him, whose hearts God had touched—so Saul had the beginning of an army to protect him now that his pending kingship had become public knowledge. Remember, the Philistine garrison is still at Gibeah.

But then there were some rebels who looked at Saul, this man who was supposed to be the great savior of the nation, and said, "Saul? *Seriously?*" It says they despised him and brought him no gifts.

The NKJV calls them rebels, but the Hebrew calls them the children of Belial. Belial is actually a composite of *beli* meaning "without" and *ya'al* meaning "profit, gain, benefit," rendering the meaning "without profit" or "without benefit." They were worthless men.

This name Belial is used frequently in the KJV, but the name isn't found in other versions. Instead the Hebrew phrase "ben Belial" is translated as rebels, scoundrels, worthless fellows, wicked, useless, vain, etc. Apart from the KJV usage, the only time we see the name Belial crop up anywhere in Scripture is in Second Corinthians 6:15 where Paul says, *"And what accord has Christ with Belial? Or what part has a believer with an unbeliever?"* So we understand that Christ and Belial represent opposite pictures—which has some implications when we apply this to what is happening in First Samuel between Saul and these children of Belial.

To give you the picture of those who have been called the children of Belial in the Old Testament, the list includes:

- The perverted men of Gibeah (Judges 19:22)
- The sons of Eli (First Samuel 2:12)
- Nabal, who refused to help David (First Samuel 25:17)
- David's men who refused to share the spoil with those who stayed behind to support the troops (First Samuel 30:22)
- A Benjamite named Sheba, who declared he would have no part of David's kingdom (Second Samuel 20:1)
- The two men who brought false charges against the innocent Naboth so that Ahab could steal his vineyard (First Kings 21:10)

The children of Belial are characterized as liars, thieves, false witnesses, perverted men, ungodly men, dissolute men given over to their passions, and rebellious men who deny the king his rightful place and would seek to usurp it. They align themselves with the wrong king and pursue a place in the kingdom the wrong way and for the wrong reasons.

These are the rebels Saul faces, but he holds his peace; which is to say, he held his tongue and said nothing.

20. Why would the savior not say anything in his own defense?

It is true that Saul was king in name, but he was not yet in possession of the kingdom. There was a battle that had to be won before the people would truly call him savior and embrace him as king.

Question for Reflection

- Have you ever found yourself in a place where you knew something wasn't right, you didn't want to be there, but you were caught up in the flood of circumstances and then had to deal with the fallout? How did it end?

LESSON 6: FIRST SAMUEL 11–12

Defeat of the Serpent King

SERIES STRUCTURE

Picture #3 (11:1-15) details Saul's first battle and coronation.

Picture #4 (12:1-25) is Samuel's indictment of Israel for having chosen Saul as king.

Like Chapters 9-10, where the last conversation is introduced in the final verses of Chapter 9 and then detailed in Chapter 10, in the same way, Saul's coronation is mentioned at the end of Chapter 11 but detailed in Chapter 12. Thus, Chapter 11 is a self-contained picture from battle to coronation, which is also a prophetic picture of Christ that connects with Chapters 9-10.

 Saul's First Battle/Coronation

READ

First Samuel 11:1–15

NARRATIVE STRUCTURE

Picture #3 and is broken into these five sections:

1) The challenge (11:1-4)
2) Saul's reaction to the challenge (11:5-10)
3) The battle (11:11)
4) Saul faces the rebels who denied him (11:12-13)
5) The coronation celebration (11:14-15)

These same elements will play out in David's first battle, ending just short of his actual coronation, and we will compare the two narratives when we get to First Samuel 17.

BUILD THE PICTURE

The Challenge (11:1-4)

1. **Who are the key characters:**

   King Nahash and the Ammonites, the people of Jabesh Gilead, and king-to-be Saul.

2. **What do we know about Nahash and the Ammonites?**

   The Ammonites are the nation on Israel's east border that Israel left alone when they came into the Land. Ammon is descended from Lot through his son Ben-ammi.

   The name Nahash means "serpent."

3. **What do we know about the people of Jabesh Gilead?**

   Jabesh Gilead is a city allotted to the tribe of Gad and situated in the middle of the rich stretch of land along the Jordan. Jabesh Gilead has a particular tie to the tribe of Benjamin that we find in Judges 20-21. It would be good to review the account because it will shed light on Saul's actions here.

   There was a heinous crime committed by the perverted men of Gibeah (Judges 19), much like what happened at Sodom and Gomorrah. A Levite and his concubine came to Gibeah late one day and were given lodging by an old man. That night, the perverted men of Gibeah stormed the man's house, demanding that he give them the Levite so that they could sodomize him. Instead, they are given the Levite's concubine, and she is abused to death. That was the crime. In outrage, the Levite takes her body home, cuts it up, and sends the pieces out to all the tribes of Israel, calling them to assemble at Mizpah to deal with this crime. All of Israel shows up except the men of Jabesh Gilead.

There is a rather one-sided trial in which Gibeah is condemned, which then sparks a war between Israel and the tribe of Benjamin who are sheltering Gibeah. When all is done, the tribe of Benjamin is left with only a remnant of men whom the LORD saw fit to spare so that the entire tribe wouldn't be lost. Then arises the question of where to find wives for the Benjamites in order to rebuild the tribe. Israel had sworn that anyone who did not show up at Mizpah to deal with this crime would be put to death. Since Jabesh Gilead did not show up, they were condemned to death.

Israel had also sworn not to give wives to the Benjamites. Because Jabesh Gilead had not been present to take the oath, their women were eligible as wives for the Benjamites.

So, Jabesh Gilead was put to the sword and their daughters given to the men of Benjamin to help rebuild the tribe. The city of Jabesh Gilead was repopulated over time as Gibeah was, but there remained a strong familial tie between Jabesh Gilead and the tribe of Benjamin because of the shared bloodlines and perhaps a sense of obligation on Benjamin's part to be merciful to Jabesh Gilead.

4. **When do the events take place (relative to the immediate context)?**

   This battle with the Ammonites happens after Saul has been proclaimed king, but before he is coronated over the kingdom. At the opening of the conflict, Saul has gone home and is tending his father's herd in the field.

5. **What is the opening conflict?**

   You will remember from the book of Judges (starting in Judges 10) that the Ammonites and Philistines have been taking turns harassing Israel in this ongoing, two-sided battle. The Philistines have been pushing their way into Israel west of the Jordan, while the Ammonites have invaded Israel east of the Jordan. This time it is the Ammonites who have risen up and established enough of a foothold in Gilead that the people of Jabesh Gilead are willing to make a covenant of peace with Nahash.

   But Nahash has a condition. Israel must consent to a mutilation of their right eye that will partially blind them, but more importantly, it will proclaim to all who see them that they are the conquered servants of Nahash. Regardless of whether the Ammonites retained their grip on Israel, the people of Israel would carry that mark of shame and reproach until the day they died.

Jabesh Gilead is given seven days to find a savior to deliver them, and immediately they send out the messengers with pleas for help.

Saul's Reaction to the Challenge (11:5-10)

6. What is Saul's response when he hears what has happened?

First, the Spirit of the LORD comes upon him, and he gets angry.

Next, he does something similar to what the Levite did in Judges 20. He takes a yoke of oxen, cuts them in pieces, and sends their parts out to all of Israel with the statement that whoever does not go out with Saul and Samuel in the battle, this will be done to his oxen. Notice, he cuts up oxen and not a human corpse like the Levite did, but the message carries the same threat and has the same effect. All of Israel assembles as one man at Bezek.

Bezek is only mentioned one other time in the Scripture, and that is in Judges 1. It is the first campaign of the tribe of Judah in taking their inheritance, and it is a resounding victory. But this Bezek may be in a different place. Many Bible maps place it closer to the Jezreel Valley across the Jordan from Jabesh Gilead.

A head count is taken at Bezek. Of Israel, there are 300,000. Of Judah, there are 30,000 (a tenth). Notice that Israel and Judah are counted separately. This anticipates the future rivalry between the two sides when David comes on the scene. Most of the tribes will remain loyal to Saul of Benjamin, whereas Judah will side with David.

The Battle (11:11)

There is only one verse dedicated to battle details. Saul puts his army of 330,000 into three companies and goes to war with the Ammonites. The battle lasts less than a day and is a rout. Saul proves he is able to deliver his people. That is all that is really said about it.

Saul Faces the Rebels (11:12-13)

7. What happens to the children of Belial who resisted Saul at first?

After the battle, the nation's eyes turn back to the children of Belial who scoffed, "Shall Saul reign over us?" Israel demands that Samuel render judgment against the rebels to put them to death, but Saul steps into the judge's shoes and rules for mercy, saying, *"Not a man shall be put to death this day, for today the LORD has accomplished salvation in Israel."* (First Samuel 11:13)

So we see the focus begin to shift away from Samuel as judge and onto Saul as king. Samuel still retains the authority of a prophet and priest, but now Saul will assume the mantle of responsibility for civic decision-making in the kingdom as he is officially coronated.

The Coronation Celebration (11:14-15)

8. Why does Samuel call everyone to Gilgal instead of Mizpah?

Keep in mind where we are physically. Saul marshals the troops at Bezek, west of the Jordan. They cross the Jordan to Jabesh Gilead and wipe out the Ammonites. From there Samuel proposes that they go to Gilgal to *renew* the kingdom. So how was the kingdom established to begin with and what did it have to do with Gilgal?

Joshua first led the children of Israel into the Promised Land at the ford near Bethabara, which is across from Gilgal and Jericho. That ford at the Jordan was the place from which they took the memorial stones that were then set up at Gilgal to remember that crossing. Then, at Gilgal, Israel renewed its covenant with the LORD and made its beginning in the Promised Land. It is because of the national significance of Gilgal that Samuel takes them back there for a renewing of the kingdom with Saul's coronation.

I don't know whether the people crossed back over the Jordan and then made their way down to Gilgal along the west bank, or if they stayed on the east bank of the Jordan and then crossed over when they came to the fords at Bethabara. It would have been more significant to cross at Bethabara, because that is where Joshua first led them into the kingdom.

Any time a prophet calls the people to Bethabara and takes them through the waters at this ford in the Jordan, it has this significant meaning for the children of Israel. It is their entry point into the kingdom. (Consider John 1:28.)

9. **Why was there a delay in crowning Saul?**

First there was the anointing in Chapter 10, which no one knew about except Samuel and Saul. Then, almost immediately, there is the grand reveal at Mizpah where Samuel proclaims Saul king and all the people (well, most of the people) hail Saul as king. But then there is this delay where everyone goes back to life as usual. Saul is in the field tending his father's herds. The people of Jabesh Gilead are struggling against Nahash the Ammonite. Then there is the war, the victory, and finally everyone goes to Gilgal for the coronation of Saul.

Saul's ascent to the throne seems like such a drawn out process, and it begs the question, why? Why wasn't Saul crowned at Mizpah when Samuel makes the big reveal? Why have all these intervening events? It is because the first king of Israel is establishing a pattern that the final king of Israel will also follow to a certain extent.

APPLY THE PICTURE

Saul's Model of Christ

The main focus of Chapters 9, 10, and 11 is the picture of Saul stepping into his role as deliverer and king. The Gospels record similar events in the life of Christ. There are three times when Christ the Lord is brought before His people in public declarations of His Messiahship and kingship:

- His baptism
- His triumphal entry
- His appearance on the Pavement (Gabbatha) when Pilate presents Him as King to the people

There is a fourth that has not been realized yet: When Christ is crowned and comes into His kingdom.

The elements of all these are pictured here in Saul's narrative, but they are blended and not in an exact timeline order. Let's walk through the Old Testament (OT) elements of Saul's life so far and compare them with the New Testament (NT) Gospel accounts.

Saul's Anointing and Jesus' Baptism

OT: Samuel is a prophet, priest, and judge. He waits for the coming of one God has chosen to be deliverer of the people, and God Himself points Saul out.

NT: John the Baptist is both a priest and prophet. He begins a baptism ministry by which God the Father will reveal the Son. John waits for the one who has been chosen to deliver Israel, and the Father Himself makes Jesus known to him.

OT: Samuel anoints Saul privately, and a number of signs confirmed the anointing, including the giving of the Spirit.

NT: John baptizes Jesus (not quite so privately), and Jesus is anointed with the Holy Spirit (see Acts 4:27, 10:38).

OT: Saul returns home, and his kinsmen are amazed to see him prophesying with the prophets. "Is Saul among the prophets? But who is their father?" they ask.

NT: Jesus begins prophesying and becomes known as a prophet. He is derided by his own family and kinsmen. "Is not this Jesus, the son of Joseph, whose father and mother we know?" (John 6:42)

Saul's Election and Jesus' Triumphal Entry

OT: Samuel makes the public statement that Saul is the king. He is the king-elect, but not yet crowned. The LORD moves the hearts of a select number of men to go with him.

NT: Jesus is publicly hailed King at His triumphal entry. He is the King-elect, but not yet crowned. He is surrounded by His disciples, men whose hearts are moved to follow Him.

OT: We would expect the Philistine garrison occupying the area to react to Samuel's announcement, but they don't.
NT: The Roman garrison in the area doesn't react to the furor over the arrival of Israel's King.

OT: The people of Jabesh Gilead cry "Save us!"
NT: The people in Jerusalem rejoice and cry "Hosanna (Save us)!"

OT: The people have mixed reactions to Saul. Many embrace him as the savior who will deliver them from the Philistines. But there are also rebels who scorn him, saying, "How can this man save us?"
NT: The people have mixed reactions to Jesus. Some think He is a prophet. Some think He is the Messiah who will save them from the Roman oppressors. There are also those who scorn and mock Him.

There is also a curious element of Jesus' servants being sent to find a donkey, which echoes Saul and his servant being sent on a similar errand.

Saul's Election[1] and Jesus' Triumphal Entry

OT: Saul wavers and hides as events begin to unfold. He is finally found hiding among the equipment.
NT: Jesus did not shirk the crowd or the crown, but we see Him in the garden alone, praying that the cup would be taken from Him.

OT: Samuel calls the people to Mizpah, the place of judgment. There he goes through the formal process of presenting Saul as king.
NT: Pilate brings Christ to the judgment seat on the Pavement to present Him to the people. Pilate cries, "Behold your King!"

OT: Samuel searches for Saul family by family (*mishpaha* by *mishpaha*). Saul sticks out like a bone laid bare or a standard on a wind-swept hill.
NT: When Jesus is presented, He has been scourged so that His bones are laid bare. He is destined for that stake planted on a wind-swept hill. By these things He is identified as the chosen one.

OT: The people reject God as King and embrace Saul as their human king.
NT: The Son of God, is rejected by the people who swear allegiance to Caesar.

---

[1] Saul's election does dual duty in presenting the imagery of both the triumphal entry and also Christ before the people on His way to the cross.

OT: Saul faces a number of mockers called the sons of Belial. They say, "How can this man save us?"

NT: Jesus faces mockers. The chief priests and Pharisees say, "He saved others; Himself He cannot save. If He is the King of Israel, let Him now come down from the cross, and we will believe Him." (Curious, how the parallel suggests the Pharisees are like sons of Belial.)

OT: The king-elect holds his tongue and does not defend himself.

NT: The King-elect holds his tongue and does not defend Himself.

Saul's Battle with Nahash and Christ on the Cross

OT: Saul has been anointed and proclaimed king, but not yet crowned or come into his kingdom. There is a battle that must be fought before he can truly be called a deliverer.

NT: Jesus has been anointed and proclaimed king, but not yet crowned or come into His kingdom. There is a battle that must be fought before He can truly be called a Savior.

OT: The battle Saul fights isn't against the Philistine occupiers. It is a physical battle over a covenant that would put His people in bondage to Nahash (whose name means "the Serpent").

NT: The battle Jesus fights isn't against the Roman occupiers. It is a **spiritual battle** over a covenant of bondage, death, and mutilation that would keep His people under the power of Satan.[2]

OT: Through Saul's victory, the LORD accomplishes salvation for His people.

NT: Through Christ's victory, the LORD accomplishes salvation for all people.

OT: When people demand judgment against the men who doubted and denied Saul as king, they appeal to Samuel the judge, but Saul the king intervenes to offer mercy.

NT: Jesus did not come as judge but as the king who offers mercy to the men who doubted and denied Him. (Think of Peter, Matthew 16:23.)

---

2 The covenant is a parallel to the Old Mosaic Covenant. Paul warns believers against "the mutilation"—those who would uphold the old covenant of works and place their confidence in the fleshly ordinances to which they were in bondage (Philippians 3).

Saul's Battle with Nahash[3] and Christ on the Cross

OT: Saul has been anointed and proclaimed king, but not yet crowned or come into his kingdom. There is a battle that must be fought before he comes into his kingdom.

NT: Jesus ascended from the grave at His resurrection and then ascended to His place beside the Father at His ascension, but as yet, He has not taken the crown or entered into His Kingdom. There is still a battle that must be fought.

OT: The battle Saul fights is against King Nahash and the Ammonites. He fights to save his people from the oppressor.

NT: The battle Christ fights will be a physical battle for a **physical kingdom** against the Dragon (Satan, the serpent) and his world kingdom. He comes to save His people (again).

OT: Saul goes to war with 330,000 of Israel and prevails.

NT: Christ goes to war with 144,000 of Israel and prevails.

OT: Samuel, who is both a priest and prophet, calls Israel to Gilgal to renew the kingdom. Perhaps they cross the Jordan at Bethabara to get there. Gilgal is the place where the kingdom was first established and where Israel's reproach was rolled away.

NT: John the Baptist, who is both a priest and prophet, calls Israel to Bethabara to baptize them, all the while announcing that the Messiah is imminent. The people flock to him, thinking that the kingdom is going to be renewed.—*Wait, isn't this out of place?*

This is what makes the Old Testament pictures difficult to identify without the New Testament clarification, because some of the details fit Christ's first advent, some the second, and some are patterns found in both. John the Baptist inaugurated Christ's first advent, and yet, when we make parallels between Saul and Christ, this event falls (incorrectly) within the millennial kingdom picture. This is why Jewish people studying these Old Testament pictures thought Jesus' baptism was a sign of His inauguration as king.

---

[3] Saul's battle does dual duty in presenting the imagery of both the spiritual battle with the cross and the physical battle in the end times when Christ comes to claim His kingdom, but this causes some ambiguity in separating Christ's first and second advent pictures.

❹ The Indictment Against Israel

READ

First Samuel 12:1–25

NARRATIVE STRUCTURE

There is a dramatic change of tone from Chapter 11 to Chapter 12. Chapter 11 ends with Israel rejoicing over her new king. Chapter 12 begins with an indictment, followed by judgment. This chapter departs dramatically from the baseline structure in that it both begins and ends with dialogue. The only narrator comment is the relating of the sign given by the LORD.

Picture #4 is built in a chiastic order (A-B-C-B-A):

(A) Samuel defends himself as judge (12:1-5)
(B) Samuel defends the LORD as King (12:6-17)
(C) The LORD gives a sign as confirmation (12:18-19)
(B) Samuel gives an assurance of the LORD's mercy (12:20-22)
(A) Samuel gives an assurance of his own mercy (12:23-25)

BUILD THE PICTURE

10. What is Israel's assessment of Samuel's performance as a judge?

He hadn't taken anything from them—not an ox or a donkey or a bribe. He had not cheated or oppressed them or judged corruptly. He had been a good and upright judge, as God and the king were witnesses.

11. Why does Samuel belabor the fact that he took nothing from the people?

Because that is what the king will do. God the King always gave to His people, and the judges He appointed never took anything, either. But the human king will take and take and take. In crowning a human king over them, Israel is agreeing to the loss of material goods, workforce, profit, and lifestyle.

Part of pursuing crowns involves knowing with which king to align yourself. Israel has pursued the wrong king, and it is going to cost them.

12. What case is Samuel building with the history lesson?

Having built a case for himself being blameless as a judge, Samuel then builds a case for God being blameless as a King.

Samuel gives Israel a detailed rundown of all the times God had delivered Israel out of bondage, beginning with Moses and Aaron. They were oppressed in Egypt, and God delivered them. When they were faithless and fell into idolatry, God judged them by selling them into the hands of their enemies. He mentions Israel being in bondage to:

- Sisera (whom Deborah and Barak defeated)
- The Philistines (who Shamgar, Samson, and Samuel himself engaged)
- The king of Moab (whom Ehud defeated)

But Samuel doesn't focus on the judges. He focuses on Israel's continuous cycle of falling away from God. When they cried out to God, God delivered them by sending the judges. The judges were just tools. God was King through all of that.

Samuel mentions four judges by name who delivered Israel from their enemies all around. It is possible that he chose these four to emphasize the "all around" effect. Some versions read Jerubbaal, Bedan, Jephthah, and Samuel. Bedan is an unknown. He is not mentioned in the book of Judges, although his name is spelled the same as Abdon in the Hebrew. There is no mention of Abdon being a deliverer, though. He was only a judge. The Septuagint changes Bedan to Barak.

- Jerubbaal (aka Gideon)—dealt with the Midianites to the south
- Bedan (or Barak). Bedan is not mentioned elsewhere in Scripture, but Barak dealt with the Canaanites to the north.
- Jephthah—dealt with the Ammonites to the east
- Samuel (or Samson)—dealt with the Philistines to the west

At any rate, Samuel's point is that the judges delivered Israel from their enemies on all sides—north, south, east, and west. Having given this summary, Samuel makes this point: God has delivered his people every time through the judges He raised up, and caused them to dwell safely all the days of the judge. So why is Israel asking for a king this time? Wasn't the LORD already King over them?

Israel has sinned in pursuing the wrong king. Even so, God has humored them in giving them their desires. But this is the bottom line. Nothing has changed. Whether they are under judges or kings, Israel is still under God. The laws for obedience and disobedience, blessing and curse, still apply to both the people and the king; and if one goes down, so does the other. The king is not exempt from God's headship.

13. What sign does God perform to validate Samuel's words?

Instead of giving Israel an abundant yield in the days of the wheat harvest, He takes it away by sending thunder and rain on the fields to ruin the crop. But then that is what kings do. They take, at a cost to the people. Pursuing the wrong king is going to cost them.

14. How do the people react to being convicted?

The people realize their sin and ask Samuel to intercede for them so that they will not die.

15. Why would it be a sin against the LORD for Samuel to cease praying for the people?

Samuel is a prophet and also a priest. Intercession is his duty before God, regardless of his own personal feelings.

APPLY THE PICTURE

Chapter 12 is written in a chiastic structure that reaches its apex at God's thunderous disapproval of His people's desire for an earthly king. They have sinned and they admit their sin, but the king has been chosen. Events will go forward. Even so, God does not abandon them to their poor choices. He is still sovereign over them, and He will not forsake them because it was the decision on His part, not theirs, to make them His people. He loved them first, and His love and mercy toward them are everlasting.

There are right and wrong kings with whom to align ourselves when pursuing a reward, and regardless of what earthly king is put on the throne, we cannot forget that God, the Great King, is still sovereign.

Samuel warned Israel that aligning with an earthly king can lead to being drawn aside after "empty things which cannot profit or deliver" (12:21). The choice of king will drive a choice of values and pursuits, and there are right and wrong rewards to pursue. But serving an earthly king doesn't override the relationship with God the King, as Samuel points out. Far from it. If Israel is going to survive her poor choice, she must continue to serve God the King in truth with all her heart; if she continues to do wickedly, Samuel warns *"you shall be swept away, both you and your king"* (12:25). I think the order of the wording there is intentional in lumping the king with Israel herself. This king is no rival to God. Israel's preservation doesn't rest on the earthly king or even on the earthly king's alignment with God. Quite the opposite. The earthly king's preservation depends on God's people serving God. If the people do wrong, whether at the king's direction or of their own volition, the king will suffer as well. For this reason, Israel is going to need heavy help from an intercessor.

Samuel's Model as Intercessor

Samuel has suffered a tremendous amount of personal affront throughout this affair. He has been rejected by the people whom he must still serve as priest and intercessor. Maybe his sons were not the best choices to fill his shoes, but that was no reason for Israel to throw off God's kingship and seek another king. The only thing that keeps him at the job is his alignment with the greater King's priorities and a dogged determination to serve the LORD whole-heartedly.

We are a royal priesthood, and Samuel's duty is our duty as well. Sometimes we have to overlook the personal hurt we endure at the hands of people and continue to serve as disciplers and intercessors for them—not out of an obligation to them but in obedience to God.

How hard is it to pray for someone who has pointedly rejected you or even hurt you, or who offends over and over and over again?

How hard is it to pray for someone who has rejected the faith and is pursuing what was right in their own eyes—and they are taking you with them down this path? How do you pray for this situation? How do you continue to teach and disciple them through the consequences of their decisions? It is a tough thing to do.

I think the key to being able to respond correctly relies in what we know of God's sovereignty and His love, and our ability to focus not on the people we are serving but on God whom we are serving. It puts things in perspective.

> ## Questions for Reflection
>
> - What does the role of intercessor look like for you?
>
> - What are some of the personal challenges you have experienced in coming alongside another person to disciple them?

LESSON 7: FIRST SAMUEL 13

The Endurance Test of Kingship

SERIES STRUCTURE

The narrative of First Samuel 13 is broken into two main pictures:

Picture #5 (13:1-15) is the account of Saul's first failure.

Picture #6 (13:16-23) is a small, intervening picture that remarks on Israel's lack of weapons and serves as a break between major narratives. Another similar break ends the next chapter as well. It gives enough information to move the narrative forward, and establish a comment on Jonathan's actions in the next picture.

 ## Saul's First Failure

READ

First Samuel 13:1-15

NARRATIVE STRUCTURE

Picture #5 is the main picture and first in a series of three tests King Saul faces. Each opens with a battle, then details how Saul reacts to the crisis. The picture is subdivided into the following sections:

1) Narrator's comment (13:1-2)
2) The catalyst: Jonathan's attack (13:3)
3) Reactions to the attack (13:4-9)
4) The judgment of Saul's actions (13:10-14)
5) Narrator's comment (13:15)

A crisis develops very quickly, and Saul must respond as a king worthy of a kingdom. Saul doesn't know it, but God is orchestrating this crisis to test his faith, and there is a tremendous reward on the table for him if he remains steadfast and obedient. Throughout the picture, there are subtle comparisons between Saul and Gideon, which the author makes by using similar phrasing in verses. By comparison, the judge will be more exemplary than the king.

BUILD THE PICTURE

Narrator's Comment (13:1-2)

1. **What time markers are we given?**

    We have a curious verse at the start of the chapter that gives us a reference to Saul's reign. Let's talk about it because there are some difficulties with the original Hebrew that have caused a variety of translations.

    Whenever the reign of a king is mentioned in Scripture, there is usually a formulaic way of describing it. It usually goes like this:

    > "Ishbosheth, Saul's son, was forty years old when he began to reign over Israel, and he reigned two years..." —Second Samuel 2:10

    > "David was thirty years old when he began to reign, and he reigned forty years." —Second Samuel 5:4

    According to Jewish scholars, First Samuel 13:1 reads in the Hebrew:

    > "Saul was...years old when he became king, and he reigned over Israel two years." [1]

    So we have a couple problems. Saul's age is missing in the original text, and the two-year time marker is clearly not referring the full length of his reign, since he reigned forty years according to Paul in Acts 13:21. Perhaps because of the difficulty with the translation,

---

[1] Jewish Publication Society, *The Jewish Study Bible,* Tanakh translation (New York: Oxford University Press, 1985), p 583. This is not a Christian text, but I use this resource for its notes on Hebrew word usage, structure, cultural indications, and textual criticisms like this.

this verse is omitted in the Septuagint (Greek). Some translations fill in Saul's missing age, saying he was thirty years old when he began to reign, but I don't know how they came to that age. The general observation of all the translations is that the events in Chapter 13 all happen after Saul had reigned two years. So, some time has passed.

2. **Who are the initial players?**

    The passage opens with a detailed description of King Saul mustering an army. Saul has chosen an army of three thousand men from Israel, which he divides between himself and his son Jonathan. He takes two thousand men, and gives Jonathan one thousand. And then it says that he sent the rest of the people away, every man to his tent—which implies that maybe there were a lot more volunteers than what he had chosen. There is an echo of Gideon's narrative in the way that the narrator describes Saul's actions (see Judges 7:8). God chose three hundred men for Gideon and sent the rest home. Saul selects three thousand men and sends the rest home.

    We will keep Gideon in mind as a comparison picture to Saul.

3. **Where does Saul position his troops?**

    Saul has stationed his troops at Bethel and Michmash, while Jonathan remains at the home front in Gibeah. All of these places are grouped very closely together in Benjamin's territory, which is under Philistine occupation. Remember, there was a garrison of Philistines at Gibeah when Saul was made king, and there is nothing to suggest that they had been routed since then.

    We have talked a little about Gibeah and Bethel, but Michmash is a new place. What do we know about Michmash?

4. **What is significant about Michmash?**

    Bethel, Michmash, Gibeah, and Geba are all in the hill country, which is cut by deep canyons running east and west. Moving a body of troops north and south across the ridges and canyons is almost impossible, so a fight ensues for those cities that occupy the small plateaus where the ridges converge and the terrain levels out a bit. Geba and Michmash are two of those cities. They sit at either end of a large plateau called the Pass of Michmash, and on opposite sides of a notable canyon that Jonathan will tackle in the next challenge. The Michmash Pass is one of the few ridges broad enough to facilitate troop movements, and the city of Michmash holds the higher ground, which makes it a strong, strategic position for command of the area. This is where Saul has stationed his army of two thousand.

Jonathan's Attack (13:3)

5. **What sets off the crisis?**

   Jonathan attacks the Philistine garrison at Geba. A garrison is like a home guard. They are there to maintain a presence in a place, but are not actually equipped to fight a battle. They maintain the position and report uprisings.

6. **Why attack the Philistines at Geba?**

   Jonathan's army is stationed at Gibeah to the south and is cut off from his father's forces at Michmash to the north by this Philistine garrison at Geba which is right between them. Capturing Geba would remove the Philistine occupier, connect the two armies, clear a front for Israel to advance, and secure the pass. It's a logical move, militarily speaking.

   The Philistines garrison would seem like a strategic and somewhat easy target, since they are just a garrison—a group of guards—and hemmed in on two sides by Israeli armies. Jonathan has the smaller army, but he is on the same side of the pass as the Philistines, so it is logical that he should be the one to attack, and he does.

Reactions to the Attack (13:4-9)

The news of the attack is immediately relayed on both sides. The Philistines hear it, and then Saul commands the trumpets to be blown throughout Israel, calling them to battle.

7. **What is the Philistines' reaction to the news?**

   The garrison reports the news of the attack to the greater Philistine army, and the army rises up in defense of its garrison. The description of the Philistine hordes is similar to the description of the Midianite hordes in the days of Gideon in Judges 7:12.

"Then the Philistines gathered together to fight with Israel, thirty thousand chariots and six thousand horsemen, and people as the sand which is on the seashore in multitude. And they came up and encamped in Michmash, to the east of Beth Aven." —First Samuel 13:5

"Now the Midianites and Amalekites, all the people of the East, were lying in the valley as numerous as locusts; and their camels were without number, as the sand by the seashore in multitude." —Judges 7:12

8. **But weren't Saul and his army in Michmash?**

   Apparently they weren't—or at least Saul wasn't. For some reason, Saul had gone down to Gilgal, as it says, *"And the people were called together to Saul at Gilgal."* (13:4b)

   It doesn't say who called the people together—if it was Saul or Samuel or someone else. For some unexplained reason, Saul has left Michmash and gone to Gilgal, with or without his troops. It's hard to say if Saul knew Jonathan's intentions beforehand, or if Jonathan simply took the initiative and caught him off guard. Regardless, Saul hears what his son has done, sounds the trumpets to call Israel's army, and then decamps to Gilgal, leaving Michmash wide open for the Philistines to take. It almost seems like a retreat on Saul's part. Nevertheless, the people are called to rally to Saul there.

9. **What is Israel's reaction to the news?**

   First, it's reported that Saul attacked the Philistines. Did Saul attack the Philistines? No. Jonathan did. So there is a little misinformation being circulated. Saul is getting credit for his son's initiative, but that's what a king does. He gets credit for these things—but then he also gets the criticism for it. Note what else it says in verse four: People started telling one another that Israel had become odious or an abomination to the Philistines.

   Think about that statement. Should Israel care what the Philistines think of them? No. But they do. It's a concern. Why? Because they have let the Philistines dominate them physically and mentally. And now that they have thrown off God's kingship and put the crown on Saul, Saul becomes the one to whom they look for strength. Except Saul has seemingly decamped in front of the advancing Philistine armies and is holed up in Gilgal. He isn't on the scene to take command of things. The Philistines have taken the high ground and are encamped in force at Michmash. This is not good.

Compared to God, the Philistines are nothing. Compared to Saul and Israel's army of three thousand, the Philistines are the bigger dog in the fight.

> *"When the men of Israel saw that they were in danger (for the people were distressed), then the people hid in caves, in thickets, in rocks, in holes, and in pits. And some of the Hebrews crossed over the Jordan to the land of Gad and Gilead . . ."* —First Samuel 13:6-7

Again, this is very like the account in Gideon's narrative:

> *"And the hand of Midian prevailed against Israel. Because of the Midianites, the children of Israel made for themselves the dens, the caves, and the strongholds which are in the mountains."* —Judges 6:2

The children of Israel see the Philistine hordes, and they panic, flee, and hide. Some head for the river. The rest rally to Saul with trembling.

10. Why does Saul wait at Gilgal?

Because that is what Samuel said to do. Back in Chapter 10, at the end of all those instructions about the signs that would be fulfilled after Saul's anointing, Samuel gave Saul a final instruction that we have not seen fulfilled yet.

> *"You shall go down before me to Gilgal; and surely I will come down to you to offer burnt offerings and make sacrifices of peace offerings. Seven days you shall wait, till I come to you and show you what you should do."* —First Samuel 10:8

It seems odd that such a long time has passed before this part of Samuel's instructions should come into play, but it is clear that these are the instructions Saul is acting on because it says: *"Then he waited seven days, according to the time set by Samuel . . ."* (13:8a) When did Samuel set the time? At the time of Saul's anointing.

Obeying God and the prophet doesn't seem like a hard thing to do until you have the Philistine hordes breathing down your neck and the people are scattering. When Jonathan attacked the garrison, it was like hitting a hornet nest. Where only a few were once buzzing around, now the entire hive swarms out of the hills.

But we have to consider why God wanted Saul to wait. God is doing something here, much like what He did with Gideon.

God defeated the Midianites with Gideon and the three hundred, but there was a selection process for the three hundred who went into battle. God took Israel's volunteers through a weeding out process to see which men of Israel would cut and run at the sight of the enemy and which would hold their ground. Only three hundred out of thirty-two thousand passed both the fear test and water test.

Saul selected his army, but they were not necessarily the men God would have selected. God is putting Israel through another fear test to see who will rally to the king as they had once rallied to the judge, Gideon. All Saul has to do is wait while the LORD chooses his army for him, just as Gideon did.

Gideon passed the test of faith. He waited two days for the sign of the fleece. He and his men stood around that enemy camp, breaking pitchers and blowing trumpets and shouting, but they waited while the LORD did the job and only moved as they were directed.

11. What does Saul do?

Saul is supposed to wait for Samuel to give him instructions about what to do next. It is understood that Samuel will offer the sacrifices as well, but the emphasis is put on Saul waiting for instruction. Events are breaking on Saul very quickly, and time is of the essence. What if Samuel doesn't come in time? What is he supposed to do in the meantime to deal with the people's panic?

Saul waits at Gilgal as he was told, <u>but</u> then he goes ahead and offers the sacrifices himself when he thinks Samuel isn't coming.

12. Why perform the sacrifice before going into battle?

Offering a sacrifice is a way of asking supplication from God—abasing yourself and admitting you can't do this without His help. The battle with the Philistines is as much mental as physical. Offering a sacrifice to God in the face of the enemy establishes God as being greater than the enemy, and that is half the battle.

It was the priest's job to offer the sacrifices, and yet both King David and King Solomon will offer sacrifices and those sacrifices will be accepted (Second Samuel 6:17, First Kings 8:62-64). I don't know when the precedent for kings offering sacrifices was set, since it seems to go against the Law. But, if waiting for a priest to officiate isn't a requirement, then why wait for Samuel to do that particular task?

13. What is compelling Saul, really?

He feels compelled because Samuel hasn't come, but more so because the people are scattering from him. Saul is losing his support base, and that fellowship table is one tool that will bring the people back to him. But is the purpose of the sacrificial offering and the fellowship table to rally the people around the human king or around God?

Saul is using the LORD's table as a way to rally the people to himself. It is a means to an end in pursuit of his own purposes and not God's, and in doing so, he profanes the offering.

Now think of Gideon. When Gideon rallied the people to fight the Midianites, he started out with 32,000 volunteers. How do you think he felt when 22,000 of them decamped in the face of the enemy because of fear? How do you think he felt when God dismissed another 9,700, leaving him with only three hundred men? Did he immediately try to do something to bring them back to him? No. God had determined the number of men Gideon needed and chose that number so that the glory would be His and not Gideon's.

Given the comparison with what God was doing with Gideon, we should ask again. Which is more important: To wait on Samuel (and God, the King) or perform the sacrifices to rally the people to Saul?

The Judgment of Saul's Actions (13:10-14)

14. At what point does Samuel arrive?

It is interesting that Samuel arrives right in the middle of all this—after Saul has offered the burnt offering but before he can offer and eat the peace offering. Samuel asks a very short question: "What have you done?" and Saul gives a very lengthy response.

15. What reasons does Saul give Samuel for not waiting as he was told?

The people were scattering from me ... you didn't come ... the Philistines have taken the high ground ... defeat is imminent ... I have not made supplication to the LORD. That last reason is an interesting one. To make supplication means to cast yourself down before the LORD as being weak and sick and in need of help. That's the sense of the Hebrew verb used here.

Is that why Saul offered the offering? Was Saul's burnt offering a way of appealing to God for help or to the people? Which relationship is driving Saul's actions?

Have you ever encountered a person who was really good at making perfectly plausible excuses for not doing what they know they should be doing? I have worked with a number of them over the years. How long do you waste time arguing with them? Samuel didn't argue with Saul at all. He cut right to the bottom line. Clearly Saul knew what the LORD's command was. It had come from Samuel himself. He had been told to go to Gilgal and wait for Samuel to give him more instructions. Therefore, he knew what he should do and he didn't do it, right?

16. What is the consequence of Saul's disobedience?

He loses the reward of an eternal kingship—the covenant that God will now offer to David. Saul didn't even know that a reward of that caliber was on the table, but it was.

Samuel judges Saul and delivers the verdict:

> "But now your kingdom shall not continue. The LORD has sought for Himself a man after His own heart, and the LORD has commanded

> him to be commander over His people, because you have not kept what the LORD commanded you." —First Samuel 13:14

Notice the repetition in the verse. Since Saul refuses to keep the commands, he loses the right to make commands. The LORD will look for another commander. This is the LORD's eye-for-an-eye kind of justice. This is very like the condemnation delivered to Eli:

> "Behold, the days are coming that I will cut off your arm and the arm of your father's house, so that there will not be an old man in your house . . . Then I will raise up for Myself a faithful priest who shall do according to what is in My heart and in My mind. I will build him a sure house, and he shall walk before My anointed forever." —First Samuel 2:31, 35

So, there is a turn-over in both the priesthood and kingship, because Israel's leaders kicked at His sacrifice and did not honor Him.

It was not the fact that Saul failed to obey that cost him the eternal kingship. Even David will do things wrong—things that he knows are wrong—and yet that covenant was never revoked from David in spite of those failings. Saul's failing is a failing of heart and a failing to identify with God. He disobeyed a simple command, but <u>the way he did it</u>—by offering that phony sacrifice to keep the people's allegiance for himself—spoke to a heart-level disdain and rebellion against the LORD's Kingship.

Narrator's Comment (13:15)

Picture #5 ended with the narrator's note in verse 15:

> "Then Samuel arose and went up from Gilgal to Gibeah of Benjamin. And Saul numbered the people present with him, about six hundred men." —First Samuel 13:15 NKJV

This wording follows the Masoretic and Targum texts, but the ESV, which follows the Septuagint and Vulgate versions, gives a more specific description of the action:

> "And Samuel arose and went up from Gilgal. The rest of the people went up after Saul to meet the army; they went up from Gilgal to Gibeah of

Benjamin. And Saul numbered the people who were present with him, about six hundred men." —First Samuel 13:15 ESV

17. Was the peace offering ever offered?

We look at what is mentioned in the text, but it is also good to note what is not in the text. It doesn't appear that the peace offering was ever made. Having interrupted the proceedings, Samuel immediately leaves Gilgal while Saul hangs back to count his people.

The burnt offering was offered profanely, and before Saul could eat of the peace offering, the eternal kingship was taken from him. There is a sense of the relationship between God and His king being left in this limbo without peace.

As I sorted through my mental database of Bible pictures, it occurred to me that this was a lot like Adam in the garden. Adam was meant to be king of God's creation, but he disobeyed deliberately, ate of the Tree of Knowledge of Good and Evil, and brought upon himself that curse. Then he was prevented from eating of the Tree of Life by which he would have lived forever in an eternal kingship. Adam and Saul have that relational model in common.

Willful disobedience is one way to lose a crown.

APPLY THE PICTURE

Saul's Model

There are many applications here, but I want to focus on four:

1) Having patience in times of testing
2) Being a people-pleaser instead of a God-pleaser
3) Respecting authority when pursuing the crown
4) Kicking at the sacrifice

Having Patience in Times of Testing

Saul's first test played out like this: He was put under pressure, felt compelled to do something, gave in to the temptation to take matters into his own hands, disobeyed, and lost the crown of an eternal kingship. His actions may have kept the perishable crown, but not the imperishable one.

It takes patience to wait on the LORD when the world seems to be falling apart, and you are the one person in charge of fixing it. Waiting patiently is part of the endurance test of a king. All Saul has to do is what Samuel told him to do—go to Gilgal and wait. Giving in to the pressure to do "something" when he should be doing nothing is what causes Saul to fail in this case.

Whenever we find ourselves in a crisis moment, we can become focused on the physical circumstances and the physical enemy fighting us. We think it is about us and them, but it is not. It is about us and God. The struggle is more than just a battle of wills between people, or a difficulty with your living situation or job or even your physical health. These struggles are God testing you—testing your understanding of Him, your faith in Him, your character, your patience, and perseverance. To pass the test, sometimes you are called to just wait. James gives us some advice that applies to Saul's challenge:

> *"My brethren, count it all joy when you fall into various trials, knowing that the testing of your faith produces patience. But let patience have its perfect work, that you may be perfect and complete, lacking nothing. If any of you lacks wisdom, let him ask of God, who gives to all liberally and without reproach, and it will be given to him. But let him ask in faith, with no doubting, for he who doubts is like a wave of the sea driven and tossed by the wind. For let not that man suppose that he will receive anything from the Lord; he is a double-minded man, unstable in all his ways."* —James 1:2-8

Saul was faced with a trial, and he was asked to exercise patience and wait for the LORD's instruction. He may be waiting at Gilgal physically, but he is not waiting for instruction, spiritually. He offers a sacrifice, but out of a desire to bring the people into the battle, not God. His lack of perseverance in waiting reveals a lack of character and hope that the testing was supposed to produce, as Paul says in Romans 5:3-4:

> *". . . we also glory in tribulations, knowing that tribulation produces perseverance; and perseverance, character; and character, hope."*
> —Romans 5:3-4

When we come to moments of crisis, we find ourselves dealing with confusion, misinformation, panicked reactions, and a lot of people flailing about, as Paul would put it. How we comport ourselves in these moments will reflect the training and discipline of our minds or the lack of it. Trials are tests. To persevere through trials without losing hope requires a certain strength of character, and it is that strength of character that the trials are meant to build. Trials are real-time scenarios into which God puts us so that we can practice making decisions as kings must, and He evaluates us along these lines:

1) How strong is our understanding of God?
    a. How well do we understand His sovereignty in our circumstances?
    b. Do we value the reward He has promised enough to pursue it, and if necessary, wait for it?
2) How strong is our character?
    a. Do we understand what is expected of us?
    b. Do we do what we are told to do as His servant?
    c. Where or to whom do we turn for wisdom, and what drives our choices? Are we single-minded or double-minded?
    d. How strong is our patience? Are we willing to persevere however long it takes?

Pursuing a crown takes patience and perseverance. It takes strength of character and a rock-solid understanding of who God is and what He expects of us.

Saul models a man who is being tested without realizing he is being tested, which reminds me of a life lesson my husband once shared with me . . .

When my husband retired from military service, he was faced with having to interview for civilian jobs, and he took some of the workshops that the Air Force provided about how to interview. One of the points they stressed was that regardless of what happened in the course of the interview, you cannot forget that the interviewer is watching. A man may look good on paper, but a good employer knows the challenges of the job. Often an employer will orchestrate a situation that is stressful, confrontational, or requires problem-solving, just to see how the applicant will react. The test can be orchestrated so smoothly that the applicant may not even realize it is part of the interview, and he will react to the stress or the confrontation true to his character, but it may not be something he would want a potential employer to see.

Never forget that the interviewer is watching. God is watching.

Being a People-pleaser Instead of a God-pleaser

There is a second aspect of Saul's actions that reflects a particular character trait that can become a stumbling stone and send us after a perishable crown instead of an imperishable one. This is how it played out with Saul . . .

Saul found himself in a crisis, and the crisis began to affect his relationship with his people. The people were scattering from him—not because of their lack of faith in him, per se, but because of their lack of faith in God. That wasn't something he could remedy. The enemy was too big. The people's faith was too small.

When his relationships began to fall apart, that is when he felt compelled—tempted—to do something to bring everyone back to the table. He tried to force a solution to remedy the relationship when he should have let them go and focused on what God wanted him to do.

Does that happen to us? In moments of crisis, when relationships are strained and falling apart, do we feel compelled to do something to somehow fix things and bring everyone back to the table? What if the relationship issue is beyond our ability to remedy? Do we still try to be the problem-solver and force a solution? How does that end?

That desire to do something to keep relationships can be a really strong temptation that can give way to sin. There is a limit to how far down that road you can go to keep or fix those human relationships before you begin to compromise your relationship with God.

This is the test that people-pleasers often fail. When people-pleasers are at that crossroad, they have to make a choice as to how far they go in pursuit of the human relationship and at what cost to themselves and their relationship with God. **People relationships are perishable**

rewards. Their support and validation are fleeting and can be gone in a day. **The relationship with God is an imperishable reward.** People-pleasers can go too far in pursuit of the wrong crown.

A lot of pressure came from people's expectations of Saul as their leader, but also from Saul's expectation of himself. What he failed to consider, which was the only thing he really should have considered, was God's expectation of him. God knew the situation was beyond Saul's ability to cope. All God expected of Saul was to sit and wait for instructions. That was something he was able to do, even though he didn't feel like he was doing anything. And that is a misconception. When you are waiting and listening for God, you *are* doing something. It may feel as if you are doing nothing. Other people might think you are doing nothing. But you are doing something.

It is a test to withstand the temptation to take matters into our own hands and force a solution in times of crisis. We have a choice to pursue a perishable crown of people relationships—popularity, validation, support—or an imperishable crown and reward from God. James says:

> *"Blessed is the man who endures temptation; for when he has been approved, he will receive the crown of life which the Lord has promised to those who love Him. Let no one say when he is tempted, 'I am tempted by God'; for God cannot be tempted by evil, nor does He Himself tempt anyone. But each one is tempted when he is drawn away by his own desires and enticed. Then, when desire has conceived, it gives birth to sin; and sin, when it is full-grown, brings forth death."* —James 1:12-15

Respecting Authority When Pursuing the Crown

A man who has no respect for authority or desire to obey commands, whether it is obeying the law or even just following instructions, is not a man who will rule justly or with fairness. He will rule by what is right in his own eyes and follow his own desires, and the people will suffer.

Anyone in pursuit of a crown needs to have a healthy respect of all levels of authority. That includes the LORD, kings, masters, employers, parents, and even elders in the church. This is why, among all the instructions given in the New Testament, respect for authority is high on the list of commandments. There are authorities that the LORD has placed in our lives to whom we are expected to submit, and a submission to these authorities reflects a submission to the LORD Himself who gave them their authority. God takes crowns away from those who don't respect the crown's authority.

When Peter talks about believers being a royal priesthood in First Peter 2, he immediately follows it with a discourse on submission to government, masters, and husbands, and even to a certain extent, each other. He summarizes this in First Peter 2:17: *"Honor all people. Love the brotherhood. Fear God. Honor the king."*

Kicking at the Sacrifice

- **Did Saul know that the reward of an eternal kingship was on the table for him when Samuel told him to go to Gilgal and wait?**

    No. He didn't.

    Whether you realize it or not, there is an eternal reward on the table for you as well.

- **If Saul had known the nature of the reward reserved for him, would he have obeyed and waited for Samuel, however long it took?**

    Maybe. Maybe not. He didn't seem too keen on being king in the first place, considering that he hid in the equipment when Samuel was presenting him to the people. I suppose it might depend on whether he valued the reward or not, or if he thought the benefits offset the responsibilities. The only problem was that the nature of the reward was never revealed to him until *after* he had lost it.

    Unlike Saul, we have been told there is a reward waiting for us if we obey, and yet the nature of our reward is not revealed to us, either, and we will not find out until *after* we have won or lost it. Even so, knowing it has been promised, is that enough to motivate us to pursue it? Maybe. Maybe not.

- **Does our lack of esteem for the reward reflect a lack of esteem for the King who offers it? Is it a way of kicking at the sacrifice, figuratively?**

I think it is. It is the endurance test of a king to persevere by faith and not by sight. Jesus spoke these words to Thomas:

> "...Thomas, because you have seen Me, you have believed. Blessed are those who have not seen and yet have believed." —John 20:29

Jesus was speaking of a belief in Himself in that instance, but I think the same principle carries into our attitude toward the reward He offers. We do not see Him, and yet we are blessed if we believe in Him. The blessing, at this point, is as intangible as He Himself is, and yet both will be realized at His return. I think our esteem of the reward is a reflection of our esteem of Him—or lack of it. Over the years, I have heard a lot of Christians say they want to be like Christ, just don't make them royalty. To those I would like to ask: What part of Christ do you want to be like, then? Christ is the King. He valued that reward of kingship and pursued it to death. Can you seek to emulate Him without embracing this side of Him? What reward do you think you are pursuing?

A Personal Thought About the LORD's Table

Granted, Saul used the Lord's table for the wrong reason, but we shouldn't overlook the importance of that communion when we are faced with battles in life. The Enemy can gain the upper hand in the battle by disrupting our relationship with God, and he does this in a couple of ways. One way is to make us avoid fellowship altogether. He scatters us. Another is that he keeps us from fellowship at the LORD's table.

I feel like I have done this at times. When life gets chaotic and everyone in my life, including me, is distracted and distressed, the last thing I want to do is go to church and sit down for communion. I want to come to that fellowship table with a sense of peace and focus on God, and if I can't, I tell myself to just let the plate pass. Just let me get past this battle that I am fighting, and then I'll do my self-reflection and whatever repentance I need to do, and *then* I will be prepared to come to that table. How can anyone sit down to a fellowship meal with God under these circumstances? And yet, shouldn't we feel compelled to seek God in moments of crisis? Isn't this a way of bringing God into the battle? I think it is, and it is something I have tried to correct in my own life.

6 No Weapons for the Army

READ

First Samuel 13:16-23

NARRATIVE STRUCTURE

Picture #6 is a transitional picture delivered almost entirely by the narrator, with the exception of one bit of Philistine dialogue around which the chiastic structure revolves:

(A) Narrator comment on the Philistines' position
(B) Philistines at the advantage (13:17-18)
(C) Israel's lack of blacksmiths (13:19a)
(D) Philistines' statement (13:19b)
(C) The Philistines' control of blacksmiths (13:20-21)
(B) Israel (seemingly) at the disadvantage (13:22)
(A) Narrator comment on the Philistine's position (13:23)

The structure brings us to a focus on a strategic ploy that will backfire on the Philistines and lead to their defeat in the next chapter. The excessive detail about Israel's lack of weapons sets us up for yet another picture comparison, this time to the judge Shamgar. The picture comparisons of Shamgar and Gideon will continue into the narrative of Jonathan's battle in the next chapter.

BUILD THE PICTURE

18. How have the strategic positions changed?

Saul, Jonathan, and the people with them (six hundred men) are now at Gibeah on one side of the Michmash Pass, and the Philistines now command Michmash on the other side.

Having achieved the strategic advantage, the Philistines begin to raid the countryside in three directions. One company heads north toward Ophrah and the land of Shual. The second company heads west to Beth Horon. The third company heads east toward the Valley of Zeboim.

Saul and the Israeli army are south of where all the action is, and they are cut off by the ravine that runs between them and the Philistine forces. While the bulk of the Philistine forces are raiding the countryside, a garrison is left to stand guard at the Michmash Pass in case Saul's army decides to make a move.

19. What hinders Israel's army from attacking?

In addition to the geographic challenge, there are no weapons for the army. Only Saul and Jonathan had swords. The rest of the six hundred did not. Why not?

Because the Philistines banned all blacksmiths throughout the land of Israel. If the Israelites needed anything sharpened, they had to pay the Philistines to sharpen it. So, the Philistines could very easily prevent the manufacture of weapons while allowing for farm tools.

It's funny that the text belabors the cost of sharpening farm tools, particularly the goads. How much does it cost to outfit six hundred men with swords? Quite a lot, I imagine, if it were even possible. How much does it cost to outfit them with goads? Roughly two hundred shekels.

20. Do you need swords to fight the Philistines?

Not necessarily. Ox goads and a little faith have been known to work. Judges 3:31 says,

> "After him [Ehud] was Shamgar the son of Anath, who killed six hundred men of the Philistines with an ox goad; and he also delivered Israel." —Judges 3:31

Shamgar, who fought alone with his ox goad, stands in stark contrast to Ehud, who had a sword and a sizable army with him. The lesson Shamgar taught is that you don't need sophisticated weapons or training to deal with an enemy. All you have to do is stand where you are, do what you can with what you have, and it will be enough— if you have faith. So, what if you had six hundred Shamgars? Six hundred men of Israel—armed only with an ox goad and the faith of

Shamgar—had the potential of killing 360,000 Philistines. Or God could just turn the enemies' own swords against them as He did with Gideon.

Only Saul and Jonathan have swords (13:22). Only one of them thinks one sword is enough to take on the Philistines.

LESSON 8: FIRST SAMUEL 14

Fighting a Good Fight

SERIES STRUCTURE

The narrative of First Samuel 14 is broken into two main pictures:

Picture #7 (14:1-46) records Saul's second failure.
Picture #8 (14:47-52) records how Saul establishes his kingdom.

The focus opens with Jonathan's exploit against the Philistines, then segues abruptly to a focus on Saul's part in the battle and subsequent failure. Jonathan presents a sharp contrast to his father and ends up in conflict with him. This will be a picture we will look at when we get to David's battle at Keilah and first conflict with Saul in Chapter 23. David will compare with Jonathan and also contrast with Saul.

 ## Saul's Second Failure

READ

First Samuel 14:1-46

NARRATIVE STRUCTURE

Picture #7 is second in the series of three tests Saul faces. The picture elements follow the same formulaic layout as picture #5 but there is an additional segment added that begins with Saul's rash oath and ends with Jonathan's trial.

The expanded judgment sequence is laid out in a chiastic structure that reaches a turning point when Saul inquires of God and gets no answer, and the episode highlights Saul's poor performance as a judge. He was, after all, made king in order to judge God's people (First Samuel 8:5), but this episode ends in a debacle.

Here is the picture's structure:

1) Narrator's note setting the scene (14:1-3)
2) The catalyst: Jonathan's attack (14:4-15)
3) Saul's reaction (14:16-23)
4) The judgment sequence
    (A) Saul's rash oath (14:24)
    (B) Jonathan's sin (14:25-30)
    (C) The people's sin (14:31-35)
    (D) Saul inquires of God, gets no answer (14:36-37)
    (C) The people on trial (14:38-40)
    (B) Jonathan on trial (14:41-44)
    (A) Judgment passed on Saul for his oath (14:45)
5) Narrator's note (14:46)

[Chiasm bracket spans items A through A under section 4]

The narrative opens with an exceedingly detailed and exemplary picture of Jonathan stepping out in faith in comparison to his father, who proves faithless to God, his son, and his people. While Saul's actions and reactions drive the narrative, I think more of the lesson application is drawn from Jonathan's example of fighting a good fight.

BUILD THE PICTURE

Jonathan Defeats the Philistines (14:1–23)

The scene opens with Jonathan and his armor bearer embarking on a skirmish with the Philistine of which Saul is unaware. The scene is set with an emphasis on the fact that all the people who should have known where Jonathan was and what he was doing didn't have a clue.

1. **Where are Saul and the army?**

    Saul and his men are sitting under a pomegranate tree at Migron just outside of Geba. He isn't where he should be or doing what he should be doing. He isn't even aware of what his son—his second-in-command—is doing.

The meanings of the Hebrew words here lend a wonderful nuance to the narrative. The pomegranate is called a *rimmon*, from the word *ramam* meaning "to be lifted up or exalted." It is called that because of its upright growth. This "exalted one" has rooted itself at Migron.

Migron means "precipice," a high place from which things are cast down. Its root verb, *magar,* means "to cast down," and in the Scriptures it is used in context of God being furious with his anointed king and His people and casting them down from an exalted place.

It is rather poignant that the scene in Chapter 14 should begin at this place. Saul is very much the picture of that exalted *rimmon* that had been lifted up but now will be cast down from the precipice of kingship as his kingdom begins its downward slide.

2. **Why mention Ahijah here?**

   We haven't heard anything of Eli's family since Chapter 4. Apparently, they are still serving in some capacity as priests since it says that Ahijah, Eli's great-grandson, was wearing the ephod at this time. The ephod was the device used by the priests for consulting the LORD. The text seems to belabor the fact that when events begin to happen, all the people who should be in-the-know are not.

3. **What obstacle does Jonathan face in tackling the Philistines?**

   Jonathan and his armor bearer are standing on the cliffs on one side of the canyon. The Philistine garrison in charge of guarding the pass is standing on the cliffs on the opposite side. The big question is how to get from point A to point B. The only way is through the heavily guarded Michmash Pass.

   Jonathan and his armor bearer go down into the canyon ravine, and they look up at the guards stationed above them. The text describes them standing between these two great cliffs in the mouth of the ravine, one facing northward opposite Michmash and the other facing south opposite Gibeah. The cliffs are even named: Bozez and Seneh.

Bozez means "glistening white." **Seneh** means "craggy or serrated (toothy)." So, for Jonathan and his armor bearer to get to the enemy, they have these cliffs of glistening white teeth to overcome.

Jonathan looks up at those guards and says, we can take them.

> "... Come, let us go over to the garrison of these uncircumcised; it may be that the LORD will work for us. For nothing restrains the LORD from saving by many or by few." (14:6)

We are getting ready to have a Gideon moment, with a little bit of Shamgar mixed in.

4. **For what sign is Jonathan looking to determine his action?**

   If the Philistines say, "Wait until we come to you," then he will stay and wait. But if the Philistines say, "Come to us," then he will go.

   Jonathan has no doubt that the LORD has delivered the enemy into his hands. He is just letting the enemy decide where they want to die, and he will be very obliging in this.

5. **What do the Philistines decide?**

   They look down at Jonathan and his armor bearer and laugh. They think they are in an impregnable position. The battle in the "toothy" ravine begins with taunting words. "Hey, look who's coming out of their hidey-holes. Come up here, and we will show you something!" the Philistines call to Jonathan.

   The Philistines never suspect that Jonathan has a sword. The most Jonathan might have for a weapon is a farm tool, like an ox goad, and so they invite him up to teach him a lesson. You don't attack superior forces with farm tools and expect to win. The Philistines have forgotten the lesson of Israel's judges, Shamgar and Ehud. Shamgar took out six hundred Philistines with a mere ox goad. One Israelite armed with an ox goad and faith can be deadly enough. And while Jonathan appears handicapped for lack of a weapon, looks are deceiving. Like the judge Ehud, Jonathan gets invited up to the upper chamber with a message for the king, all the while hiding the fact that he is carrying a sword. Like Ehud, the message he delivers is a sword in the belly.

6. **What is Jonathan's strategy?**

   Instead of following the canyon up to the Pass and crossing there as the Philistines expect, Jonathan tackles those taunting, glistening teeth head on. He goes straight up the serrated face of that cliff on his hands and knees with his armor bearer behind him.

   He hits the top of that hill and starts swinging, and the men he takes down are finished off by his armor bearer coming behind him. He plows right through them and kills twenty men "within about half an acre of land," that is, what can be plowed by a yoke of oxen in a day's work. That was the first slaughter. And now we come to our Gideon moment...

7. **What is God's response to Jonathan's step of faith?**

   "And there was trembling in the camp, in the field, and among all the people. The garrison and the raiders also trembled; and the earth quaked, so that it was a very great trembling." (14:15)

   The Hebrew word for trembling is equated with fear and terror, and it takes over the men in the camp. It spreads to the men in the field. It goes through all the people. The garrison and the raiders trembled in fear. Even the very earth quaked. When God had put his foot down on the battlefield, there was chaos. Philistines scatter like ants, every man's sword is against his neighbor, and they run to and fro in complete confusion.

   Can you imagine this moment from Jonathan's eyes? He was like a little dog that goes charging at a pack of wolves only to have the wolves turn and flee. What just happened?

   He purposed in his heart to do what he could with what he had, but he gave God the glory for the deliverance. He went up that hill, plowed through the enemy, and when he came to a standstill, BA-BOOM. The world rocked around him, and all his enemies fled before him. Can you image the power he must have felt at that moment? It wasn't his power but God's power, but it was God's power working side by side with him.

8. **What is Saul's response?**

    The watchmen from Israel's side of the canyon undoubtedly felt the quake and heard the noise of battle. So that was the wake-up call. There was a battle being fought in the Philistine camp, and they were just sitting around. So if they weren't fighting, who was?

    Saul immediately calls the roll and finds that Jonathan and his bodyguard are missing.

    I imagine there must have been a moment of horror for Saul at finding Jonathan gone. Jonathan had taken this kind of initiative before in starting a war with a Philistine garrison, and that engagement had ended badly for Saul. The Philistines had taken Michmash, the people had scattered from him, and his unlawful sacrifice in that event had lost him the everlasting kingdom.

9. **What does Saul do this time?**

    As it reads in the Hebrew text, he tells Abijah to send for the Ark of God, but then Saul countermands his order. He tells Abijah to withdraw his hand. In other words, stop inquiring of the LORD. Why? Because there is neither time nor need. The battle was increasing, and he just needed to get into the field. Instead, he assembles his men, and they head for the battle.

    We should note that the last time the narrative talked about the Ark of God, it was at Kirjath Jearim being tended by Eleazar in Abinadab's house. Kirjath Jearim is a good distance from the battle at Michmash. While the text says that Saul sent for the ark, it was not likely that it would return in time. Apparently Abijah had the ephod with him by which he could inquire of the LORD, and it is implied that he was about to cast lots when Saul says, "Withdraw your hand."

    All the Hebrew texts maintain that Saul did indeed send for the Ark itself, but the Septuagint says he sent for the ephod, based on the context of what Abijah actually did and the fact that it was customary to inquire of the LORD before going into battle.

10. **Why would Saul send for the Ark of God and not the ephod?**

    The phrasing is forcing your mind to connect with another instance of this happening—when Hophni and Phinehas brought the Ark out to the battlefield.

Why did they do that? Because the Ark represents God's presence on the battlefield. They were using the Ark as a way of rallying the people and forcing a solution by getting God to act.

How did that end? The Philistines won the battle and captured the Ark, the glory departed from Israel, and Hophni, Phinehas, and Eli died.

Knowing that end, what judgment can we make of Saul's actions here?

It was a bad thing. The author is making a point of highlighting Saul's poor judgment by linking his actions to the actions of previous leadership who made this error in judgment. Sending for the Ark is another instance of Saul mishandling the LORD's things, and the fact that he sends Phinehas' grandson after it is like history repeating itself. And it is a senseless act.

Why bring the Ark to the battlefield? To bring God to the battlefield. But God is already on the battlefield, so why bring the Ark to the battlefield? What is the point?

Saul wants to inquire of God—but there isn't enough time. Why isn't there enough time? Because God is already acting.

The text belabors the fact that Saul is the one caught lagging behind the action in a place where he shouldn't be, and by the time he gets into action, there isn't anything he needs to do. But then there was never really anything he needed to do to begin with except take the same step of faith that Jonathan did.

11. How does the battle sequence end?

God rallied the people to Himself, and Saul and his army are swamped with volunteers flooding to the battlefield. It says that all of Israel came out of hiding and joined the battle. Even the Hebrews who were serving in the Philistine camp switched back to Israel's side and started fighting. The LORD saves Israel, and the battle shifts to Beth Aven, which is a retreat on the Philistines' part.

Beth Aven means "house of vanity" in the sense of being associated with futile acts such as idolatry, iniquity, or where rash oaths are made before the LORD. It is spoken of by the prophet Hosea:

> "Though you, Israel, play the harlot, let not Judah offend. Do not come up to Gilgal, nor go up to Beth Aven, nor swear an oath, saying, 'As the LORD lives'—" —Hosea 4:15

In later days, both Gilgal and Beth Aven become places of idolatry and harlotry in Israel. The LORD warns Judah of following Israel's model as the Babylonian Captivity looms on the horizon, but the making of that model begins here with Saul, and has to do with a rash oath that begins with the phrase "As the LORD lives . . ."

As the battle shifts to Beth Aven, the "house of vanities" where rash oaths are made, the narrative takes a turn as Saul takes over command of the battle from God and Jonathan.

Saul's Rash Oath (14:24–46)

12. God has routed the Philistines, and victory should be easy. Why are the people in distress?

Because now Saul has stepped into the battle and assumed control. He has cursed anyone who eats until he has taken vengeance on his enemies.

13. To whom did the battle and the vengeance belong?

The battle is the LORD's, and the LORD should get the glory for taking down the enemy. It wasn't Saul who climbed that canyon to tackle the Philistines. It wasn't Saul's idea to go into battle at all. So, who is Saul to come charging into the middle of things in the eleventh hour and declare, "I will take vengeance on my enemies!"

This is the first rash oath, but there will be another.

14. Why does Saul say this?

Pride. Posturing. A greed for glory.

15. How well do hungry people perform the task they are given?

Not very well. Hunger for physical food affects the body physically but also mentally because hunger then becomes a distraction and a point of temptation. When the body is craving necessary nourishment, and it is presented with food it cannot eat, then all of a sudden you have different kind of battle on your hands—an internal battle that distracts from the battle with the enemy. Notice how the narrative ceases to record the battle with the Philistines and suddenly focuses on the internal strife in the body (the congregation) of Israel.

16. The text belabors how the people came into the forest and found the honey on the ground. What is the significance of the honey?

God was giving Israel this rich, verdant land flowing with milk and honey so that they may enjoy the bounty of it once they had taken it from the Canaanites. This was their reward. For what are they fighting if not for the honey—the sweetness of taking the land and defeating their enemies?

But when the people chose a new king for themselves, that king placed a curse on what should have been a blessing and did not allow the people to partake of the spoil under pain of death. He institutes this fast, but to what purpose?

17. What is the purpose of fasting, in general?

Fasting is meant to be a physical reflection of a spiritual hunger for the LORD. A person may fast:

- In preparation to meet the LORD
- While waiting for an answer from the LORD
- While mourning the loss of a relationship

Fasting is meant for God's eyes only (Jesus tells us that). But abstinence can become a form of self-glorification when it is performed for men's glory or to receive their approval.

The physical hunger and abstinence is an outward manifestation of the internal hunger and loss. Is a fast appropriate at this point in the battle? No. Why would the people mourn as if they had suffered loss when the LORD has given them victory over their enemies?

Was Saul's proclaimed fast for any of the appropriate reasons? No. Was the fast about drawing closer to the LORD in any way? No.

Saul wanted their hunger to drive them to accomplish the task for his own glory. Again, Saul misapplies a spiritual act, and it is going to cause the people to sin, beginning with Jonathan.

In verses 27-28, we see that Jonathan is absent again. We don't know where he is in the battle, but he didn't get message that he wasn't supposed to eat. He sees the honey, and he eats it, and it strengthens him. But someone sees him eat it and rebukes him for transgressing his father's command.

18. What is Jonathan's response to being rebuked for this?

Jonathan is angry, and he is critical of his father's judgment. He sees the people struggling because they are hampered by an arbitrary command that is actually doing them harm and hindering the mission. This is not a requirement that the LORD demanded of them. His father is in pursuit of his own glory, not God's glory.

Jonathan points out that his father has done wrong—he has troubled the land—and then he points out the obvious truth, that eating the food isn't bad. Look how it has benefited him. Food is necessary for the mission they had been given. And it was meant as spoil—the reward—for having won the battle.

19. Why wouldn't a king allow the people to share in the spoil?

Saul is pursuing a crown for himself without sharing the reward of it with his people. This behavior is typical of a man that the Hebrew text would call a son of Belial. We will see a similar behavior in the four hundred men who fight with David for Ziklag, who the Scripture also describes as sons of Belial. The men who fight do not want to share the spoil with those who remained behind because they were too weary to fight. David rebukes this kind of unmerciful greediness and shares his spoil with the weary. Saul's behavior is not the behavior of God's king, and it is not the way to keep a kingdom and crown.

20. What happens when the people finally accomplish their mission?

Verse 31 belabors the distance that the battle had traveled. From Michmash they had pushed on to Beth Aven and to Aijalon—roughly fifteen miles—and the people were faint.

The name Aijalon adds an interesting dimension to the text. Aijalon means the field of stags, stags being among those which are examples of strength. And yet in this place of the strong ones, we find a people who are not strong. They are faint and hungry, and they seek strength by rushing upon the spoil and eating the meat, blood and all, off the ground in their desperate hunger.

21. Why is slaughtering meat on a stone acceptable but slaughtering meat on the ground not?

This is a technical point that explains why Saul called for a stone to slaughter the meat upon. God told His people not to eat the meat with the blood. When you slaughter meat on a stone, the blood drips down and away from the meat, so you can separate the meat from the blood. If you slaughter the meat on the ground, the blood pools beneath the meat and gets mixed in with it. So, the people were defiling themselves in their haste. Sometimes, acting upon urgency causes sin.

22. Why would Saul say that the people had dealt treacherously?

The Hebrew word the author uses is the word *bagad* which means to act treacherously, deceitfully, or offensively, or to act unfaithful. We understand that the people have done wrong by breaking the Law, but the Hebrew word has a deeper nuance to it. It suggests that the offense was done covertly with an intention to cover it up—as if they knew what they were doing was wrong and yet they did it anyway. The cover-up aspect doesn't seem to bear out in the text. They were clearly eating the meat openly. And yet there has been a cover-up of sorts in all of this. Saul doesn't know it yet, but Jonathan had eaten honey earlier in the day; and some of the people had seen it, but no one had said anything about it. The people had covered it up. But God is going to uncover it.

Once the people have eaten, Saul builds an altar. The text notes that this is the first altar he has built, which makes it an unprecedented act. The Hebrew word translated as "first" is a significant one. It is the word *chalal*, which means to make a beginning, but also to profane. The beginning most often leads to tragic events, like the piercing of a body leads to death. Here are some other notable *chalal*-ing moments in Scripture:

- *"Then men began to call on the name of the LORD."* —Genesis 4:26 This leads to idolatry when men begin calling other things "lord."
- *"Now it came to pass, when men began to multiply on the face of the earth, and daughters were born to them,"* —Genesis 6:1, leads to the Flood.
- *"And Noah began to be a farmer, and he planted a vineyard."* —Genesis 9:20, leads to a curse on Canaan.
- *"And the LORD said, 'Indeed the people are one and they all have one language, and this is what they begin to do; now nothing that they propose to do will be withheld from them.'"* —Genesis 11:6, leads to the dispersion at the Tower of Babel.
- *". . . and he shall begin to deliver Israel out of the hand of the Philistines."* —Judges 13:5, speaking of Samson whose life would end tragically even as he defeats the Philistines. The word *chalal* appears four times in Samson's narrative.
- *"In that day I will perform against Eli all that I have spoken concerning his house, from beginning to end [Hebrew phrasing: when I chalal, I will also make an end]."* —First Samuel 3:12
- *"But He was wounded [chalal-ed] for our transgressions, He was bruised for our iniquities; The chastisement for our peace was upon Him, and by His stripes we are healed."* —Isaiah 53:5

The events have an innocent—even laudable—beginning, but an opening is made by which sin and the profaning of God's name and His holy things then enters the picture. Saul makes a beginning with this altar, and the use of the word *chalal* lends a foreboding to the events which now begin to transpire from this point.

Immediately upon making the altar, Saul proposes to press on with battle. He wants Israel to go after the Philistines all night until morning and kill them all.

23. From whom does Saul ask for approval?

From the people. Saul has just built an altar to God, but he doesn't address God or ask for direction. He proposes his plan to the people first. Note that it is the priest who suggests they ask God as a secondary measure. So Saul asks God for counsel, but God doesn't answer—for a couple of reasons. First of all, why would God answer if Saul has already received an answer from the people? Why does Saul bother to seek a second opinion if he already has the answer he seeks? Saul is what James would call a double-minded man:

> *"If any of you lacks wisdom, let him ask of God, who gives to all liberally and without reproach, and it will be given to him. But let him ask in faith, with no doubting, for he who doubts is like a wave of the sea driven and tossed by the wind. For let not that man suppose that he will receive anything from the Lord; he is a double-minded man, unstable in all his ways."* —James 1:5-8

Secondly, any time God refuses to answer His people or sends them into battle to be defeated, it is because there is sin among them that needs to be addressed.

24. What is Saul's next rash oath?

Saul is frustrated. He wants to move forward, but God isn't speaking to him, and he can't very well move forward at this point without the LORD's okay. That would be a flagrant overstepping of authority. So he is put in a position of having to sort things out. He calls the chiefs of the people together and says, I don't care if it is my own son, but whoever broke the commandment is going to die. We will settle this so that we can move on.

> *"For as the LORD lives, who saves Israel, though it be in Jonathan my son, he shall surely die."* (14:39)

This is another rash oath. The phrase "as the LORD lives" occurs 38 times in the Old Testament in conjunction with oaths being made, but it is a meaningless phrase coming from a man who does not give God glory or is at cross-purposes with Him. It is mentioned twice in this passage and bookends this instance of Saul's failure in judging his own son.

Saul wants to know who has sinned, and, of course, no one answers him. I can imagine all the people shifting uneasily on their feet and glancing worriedly at one another because they know Jonathan is actually the guilty party. This is going to be a major embarrassment for Saul, who doesn't have a clue.

25. **How does Saul go about discovering the guilty party?**

Saul sets himself and Jonathan on one side and the rest of Israel on the other side, and then asks the priest to cast the lot. Is it my side or theirs? In the NKJV, verse 41 is rendered as it is in the Masoretic text, "Give a perfect lot," but the ESV (that follows the Septuagint translation) add this explanation:

> "Therefore Saul said, 'O LORD God of Israel, why have you not answered your servant this day? If this guilt is in me or in Jonathan my son, O LORD, God of Israel, give Urim. But if this guilt is in your people Israel, give Thummim.' And Jonathan and Saul were taken, but the people escaped." —First Samuel 14:41 ESV

By this we understand how lots are cast. It was similar to flipping a coin and calling heads or tails. The people would be divided into two groups, which then corresponded to one of two lots, the Urim and Thummim, which were kept in a pouch on the priest's ephod. The leader would ask God: "If it this one, show Urim, or if it is that one, show Thummim." Then the priest would pull a lot from his ephod and cast it down. The lot would either be the Urim or the Thummim. (I am not sure what would show for a non-answer like God gave Saul initially.)

It must have been a shock for Saul to see the lot come up for himself and Jonathan. Which of them was guilty and of what? If you were Saul, would you do a moment of soul-searching at this point?

Saul asks the LORD to choose between himself and his son, and Jonathan is taken. Then he looks at his son and says, "What have you done?" So, Jonathan tells him. It was an unintentional sin.

26. **Why is Saul merciless to his son?**

Perhaps because it is a matter of saving face at this point. He said he would kill the one who transgressed his rule, and if he doesn't follow through, he loses credibility. But think of the heartache his rash words caused. He will have to kill his own son.

This lack of mercy is in stark contrast to the mercy he offered the sons of Belial after he defeated the Ammonites. Then he said:

> "... Not a man shall be put to death this day, for today the LORD has accomplished salvation in Israel." —First Samuel 11:13

27. How does Saul's vow compare to Jephthah's vow in Judges 11?

Saul's rash vow is a lot like Jephthah's rash vow that afflicts his own child, but there are some key differences.

In Judges 11, Jephthah vows that if the LORD will give him victory, he will offer to the LORD whatever (or whoever) comes out of his house to greet him on his return from battle. Jephthah offers an offering to the LORD and acknowledges the LORD as the victor in the battle.

There is no acknowledgment of the LORD in Saul's vow. Saul had taken glory for the battle, afflicted his own people to get that glory, and now he is killing his own son as a punishment, not as an offering to the LORD but to preserve his own glory. Also, the Scripture says that Jephthah followed through with his vow, to his own grief, whereas Saul does not. Why not?

28. Why isn't the punishment carried out?

Because the people intervene on behalf of Jonathan and rescue him. As one man, they stand up to Saul and rebuke him because they see Jonathan as the one who was doing God's will and not Saul. They credit Jonathan with delivering Israel and showing better judgment than his father.

> "... Shall Jonathan die, who has accomplished this great deliverance in Israel? Certainly not! As the LORD lives, not one hair of his head shall fall to the ground, for he has worked with God this day." (14:45)

Saul is swayed by the people and the popular consensus. His behavior is always reactionary and often emotional in nature and almost always trained toward what would make him look good in the people's eyes, which is why he backs off now and does what the people want. He gives up pursuit of the enemy, and the enemy goes back to their place.

This is the problem with rash oaths. Both Saul and the people invoke the LORD's name to accomplish the oath, and yet the oaths have opposing purposes. Which does the LORD honor—to kill or not to kill? Of course, He honors the one that aligns with His purpose, but you can see the futility with which Saul uses the LORD's name—first His holy things and now His name. That is a *chalal*-ing act.

29. Was Jonathan's sin worthy of death?

No, it shouldn't have been. Jonathan's sin was an unintentional sin. He did it in ignorance. According to the Law, if a man commits a sin in ignorance, when he realizes it, what should he do? Confess his sin and offer an offering. Atonement can be made for sins committed in ignorance. They do not incur the penalty of death as deliberate sin does. Even so, Jonathan has broken the king's command, and so he is guilty.

30. Is Jonathan the only one guilty in this case?

> *"If a person sins in hearing the utterance of an oath, and is a witness, whether he has seen or known of the matter—if he does not tell it, he bears guilt."* —Leviticus 5:1

That means that if someone knows about a commandment or oath (like the one Saul made) and he knows someone has transgressed the oath (like Jonathan did), if he refrains from coming forward with testimony when he has been a witness to the crime or has indirect knowledge of it (such as hearing it from an eyewitness) and he doesn't speak up when he is asked publicly, then he is guilty of trespass.

There were at least a few people who witnessed Jonathan breaking the command and yet didn't say anything. They, too, were guilty.

> *"Or if a person swears, speaking thoughtlessly with his lips to do evil or to do good, whatever it is that a man may pronounce by an oath, and he is unaware of it—when he realizes it, then he shall be guilty in any of these matters. And it shall be, when he is guilty in any of these matters, that he shall confess that he has sinned in that thing; and he shall bring his trespass offering to the LORD for his sin which he has committed..."* —Leviticus 5:4-6

This means that if a man takes an oath to do something, and fails to do it for whatever reason, when he realizes he did not follow through on his oath, then he becomes guilty of breaking that oath. That requires a trespass offering as well. So the king trespassed just as the people and Jonathan trespassed. All had sinned.

In the end, the enemy is forgotten, and everyone returns home in a very anti-climactic fashion.

For the sake of comparison, consider the episode with Jesus and the adulteress (John 8). The Pharisees brought the adulteress before Jesus for condemnation, and Jesus said, let he who is without sin cast the first stone. And what was their response? All of them were convicted of their own sin in the matter and no one cast any stones. Why? If adultery had been committed, then both the man and woman were to be judged, not just the woman, and if they knew of the woman, they surely knew who the man was also. So the Pharisees knew the truth of the matter but did not bear witness of the whole truth nor did they judge rightly or with the right motive. Though the adulteress was guilty, she walked away forgiven, in a somewhat anti-climactic ending. It is kind of an interesting parallel.

❺❼ Picture Comparison of Jonathan's Battles

Picture #5: In Chapter 13, Jonathan attacks the Philistine garrison at Geba, sparking the war. God puts Israel to the fear test as He did with Gideon, but Saul interferes. Saul:

- Takes credit for Jonathan's initiative, but also the criticism
- Tries to rally the people around himself instead of God by offering a profane offering.

In this instance, Saul held the high ground with the superior forces, and yet he doesn't press the advantage against Israel's enemies when he is in a position to do so. Instead, Jonathan sallies out with a little conviction and a lesser force to engage the enemy in a small venue.

Saul loses the advantage, and yet the ground Jonathan gained wasn't lost. Gibeah and Geba remained in Israel's hands while Michmash was taken by the Philistines. True, Saul left Michmash for Gilgal, but God would have given Michmash back to him with so much more if he had only followed through and obeyed. Saul stepped out, but then stumbled, and ended up disqualified.

Picture #7: In Chapter 14, Jonathan attacks another Philistine garrison at the canyon of Michmash and sparks another war. It is another Gideon moment. This time God sends the fear among the Philistines, and they begin to flee while the Hebrews rally to Jonathan. Saul steps in and:

- Takes credit for Jonathan's initiative and takes glory from God by owning the victory.
- Tries to rally the people around himself by force and by instituting the fast.
- Takes criticism for his rash oath, misjudgment, and lack of mercy for his son, and loses the people's regard.

In this instance, Saul has an army of six hundred and a priest with him. He has all the advantages he needs by the LORD's estimation, and yet he gathers all his men to him and sits doing nothing under a pomegranate tree at Migron while the enemy taunts Israel from across the canyon. Instead, Jonathan steps out and tackles the canyon head-on with tremendous conviction, one sword, and one faithful friend for backup. When he got past the teeth, he took his stand and laid into the enemy, and God rewarded him with a victory, which his own father then undercut.

In the comparison between father and son, Jonathan is more exemplary. Let's look at what he models when it comes to fighting a good fight.

APPLY THE PICTURE

Jonathan's Model

Jonathan faces an external enemy and an internal enemy, just as we do.

In regards to the external enemy:

Jonathan fights a good fight in terms of engaging the physical enemy. He steps out in faith, gives God glory, and tackles those enemies with perseverance. Like Jonathan, we face an enemy that taunts us from a high place and from behind the teeth as well. In our case, we fight a war of words more often than we fight a physical war, and the sword that we wield is the truth of the Word of God. The Word of God can seem like a weak weapon—an ox goad—that only serves to prick and drive the enemy to anger when we use it. But even a goad can be as effective as a sword for those who wield it with conviction. The Word of God is a goad, but it is also the only sword that we need to carry into battle when engaging the enemy hiding behind the teeth.

- Are we called to play defense or offense? It's an uphill climb to get past the teeth and deal with the enemy hiding behind them. Are we called to take the initiative in tackling the enemy and gaining ground for God like Jonathan, or do we huddle together in defensive positions and fight only as a reaction to the enemy like Saul?

- Is one sword enough? I suppose that depends on the nature of the sword you are using. Is it a physical sword, a panel of trained experts, or is it the Word of God? A believer in pursuit of a crown knows which weapon to use in engaging the enemy, and he trains himself in the use of that weapon.

As Christians, we can take the high ground, get in our holy huddle, and play the defensive game. And it always seems to surprise us when one or two actually venture out on their own armed with just one sword and have a resounding success. And we see the LORD moving in those circumstances and marvel at it, and then we want to get into the battle with them after the fact. Why aren't we the ones stepping out? Why are we the ones still in the huddle?

Playing defense is not the way to pursue the crown. Grip the sword, step out of the huddle, and tackle the teeth. Let the world think you are carrying an ox goad, and then wield it like a sword—with conviction.

In regards to the internal enemy:

Jonathan faced an external enemy in the Philistines, but then he also faced his father who was supposed to be on his side but wasn't. Saul assumed a place in the battle as if he were fighting for Israel, but his actions which came out in the course of battle showed a very different motivation. He was in it for his own glory and pursuits, and not for God's glory or even the well-being of God's people. And Jonathan saw it and reacted to it by speaking the truth to the people in rebuke of his father.

When we are engaged in a spiritual battle with the enemy, there are those who present themselves as co-laborers with us in the battle, even assume the place of leadership among us, and yet are not after God's glory but their own. They can become oppressive rulers over us, instituting rules over what we eat or drink, forbidding marriage, and all manner of requirements that do more harm than good and hinder the mission. When these leaders' rules are challenged, those who challenge them may not face death as Jonathan did, but they certainly face persecution and are often cut off from the congregational body. What kind of leaders am I talking about? False prophets or false teachers.

Paul warns the Colossian church against the wrong pattern of self-denial and neglect of the body that false leaders can impose on us when we are in pursuit of the crown. Pious abstinence can become a self-glorifying humility. Self-denial can force a person's focus inward on him or herself instead of outward on the mission, and lead to sin and dissension in the congregational body.

Paul warns:

> *"Let no one cheat you of your reward, taking delight in false humility and worship of angels, intruding into those things which he has not seen, vainly puffed up by his fleshly mind, and not holding fast to the Head, from whom all the body, nourished and knit together by joints and ligaments, grows with the increase that is from God. Therefore, if you died with Christ from the basic principles of the world, why, as though living in the world, do you subject yourselves to regulations—'Do not touch, do not taste, do not handle,' which all concern things which perish with the using—according to the commandments and doctrines of men? These things indeed have an appearance of wisdom in self-imposed religion, false humility, and neglect of the body, but are of no value against the indulgence of the flesh."* —Colossians 2:18-23

Saul demanded that the people abstain from that which was good so that he might indulge his own vanity and greed for vengeance, and he almost killed his followers in his pursuit. He built an altar but did not seek God's counsel. He would put his own son to death for unknowingly disobeying his arbitrary rule as a matter of face.

> *"Beware of false prophets, who come to you in sheep's clothing, but inwardly they are ravenous wolves. You will know them by their fruits . . ."*
> —Matthew 7:15-16

So . . . Is Saul also among the prophets? I snicker at that a little.

Jonathan, Saul, and First Timothy

Fighting a good fight involves defending God's people not just against the external enemy, but being on guard against the internal enemy. First Timothy pairs well with Jonathan's example in these chapters of First Samuel, particularly in regards to fighting a good fight.

> *"This charge I commit to you, son Timothy, according to the prophecies previously made concerning you, that by them you may wage the good warfare, having faith and a good conscience, which some having rejected, concerning the faith have suffered shipwreck,"* —First Timothy 1:18-19

Jonathan models a young man who steps into battle with faith and a good conscience. The battle he faces with the external enemy is fairly straightforward, and that enemy is easy to identify. The internal enemy is a little harder because for Jonathan, he is 1) the king, 2) a co-laborer in the battle, and 3) family.

Much of Paul's instructions to Timothy have to do with setting a standard in relating to authorities that includes 1) kings and masters, 2) leadership in the church, and 3) the family—often in overlapping capacities.

Jonathan runs up against an authority who has "suffered shipwreck," as Paul puts it. Saul has been carried away from the faith by his greediness for glory in the kingdom to the point where he speaks rash oaths in the LORD's name (blasphemy) and brings the people under cruel rules. Paul draws a similar parallel to Alexander and Hymenaeus whom he delivered to Satan so that they may learn not to blaspheme. (Spoiler alert! Saul will continue his resistance to God to the point that God causes him to struggle with an evil spirit who terrifies him.)

Paul warns Timothy against authorities who speak "lies in hypocrisy, having their own conscience seared with a hot iron, forbidding to marry, and commanding to abstain from foods which God created to be received with thanksgiving by those who believe and know the truth" (First Timothy 4:2-3). Jonathan runs into this very issue with his own father. Saul is a hypocrite in how he demands the people abstain from needful things while he himself indulges in his own craving. Saul has not the least pangs of conscience over the harm he is doing to his own people. He pursues a battle for his own glory and forces the people to abstain from food that Jonathan points out is meant for good. Jonathan's own conscience doesn't bow to such tyranny, and he speaks the truth to the people, just as Paul exhorts Timothy to do—to nourish the people with words of faith and good doctrine.

Just as Paul warns Timothy that he will both labor and suffer reproach for pursuing godliness and trusting in the living God who is the Savior of all men, so Jonathan labors but also suffers reproach from a man who, ironically, prefaces his judgment of Jonathan with the words "as the LORD lives, who saves Israel . . ." But that is the hypocrisy and blasphemy of an enemy who has rejected the LORD as master.

In First Samuel 14, we saw the effects of Saul's policy on the congregation of Israel. The mission was derailed as the people's attention diverted into internal struggles. Saul's unwholesome words created a sense of envy in the people for something that was being denied them, and the envy progressed into sin, strife, disputes, reviling, and wrangling over policies. It all began with a leader who threw off God's headship over him and set off to pursue his own glory and gain.

Paul warns Timothy in First Timothy 6 of the same thing happening in the church at the instigation of men who would throw off God's headship and wholesome doctrine. They pursue a reward that they have defined for themselves and embroil others in their rebellion. Paul says, from such withdraw yourself.

It's hard to withdraw when it is your own father, the king, doing this to you, and yet Jonathan begins a very subtle withdrawal from his father from this point on in regards to where his loyalties lay.

8 Saul Establishes His Kingdom

READ

First Samuel 14:47-52

NARRATIVE STRUCTURE

Picture #8, like Picture #6, is delivered by the narrator and provides a hard break between pictures in the series while providing the necessary information to move the narrative forward.

BUILD THE PICTURE

31. What is Saul's focus now?

Saul establishes himself as king over Israel, and he fights for his temporal kingdom because it is the only kingdom he will have now that he has lost the imperishable crown of an eternal kingship. He presses every strong man he finds into service and fights fiercely for it, but he is grasping after a perishable crown.

There is a specific note in verse 48 that Saul gathered an army and attacked the Amalekites. This battle will become the focus of the next chapter and lead to the kingdom being taken from Saul and given to David. We are also given a picture of Saul's family tree to introduce some new characters, who will join the narrative in the next chapters. Saul marries Ahinoam and has three sons and two daughters. He makes his uncle, Abner, commander of his army.

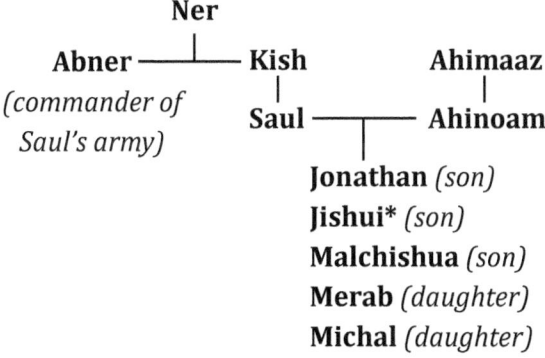

*Jishui is called Abinadab in First Chronicles 8:33 and 9:39. The Chronicles verses also list a fourth son, Esh-Baal, who may be Ishbosheth in Second Samuel 2. I think the sons listed here are relative to the First Samuel narrative and will be the sons who will die in battle with their father in Chapter 31.

LESSON 9: FIRST SAMUEL 15–16

The Cost of Disobedience

SERIES STRUCTURE

Picture #9 (15:1-35) is the third and final test of King Saul in which he loses the kingdom.

Picture #10 (16:1-23) records David's anointing as the new king.

I put these two pictures into one lesson because they are tied together in structure and theme. Both Chapters 15 and 16 open with a command from the LORD, which is unique in the First Samuel narrative. Pictures typically open and close with narrator notes; a few open with dialogue, and that deviation points to a significant picture parallel. But only these two pictures open with the LORD issuing a command, and His voice lends a grandeur to the events as the great King now transfers the crown from Saul to David. The structural similarity is a pointer that these two chapters are thematically tied together. The theme of ascents and descents will continue as David begins his rise and Saul his descent.

The author intentionally draws comparisons between David and Saul from here on, and he points us to the parallels in how he structures the pictures in David's narrative. Both David and Saul will have anointing, first battle, and celebration sequences with many narrative elements in common, but there will be some differences or additions to David's narrative that are not included in Saul's accounts. We will look for those differences, because they are intentional for application.

❾ Saul's Third Failure

READ

First Samuel 15:1-35

NARRATIVE STRUCTURE

In **Picture #9**, the picture elements follow the same basic formula as Pictures #5 and #7 but with some variations. Instead of an opening narrator's note, we have a direct command from the LORD to attack the Amalekites. Instead of Jonathan going into battle and Saul reacting, Saul himself goes to war and then we see the LORD's and Samuel's reactions.

Picture #9 has a tightly structured narrative:

1) Command from the LORD (15:1-3)
2) Saul's battle (15:4-9)

Inclusio

3) The LORD's regret and Samuel's reaction (15:10-11)
4) The judgment sequence

Chiasm

- (A) Samuel seeks Saul (15:12-13a)
- (B) Saul declares he has performed the LORD's command (15:13b)
  - (C) Samuel rebukes Saul (15:14)
  - (D) Saul's excuse #1 (15:15)
  - (E) Samuel announces judgment (15:16-19)
  - (F) Saul's excuse #2 (15:20-21)

Inclusio

  - (G) Samuel pronounces judgment for disobedience (15:22-23)
  - **(H) Saul's excuse #3 (15:24-25)**
  - (G) Samuel affirms the judgment for disobedience (15:26)
  - (F) Saul tears his robe (15:27)
  - (E) Samuel reaffirms the judgment (15:28-29)
  - (D) Saul's confession and request #2 (15:30)
  - (C) Samuel grants Saul's request (15:31)
- (B) Samuel performs the LORD's command (15:32-33)
- (A) Samuel seeks Saul no more (15:34-35a)

5) Narrator's note: Samuel's grieving and the LORD's regret (15:35b)

The focus of Chapter 15 is on the running dialogue between Samuel and Saul. Saul opens the dialogue, but Samuel dominates it from then on with four main rebukes of growing intensity that end with his statement that God has torn the kingdom from Saul. The apex of the chiasm is Saul's confession (H), but it is enclosed in the inclusio of Samuel's repeated statements "the LORD has rejected you from being king" (G-G). As we work through the dialogue, we will focus on what Saul's words reveal about his character, and how Samuel responds to deal with the disobedience.

BUILD THE PICTURE

Command from the LORD (15:1–3)

1. **When was the last time we saw Samuel in the text?**

    The last time we saw Samuel was at Gilgal with Saul. The LORD had given Saul a command through the word of Samuel to wait seven days for Samuel to come and offer the offerings. When Samuel gets there, he discovers Saul had wrongly offered the burnt offering to keep the people from scattering from him during the Philistine attack. At that time, Samuel told Saul that he had lost the reward of an eternal kingship and his kingdom would not be established.

    Since then, Saul has been trying to establish an earthly kingdom by his own will and power. He pitched himself into wars with all his enemies, and he established his sovereignty over the people.

    Now we find out that there had been another command that God had given to Saul through the words of Samuel:

    > "Thus says the LORD of hosts: 'I will punish Amalek for what he did to Israel, how he ambushed him on the way when he came up from Egypt. Now go and attack Amalek, and utterly destroy all that they have, and do not spare them. But kill both man and woman, infant and nursing child, ox and sheep, camel and donkey.'" (15:2-3)

2. **Who are the Amalekites and what is Israel's history with them?**

    The Amalekites inhabit the southern deserts of Judah and down into the desert wilderness as far as Mount Sinai. They share the desert with the Midianites and Kenites.

Amalek was among those nations who fought Israel when they came out of Egypt. In Exodus 17, Joshua defeated Amalek, and the LORD pronounced a condemnation on Amalek.

> "Then the LORD said to Moses, 'Write this for a memorial in the book and recount it in the hearing of Joshua, that I will utterly blot out the remembrance of Amalek from under heaven.'" —Exodus 17:14

The LORD swore to have war with Amalek from that point forward from generation to generation. The curse was renewed in Numbers 24 with Balaam's fourth prophecy.

> "Then he [Balaam] looked on Amalek, and he took up his oracle and said: 'Amalek was first among the nations, but shall be last until he perishes.'" —Numbers 24:20

There is a final commandment given to Israel in Deuteronomy 25:17:

> "Remember what Amalek did to you on the way as you were coming out of Egypt, how he met you on the way and attacked your rear ranks, all the stragglers at your rear, when you were tired and weary; and he did not fear God. Therefore it shall be, when the LORD your God has given you rest from your enemies all around, in the land which the LORD your God is giving you to possess as an inheritance, that you will blot out the remembrance of Amalek from under heaven. You shall not forget." —Deuteronomy 25:17-19

When Israel came into the Promised Land, the Amalekites were among the many aggressors the LORD left in the land along with the Canaanites who He used to punish Israel for their idolatry and wickedness. They joined Midian and the other desert tribes in harassing Israel in Gideon's day. But now the LORD tells Saul through Samuel, it is time to end them. Go, strike the Amalekites.

So, Saul musters the army. He has 200,000 foot soldiers and 10,000 men of Judah (again, we have the distinction made between Judah and the rest of Israel that sets up the future rivalry).

Saul Battles the Amalekites (15:4–9)

3. Who are the Kenites and how have they been kind to Israel?

Kenites are Midianites by nationality, but they break away from Midian to be associated with Moses and Israel. Moses' wife, Zipporah, was from the Kenite clan, and he maintained ties with the family as Israel begins their exodus from Egypt. In Numbers 10:29-32, Moses makes a promise to his brother-in-law Hobab that if he will come with Israel, then the family will be given a share of the good that the Lord promised Israel. The Kenites reappear in Judges 1. They come into the land with Israel and are allowed to settle in the southern deserts of Judah. They are the only Gentile people granted a place in the land. Since they are not Canaanite, they are not on the list of those to be thrown out of the Land. They were a great help to Deborah and Barak when they were battling Sisera and Jabin. Jael the Kenite is the one who killed Sisera. Historically, the Kenites have been loyal to Israel, so Saul spares them.

4. What did Saul do and not do in the campaign?

Saul goes to war with the Amalekites in the lower deserts via the Way of Shur. There are three main routes that run across the Sinai Peninsula between Israel and Egypt. There is the coastal route referred to as the way of the Philistines. There is the Way of Shur, which runs inland through the Wilderness of Shur. Then there is the southern route that Israel took on their way to the Promised Land. Havilah is unknown, but it is thought to be the land encompassed by that circuitous route that Israel wandered those 40 years in the desert, and Shur is the wilderness just above it that butts up to Egypt. Saul pretty much cleaned the Amalekite presence out of the Sinai deserts. He destroyed all the people, except King Agag, and everything that was weak and worthless. But all the good stuff that he valued he brought home as trophies.

He also set up a monument for himself in Carmel in Judah. There's some grandstanding and self-glorification in it for Saul, in what should have been a moment for glorifying God and God alone. This monument is a slight to the tribe of Judah, which was the largest and most powerful of the tribes, whereas Saul's tribe of Benjamin is the least. There is a rivalry there, and Saul has scored a coup in defeating Judah's enemies on their own turf.

I want you to remember this monument at Carmel and the warning it represents: A man in pursuit of a crown can lose the crown when he takes glory for himself instead of giving glory to God. David will face a similar test in the shadow of that monument when he comes into conflict with Nabal at Carmel.

There is one final action that Saul takes, but we find out after the fact when it is reported to Samuel. After setting up his monument, Saul *"has gone on around, passed by, and gone down to Gilgal"* (15:12). The Hebrew text belabors the fact that Saul has deliberately skirted Samuel at Ramah and doesn't report to him that the job was done. Instead of going to Samuel, he forces Samuel to seek him out. It's a good indicator that Saul knows that he has done wrong and is avoiding Samuel because of it.

The LORD's Regret, Samuel's Reaction (15:10–11)

Meanwhile, God and Samuel are having a discussion about Saul. God says that He regrets making Saul king. The Hebrew word for regret is *naham*, which means "to sigh heavily."

5. **What does a heavy sigh communicate?**

    It can communicate a number of things, depending on the context: Regret, frustration, anger, resignation, comfort (a sigh of relief).

6. **What is Samuel's reaction?**

    In the NKJV, it says he was grieved, which sounds like Samuel is feeling grief or sorrow, but that is not the word in the Hebrew. The Hebrew word used here is *hara*, which means to be hot, furious, burn, become angry, or be kindled. Why would Samuel be angry with Saul? Some leniency might have been offered for the first offense, but this is the second offense. Saul hasn't learned anything.

Samuel Seeks Saul (15:12-13)

To add to Samuel's frustration, Saul doesn't return to him when the mission is accomplished. Samuel finds out what Saul has been doing from a second hand source and has to go looking for him, like a parent having to go after a naughty child.

7. **What does Samuel find when he gets to Gilgal?**

    The scene is almost a repeat of the last time Samuel found Saul at Gilgal, except then, Saul had already offered a burnt offering. This time the offering hasn't been offered yet. Samuel can hear the bleating of the animals in the background. And there is Saul, coming out to greet him.

Rebuke #1, Excuse #1 (15:13–15)

Saul announces that he has performed the commandment of the LORD, just like he should have. Samuel then remarks on the obvious. Where did all these animals come from then?

8. **What reason does Saul give for bringing back spoil from the war?**

    Look very carefully at the pronouns being used.

    > "And Saul said, '**They** have brought them from the Amalekites; for **the people** spared the best of the sheep and the oxen, to sacrifice to the LORD **your** God; and the rest **we** have utterly destroyed.'" (15:15)

    Notice that Saul deflects the blame to the people, although he himself is among the people, even leader of the people. Also notice how Saul said "the LORD *your* God" (Eloheka) and not "the LORD *my* God" (Elohay) or "the LORD *our* God" (Elohenu). That is significant.

    Saul could argue: what did it matter if the animals were slaughtered on the battlefield or at Gilgal, so long as they are slaughtered? The people took the spoil to sacrifice to God, so really what we did was for God's glory.

    The LORD didn't want the offerings offered at Gilgal. He wanted them destroyed where they were taken on the battlefield. But if Saul had killed the Amalekites in the desert, he would have come home with nothing to show for it. Instead, he takes the spoil and glory that should have been God's for himself and parades it the length of Judah's territory on his way to Gilgal for all the people to see. He steal's God's thunder, so to speak, but God does not share his glory with anyone.

Rebuke #2, Excuse #2 (15:16–21)

The second rebuke is quite forceful. Samuel tells the king, in essence, to shut up and listen to what God has to say about his actions. Samuel isn't the one to whom Saul has to justify his actions. God is the one who issued the command and He is the offended authority here. This is Saul's third offense in taking glory from the LORD.

9. **What charges does Samuel lay against Saul?**

    First he addresses the pride, and then the failure to obey.

    > *"When you were little in your own eyes, were you not head of the tribes of Israel? And did not the LORD anoint you king over Israel?"* (15:17)

    Saul was never "little" to begin with, and God lifted him up even more. But now Saul has lifted his own self up beyond that, all the while making a show of giving God glory. Again, this is false humility and pride. Then Samuel brings up Saul's failure to complete the mission, which was an act of disobedience, and the fact that Saul dipped his hand into the King's spoil and took it for himself and his own glory. The charges are pretty condemning, but Saul protests his innocence.

    > *"... But I have obeyed the voice of the LORD, and gone on the mission on which the LORD sent me, and brought back Agag king of Amalek; I have utterly destroyed the Amalekites. But the people took of the plunder, sheep and oxen, the best of the things which should have been utterly destroyed, to sacrifice to the LORD your God in Gilgal."* (15:20-21)

    He went on the mission as commanded and destroyed the Amalekites. But then he adds something to the LORD's command that the LORD didn't actually command. He brought back King Agag. Then Saul repeats his earlier argument, deflecting the blame to the people. It was the people who took the plunder and sheep and oxen. They did it to sacrifice to the LORD—at Gilgal. Again, he adds to the command of the LORD. And he still is not taking responsibility for the people as a leader. He divorces himself from their actions.

    Notice, again, the very fine wording in verse 21: *"to sacrifice to the LORD your God in Gilgal." Your* God? Is God not Saul's God as well?

Judgment and Excuse #3 (15:22–26)

Saul has twice used the excuse that the animals were meant as a sacrifice to the LORD, as if that would excuse the behavior, so Saul refutes that aspect of his argument. *"To obey is better than sacrifice."* Then Samuel names Saul's behavior for what it really is—rebellion and stubbornness—and delivers the judgment. The poetic structure of verses 22-23 sets Samuel's judgment apart from the rest of the dialogue, emphasizing their significance, and Samuel's repeated statement, *"the LORD has rejected you from being king,"* in verses 23 and 26 create the inclusio that encloses Saul's confession that he has indeed obeyed the people over God. This is the pivotal moment.

10. What does Samuel mean by "to obey is better than sacrifice"?

Doing right is better than performing rites. Samuel is the first of the prophets to declare this precept of right over rite. (Others include Amos, Hosea, Isaiah, Jeremiah, and Micah.)

Where other prophets like Hosea stress moral behavior (*"For I desire mercy and not sacrifice, and the knowledge of God more than burnt offerings."*—Hosea 6:6), Samuel and Jeremiah are unique in demanding simple obedience to the LORD over performing rituals.

The LORD declares through Jeremiah:

> *"For I did not speak to your fathers, or command them in the day that I brought them out of the land of Egypt, concerning burnt offerings or sacrifices. But this is what I commanded them, saying, 'Obey My voice, and I will be your God, and you shall be My people. And walk in all the ways that I have commanded you, that it may be well with you.'"* —Jeremiah 7:22-23

Before God brought Israel out of Egypt, He did not first deliver the Laws about the burnt offerings and peace sacrifices. He instituted the Passover sacrifice, but the rest of the sacrificial laws were not given until several months later at Mount Sinai. What He did demand was obedience to His voice as He led them. The command to obey the voice of the LORD precedes the command to offer sacrifices, making it the greater commandment. I think perhaps this is because obedience can only be performed from the inward heart. Performing the sacrifice is an outward task that can be performed with or without an inner heart for God, for selfish reasons or man's approval, as Saul has already demonstrated. But God is looking at the heart. He has already told Saul this in so many words when the first judgment was rendered.

> "... The LORD has sought for Himself a man after His own heart..."
> —First Samuel 13:14

11. Why is rebellion like the sin of divination (witchcraft) and stubbornness like iniquity and idolatry?

It is an important skill when studying the Old Testament to be able to see the connecting thought in analogies like this. What is the common or source behavior that characterizes both rebellion and witchcraft? Saul's rebellion is a bid to rid himself of God's authority and power by assuming that power and authority himself, and it is this that rebellion and witchcraft have in common. They both involve turning away from God to seek power by another means (by your own strength or by demonic power), and seeking to replace God with another authority figure.

Stubbornness is persistent and aggressive in its willful pursuit of lusts, just like sin and idolatry. God is just as stubborn as Saul, and delivers him a tit for a tat. Since Saul rejected God's authority, God rejects Saul's authority and takes him off the throne. (15:24b)

12. How does Saul try to avert the judgment?

> "I have sinned, for I have transgressed the commandment of the LORD and your words, because I feared the people and obeyed their voice. Now therefore, please pardon my sin, and return with me, that I may worship the LORD." (15:24)

Saul's confession, or at least partial confession, is sandwiched between Samuel's repeated phrase: *"you have rejected the word of the LORD, and the LORD has rejected you from being king."*

Saul confesses he has sinned, but then blames the people again. There is always the excuse. The people wanted to do this thing, and he couldn't stand up to them. He feared the people more than God, so he obeyed their voice. What kind of a king can't stand up to his people?

One who was elected based on popularity. But in reality, he is their commander and representative before God. He can't deflect the blame on the people without being equally guilty.

There is an echo of the model of Adam who, in addition to adding his own twist to the LORD's command, listened to the voice of the woman, willfully disobeyed, and lost the kingdom.

Saul wants to be forgiven for his sin, but he also wants Samuel to go with him to worship the LORD. That's an odd request. Why would Saul want to worship a God he has rebelled against?

13. Why does Saul want Samuel to return with him?

It's still about the glory and saving face. If Samuel is there, then the people won't think there is anything wrong, right? Saul says he wants to worship the LORD (by worship, he means bow down before the LORD), but it is a hypocritical act. Saul is only bowing outwardly, but his words clearly indicate that he is still in rebellion and denial. So it's still about keeping up appearances. He wants to look good and not be embarrassed in the eyes of the elders and before Israel.

14. What is Samuel's response to Saul's request?

> *". . . I will not return with you, for you have rejected the word of the LORD, and the LORD has rejected you from being king over Israel."* (15:26)

Saul isn't repentant, and Samuel knows it. He is not going to perpetuate the charade and be party to Saul's sin. Samuel knows the King to whom he owes allegiance and loyalty, and it's not Saul. He repeats the charge and turns to go.

Saul Tears Samuel's Robe, Rebuke #4 (15:27–29)

15. How does Saul try to keep the kingdom?

In his desperation, Saul resorts to physical force. He escalates from passive-aggressive excuse-making to outright aggression, and his true animosity toward Samuel and God is finally revealed. I think it is funny that he tries to stop Samuel, as if that will do any good. Samuel is just the messenger. He has no power to override the King's command. It is God with whom Saul is truly wrestling.

16. What is the significance of Saul tearing Samuel's mantle?

The cutting or tearing of cloth is symbolic of cutting covenant or alliance with someone or something. Samuel tells Saul that because of his grasping, the LORD is cutting His covenant with him and tearing the kingdom from his hands.

Then Samuel says:

> "And also the Strength of Israel will not lie nor relent. For He is not a man, that He should relent." (15:29)

The Hebrew word translated as "strength" is *netsak,* which embodies splendor, glory, truth, sincerity, and an attribute of "continuing" or eternality. The Strength of Israel does not lie, because He is truth. He does not relent, that is, He is constant and unchanging.

Again, God delivers a tit-for-tat, this time in a rather passive-aggressive statement. God is not a man (like Saul) that He should relent—implying that God will follow through with His words, unlike inconstant Saul who did not follow through with anything.

But the Hebrew word for "relent" is the same word translated as "regret" back in verse 11. Regretting and relenting are two unrelated acts in the English usage, so Samuel's statement seems to contradict what God Himself says. God says in verse 11 that He *nahams* making Saul king, but then Samuel says that God is not a man that He should *naham*. How do we reconcile these statements?

Keep in mind that the Hebrew word simply means "to sigh heavily" which is one act, but it can express different things, depending on the context. It can be a sigh of relief. It can be a sigh of frustration or regret. It can be a sigh of resignation and relenting (*"fine, we will do it your way."* *sigh*). The context is what defines the action and drives the translation. So we see that God can *naham* in one sense of regretting, and yet not *naham* in the sense of relenting. Verse 29 might be translated: The Strength of Israel does not lie and He does not sigh [as if He is without strength to follow through]. For He is not a man, that He should sigh.

Saul is a man who flails about. If truth does not achieve his objective, he resorts to lies. If a show of force does not work, then he retreats or relents. If going to the right doesn't work, he turns to the left. Men like Saul seek strength however they can lay their hands on it. God is not like double-minded man. God does not flail about. He sets his mind with single purpose and follows through.

17. Didn't Saul already lose the kingship already? How is it different this time?

Compare these two statements. Are they speaking of a loss of the same crown, or is there a difference?

The first time Saul disobeyed, this was God's response:

> "... For now the LORD would have established your kingdom over Israel forever. But now your kingdom shall not continue. The LORD has sought for Himself a man after His own heart, and the LORD has commanded him to be commander over His people, because you have not kept what the LORD commanded you." —First Samuel 13:13-14

This time when Saul disobeys, this was God's response:

> "Because you have rejected the word of the LORD, He also has rejected you from being king ... The LORD has torn the kingdom of Israel from you today, and has given it to a neighbor of yours, who is better than you." —First Samuel 15:23, 28

The first time, Saul lost the imperishable crown—the crown that would have lasted forever—but he was still an earthly king over an earthly kingdom (a perishable crown). The second time, God takes away the perishable crown from him, too.

Saul Confesses, Samuel Relents (15:30-31)

Saul's final request doesn't shift blame. He confesses his sin, and only asks not to be publicly humiliated in front of the people.

18. Why does Samuel relent?

Think about this from Samuel's perspective. Both Saul and Israel as a congregation have snubbed him, and he has every inducement to humiliate Saul by snubbing him back, and yet he does not take personal vengeance in this way. It is enough that the LORD has vindicated him. To take his own shot at Saul would be the same sin of self-glorification of which Saul was guilty. And it is right that every knee bow in acknowledgment of the LORD's righteous judgment, regardless of their heart.

So, Samuel relents and goes with Saul to bow before the LORD. But just because Samuel goes does not mean God has relented in His judgment. Samuel also returns to perform the deed that Saul refused to do. He goes to kill Agag, and fulfill the command of the LORD which Saul failed to do.

Samuel Performs the LORD's Command (15:32-33)

19. What does Agag think will happen when he approaches Samuel?

He thinks his life will be spared. The NKJV translation says he approached cautiously or with faltering steps, but the Hebrew can also be translated as he approached with delight or fawning steps, perhaps with arms open wide in appeal. *". . . Surely the bitterness of death is past."*

Samuel hacks Agag to pieces before the LORD in Gilgal, in front of Saul and Israel, then goes home. What God had commanded was done, but by the priest, not the king.

Narrator's Closing Comment (15:34-35)

The narrator's final note is that Samuel and Saul parted ways at this point, and Samuel never went to Saul again until the day of his death. The relationship is cut off, and yet Samuel mourns over it. And, again, God regrets—*nahams*—making Saul king.

The Hebrew word *naham* is used here for a third time in this closing comment forming the inclusio that frames this segment (15:11, 35). The entire episode is described as one heavy sigh.

APPLY THE PICTURE

Rebellion

Have you ever dealt with someone who does what you ask...

> ...in part but not in whole?
> ...in their own time and not when you asked them to do it?
> ...in their own way and not the way you told them to do it?
> ...but twists it so that the credit falls to them and not you?

It's a rebellion and pride issue. It's a willful refusal to submit, but done in a passive-aggressive way that doesn't challenge the authority outright, but is wearying to the one in authority, like water on stone.

This kind of rebellion stems from anger, resentment, and pride, but the feelings are expressed indirectly, in a very passive-aggressive way. Saul appears to comply with God's commands but doesn't follow through. He disobeys, makes intentional mistakes, avoids responsibility with excuses and blaming others, and generally acts stubborn and sullen. This kind of rebellion alternates between hostile defiance and contrition, and may also include verbal resistance in the form of sarcasm and back-handed "compliments." When the passive form of rebellion is challenged, it can erupt into outright aggression, as it did with Saul.

I have always struggled in life with passive-aggressive people because I didn't realize right away that I was dealing with a rebellion. They were just accommodating enough to make me think they were being agreeable, and yet, like Samuel, I found myself constantly having to clean up the mistakes or misunderstandings or jobs they left half finished. And then there were the excuses, always the excuses, and snide remarks and the sarcasm, all of which I endured until the day it finally added up, and I realized what was going on. But by then I was so frustrated with them that I boiled over, which then got *me* in trouble, while they just sat back and smiled. Augh! So frustrating! (That's me *naham*-ing.)

I think Samuel's response gives a good model for dealing with rebellion that presents itself in this passive way:

1) Samuel is angry, but he doesn't let his personal anger and grievance

with Saul drive the confrontation. This isn't a battle of wills between the prophet and king. It's a fight between king and King.

2) He establishes who is the authority that Saul is challenging. It is not himself, in this case. It is God.

3) He stays focused on Saul's disobedience to God, and addresses the spiritual issue at the heart of Saul's actions.

4) He lays out a very clear case of what was expected and where Saul crossed the line. He establishes the boundary.

5) He puts the accountability back on Saul to explain why he didn't follow through with what was commanded.

6) He hands down the verdict for the behavior, but, when given an opportunity, doesn't humiliate Saul to vent his own frustration.

Humiliation

This is the second thing that Samuel models that I thought was notable. As God delivers judgment on Saul through Samuel, Saul makes a request of Samuel. He asks Samuel to return with him to worship God. Think about that for a moment. Both Saul and Samuel know that nothing in Saul's heart has changed. It's a hypocritical act, at best. But the request presents Samuel with the perfect opportunity to humiliate Saul by doing nothing more than simply walking away and leaving him to face the people's reaction. The first time Saul asks, Samuel is determined to go, but then Saul is still making excuses (15:24-26). But the second time, when Saul confesses in full without deflecting the blame, Samuel relents (15:30-31).

Why relent? Samuel had every right to walk away from Saul, for personal reasons as well as for Saul's rebellion against God. But he didn't.

This is something that the Word teaches, and I, personally, have seen the truth of in life. There are times when the breaking of a person is necessary to achieve repentance, but once the breaking is done, to add humiliation on top of it does more harm than good.

It says in Deuteronomy 25:3 that a man under judgment should be given forty blows and no more *"lest your brother be humiliated in your sight."*

Humiliation was never permitted as part of punishment in the justice process, because it goes beyond godly justice into the realm of selfish vengeance and retaliation. God delivers justice, but man often heaps on humiliation for his own pleasure.

Humiliation is a stumbling block to healing and reconciliation. In Isaiah 54:10, the LORD speaks of removing the humiliation of barren women, who are likened to fruitless Israel. Part of returning a person to wholeness and reconciling them to God and the congregation is the removal of humiliation associated with sin. It is one thing to incur and endure a punishment for sin. It is another to be tormented mercilessly for another's vindictive pleasure.

When you heap humiliation on a person, that is a case of you glorifying yourself over your brother. If God has already dealt with the issue, then you are glorifying yourself over God as well, because your actions suggest God's justice was insufficient. Don't do that.

Lessons Learned

Wearing a crown confers power, but what is the source of that power, how do you achieve that power, and how do you keep it?

God gave Saul the power initially, and that by grace alone, but then Saul quickly turned to the task of keeping that power by his own works. Although he knew God, he did not glorify God: nor was he thankful, but instead became futile in his thoughts. He rejected God as King and his source of power and relied instead on the power of the created crown he had been given, thus changing the glory of an incorruptible God into a crown made like corruptible man. While he did not acknowledge God, he lifted himself up by using the holy things of God for his own glory, and established himself through the wealth of material plunder, the might of his army, and a changeable heart that secured his popularity in the people's eyes. He wanted what he wanted, and he took what he wanted because that's what an earthly king does, and he used whatever force was necessary. But his sights were ever set on a perishable crown.

Saul will learn in a future lesson that if the source of power resides in the earthly realm, then that power has limits. You are only a big dog until a bigger dog enters the fight. Saul will try to retain his own power by force and fear and promises of earthly rewards, but those measures will fail when he find himself overpowered by the Philistines at a later date. He will then seek power from a spiritual source, but because he has rejected the LORD as his source of power, he cannot go through godly channels and will have to consult a witch to access it. His rebellion here in First Samuel 15 is the point where his descent begins.

Rebellion is as the sin of witchcraft. If you reject God as the source of power and authority, then you will have to find a replacement for Him, either in yourself or in the people with whom you surround yourself (and you are going to need an army). If those fail—and they will—then you will have to seek a source of power in the spiritual realm, but not from God. The only other spiritual source of power will be a satanic one.

Another way to lose a crown is by taking glory for yourself at the expense of God's glory. This includes taking vengeance and dealing in humiliation, both of which stray beyond justice into personal vindictiveness. Saul will become infamous for his vengeful dealings with those he considers enemies. How to deal righteously and justly with aggressors and enemies is one of the major lessons that a person pursuing a crown must learn before God grants them the power to command and rule.

There are right and wrong kings with which to align yourself, right and wrong crowns to pursue, and right and wrong ways and reasons to pursue them.

Saul did everything the wrong way, and there was nothing Samuel could do to convince him that he was going to lose the kingdom if he persisted. Samuel instructed, warned, rebuked, raged, and wept over Saul in vain. We do the same thing.

Like Samuel, God sends us out to grapple with the Sauls of our world who are grasping after an earthly kingdom they value for its power and glory, validation and riches. These aren't wrong rewards to pursue, but where they are sourced makes all the difference. Apart from God and a relationship with Christ, these crowns are worthless and fleeting. And yet, the Sauls of this world pursue them tirelessly, in the wrong way, and for all the wrong reasons. They look for strength and empowerment in themselves, from the supporters with whom they surround themselves, from armies, maybe even from a spiritual source, but not from God. In the event that they achieve some form of an earthly crown, they try to hold onto it by any means they can, forcibly if necessary. God tells us to warn them, "You are going to lose the kingdom!"

They scoff at the thought. Kingdom? What kingdom? This is the kingdom!

How do you explain to them that this world in its present form is dying—it's passing away? They are desperately trying to preserve it, but they aren't going to succeed. And after that death, a new form of eternal life will begin, this time divided between two kingdoms from which they will have to choose. One will be more glorious than anything they can imagine, but ruled by a King with a very different set of values than they currently embrace; the other, a hell of fiendish horror.

They have a choice to make, but they have to make it in *this* life. It all begins in *this* life. That means casting their vision beyond the next week or month or year, beyond the next promotion, beyond their five-year plan, beyond retirement—beyond death. They have to start thinking *beyond.* That means wrapping their head around the world to come, what it has to offer, and what it takes to excel in that kingdom. It means aligning themselves with the King, valuing what He values, obeying His rules, and submitting to His authority. It all begins in *this* life.

But here's the kicker. Having established that a new, glorious King is coming, explain to them that the first king that will come onto the world stage and begin a new world order will not be this King, however glorious he may look to them. The first king may have all the wealth and power and glory in the people's eyes, but he will not be the King.

Heavy sigh

Questions for Reflection

There is the picture presented by Saul and Samuel in the more eternal scheme of things, but then there are some practical points we can apply to everyday life that I think are valuable. They have to do with submitting to authority, and dealing with those who don't want to submit.

One of the chief stumbling points for Saul was his disobedience to an authority that he didn't like and didn't want to acknowledge. Though he was a king, Saul was still an underling, and his childish behavior underscored that.

The chief struggle for Samuel was dealing with a person like Saul. Samuel is like middle management—tasked as the go-between delivering the commands from the Higher-up but with little power to make Saul do what he should except by instruction, warning, or rebuke, all of which failed.

We can look at the issue from the shoes of the authority, or the one under authority. Let's consider the authority first.

- Are there people in your life over whom you have been given authority? Who are they?
- Did God play a role in your being placed in your position of authority?
- When was the last time you sighed heavily over one of your underlings? What was the issue?
- How did they react when you confronted them?
- How do you deal with people who constantly make excuses for not doing what they should be doing or challenging your authority?
- Do you ever resort to using humiliation to control them?
- If your final resort is to pass them on to a higher authority to deal with, who is next in your chain of command?
- Do you ever appeal to God as the higher authority?

Now, step into the underlings shoes (we are all underlings, even if we are kings). Is there an authority in your life with whom you are struggling?

- If so, why are you struggling with them?
- How do you express your dissatisfaction with what they are asking you to do (in words or actions)?
- If you were given a chance to embarrass them, would you do it?

⑩ David's Anointing

READ

First Samuel 16:1-23

NARRATIVE STRUCTURE

Picture #10 is divided into three basic sections:

1) Command from the LORD (16:1-3)
2) David's anointing (16:4-13)
3) Saul's distressing spirit (16:14-23)

This picture sets up the first comparison between David and Saul, beginning with the transfer of the Spirit from one to another. The first half of the chapter focuses wholly on David and his family. The section ends with the phrase: *"... and the Spirit of the LORD came upon David..."* (16:13). The chapter then segues abruptly to focus on Saul, but keeps the connecting thought: *"But the Spirit of the LORD departed from Saul..."* (16:14). Thus, the chapter's focus revolves around the comparison of the kings' spiritual conditions, more so than their physical comparisons.

In addition to the comparison found within Picture #10, there are a wealth of comparisons between Saul's anointing sequence (Pictures #1 and #2) and David's anointing here in Picture #10. Once we get through an examination of the text, we will look at the greater picture comparisons.

BUILD THE PICTURE

David's Anointing (16:1–13)

The conflict in Chapter 15 ended with Saul and Samuel going their separate ways. Samuel returns home to Ramah, and Saul to Gibeah, and that would be the last time Samuel would go to see Saul.

20. Why does Samuel mourn for Saul?

I think most people in Samuel's shoes wouldn't mourn for a man like Saul. Saul is a disappointment and a fool. He has snubbed Samuel personally and acted aggressively toward him. He failed to learn anything from Samuel's instruction or rebukes. Saul troubled his own people, wanted to kill his own son to save face, kicked at God's sacrifices, and rejected God's authority outright. He was arrogant, fool-hardy, a glory-hound, and a man given over to his own lusts. Wouldn't you just wash your hands of a man like Saul and say good riddance?

Samuel mourns for Saul, almost as if Saul had died. But then, Saul has died, in a way. The death of a relationship has taken place. Now, in Chapter 16, we see that the LORD has moved on, but Samuel hasn't.

Samuel no longer has a relationship with Saul, and yet he is still in mental bondage to him. He can't move forward for fear of Saul and what Saul might do to him. Fear can overwhelm even the strongest believer, and I think the fear adds to Samuel's melancholy.

21. How does God get Samuel moving forward again?

God sends Samuel on a mission to anoint the new king. The command brings Samuel's fear into the open as he voices his concern.

22. What is Samuel's concern?

That Saul will kill him if he hears about it. Bethlehem is in Judah, not Benjamin, and quite a ways off of Samuel's usual circuit of Bethel, Mizpah, and Gilgal. The deviation in routine would quickly be noted and reported to Saul, and Saul would immediately suspect what Samuel was doing. This would place not just Samuel in danger, but the new king as well. Saul knows the prophetic word that was spoken will come true and he lives in fear of it, much the same as Herod did in Jesus' day, or even Satan himself does.

To deal with Samuel's fear, the LORD gives him a plausible excuse for going down to Bethlehem. He is to take a heifer with him and tell the people he is there to offer a sacrifice. He is to play the priest and not the prophet in this scenario.

23. Why do the elders of Bethlehem tremble at Samuel's coming? What do they have to fear?

The king and prophet are now at odds. When there is division within leadership, it affects the congregation. We don't really know what was driving the fear, but I imagine word has spread of Samuel's displeasure with Saul over bringing the spoils back—an act in which the people participated. The conflict between Saul and Samuel has escalated. Saul may be the king, but he isn't a very wise one nor is he in favor with the LORD. Samuel, on the other hand, is God's man, and wields a significant amount of authority among the people. Samuel's appearance in Bethlehem is definitely not normal and portends unusual events.

Samuel carries on with his duties as if what he is doing is completely normal. He consecrates Jesse and his sons and invites them to the sacrifice, just as he once invited Saul to the sacrifice. But before they sit down (or gather around the table) for the sacrifice, Samuel seeks the son to anoint as king.

24. Why did Samuel think Eliab would be the next king?

Because he is the image of Saul—the tall, good-looking, favored, first-born son. Eliab fits the image. But God says He has refused Eliab. The word for "refused" is the same word as "rejected," when God said He had rejected Saul. The LORD sees in Eliab the same qualities as Saul that made him unsuitable for kingship.

The selection process is rather drawn out. The author names the passing-over of the first three sons by turn then fast-forwards to the seventh, who is also passed over. David would be son number eight, but he is absent because he is keeping sheep in the field.

The LORD tells Samuel not to look for appearances or physical stature. God chooses a man for his heart, which in this case will be David. I think it is funny that after telling Samuel not to look at appearances, the LORD then picks a handsome young man, who *"was ruddy, with bright eyes, and good-looking."* I imagine Samuel was expecting him to be the ugly duckling of the group.

Like Saul, the LORD announces to Samuel "this is the one!" Samuel anoints David in front of his brothers, the Spirit comes upon David, they have the sacrifice meal, and then Samuel hurries home to Ramah.

Saul's Distressing Spirit (16:14–23)

25. What happens to Saul when the Spirit is taken from him?

Just as Saul changed and became a different man when that Spirit entered him, he now changes again. This time the LORD allows a *ra* spirit—an evil or bad spirit—to trouble him, and by trouble, the Hebrew word means to frighten or terrify. Saul begins his descent from the throne into fear. It is a nightmarish existence of mental disorder brought on by a supernatural source. That is the reality of being separated from God.

26. What help did Saul's servants seek to deal with his terror?

A skilled harpist. They suggest music therapy in treating his mental disorder. It is interesting that Saul didn't have any advisors or ministers or even a priest to give him advice. Instead, he takes the advice of his servants, just as he did at the beginning when he was searching for donkeys in the wilderness. He has returned to a wilderness-like wandering.

27. What else did David have to recommend him to Saul?

David is a mighty man of valor and a man of war, and Saul coveted men of valor for his army. David is prudent in speech. That means he speaks well and with discernment and perception. He is handsome, and the LORD is with him. Whenever Saul is beset by the distressing spirit, David's playing on the harp would refresh him and drive the spirit away. David immediately meets with Saul's approval, and Saul loves him greatly, to the point of asking Jesse to let David remain in his presence and be his armor bearer.

❶❷ / ❿ Picture Comparison of the Kings' Anointings

I have outlined the elements from each event as they unfold. The details are not exactly the same, but on a high level, Samuel structures the two narratives with chiastic symmetry.

Let's first compare how Saul and David are presented initially. Saul is given a detailed introduction, including his genealogy; David's family, not so much. We know his father and three older brothers, but that is all. David's own name isn't even mentioned until the end of the anointing (16:13).

When Saul meets Samuel, he professed himself to be of lowly station—son of the least of all the families in the least of all the tribes of Israel—when in fact he was well-known, the firstborn son of a very wealthy man. David, by contrast, truly is the last and least-esteemed son in his family.

Now let's compare the overall structure.

① ② SAUL

9:1-14	Saul's father sends him on an errand (to find donkeys)
9:18-24	Saul and Samuel sit down to the feast
10:1-16	Saul anointed privately with oil and the Spirit, with signs but no witnesses
10:17-27	The process of singling out Saul as the king-to-be in front of the nation

⑩ DAVID

16:6-12	The process of singling out David as the king-to-be in front of his family
16:13	David anointed privately with oil and the Spirit, with witnesses but no signs
(16:11)*	David and Samuel sit down to the feast
16:14-23	David's father sends him on an errand (to play music for Saul)

The singling out of David appears to happen as they are arriving for the feast and Samuel is consecrating the family. Samuel declares they will not sit down (gather around the table) until David comes. Sitting down to the feast, therefore, must follow.

In both anointings, the LORD gives Samuel a heads-up and announces His pick in much the same way: "This is the one!" When Samuel anointed Saul, he did it privately so that only Saul knew, not even his family, perhaps because of the Philistine presence in Gibeah. Samuel then presented Saul to the nation with a tremendous build-up, going family by family to call out Saul in a grand reveal.

At David's anointing, there is also a tremendous build-up in the narrative, but on a smaller scale as Samuel passes from brother to brother until he comes to David; but there is no grand presentation of David to the nation.

There is only the reveal to David's immediate family but perhaps for the same reason that secrecy was needed with Saul, to limit the spread of the news because of the danger not just from the Philistines but from Saul as well. Where God grants Saul a small contingent of men to guard him, David has only his family.

There is an anointing not just with oil but also with the Spirit in both. Saul had confirming signs but no witnesses; David has confirming witnesses but no signs. That's a reversal. Just as the Spirit entered Saul, the Spirit now departs from Saul and enters David.

The chapter contains a good number of physical details, but the main contrast of the kings is in their spiritual state. The Spirit entering David and departing Saul is a breaking point in the narrative as the focus on David switches to a focus on Saul at verses 13-14. But the detail at the end about Jesse sending David on the errand helps round out the picture comparison with Chapter 9 (Saul's father sending him on an errand) and is purposely added for this reason. These same details about David's family will be repeated in the next chapter and will seem redundant, but that is only because they are needed for Chapter 17 to be compared to Chapter 2.

I think it is noteworthy that all the time Saul was king, the Spirit was present in him, and yet that indwelling Spirit seemed to have little influence over Saul's behavior. It empowered him to an extent, convicted him little, but the choices Saul made were still an outworking of his own carnal nature. Now, as the Spirit departs from him, whatever restraint he once had will be taken away as well.

Desire vs. Love

At the beginning of First Samuel, we contrasted the meanings of the names Peninnah and Hannah, rubies and grace. Now we have a contrast between the names Saul and David.

The name **Saul** means **"desired"**.
The name **David** means **"beloved"**.

Isn't it curious that these particular emotions of desire and love would be embodied in these first two kings of Israel?

What is the difference between desire and love?

To me, they are similar, but desire has a less noble quality than love. If I were to define it, I would say that desire is about taking. It is driven by lusts and selfishness and often objectifies the person or thing that is loved. There is a changeability and fleetingness to desire that often ends with emptiness on both sides. Desire says, "I want you. I desire you. But if you change, my desire for you may change."

Saul is a man desired by many for what he could give them, but their desire for him is based on their expectation of him more than on who he is as a person. Saul himself is the embodiment of desire in that he is driven by his lust for glory and the superficial validation of popularity. He wants what he wants, and he will take it by force if necessary, right up to the point where it makes him unpopular, and then he wants what will make him desirable in people's eyes again.

Love is a richer emotion of a less changeable and self-serving nature. When someone is beloved, they have an approval and acceptance for who they are at heart and the qualities they embody beyond just the surface appearance or offering. People will make sacrifices for the sake of a beloved one's well-being, comfort, or safety, even at the cost to themselves (as we will see with Jonathan). Love is about giving and often ends with a sense of inner peace and fulfillment on both sides.

We have not seen much of David in action yet, but we will look for this comparison between how people relate to David versus how people relate to Saul as we continue through the text.

APPLY THE PICTURE

Saul's Model

From this chapter forward, Saul is going to model for us what happens to a child of God when they give up a pursuit of an imperishable crown and become obsessed instead with keeping the perishable one. One of the outworkings of Saul's choice is that his life is now beset by fear, and it will rob him of power, love, and a sound mind.

The Spirit of God and the spirit of fear are opposed to one another. Paul tells us this unequivocally in Second Timothy 1:7:

> *"For God has not given us a spirit of fear, but of power and of love and of a sound mind."* —Second Timothy 1:7

In the last lesson, I talked a lot about power and where it is sourced, and it comes up again now. The power, love, and sound mind of which Paul is speaking are all granted by God and sourced in the Spirit. Without the Spirit, you will have to find another source for these things. You can try to empower yourself by your own strength, wisdom, or sheer force of will, but in the end, it will make you a controlling tyrant. Your love will twist into jealousy and desire, and the sound mind . . . well, that is just gone, and with it, self-control. All rationale is driven by fear of losing what you have, and your thought life will fixate on that goal. Once the fear takes you, there will be no comfort apart from the presence of the Spirit of God.

> *"There is no fear in love; but perfect love casts out fear, because fear involves torment. But he who fears has not been made perfect in love."* —First John 4:18

Saul now descends into a world of torment that is only relieved by the presence of the Spirit. Not David, but the Spirit in David, and that is an important distinction to make. David is not the solution to Saul's problem. In fact, David will become Saul's biggest problem. Because of the fear, the love that Saul professes for David here will quickly turn to jealousy and bitterness, and he will begin to fight a very one-sided battle with David for possession of the kingdom that God has taken from him.

Imagine how hard it would be for someone like Saul who, having achieved the crown and lost it, must now hand over his kingdom and align himself under a new king of God's choosing. You can almost hear him cry, "Over my dead body!" As the parables say, there will be weeping and gnashing of teeth for the unprofitable servant.

There are right and wrong kings with whom to align yourself, and you battle God's anointed king at your own peril.

LESSON 10: FIRST SAMUEL 17–18:7

⑪ Defeat of a Giant (and a Critic)

READ

First Samuel 17:1–18:7

NARRATIVE STRUCTURE

Picture #11 (17:1–18:9) records David's first battle and subsequent honoring (not quite a coronation, but almost). We will compare it with Saul's battle and coronation sequence in First Samuel 11 (Picture #3). Where Saul's battle narrative is related in a short, succinct narrative of 15 verses, David's corresponding narrative is told with decadent detail in 65 verses. (There are 58 verses in Chapter 17 alone, making it the longest chapter in the book.)

Picture #11 is divided into seven basic sections:

1) The enemy's challenge (17:1-16)
2) David enters the scene (17:17-22)
3) David questions the people (17:23-30)
4) David accepts the challenge (17:31-40)
5) David in battle (17:41-52)
6) The reward (17:53-58)
7) David is honored above Saul (18:1-7)

There is an oddly placed comment in First Samuel 17:12-15 that seems like an unnecessary repetition of David's family information from the previous chapter, but it isn't. It is part of the author's literary style to employ randomly placed comments as clues to what the key issues or comparisons are, or to mark pivotal points in the greater narrative. The information in this particular note sets up the dialogue between David and his brother in later verses—with a thematic point to make.

There is a distinct departure from the chronological timeline between the previous picture and this one, and that departure is something that has brought Chapter 17 under criticism by Bible scholars. I will talk about that at the end of the chapter.

BUILD THE PICTURE

The Enemy's Challenge (17:1-16)

From the anointing, we now move into a battle scene. Just as Saul immediately launched into war against the Ammonites in Chapter 11, now David will take on the Philistines. Chapter 17 opens with a detailed description of battle lines being drawn between Israel and the Philistines.

1. **Where does the battle set up?**

    The battle sets up in the foothills that are the buffer zone between the Philistine holdings on the coast and the hill country of Judah. The battleground is the Valley of Elah (Valley of the Oak). If the Philistines take this valley, it would give them access to the hill country leading toward Bethlehem and Hebron and would cut Judah off from Saul's Benjamin-based monarchy. The Philistines are employing a divide-and-conquer strategy. For Saul to keep Judah's support, he needs a victory in this battle.

    The Philistines encamp to the southwest of the Elah Valley. Saul and Israel encamp on the hill on the northeast side of the Elah Valley.

    It was a practice in ancient warfare for a champion from both sides to meet and fight it out instead of pressing entire armies into battle, thus preventing an unnecessary loss of blood on either side.

2. **Who is the antagonist on the Philistine side? How is he described?**

    The antagonist is Goliath of Gath, whose name means "splendor" (splendor of the winepress), and he is described in glorious detail. He is tall—six cubits and a span, which is roughly nine feet tall (taller than Saul). He is covered in bronze—helmet, coat of mail, leg armor, and a bronze javelin. The coat alone weighs five thousand shekels of bronze (approximately 130 pounds). He has a spear like a weaver's beam with an iron head weighing six hundred shekels (about fifteen pounds). And a shield-bearer goes before him.

So, he's like a walking fortress. He is the great lone oak that has planted itself in the middle of the Elah Valley.

3. **Who is the champion on Israel's side?**

   No one, at first. Goliath stands in the valley taunting Israel for forty days without any man of Israel approaching him. Saul won't fight him. Instead Saul offers a reward for any man willing to fight him, and there are no takers.

   Now we come to our oddly placed note. The dialogue could very easily skip from verse 11 to verse 16 without missing a beat.

   > *"When Saul and all Israel heard these words of the Philistine, they were dismayed and greatly afraid . . . And the Philistine drew near and presented himself forty days, morning and evening."* (17:11, 16)

   But between these verses, the author inserts a curious interlude in which David and his family are described.

4. **What information is given about David and his family?**

   > *"Now David was the son of that Ephrathite of Bethlehem Judah, whose name was Jesse, and who had eight sons. And the man was old, advanced in years, in the days of Saul. The <u>three oldest sons of Jesse had gone to follow Saul</u> to the battle. The names of his three sons who went to the battle were Eliab the firstborn, next to him Abinadab, and the third Shammah. David was the youngest. And <u>the three oldest followed Saul</u>. But David occasionally went and returned from Saul to feed his father's sheep at Bethlehem."* (17:12-15, emphasis added)

   David is given a more formal introduction than he was given in the previous chapter. This is reminiscent of Saul's introduction in First Samuel 9, only without the father's extensive genealogy mentioned.

Jesse's genealogy will remain undefined throughout First Samuel and have some implications in future chapters.

There is a repetition of information from the previous chapter about David's three older brothers and the fact that David was the youngest. An inclusio marked by the phrase "the three oldest followed Saul" frames their names: Eliab, Abinadab, and Shammah. These three went to war with Saul while David remained home tending the sheep at Bethlehem. The redundant details about David and his family cause some questions about the timeline that we will resolve at the end of the lesson, but the oddly placed information is not without point.

5. **Why focus on David's brothers now?**

    The information should serve as a reminder of what we already know about them from an earlier passage. These three brothers were passed over by Samuel as the next king. Eliab in particular was rejected by God in the same way Saul was rejected and for much the same reason. More importantly, these three men are the only men on the battlefield who know that David has been anointed as the new king.

    Think about the choice they must make in light of this knowledge. They have followed Saul into this battle. They are in his army. They have sworn allegiance to him. They are facing a national enemy, but the circumstances have put them into potential conflict if David should show up on the battlefield for some reason and decide to act. The brothers will then have to decide with which king their loyalty lies: Saul or David. They can't serve two kings. Fortunately, David has been left home tending sheep, far from the battle, so there is little danger of his kingship being brought into the limelight. Right?

    Wrong. David will show up on the battlefield and that loyalty will be tested. Eldest brother Eliab will have a serious reaction.

    So, you can see that the inclusion of this information about David and his brothers sets up a challenge on another level and fits with the overall theme. There are right and wrong kings with whom to align yourself, and at some point, you will be put in a position of having to declare your loyalty—or not. Either choice will have repercussions.

David Enters the Scene (17:17-22)

6. How does David enter the scene?

At the opening of the scene, we find David out in the field, tending sheep. He has been anointed king, but then he returns to life as usual, just like Saul did in First Samuel 11:5: *"Now there was Saul, coming behind the herd from the field..."*

Now, Jesse sends David on an errand to take supplies to his three brothers who are fighting with Saul on the battlefield. From Bethlehem to the battlefield is roughly 15 miles, so it is the better part of a day's journey. When David arrives, the armies are just drawing up in battle array and Goliath is delivering his evening challenge. David leaves his supplies with the supply clerk and runs out on the ridge to join his brothers.

When Goliath strides out to defy Israel, David hears him. He also sees the men's distress and hears them talking about the reward that Saul is offering for the man who kills Goliath.

David Questions the Men (17:23-30)

7. What reward is Saul offering for a champion to kill Goliath?

The reward is great riches, marriage to one of Saul's daughters, and exemption from taxes for his father's house. That's a pretty rich reward, but not enough to tempt any of the men of Israel. What good are earthly riches if you lose your life in pursuit of them?

David questions the men around him, and the truth of the reward is confirmed. The reward is mentioned first in verse 25, then David questions the men, and it is reiterated in verses 26-27, and then it is confirmed a final time in verse 30. David is in relentless pursuit of an understanding of the reward.

The text belabors David questioning people. There is a reward, isn't there? It is an awkward question to ask a person bluntly, because it is easy to read into it an expectation that the people should be pursuing the reward when they aren't. There is a reward, right? It is a rich reward. Why wouldn't you pursue the reward? Those kinds of questions can be a little convicting, because the people know they ought to value the reward and pursue it, but they count the cost of the battle and shy away.

8. **Why does David's oldest brother, Eliab, rebuke him angrily?**

    I think Eliab is in a very tenuous position. He knows David is the king-to-be, and David being on the battlefield and drawing attention to himself like this puts him in danger. If David starts something, it's going to get back to Saul (which it does). What if David demands that his brothers rally to him? What will Eliab do?

    Eliab wants David to leave, so he pulls rank on him—family rank. As the eldest brother, he is David's superior and an authority over David in his father's absence, and he doesn't know that David has been sent by their father with supplies. He gets angry with David and accuses him first, of shirking his duties at home by leaving his sheep, and, second, of pride and "wickedness" or insolence of heart—as if David has lifted himself up above his station. That is a very telling remark.

    There is that character about Eliab that is patterned after Saul's character and is the reason why God rejected him as king. Eliab's words betray his own focus on personal glory and his pride. David may be his younger brother, but he is also the anointed king. To speak to the king as Eliab has spoken to David would definitely qualify as lifting oneself up above one's station and reveals that Eliab has chosen loyalty to Saul over his brother. And perhaps Eliab feels a little conviction over shirking of his own duties. He is, after all, one of Saul's soldiers, and yet he is unwilling to fight, even when offered a reward. David clearly isn't afraid of the enemy and values the reward. David is making him look bad.

9. **What is David's reaction to his brother's rebuke?**

    I love how David stands up to his brother. He has not shirked his duties. He has delivered the goods and accomplished the mission on which his father sent him. He has a reason for being here, as he tells Eliab bluntly, and then he goes back to asking about the reward. He isn't cowed in the least by his brother.

David Accepts the Challenge (17:31-40)

News gets back to Saul that someone is asking about the reward, and Saul has David brought to him.

10. What is Saul's assessment of David?

Saul is openly skeptical. How can this young man go to battle against such a giant and save Israel? He is too young and inexperienced at war to fight. That seems an odd thing to say, since David was described as a valiant man of war when he came to Saul as a harpist. Why would Saul say that? And why is it that David isn't with Saul at the battle if he had been made Saul's armorbearer? Saul doesn't even seem to know him. These seem like inconsistencies in the text, and we will come back to this issue once we get through the chapter.

11. What case does David make for his abilities?

He has defeated lions and bears—but not by his own strength. He gives the credit to God for having delivered him. If God delivered him from the paws of the lion and bear, God will certainly deliver him from Goliath, who is nothing more than another unclean animal to David.

Saul accepts David's argument with the simple statement, "Go, and the LORD be with you!" David is a raw volunteer without any combat experience, but if he wants to tackle the giant, he can go for it. No one else is stepping up. Then Saul considers the issue of arming David to face Goliath. Unlike his brothers, David isn't kitted out for battle.

12. What armor does David wear into battle?

Saul tries to arm David with what Saul thinks will protect him, but Saul's armor is cumbersome, and David rejects it. It's too cumbersome and he can't move freely in it. Instead, he arms himself with five smooth stones from the brook and heads for the battlefield.

I have always wondered why David chose five stones. With that amount of conviction motivating him, I would have thought one stone was all he needed. Perhaps the stones were symbolic. The first stone took down Goliath, but the giant had four other brothers, according to Second Samuel 21:22. In addition to Goliath, King David and his men would kill the other four as well, making five total, one for each stone. But that is just conjecture.

David in Battle (17:41-52)

13. The narrative contrasts David the shepherd and Goliath the giant. What are the differences?

David doesn't fight the way Goliath and Saul fight. David rejects Saul's armor and weapons in favor of the simple tools of a shepherd's sling and five smooth stones. These make him lighter on his feet, where Goliath is ponderous, and able to fight from a distance, where Goliath's strength is at a disadvantage. David is small, whereas Goliath is gigantic. David is relatively unarmed, whereas Goliath is a fortress. David is untested on the battlefield, whereas Goliath is a veteran fighter.

Goliath judges his own strength, weapons, and skill as superior to David. He sees David as a cocky youth who doesn't know any better, and takes it almost as an insult disrespect that Israel would send out such an unworthy adversary. *"Am I a dog, that you come to me with sticks?"* (First Samuel 17:43)

Goliath sees the battle as a man against a man with physical weapons, and he curses David by his gods. David sees the battle as man against God and without physical weapons and rebukes him with like wording. Goliath is fighting the LORD and the battle is the LORD's. David glorifies the LORD as Israel's real champion, and he enters the battle alongside the LORD.

14. How did David win the battle?

David struck Goliath with one stone in the middle of the forehead, then finished him off with his own sword—but the battle was not won by the sword.

I think David won the battle long before that stone struck home between Goliath's eyes. He won the battle simply in seeing himself and Goliath the way God saw them. The battle is a matter of mental perspective—how the enemy is seen—and in this David is a contrast to Saul.

Saul judged Goliath by his estimation of himself and found himself wanting. Goliath was taller than he was, more heavily armed, and more skilled. Saul relied on his own strength and army to win him victories, and he had met his match in Goliath. He relied on what his eyes told him, judged the enemy by appearance, and refused to step out in faith. For forty days he had done nothing except offer a reward to any man willing to tackle the giant.

David did not look at himself in comparison to Goliath. He looked at Goliath in comparison to God. Goliath may have been a giant to him, but he wasn't a giant to God. Goliath's physical strength and weapons were nothing compared to God's power. All David saw was an enemy who defied God and wanted to make God's people his servant, and that is what sent David into battle when Saul (and Eliab) wouldn't fight.

The Reward (17:53-58)

15. How does the battle end?

Once the champion is defeated, the Philistine army scatters and Israel and Judah pursue them to the entrance to the Valley of Elah, and then as far as Gath and Ekron.

Gath means the "winepress," and Ekron means "torn up by the roots." Goliath of Gath, the splendor of the winepress, had planted himself like an oak in the Valley of Elah. David has cut him down and now his people are being trod upon like grapes in a winepress and thoroughly uprooted. The imagery within the words paints the clear picture of a thorough rout.

16. Israel returns and takes the plunder. What does David take from the battlefield for his trophies?

David keeps Goliath's armor and takes his head to Jerusalem. Jerusalem seems like an odd detail and out of context. Why take the head to Jerusalem? Jerusalem hasn't been mentioned since the days of Joshua, and it was still considered a Jebusite town in the days of the judges. It doesn't have any prominence at this time that it should be a place of honor to hang a trophy.

Usually the king would take it back to his city to put it on display, but was it Saul's trophy or David's? Who gets credit for it, the Benjamite king or the Judean king?

Jerusalem is situated on the border of Benjamin and Judah. Technically it was allotted to Benjamin's lands (Joshua 18:28), but members of the tribe of Judah reside there and have some claim to it. I think it is curious that David should pick a border town between himself and Saul, in a location shared by both tribes, almost as if he is sharing the honor with both sides. Jerusalem will become the City of David when King David conquers it in Second Samuel 5, and this is the first mention of David's identification with Jerusalem.

David's action here is even more magnanimous considering he has dealt with Saul's enemy for him—a little like Saul did with Judah's enemies, the Amalekites. Do you remember what Saul did to Judah after the battle with Agag? He set up a monument to himself in Judah's territory to remind them to whom they owed the victory. David could easily have used this moment to self-aggrandize, and yet he shares the victory and the spoil.

17. Why does Saul ask Abner about David?

Verses 55–58 record a curious exchange between Saul and Abner as they watch David sally out to confront Goliath. "Whose son is this youth?" Saul asks. The question is repeated three times, finally to David himself. This is odd since David became his harpist and armorbearer in Chapter 16. Why doesn't Saul know him? The events don't seem to fit the timeline. The final interview between Saul and David is a bit puzzling for this reason, but it fits perfectly with the overall theme of the reward and also as a structural element for the picture comparison of Saul and David's first battles.

In regards to the theme, David has taken his spoil, the soldiers have taken theirs, but the reward isn't complete yet. There is still that promise that Saul made to grant exemption from taxes to the house of the victor's father. This is perhaps why Saul seeks to know who David's father is in the final section of the chapter, that the reward might be granted. This also fits with the greater picture of David as a king who shares his spoil with all the people and sees that no one who had any part of the effort goes unacknowledged. We will see this same behavior pattern in First Samuel 30, when David shares his riches not just with his men but sends gifts of spoil to the elders of Judah and his extended list of friends.

We will get to the picture comparison shortly, and address the timeline issue as well, but first let's finish with David's being honored after the battle.

David is Honored Above Saul (18:1-7)

David isn't coronated as king after the battle the way Saul was, but his ascent into public recognition is on par with it. He is first approved by the king and army commander, then by the king's son, then by people, and finally by king's servants. Lastly, he is lauded by the women in song.

This time it states that he is loved not by the king but by the king's son Jonathan. An inclusio marked by the phrase "Jonathan loved him as his own soul" in verses 1 and 3 highlights the covenant that Jonathan makes with David.

18. What does it mean that Jonathan's soul was knit with David's?

We have seen Jonathan in action and now David, and they fight with similar tactics and a similar faith in God. I think this is part of what knits Jonathan to David—he identifies with David as a warrior.

They are similar in several ways:

- Both faced enemies who were superior in the eyes of men, and yet saw their enemies as inferior because they looked at them from God's perspective. Jonathan recognized in David a man who saw life from the same perspective as he did.
- Both gave God glory in the battle and aligned themselves with God's priorities.
- Both stepped out on their own in faith despite the odds.
- God validated both of them with a resounding victory.

There are a couple of differences between them:

- Jonathan had been in formal battle before, whereas David had only fought lions and bears (according to the narrative in this picture).

- One fought with a sword and one with a sling and stone. Both weapons were equally effective and appropriate for the kind of challenge they faced, but they were also appropriate to David and Jonathan's skill levels. Each man used what he had to its best advantage.

19. How does Jonathan honor David?

Jonathan literally clothes David in honor with his own clothes (the clothes of royalty). He gives him his robe and armor, and even presents him with his sword, bow, and belt.

From this point on, David begins to receive tremendous recognition and approval. Even though David is not crowned king at this point, the people honor him above Saul in the victory celebration. David has achieved a certain momentum that is rocketing him toward a crown, but he can't claim the crown until the king who currently wears it gives it up.

These are some picture comparisons between David and Jonathan, but the author's intent is to compare the two kings. Now let's look at David's comparison to Saul.

③/⑪ Picture Comparison of the Kings' Battles

The picture of Saul's first battle and coronation (Picture #3) and David's first battle and subsequent honoring (Picture #11) are structured very closely. It is good to look at the elements that compare, but also at what is added to David's narrative that isn't in Saul's account.

The Enemy's Challenge

Both narratives begin with the opening challenge and introduction of the people's dilemma.

③ Nahash taunts the people of Jabesh Gilead. (11:1-4)
⑪ Goliath taunts Saul and the armies of Israel. (17:1-16)

There is an addition here in David's narrative. We have the oddly placed note introducing David that is patterned vaguely after Saul's introduction in Chapter 9 but with the repeated information about David's older brothers from Chapter 16. The information is redundant but with a point. It sets up the narrative for the new king to make his debut in battle, and with his arrival comes the choice these brothers must make over which king they will follow into battle, Saul or David. There are right and wrong kings with which to align themselves, and in the end, they choose the wrong king. David steps up to the battle with God alone.

The King Enters the Scene

❸ Saul is at home tending herds. He comes in from the field to hear the news of Nahash's challenge. (11:15)

⑪ David is at home tending flocks. He arrives at the battlefield to hear Goliath's challenge. (17:15-22)

Both kings have been anointed, and yet they have gone home to resume life as usual. Both come in from the field to hear of breaking events. This is one of those very fine details that helps cement the comparison between the two pictures.

The King Reacts to the Challenge

❸ Saul questions the people and reacts to the threat by sending a threat of his own to Israel—rally around me or else. God then sends His fear upon the people that prods them into supporting Saul. (11:6-7)

⑪ David reacts to the news by questioning the men about the reward. There's a reward, right? The text belabors David's focus on the positive goal rather than issuing a negative threat. (17:24-30)

Eliab's rebuke of David is an added element without a parallel in Saul's narrative, but it develops the theme of the reward. Eliab shuns the reward that David values, and follows Saul's lead in not stepping up to deal with the enemy.

The King Accepts the Challenge

❸ Saul sends word to Jabesh Gilead that he will fight the enemy. (11:9-10)

⑪ David declares to Saul that he will fight the enemy. (17:31-40)

In both narratives, the kings have a rebel faction opposing them who doubt their ability to save the people. For Saul, it is the men of Belial.

> *"But some rebels [men of Belial] said, 'How can this man save us?' So they despised him, and brought him no presents. But he held his peace."* —First Samuel 10:27

In David's narrative, it is Saul who expresses this doubt.

> *"And Saul said to David, 'You are not able to go against this Philistine to fight with him; for you are a youth, and he a man of war from his youth.'"* —First Samuel 17:33

So, the two narratives share this element of the rebel doubters, leading to a comparison between Saul and the men of Belial. Hold that thought.

The King Goes to Battle

- **(3)** Saul goes to battle with Israel around him. (11:11)
- **(11)** David goes into battle with God alone. (17:41-52)

Saul has the more majestic army, but the battle is described in one verse; David is alone but his battle is described in eleven verses. David's epic confrontation completely eclipses Saul's victory with an army of multitudes. That is a comparison of values. God would rather honor the man who steps out alone in faith than a rebel bolstered by an army. It's a glory issue.

The Reward

- **(3)** Apart from saving Jabesh Gilead from Nahash, there is no record of Saul or the people taking the spoil of their enemies.
- **(11)** David takes his spoil, the people plunder the Philistines, and David claims the portion of the reward for his father's house. (17:52-54) The reward is only mentioned in David's narrative.

The King Confronts the Rebels Who Refused to Acknowledge Him

- **(3)** At the end of Saul's battle, the people call for the rebels who had refused to acknowledge Saul as king. (11:12-13)
- **(11)** In David's narrative, we have the curious closing discussion between Saul and Abner over the question of who David is. (17:55-58)

The main theme of this element is about the reward, but there is a secondary purpose in recording this conversation—it creates the final parallel with Saul and the men of Belial. Just as the men of Belial were brought face to face with Saul, the king they refused to acknowledge, so Saul is brought face to face with David, the king he will refuse to acknowledge. David has done everything that Saul did to validate himself as a legitimate savior of the people, but Saul doesn't see it, and David doesn't enlighten him. He, too, holds his peace and simply says, I am the son of Jesse.

Saul's lack of recognition of David is emphasized to the point where the entire episode seems out of place in the timeline. But remember this author's literary style. Whenever a set of verses seems out of place, they are not. In this case, David's narrative was purposely written to parallel Saul's narrative, to create this comparison between Saul and the men of Belial. It is a subtle but powerful detail in its implications.

The King's Coronation

❸ The people take Saul to Gilgal, and he is coronated there. There is much rejoicing and celebration (11:14-15). The coronation continues into Chapter 12 as Israel covenants herself to her new king.

⓫ David isn't coronated, but he might as well be. The honor he receives outstrips Saul (18:1-7). Jonathan covenants himself to the new king.

APPLY THE PICTURE

The Focus on Appearances

When I look through David's narrative so far, this issue stands out as a point for consideration. The contrast of how God sees as opposed to how man sees marked the start of David's narrative in Chapter 16:

> "... For the LORD does not see as man sees; for man looks at the outward appearance, but the LORD looks at the heart." —First Samuel 16:7

Examples of how this theme of judging by appearances runs through Chapters 16–17 include:

- » Samuel's choice of Eliab for king (16:6-12)
- » Goliath's appearance (17:4-7)
- » How Saul sees David compared to Goliath (17:8, 21)
- » How Goliath sees David (17:42)
- » How David sees Goliath (17:45-47)

Let's look at the David and Goliath scenario.

Goliath's Model

We live in a world that is actively engaged in challenging God's authority, the authority of His Word, and our faith in Christ; and the champions who step up to fight for that worldview come in myriad forms. They can be news media, government officials, scientists, and medical experts, or even just the weight of public opinion and social media. Our giants can be personal combatants at work, in our social groups, at our schools, or even at home or within the congregational body.

When we face our Goliaths, how does their appearances affect us? (How did Goliath's appearance affect Saul and David?)

Think about how much of our reaction is based on appearance or perception of strength, and how that appearance influences our desire to engage them. Fighting a good fight—fighting effectively—begins first with seeing ourselves rightly and then, seeing our enemies rightly. Getting past appearances can be one of the hardest parts of the battle.

- **How do we see ourselves?**

    Do you judge yourself compared to them, or do you judge them compared to God? You-against-them is a physical battle, but them-against-God is a spiritual battle; but then physical battles are really spiritual battles at heart. For us, the battle isn't fought with swords so much as with words, which can be daunting if you are not a good debater. I admit I am not. I don't speak off the cuff well because I have to think about things, and I admit I don't like engaging in verbal combat. But this is something I have learned. You don't always have to meet an enemy's argument with an argument. The truth can be a sword, but it can also be a stone—a simpler challenge that can cause the argument to collapse simply by finding a weak spot and poking a hole in it. I'll talk about some stone-slinging strategies in a moment, but this is the most important point to understand. All God asks is that we stand where we are, and do what we can with what we have. When we start making comparisons of our abilities to those of our combatants, we lose the battle before it begins.

- **How do we see our combatant?**

    Inevitably we have a gut reaction to a person yelling in our face, or maybe they repulse us in other ways. Maybe they are openly engaged in a sinful lifestyle. Maybe they are physically abusive. Maybe they don't look so good or smell good. Maybe they have built this impregnable fortress around themselves that keeps us from penetrating who they are behind all that armor.

Goliath fought a physical fight behind a fortress of armor. We fight a spiritual fight that is often more a battle of words, and yet there are ways our combatants can build fortresses around themselves in the way they communicate.

- **What forms do these fortresses take?**

    The fortress can be a bulwark of knowledge, public opinion, or simply personal beliefs or a refusal to acknowledge God. Anger, silence, excuses, sarcasm, self-pity, and a victim mentality can become defense mechanisms our combatants use to keep us from getting to the heart of the battle which is the spiritual relationship with God.

- **How do we fight these things?**

    We can get sucked into a battle against the armor, which we cannot win, but then that is what the enemy wants. He wants us fighting according to his strengths and his terms. That is the strategy with which Saul approached Goliath, and it kept him at a stalemate. You can't fight Goliath on Goliath's terms. If the enemy is angry or silent, we don't fight anger with anger and silence with silence. So, how do we get past the defenses, then? I am not a skilled counselor to offer advice on this, but I think each battle has to be tackled individually and in its own unique way. Sometimes you just need a well-placed stone instead of a sword.

- **How do we dress for battle?**

    Ephesians 6:10-20 lists our battle dress:
    - » Belt of truth
    - » Breastplate of righteousness
    - » Shoes of preparation of the gospel of peace
    - » Shield of faith
    - » Helmet of salvation
    - » Sword of the Spirit (Word of God)

The list ends with this final instruction:

> *"praying always with all prayer and supplication in the Spirit, being watchful to this end with all perseverance and supplication for all the saints—and for me, that utterance may be given to me, that I may open my mouth boldly to make known the mystery of the gospel,"* —Ephesians 6:18-19

Don't be afraid. Speak boldly! That's what David and Jonathan did.

David's (and Jonathan's) Model

David and Jonathan knew how to fight a good fight against the loud-mouthed Philistines of their day. We, too, face battles like David and Jonathan did, but ours are usually limited to the verbal kind. We battle over words, particularly over the Word of God. The Word of God is the sword that we carry into battle, but the enemy seeks ways to blunt that sword, just as the Philistines found ways to blunt Israel's weapons as we saw in First Samuel 13:16-23. A sword is only effective if it has an edge.

It takes skill and a great deal of courage to face an antagonist in a battle over the Word of God. Some of us are like Jonathan. We have been through these battles before, and we may have more extensive knowledge of the Word and can meet an enemy sword for sword. Others of us are like David. We have a simpler knowledge and skill level, are untested in formal battle, and may not be able to meet the enemy sword for sword, but we can meet the enemy stone for sword and still be just as effective.

Defeating Critics: Handling Scriptural Criticism

Critics of the Bible are a version of Goliath for us today. They love to point out that this text we tout as the inspired Word of God is full of contradictions and "inconsistencies." They will then argue that to explain the inconsistencies, one must say that the Word of God is the work of many authors and also many editors who, over the years, have redacted and revised portions of the text. I see this argument a lot when I am researching Bible studies, and it is put out there by "giants"—leading scholars and Bible experts who have a very deep knowledge of the Scripture.

In regards to the issue of many authors, it is true that the Bible as a whole is a compilation of writings from different authors over the years. That is without dispute. But then the critics add that the text was then edited or redacted over hundreds of years. That becomes a problem.

Paul offers this rebuke to the Galatian church: *"Having begun in the Spirit, are you now being made perfect by the flesh?"* (Galatians 3:3) While that rebuke is given in context of not returning to the law, it presents a principle that what was Spirit-inspired and Spirit-delivered is not then perfected by men's efforts.

I fully believe that the Spirit of God inspired the original authors, who delivered the text as it was meant to be read without need for man's addition, redaction, or revision. Having begun in the Spirit, the text has not been perfected by man's editing. We are warned against adding or removing text from God's Word. Biblical transcriptionists have been exceedingly exacting in maintaining the integrity of the text, and while errors in copying may have occurred, they do not affect the overall intent of the passages, nor do they alter passages in their entirety.

The problem occurs when scholars start using this "other author" argument in order to reconcile what they consider to be discrepancies in the text, and this will be an inconsistency in their argument. On the one hand, they will attribute the writing of First Samuel to Samuel, but when they get to Chapter 17 and find information repeated—and seemingly inconsistent with the previous chapter—they will say: "Another author must have written this part of the account, perhaps at a later date or without knowledge of Samuel's text. We don't know who the author is, when he wrote, or why he wasn't aware of Samuel's writing, but it doesn't fit the timeline and it has redundancies; therefore, another author must have written it." They completely undercut Samuel's authorship of this passage, when in fact, the inconsistencies and redundancies are completely in keeping with Samuel's literary style, structure, and purpose, as I have shown you with the narrative structure explanations and picture comparisons.

This is how God's Word becomes blunted. Critics undermine its character as an inspired work given to a particular author and transform it into something written by an unknown number of unidentified authors, revised, redacted, and even expanded over history. Farther down the line, this argument becomes the means by which they begin to explain away prophetic Scripture by saying "other authors" wrote parts at later dates in history after the prophetic word had been fulfilled (therefore, it must not be prophetic at all). The "other authors" argument can lead us away from viewing God's Word as an inspired work of the Spirit and give that credit to men, thus relegating it to the "traditions of men." Having begun in the Spirit, is the text now perfected by men? No, it is not.

You can't just throw in the "other authors" argument whenever it seems to suit a difficulty in the text. **That is the blunting of the sword of the Word of God.**

You cannot say that the redundancies are without purpose. **That is a blunting of the sword of the Word of God.**

I am going to give you some strategies in how to fight a good fight against critics who come at us with this critical argument over the supposed "inconsistencies" in the Biblical text by giving you some stones for slinging at this enemy argument. So, let's take a stab at the criticism of First Samuel 16–18.

The argument: There are inconsistencies in the timeline between First Samuel 16 and 17-18:7; therefore, "another author" must have written First Samuel 17. The gist of this argument hinges on the fact that Saul knew who David was in Chapter 16, but he doesn't know who he is in Chapter 17. Here are a few points they note:

- David is described as a mighty man of valor in 16:18, but according to David's own words in 17:34-37, he has only ever battled lions and bears as a shepherd.

- David came to Saul and is made Saul's armor-bearer in 16:21. Compare that with David's absence by Saul's side in the battle with Goliath. According to 17:15, David is still at home and only makes occasional forays to see Saul—and most certainly isn't his armor-bearer at this point.

- Saul knows Jesse is David's father in 16:22, but doesn't know who his father is in 17:55-58.

- In addition to these, critics point out the redundant information about

David and his family between Chapters 16 and 17. Why repeat the information?

Sounds like a pretty solid argument, doesn't it?

How do we reconcile the seeming inconsistency without using the "other authors" argument?

Very simply. We know Samuel is a very exacting writer who structures his accounts very carefully, and he is known to forgo a linear timeline in favor of chiastic structures, inclusios, and parallels when he creates the pictures in his narrative. If he deviates from a timeline, it is because there is another literary structure in play. This is why I have made it a point to stress Samuel's way of structuring his narratives—so that you will not be confused when he switches gears between Chapter 16 and 17.

First Samuel 16 presents contrasting pictures that support Samuel's theme of ascents and descents. As David begins his ascent, Saul begins his descent, and it is facilitated by the Spirit. This theme is in keeping with the rhythm that Samuel has perpetuated throughout the narrative.

First Samuel 17-18:7 is a separate picture and is written as a parallel picture to Chapters 11-12, not Chapter 16. The comparison validates David's rise to kingship by showing how he follows the pattern of Saul, with some significant differences.

This chapter is not the work of another author who wasn't aware of Samuel's writings. This chapter is wholly in keeping with Samuel's established writing style and structuring of his narratives. His method of picture comparison is consistent with how he presented the wives of Elkanah, then the priesthood, and now the kings.

By the same token, the redundant details about David's family in Chapter 17 is another of Samuel's literary devices for drawing attention to a particular theme or pivotal moment by inserting oddly placed information. He does this in First Samuel 21:7, 23:6, 25:1, and 28:3.

The critics' "another author" argument is unfounded.

We should note that Samuel isn't the only biblical author to pick and choose elements out of a timeline to fit a particular theme he is following. We see this same thing happen with the four Gospel accounts. All four reference the same timeline, and yet the authors don't necessarily hold to a strict linear order of events because they are painting different pictures of Christ.

Five Smooth Stones

You can meet the critics' sword with a sword and answer their arguments with a deeper knowledge if you have it. Or you can deflate an argument by poking a hole in it—creating some doubt that makes them step back and think. So, here are five smooth stones you can cast at an antagonist who challenges you about inconsistencies like this in the Scriptural text:

1. Ask them why they assume the Bible is structured only in a linear timeline order.
2. If the narrative doesn't follow a timeline order, it is usually because the author is using another literary structure in keeping with the author's writing style.
3. Details are repeated to create parallels with other pictures or cause the reader to recall previous details (like David's brothers being the only men on the battlefield who knew David was king).
4. The author may be pulling together select parts of the timeline to build his theme.
5. The Old Testament is about building and comparing pictures. You may not be comparing the right pictures. First Samuel 17 wasn't meant to be compared with Chapter 16. It is too be compared with Chapter 11.

That will give most of them pause to think because they might not know about the Bible's literary structures (chiastic structures, inclusios, and parallelisms)—but you do, because I have taught you. This is why I teach aspects of Bible study like structure—so that when you face this enemy argument, you might be able to speak boldly from knowledge of God's Word. I have just given you five smooth stones. They don't require you to explain everything. They merely poke holes in the giant's argument.

Inconsistency Between the Masoretic and Septuagint Texts

This issue over what to do with inconsistencies goes back to the earliest translations, including the Greek Septuagint. All the verses in Chapters 17 and 18 where these "inconsistencies" and "redundancies" occur in David's narrative are kept in the Masoretic (Hebrew text) but omitted from the Septuagint (the Greek version of the Old Testament). The Septuagint's omissions include the repeated details about David's family along with all of David's discussion on the battlefield with the men about the reward and Eliab's rebuke of David. The Septuagint cuts out verses 12–31. It also cuts out Saul's conversation with Abner in 17:55-58 and 18:1-5 where it talks about Jonathan's heart being knit to David—a detail that crops up again a couple chapters from now.

While the details in the Hebrew seem redundant, the Septuagint loses the parallelisms by omitting them and destroys much of Samuel's structure. I think this is a grave error, and one reason to study the Old Testament in its original Hebrew and not the Greek, however venerably the Septuagint is regarded. It is only another translation, after all. I realize I am like David, slinging stones against the giants of biblical scholarship in my criticism of the Septuagint, but there it is.

Questions for Reflection

- In general, do we see people as God sees people? What should we be looking for when we evaluate people for leadership roles?

- Who has been a Goliath for you in your life?

- Did you try to tackle them alone, or did you join God in the battle?

- Did you battle them on their terms (anger for anger, silence for silence) or did you choose a different tact? How successful were you?

- If God gave you victory over them, did you give God credit?

- Do you believe that the Word of God is written as God intended, or do you think it has been refined by many editors?

LESSON 11: FIRST SAMUEL 18:8-19:24

My Worst Enemy

SERIES STRUCTURE

In Chapters 18 and 19, we return to the theme of ascents and descents as the narrative alternates between Saul and David, much like it did with Samuel and the house of Eli in Chapter 2 but with even sharper structure.

Picture #12 (18:8-30) highlights Saul's descent into fear as David ascends in honor at every turn.

Picture #13 (19:1-24) focuses on Saul's further descent into persecuting David.

⑫ Saul Fears David

READ

First Samuel 18:7-30

NARRATIVE STRUCTURE

Picture #12 details Saul's three-fold effort to remove the threat of David's rivalry. Each time, David gains more popularity and honor in the eyes of the people, and as a result, Saul becomes more afraid of him. That is the repeated phrase throughout, that Saul was afraid of David. The aggression is all on Saul's side and the author provides us with a transparent view of Saul's thoughts.

Picture #12 is divided into five main sections:

1) Narrator's opening comment: Saul's resentment (18:8-9)
2) Saul's first attack (18:10-12)
3) Saul's second scheme (18:13-16)
4) Saul's third scheme (18:17-29)
5) Narrator's closing comment: David's honor (18:30)

BUILD THE PICTURE

Saul's Resentment

1. **What begins Saul's turn of heart away from David?**

   Jealousy. The women had lauded David for having killed ten times the number of enemies as Saul. Of course, the women's words are hyperbole, but it rankles Saul even so.

2. **What did Saul have to be jealous about?**

   Nothing really. He wasn't the one who had wanted the fight. He had offered a reward to anyone else who was willing to fight Goliath. He waited forty days without acting, and stepped up to the battlefield only after David slew the giant. So why should he get any credit at all? Because it is in the nature of a king to take things. He takes men for his army, and he takes credit for the victory those men achieve when they win the battle on his behalf. The victory is theirs, but the glory is his, and a king does not like to share his glory, particularly not with a young shepherd from Bethlehem.

   Notice that when David was challenging Goliath, he never mentioned fighting for the glory of King Saul? He called Israel's army the army of the living God. He gave all the glory to God, and he fought as a warrior for God, not Saul. Saul has been cut out of the credits throughout this whole incident, which marks the beginning of his descent.

   Also notice here how Saul's jealousy over David being ascribed a greater conquest quickly changes to a suspicion of David's loyalties and motives. What more can David have but the kingdom?

Saul's First Attack

Saul's first attempt to rid himself of his rival is an open attack while under the influence of the distressing spirit.

3. **The scene opens with a note that Saul was prophesying under the influence of the distressing spirit. Is his prophesying a divine act of revealing God's inspired instruction?**

    No. This is more along the lines of ecstatic ranting. The word for "prophesy" here is the Hebrew word *naba*, which describes an act of bubbling up and pouring forth, but it can apply to false prophets as well as godly prophets. Is Saul among the prophets? Which spirit is driving him? The one that terrifies him.

    The fear has come upon Saul, and the fear focuses on David. Where David's music had once brought Saul comfort, now Saul seeks comfort in killing David and removing his rival. The text emphasizes what each man held in his hand: David, a musical instrument, and Saul, a spear. Saul catches David in an unguarded moment and attacked.

    There are right and wrong ways to keep a crown.

4. **David escapes twice when Saul had him cornered, and Saul becomes afraid of David. Why?**

    The text says it is because the LORD was with David and had departed from Saul. This is an echo of the wording in First Samuel 16:14: *"But the Spirit of the LORD departed from Saul..."*

    I don't think Saul had recognized initially that the Spirit had left him. He found himself unexpectedly beset by a faceless fear, and David's harp-playing helped ease it. But now a thought has been planted in his mind that David might be his rival for the throne. David has eclipsed him in popularity and escaped twice when the spear should not have missed. There can be no other conclusion but that the LORD is with David. *He has been harboring his rival in his own house all this time!* The horror of it must have gripped him.

Saul's Second Scheme

5. **What is Saul's next scheme to get rid of David?**

   Saul promotes David. He makes him a captain of thousands so that David wouldn't always be in his presence. Out of sight, out of mind. But David's new position only puts him in the eyes of the people more, and he increases in popularity. Israel and Judah alike love David.

6. **What was the source of David's success?**

   It wasn't so much his visibility with the people, but because the LORD was with him, and he behaved wisely in all his ways. This is a stark contrast to Saul, who hasn't behaved wisely at all.

7. **What does it mean to behave wisely?**

   It means to think before you act, to consider what is the better way and thereby prosper from a wise decision. David was a thinking man, and he comes across as superior to Saul who is more given to hasty decisions and reactions. And Saul fears David for this reason. There is something really scary about a thinking man.

Saul's Third Scheme

8. **What is Saul's final scheme to get rid of David?**

   Alliance by marriage. He offers David his oldest daughter Merab as wife. The name Merab means "increase," from the root, *rabab*, meaning "to be multiplied or become great"—to become ten thousand *[rabab]* on top of a thousand, as David writes in Psalm 144:13. Curiously, the context in which the word *rabab* appears, with a few exceptions, is usually in regards to enemies or troubles increasing.

   When Saul offers his daughter to David in marriage, doesn't it seem like he is adding honor to David rather than trying to kill him? After all, this was supposed to be part of David's reward for killing Goliath—and for David killing his ten thousands on top of Saul's thousands. But Saul makes a condition to the marriage arrangement. David must be valiant for Saul and fight the LORD's battles if he is going to become the son-in-law of the king. Saul could have sent David to the front lines without using the marriage to his daughter as an excuse to do it. But instead, he uses his daughter's marriage covenant to trap David and bring him into a form of bondage meant to secure David's death and the loss of his crown. Saul is forever treading on God's ordained covenant relationships.

The author reveals for us what is truly in Saul's thoughts. Saul wants David dead, but in a way that the blame won't fall back on him. His tactic is to send David out to battle the Philistines and hope that he dies in battle. Let him die at the enemy's hand, not the king's hand. Then the death can be chalked up to an act of God. (We should note that this tactic is the same one David will use on Uriah the Hittite in Second Samuel 11. He will put Uriah on the front lines so that he will die in battle, just so that David can take Bathsheba for himself.)

Saul's condition seems absurd. Being valiant for Saul goes without saying for a soldier in the king's army, but when does David *not* fight the LORD's battles? There is a mixed message here. Has David already earned the reward of Saul's daughter for fighting Goliath? Why then is the reward now contingent on future service? And if he is judged in the end not to have fought valiantly enough or fulfilled his obligation to the LORD, does that mean the status of son-in-law will be denied?

This is a very subtle scheme meant, in essence, to get David to kill himself in pursuit of a goal he has already achieved. David has already been granted the crown to the physical kingdom by God Himself. He doesn't need an alliance with the earthly king through a marriage contract to accomplish this. But now the earthly king (his enemy) comes to David and presents this alternative way to secure the physical throne, if he agrees to certain conditions.

On the surface, the same kingdom is being pursued, but that fact is misleading. There are actually two "rewards" in the picture. One is a throne in an earthly kingdom and the second is an eternal kingship. The first one has been granted to each of the kings by God Himself, apart from their merit. The second is the reward of an eternal kingship and *that* must be merited. Saul did not find out about the eternal kingship until he had lost it, and David doesn't know it's on the table for him, too, at this point. The eternal kingship is the true reward, but because it remains unknown, the only goal that the kings see is securing the earthly kingdom. Thus, the first "reward" that was granted while unmerited is now pushed forward to become a reward that must now be merited. Where there were once two, now there is only one reward.

There is a twist in how the reward is defined; there is also a change in king granting it. The earthly crown is no longer something God has given David; it now seemingly becomes something he must negotiate with Saul. Think about how this changes the reward dynamic.

God gifted David his place in the physical kingdom by grace, and it was assured by God's authority. But God alone offers the greater reward of an eternal kingship, which is still out there if David remains obedient to Him as King. Saul's "gift" mimics God's gift, *but* it is limited to the physical kingdom alone. The irony is that Saul is offering David something that Saul has already lost to David. The eternal kingship, on the other hand, is the reward that Saul cannot offer.

The reward of the physical kingdom isn't something for which David should be negotiating with Saul, and yet this is where Saul seeks to embroil him. Saul offers the bride and the inheritance of the throne conditionally by making them contingent on David's future loyalty, obedience, and service to himself. With Saul, the inheritance is granted and yet not granted, suggesting that even if David fights the LORD's battles valiantly all his life, in the end, David's effort to secure the crown may fall short. Basically, Saul is saying, bow to me and I will give you the kingdom.

In response to Saul's offer, David makes a very self-effacing statement that he isn't worthy of the honor of being the king's son-in-law (much like the self-effacing statement that Saul made to Samuel at the time of his anointing). The text does not indicate whether David's response constitutes a yes or a no, and yet, from verse 19, it appears that the marriage is brokered. Then Saul reneges on the agreement and gives Merab away to another man, without any explanation as to why David was denied his reward.

9. **Why does Saul give Merab to another man instead?**

   First, let's consider the man to whom Saul gives her. His name is Adriel the Meholathite. A little digging into Scripture reveals that he is the son of Barzillai the Gileadite and comes from the town of Abel Meholah, near Jabesh Gilead. Now, the people of Jabesh Gilead were the ones Saul saved in his first battle, and they are loyal to Saul. Perhaps Adriel fought alongside Saul in that first battle. That is pure conjecture, but for whatever reason, Saul decides to visit the reward of a champion on Adriel and gives him Merab as a wife.

   Call it favoritism or political maneuvering, Saul's act is a slap in the face to David and somewhat self-defeating. It is a dishonorable thing to break a covenant like this. In fact, it is a very Philistine-like action. A similar thing happened to Samson in Judges 15, and a picture comparison might shed a little light on why Saul did what he did.

   There had been a falling out between Samson and the Philistines over the solving of Samson's riddle at his wedding. Samson uncovered their treachery, and when he delivers their reward, instead of giving them the thirty sets of clean linen garments, he gives them bloody, used garments taken off of thirty dead Philistines. Later, when Samson returns to collect his wife, he finds that his Philistine father-in-law has married her off to another man. Just as Samson had delivered a less than honorable reward for solving the riddle, the father-in-law denies him his reward—his wife—and offers a second-best option of his younger daughter.

   The Philistine father-in-law did this out of resentment and a desire to humiliate Samson the way Samson had humiliated the Philistines. It was nothing to him to break a marriage covenant for a little personal, petty vengeance. I think the same motives are driving Saul in this case. Out of his resentment and jealousy, he delivers this humiliation in breaking the betrothal and not delivering the promised bride. Instead, he puts forward his second daughter Michal as a consolation prize in Philistine fashion. Perhaps he feels that David has been disloyal to him and broken covenant with him and, therefore, he is justified in breaking covenant with David in retaliation. I don't know. Any number of excuses can be made, and none of them are valid.

Having delivered David the slap in the face, Saul comes to him again with open arms and the offer to become his son-in-law as if nothing had happened between them. But his intent is the same as with the first marriage offer. He is trying to use Michal to ensnare David by playing on David's desire for this woman who loves him.

Saul is living up to his name in this. Saul, who name means desired, is the son of Kish, whose name means one who is bent like a snare. God appointed Saul, the desire of Israel, as a snare and an object lesson to teach the children of Israel not to follow after their desires. David is not exempt from this test, only the adversary comes at him a much more personal and direct way. There is the outward offer of a kiss, but behind it, the sword.

10. What do we know about Michal?

This section of the narrative (18:20-28) is bookended by the phrase "Michal, Saul's daughter, loved David," which explains the reason why Saul used her in his scheme. Michal is a unique character in that she is the only woman in all of Scripture of whom it is specifically stated that she loves a man. Typically, it is the man expressing love for a woman (e.g., Samson loved Delilah).

The meaning of her name can be taken one of two ways. Like the name Micah, it can reflect the question "Who is like God?" and suggests a rather wry comment on God's hand in thwarting Saul's scheme. Saul thinks he is outwitting David, but is blind to the fact that God has chosen David and isn't going to let Saul win.

The word, *mikhal*, also means "little brook." Its meaning lends little to the immediate context, but it connects us to another picture in Second Samuel 17:20 with a similar context. In this context, a woman deceives Absalom's servants to draw them off of David's men. As we will see in the next chapter, Michal will deceive her father's men in a similar fashion when they come seeking David.

11. How does Saul alter his tactics this time?

After telling David, "You shall be my son-in-law today," Saul sends his servants to David to flatter him. Saul has long subscribed to his servants' suggestions, more so than he should, and I think it is funny that David isn't swayed in the least by their words.

12. What is the reason David gives for not marrying Michal?

He responds similarly to what he said the first time, but he adds the comment that he is poor and lightly esteemed. There is a play on words in David's rebuke. He asks Saul's servants if they think that being a king's son-in-law is a slight *[qalal]* thing seeing as how a slighted *[qala]* man is being offered the honor. Quite a pithy statement.

It is not a light thing to be a king's son-in-law. Dangerous obligations come with it. Nor is David fooled into believing he has the king's esteem. He understood the slap Saul had given him. He isn't taking any handouts from Saul since Saul is a man who reneges on his promises.

13. How does Saul alter the offer this time?

Last time, Saul attached the condition of perpetual loyalty, obedience, and battle service to himself in return for Merab as wife. For whatever reason, perhaps by divine providence, that offer fell through.
The whole point was to get David into battle, and waiting for the opportunity to happen in the course of time was not ideal. This time Saul foregos a demand for a dowry and sets the bride-price on Michal of one hundred Philistine foreskins. (The Philistines were uncircumcised, so Saul would know that David had killed the enemy and not his own countrymen to get the prize.) This will immediately catapult David into battle where odds are that he would die before being able to claim the bride and, thus, secure an inheritance to the throne. So, the marriage will be a simple transaction this time, at a price that a poor man like David would be able to pay.

David goes for it. Not only does he pay the bride price, but he pays it twice over by delivering 200 instead of 100 foreskins. This shows his prowess in battle and marks his third success at eluding Saul's schemes.

14. Why would David agree to do this? Why bind himself in marriage to the house of Saul?

The first marriage contract would have put him in bondage to Saul and in conflict with God's sovereignty. Paying the bride price, on the other hand, is a transaction that carries no obligation to future loyalty or obedience to the earthly king while at the same time securing the bride. And, since Saul and not David initiated the marriage transaction, Saul is now required to acknowledge David as a rightful heir to the throne. Of course, Jonathan's right takes precedence, but if something should happen to Saul's sons, then David could legally take the throne. This arrangement actually works toward David's advantage, without bringing him in bondage to Saul.

David has had three successes. He has escaped Saul's personal attacks. He has become a great man in the eyes of the nation as Saul's front man and the leader of the men of war. And now, he has escaped a scheme to bring him into bondage, succeeded in defeating the Philistines (again), and become a royal heir in the physical kingdom. (Keep in mind: God's reward of an eternal kingship is still on the table.)

15. Why does Saul fear David?

The final mention of Saul's fear has a dual reason. He sees that the LORD is with David to give him success in battle, so any hopes he has of David dying at the hands of the Philistines will come to nothing. Secondly, his own daughter loves David, as does his son, Jonathan. He has lost the loyalty of his own family, and with it, the ability to use them as allies and tools against David. His enemy has established a foothold in his own house and is that much closer to taking the throne from him.

The final verse in the chapter lauds David. Whenever the Philistines went to war, David battled more wisely than Saul's servants and became highly esteemed.

And so we see the pattern of ascent and descent similar to the account of Samuel and Eli. Saul goes from loving David, to eyeing him suspiciously, to finally counting him as a perpetual enemy. In the next picture, Saul abandons all semblance of civility and his animosity breaks out in open aggression.

APPLY THE PICTURE

Saul and David: The Third Temptation of Christ

I think the reason why Saul's offer of Merab is contrasted with his offer of Michal is because they represent two different ways to pursue a crown. One would have placed the king-to-be in perpetual bondage to the ruler of the earthly kingdom and disqualified him from the eternal kingship. The other came at a greater cost, but by paying the bride price, the king-to-be retained his alignment with God the King and claimed the bride.

This reminds me greatly of Christ's third temptation. Satan came to Christ with the offer of kingship over all the kingdoms of the world if Christ would just bow down and worship him. Satan, like Saul, is a glory-hound, and his ultimate goal was to derail the King from claiming His throne. But the kingdoms Satan was offering had already been lost to Satan, and he knew it. For all its potential glory, the offer was an empty one. In reality, Christ had already been made the same offer by God the Father in return for obedience, but it was not an empty offer. God the Father intended to take the kingdom from Satan and give it to Christ, and in addition, He held out the reward of an eternal kingship.

The whole issue revolved around which king Christ would choose to align himself with: the king offering a fleeting kingdom without an eternal kingship, or a King who offered a permanent kingdom and eternal Kingship. Christ chose to remain aligned with God the King, though the cost to Himself was greater.

Kingdoms aside, there remains the issue of securing the bride. Is the bride's place in the kingdom contingent on the king's continued allegiance to the ruler of the earthly realm, or is it guaranteed because the bride price has been paid? It is guaranteed.

The Brides: Merab and Michal

Like the king, there are right and wrong ways for the bride to secure a crown, and it begins with understanding of what reward is being pursued. As the Bride of Christ, there is the award of a place in the kingdom, which comes to us without being merited because the bride price has been paid. We are brought into the kingdom by grace alone, based on our marriage to the King. There is the second reward: an added glory offered to us as co-heirs with Christ, and like the eternal kingship, this crown must be merited—earned by works.

These are two different awards, one granted apart from works and one earned, but the ruler of this realm can twist our understanding into thinking of them as one—the one we must earn. Thus, we can be convinced that the salvation we were granted by grace now becomes the reward we must earn after a lifetime of service—but to which king? There is the rub. Are we truly fighting the LORD's battles, or are our efforts just an underhanded way that the Enemy keeps us bound to him and takes his own glory from our works?

Our marriage contract is like Michal's. We are purchased at the bride price, thus relieving us of further allegiance to the ruler of the earthly realm. But we can end up in a marriage contract like Merab's, living our entire life trying to validate ourselves by our own works to secure our place in the kingdom.

Always remember, there are two awards: One that is unmerited and granted by grace, the other that is earned by works. Keep salvation by grace and the reward for works separate in your thoughts. **When you turn salvation into something that has to be earned, it brings you into bondage to the wrong king, and becomes the wrong reason and the wrong way to pursue the final crown.**

Side note: The Septuagint omits verses 17-19, making no mention of Saul's offering of marriage to Merab. Instead, it skips straight to Michal. I think this is a grave omission because the comparison between the ways of pursuing a crown is then lost, and with it, the picture of Christ's temptation.

⓭ Saul Persecutes David

READ

First Samuel 19:1–20:1

NARRATIVE STRUCTURE

Picture #13 (19:1-24) details Saul's increasing persecution of David. This time, the narrative is structured around a series of three interventions by which David escapes Saul's plots, with the last intervention divided into four stages. The phrase "David fled and escaped" is repeated three times—once after Jonathan's attempted intervention, and twice within the narrative of Michal's intervention. There is a fourth mention of David fleeing when Saul seeks him at Naioth, found in 20:1, bridging the concluding action in Chapter 19 with Chapter 20 as David returns to Jonathan. He comes full circle, so to speak.

Picture #13 is also divided into five main sections:

1) The opening comment establishing Saul's plotting (19:1)
2) Jonathan's intervention, David's escape (19:2-10)
3) Michal's intervention, David's escape (19:11-18)
4) The Spirit's intervention (19:19-24)
5) David's escape (20:1)

BUILD THE PICTURE

Just as Chapter 18 was divided into two sets of three—three accounts of David's success set off by three accounts of Saul's fear—Chapter 19 is divided up into another series of threes. This time we have three interventions with the last intervention divided into four stages. Each intervention is separated by the phrase that David "fled and escaped."

Jonathan's Intervention (19:1-10)

The opening verse sets up the contention between father and son over David that will carry over into the next chapter. Saul wants David killed, but Jonathan loves David greatly.

16. Where does the first intervention take place?

Jonathan chooses a field, then tells David to hide there while he arranges to speak to his father. The field is neutral ground and somewhat private, an open place away from listening ears (except for the ears of David who is hiding nearby), and so Jonathan can speak candidly to his father.

17. How does Jonathan intervene on David's behalf?

He speaks to his father to reason with him, but in the reasoning there is a warning for Saul. Jonathan points out that what Saul is doing is not justified. Saul has sinned against David, but David has not sinned against Saul. David took his life in his hands and brought about deliverance for Israel. Saul, as the king with ultimate authority, has the right to put wrongdoers to death, but the king sins against innocent blood in seeking to kill David without cause. There are three repetitions of "sin" (19:4-5), which drives home the fact that in killing an innocent man, Saul will fall into a very grave sin. This picture will contrast to a later picture when David refuses to kill a guilty man.

I imagine Saul saw plenty of reasons for killing David and had even rationalized it in his mind, but Saul is a man who is swayed by whatever person is working on him at the moment. He relents under his son's admonishment, but then goes a step farther by invoking the LORD's name in a hasty oath. *"As the LORD lives, he shall not be killed"* (19:6). This is a contradiction of his previous command.

Jonathan foolishly thinks his reproof has had some effect on his father and calls to David. David then comes out of hiding to join them and returns to Saul's presence. I can imagine Saul's shock at finding David waiting in the field, and I wonder if this didn't cause him to look at his own son with a little more suspicion for having orchestrated the intervention. All seems well for a period of time, but nothing is solved.

18. What sets Saul off again?

There is a catalytic moment when war breaks out with the Philistines again and David has another success. At the same time the distressing spirit returns to Saul and ignites his fear again, and he tries to kill David. But David flees and escapes.

The reality of anger is that whatever level you achieve in one instance, that will become your beginning level the next time something happens. Saul goes from a nominal peace with David to full-blown violence the moment the fear takes him. This is almost a replay of the first scene in the previous chapter.

Michal's Intervention (19:11-17)

19. Where does the second intervention take place?

From the neutral setting in the field, we move now to the more intimate setting of David's house, which brings David's wife, Michal, into the conflict.

20. How does Michal intervene on David's behalf?

She lowers David out the window, and he flees and escapes. But then she delays the discovery of his absence by taking a household statue, dressing it as a man, and hiding it in the bed under the covers.

21. How is Michal's approach to her father different than Jonathan's?

Jonathan hid David in the field, but then pleaded on his behalf very openly and candidly. Michal, on the other hand, uses tactics of deception and misdirection.

I find it a bit shocking that an idolatrous image would be found in David's house. Perhaps it is something that Michal brought with her from her father's house. It is also a bit ironic that she used it to impersonate David. Saul has made something of an idol out of David in his pursuit of him.

When confronted, Michal lies. She makes the excuse that David cannot get out of bed because he is sick—an excuse which Saul doesn't accept. Saul discovers Michal's deception for himself and accuses her, and she lies again to escape the consequences of her father's wrath by blaming David (bearing false witness). She is a little self-serving in throwing David under the bus like that, and in a way, she is her father's daughter. She uses Saul's own tactics against him.

Michal's delaying tactics are framed by the repeated phrase "David fled and escaped" (19:12, 18).

We don't have any sense of David's thoughts or emotions here in the narrative, but Psalm 59 is written about this particular episode. Here are some select verses from the psalm:

> *"To the Chief Musician. Set to "Do Not Destroy." A Michtam of David when Saul sent men, and they watched the house in order to kill him. Deliver me from my enemies, O my God; defend me from those who rise up against me. Deliver me from the workers of iniquity, and save me from bloodthirsty men. For look, they lie in wait for my life; the mighty gather against me, not for my transgression nor for my sin, O LORD. They run and prepare themselves through no fault of mine. Awake to help me, and behold! . . . But You, O LORD, shall laugh at them; you shall have all the nations in derision. I will wait for You, O You his Strength; for God is my defense. My God of mercy shall come to meet me; God shall let me see my desire on my enemies . . . Consume them in wrath, consume them, that they may not be; and let them know that God rules in Jacob to the ends of the earth. Selah . . . But I will sing of Your power; yes, I will sing aloud of Your mercy in the morning; for You have been my defense and refuge in the day of my trouble. To You, O my Strength, I will sing praises; for God is my defense, my God of mercy."* —Psalm 59:1-4, 8-10, 13, 16-17

The Spirit's Intervention (19:18-24)

22. Where does David flee next?

He flees to Samuel, who is in Ramah, in a section of the city called Naioth where the prophets live. He flees to God's turf for protection.

23. What happens when Saul sends his deputies after David?

As soon as the first set comes among Samuel and the prophets, the

Holy Spirit comes upon them and they begin to prophesy. Saul sends a second and third dispatch of deputies, and the same thing happens three times.

Finally, Saul himself goes, and the same thing happens to him. As soon as he leaves the well at Sechu, he begins prophesying until he comes to Naioth. The Spirit forces the king to abase himself before Samuel just like his men. This abasement is thorough and humiliating. He strips off his clothes and lies down naked in the dust for the rest of the day and night. Is Saul among the prophets?

The final note of David fleeing to escape appears in the first verse of the next chapter. By ending this picture with an intense focus on Saul flat on his face before Samuel, the author is making a strong comment. Saul prophesying among the prophets under the power of the Spirit had once been a confirming sign of his own kingship. What an irony that it now becomes a confirmation of David's kingship and a reminder of God's sovereignty.

APPLY THE PICTURE

Saul's Model: Fear

The narrative has been building a severe contrast between these two kings. Saul descended into anger, fear, and jealousy over David's successes. Everything David did increased his honor and reputation, while everything Saul did was thwarted and defeated. David is presented in a passive role, speaking only twice in the space of two chapters. By contrast Saul's character and motivations are presented very vividly as he tries devious ways to snare and kill David before finally resorting to an open pursuit of him.

Fear can be our worst enemy and a sign that our pursuit of the crown has shifted down the wrong channel. There is an interesting interplay of power, love, a sound mind, and fear on display in these passages, and I want to revisit a verse in Second Timothy that we previously discussed.

> *"For God has not given us a spirit of fear, but of power and of love and of a sound mind."* —Second Timothy 1:7

Fear is a negative emotion that progresses in stages from guilt, to worry, to anxiety, and finally to paranoia in its extremity. Saul is very much the picture of fear, and we see the difference fear makes between Saul's model and David's model when we compare them in terms of power, love, and a sound mind. Using Saul as a case study, let's examine the dynamic of Second Timothy 1:7.

Fear and Power

Instead of feeling empowered, fear makes a person feel powerless.

- **In what ways did Saul become powerless?**

    God took his kingdom from him and with it, his hope. This impacted Saul's sense of self-worth in a way because his self-worth and validation were wrapped up in his worldly possessions and status. God took His Spirit from Saul and put him at the mercy of a distressing spirit who terrified Saul—an adversary he could not overcome on his own. He also lost the support of Samuel, his own family, and the people. God took away all the crutches that had been supporting Saul's sense of power. Even Saul's deputies were taken over by the Spirit, and in the end, God brought Saul himself to his knees. Only a sovereign God could do this.

- **How does Saul try to take back the power?**

    With anger, aggression, and murder. He schemes. He uses people. He breaks covenants.

Fear and Love

Saul started out loving David, but fear twisted that love into hate and jealousy. Fear can make a person incapable of giving or receiving love.

- **What is jealousy?**

    A feeling of resentment against someone because of that person's rivalry, success, or advantages, characterized by or proceeding from suspicious fears. Jealousy can also display as a fiercely protective or vigilant grasping of one's own possessions or rights and a lack of tolerance toward rivals. Jealousy, in this sense, is an attribute of God.

God is described as a jealous God eight times in the Old Testament[1]. God's jealousy is not any indication that He is powerless to deal with His rivals, but He models it for us so that we can see how jealousy works itself out in destructive anger.

- **What happened to Saul's love when fear entered the picture?**

    The person he once loved became the person he hated themost, even pursued as a quarry to be taken as a prize. The relationship was poisoned. As he grew suspicious of David's rivalry, other loyalties began to be questioned. Jonathan's and Michal's love of David became a new source of fear and frustration. As Saul's relationship with David crumbles, he loses relationships with his own family as well.

    A person can be jealous over possessions or glory, but jealousy can also infect human relationships when the jealous person objectifies the thing they love—make them into a possession to be attained and kept—which then brings on the fear of losing that possession to a rival. Jealousy points to the fact that the relationship isn't really based on love but on desire for a possession. And so we are back to the contrast of something loved versus something desired. Saul's character is running true to his name.

Fear and a Sound Mind

A fearful person does not exercise sound judgment or self-control because fear and panic drive his decision-making. It will make a person do what is right or expedient in their own eyes and seek their own personal good over the greater mission. Saul's lack of a sound mind is clearly evidenced in these chapters, particularly under the influence of the distressing spirit.

Fighting a Good Fight Continues

Second Timothy is a follow-on to First Timothy with its discussion of fighting the good fight. Dealing with fear is part of the endurance test of kingship.

Remember that your place in the kingdom has been granted by grace and not by your works. That truth is meant to remove fear on that level.

---

1   Exodus 20:5, 34:14; Deuteronomy 4:24, 5:9, 6:15, Joshua 24:19; Nahum 1:2

> *"Therefore do not be ashamed of the testimony of our Lord, nor of me His prisoner, but share with me in the sufferings for the gospel according to the power of God, who has saved us and called us with a holy calling, not according to our works, but according to His own purpose and grace which was given to us in Christ Jesus before time began,"* —Second Timothy 1:8-9

Remember that you have an indwelling Spirit that can battle the fear by bolstering us with an understanding of God's power and love, and with a sound mind.

> *"Hold fast the pattern of sound words which you have heard from me, in faith and love which are in Christ Jesus. That good thing which was committed to you, keep by the Holy Spirit who dwells in us."*
> —Second Timothy 1:13-14

Remember the nature of the reward you are pursuing. It is an eternal crown, not an earthly crown, and there is a right way to pursue that crown. The enemy will seek to embroil you in a fight for an earthly crown, which then becomes a possession to be grasped by our own power and will. When that happens, fear quickly enters into the equation.

> *"No one engaged in warfare entangles himself with the affairs of this life, that he may please him who enlisted him as a soldier. And also if anyone competes in athletics, he is not crowned unless he competes according to the rules."* —Second Timothy 2:4-5

Remember that there are two awards. There is one that has been purchased for us by Christ's death on the cross. Our identification with Him through that death assures our salvation—our position in the kingdom—and is granted by grace apart from our merit. There is a second award is for our works in passing an endurance test. If we endure, then we will reign with Christ.

> *"This is a faithful saying: For if we died with Him, we shall also live with Him. If we endure, we shall also reign with Him. If we deny Him, He also will deny us. If we are faithless, He remains faithful; He cannot deny Himself."* —Second Timothy 2:11-13

Questions for Reflection

- Is there fear in your life?
- What is driving the fear?
- What affect has your fear had on your family or close relations?
- What helps you combat the fear?

LESSON 12: FIRST SAMUEL 20

⑭ A Choice Between Crowns

READ

First Samuel 20:1-42

NARRATIVE STRUCTURE

Picture #14 (20:1-42) begins with David fleeing back to Gibeah in search of his best friend, Jonathan. This chapter is a major turning point in the narrative for David, but also for Jonathan who must decide where his loyalty lies between Saul and David. Jonathan will only make one more brief appearance in First Samuel 23 before his death in Chapter 31. This is his signature moment in the narrative.

Picture #14 is divided into three sections arranged in a chiastic structure:

(A) David confronts Jonathan in the field with a request (20:1-23)
(B) Jonathan confronts Saul at the feast (20:24-34)
(A) Jonathan returns to David in the field with a verdict (20:35-42)

BUILD THE PICTURE

David Confronts Jonathan in the Field (20:1-23)

1. **When we last saw Jonathan in Chapter 19, what was he doing and how did it end?**

   He was standing in a field where David was hidden, trying to intervene on David's behalf with his father Saul. Jonathan reasons with his father about his irrational hatred of David. He points out that David has not committed any sin or act of faithlessness toward Saul, and therefore, Saul is sinning by seeking to hurt David without cause. Saul seemingly relents and swears an oath not to kill David, so Jonathan brings David to Saul, and there is a reconciliation. But is that the end of the issue? No. David is successful once again, and Saul's resentment springs to life again. Saul pursues David to his house and even to Ramah.

2. **Do you think Jonathan knows about Saul's actions after their conversation in the field?**

   I don't think he does. In First Samuel 19:1, it says that Saul told Jonathan and all his servants to kill David, at which point Jonathan intervenes. There appears to be a reconciliation, and everything seems fine. Afterward, in verse 11, it says Saul only sent his messengers—his deputies—to track David's movements at his house. There is no mention of Jonathan, nor is there any reason for Jonathan to be involved with his father's tasking of "messengers." Again, in verse 20, Saul sends only deputies to Ramah to bring David back.

   As far as Jonathan is concerned, David and Saul are reconciled and back to business as usual; only now David comes running to him, demanding to know what he has done wrong.

   Jonathan's immediate reaction is to insist that nothing is wrong. He is clearly in the dark over what has been going on. It must come as a shock to find out that things weren't right at all. Jonathan had believed his father when he said "David shall not die," and he doesn't believe his father would hide anything from him.

3. **If it is true, then what does that mean for Jonathan in his relationship with his father?**

   When you discover that a family member has been hiding things from you and doing things that jeopardize your relationships with others, what does that do to the family relationship?

4. **What reason does David give for Saul hiding his intentions from Jonathan?**

   David points out that Saul knows that he has found favor in Jonathan's sight, and Jonathan would be grieved if his father did something to David. David tempers the betrayal with a reason that doesn't alienate Jonathan from his father.

5. **From what we have read so far, do you think Jonathan knows about David's rivalry for the throne?**

   I don't think Jonathan realizes initially that David is his father's rival or his own rival. He doesn't know that David has been anointed as the new king, and while David is technically an heir to the throne for having married Michal, he can assume the kingship only in the event that something happens to Jonathan. So Jonathan's actions aren't driven by a sense of rivalry the way Saul's actions are. He doesn't understand the nature of the conflict between David and his father, and as a result, he doesn't see that his sense of loyalty to David will cause conflict with his loyalty to his father.

6. **Why doesn't David tell Jonathan the truth that Samuel has already anointed him king?**

   It would be perfectly natural to disclose the full truth of what is causing the conflict, especially to someone who is an intimate and trusted friend. But if David brings up the issue of Saul losing the kingship, what effect would that have on Jonathan?

   It would suddenly have focused Jonathan's attention on a physical kingdom that was already lost to him. It might have wrecked his world and sent him down the same path of desperate possessiveness as his father. Or it could have caused Jonathan to base his loyalty toward one king or the other on which one he felt would ultimately prevail and guarantee him a place in the kingdom. But all the focus would have been on the physical kingdom. Jonathan's decision could not be motivated by a desire to keep a physical kingdom. To bring up the source of the rivalry would have created a stumbling block.

7. **Where does David focus his case?**

   David begins the conversation with the discussion of sin, and he keeps the focus there. *"What have I done? What is my iniquity, and what is my sin before your father, that he seeks my life?"* (20:1) The physical conflict between David and Saul ultimately stems from the spiritual

   Lesson 12: A Choice Between Crowns | 263

one. Sin is sin, regardless of the reason why you do it. Saul had justified his sin in his pursuit of the kingdom.

It would have been very easy for Jonathan to feel defensive on his father's behalf and rationalize Saul's behavior if the cause seemed reasonable to him. David refrains from making the issue about the kingdom, but neither does he alienate Jonathan from his father. He emphasizes Saul's affection for his son in not wanting to grieve him, and yet the father's behavior is undeniable.

8. **What is Jonathan's response?**

   Jonathan has no reason to distrust David, but then he can't imagine his father acting with such treachery towards himself, let alone David. Jonathan is in limbo, but he has covenanted himself to David, which demands loyalty. He asks David, *"What do you want me to do?"*

   When someone says to you "I'll do whatever you want me to do," what do those words imply? I feel like these are the words of resignation. This is something a person says when they are submitting to another's will but are not convinced. Jonathan can't reconcile the issue in himself, but he has covenanted himself to David and is obligated to him.

9. **For what does David ask?**

   David could have asked for any form of help, any degree of loyalty, any sacrifice on Jonathan's part, but all he requests is that Jonathan seek the truth for himself. And so he proposes a way for Jonathan to test his father. How will his father react if David doesn't show up for the New Moon feast, even if there is a plausible reason for it? Whether he sits at Saul's table for the sacrificial feast, or at the LORD's table at Bethlehem, it's about worshipping the LORD, right?

   We know that Saul is not one to regard the LORD's sacrifices with much reverence, especially when they become obstacles to his own goals. It would mean nothing to Saul to use the gathering for the holy day as a means of snaring David to kill him.

10. **What does David propose Jonathan do when he discovers the truth about his father?**

    If there is no sin in David, then he asks Jonathan to honor the covenant between them and be merciful to him. But if Jonathan discovers from his father that David has sinned and is worthy of death, then let Jonathan kill David himself. Just don't take him back to Saul like Jonathan did last time. David has already made the effort to reconcile, and it ended this way. Jonathan needs to reconcile himself to the fact that things aren't going to get any better between Saul and David and stop trying to force the issue.

11. What is David's concern in verse 10?

David is worried that Saul will kill Jonathan or prevent him from communicating with David when the truth of his treachery comes out. So a way must be found for Jonathan to communicate with David without been seen or suspected of it.

Jonathan proposes a solution, but first he enters into another covenant with David. The first time the text mentions Jonathan covenanting himself to David was after the battle with Goliath, but no details were given as to the nature of their agreement. Now, details are given.

12. What are the conditions of this covenant?

1) David should show Jonathan personal kindness all the days of his life, that he should not die. This implies David rescuing him and giving him refuge and help of like kind should Jonathan need it.

2) David's house—his descendants—should keep the same covenant with Jonathan's house throughout their generations. Jonathan expresses his certainty that the LORD will establish David by cutting off David's enemies, and he doesn't want his house named among the enemies, even though his father may prove to be an enemy of David's.

13. Why make a covenant with David before and not after the truth has been ascertained?

It is a statement of faith that 1) Jonathan believes David is innocent; 2) he believes that David's life will be preserved and his house will continue even to future generations; 3) David will be established when God puts his enemies beneath him; and 4) the house of David will bring a reign of peace.

Jonathan isn't just thinking about himself and what he has to gain physically from the relationship. He is thinking along eternal lines of an everlasting peace between his house and David's. However things turn out with his father, whatever his own future will be in the physical kingdom, he values a more eternal reward. In reality, Jonathan has no idea that he is about to lose his physical inheritance to David, but in losing one kingdom, he is gaining another because of this covenant. That is the reward on the table for Jonathan as a result of this step of faith.

Personally, I think that there is an even greater reward waiting for Jonathan in Messiah's kingdom. Jonathan is at heart a man of peace and a peacemaker, and Jesus said, "Blessed are the peacemakers, for they shall be called the sons of God." (Matthew 5:9)

14. What is Jonathan's plan?

David must disappear out of sight for three days. On the third day, he is to station himself at the stone of Ezel. The stone of Ezel is a memorial stone of some sort. The name Ezel means "departure." On that day, Jonathan will make a show of going to the field for some archery practice and take with him a young man to fetch his arrows. The directions he gives to the young man will be a message to David. "Get the arrows and come" will be the signal that all is well. "The arrows are beyond you" will be the signal to flee.

Jonathan Confronts Saul at the Feast (20:24-34)

15. What is the New Moon feast?

The Hebrew word for "moon" (Hebrew: *chodesh*) also means "month," and the New Moon marks the first day of the Hebrew month. It is treated like a minor festival in itself and includes offering a sacrifice (Numbers 28:11), blowing the trumpets over the sacrifice (Numbers 10:10), and suspending work and trade (Nehemiah 10:31). It is similar to the Sabbath in many ways.

The new moon symbolizes a new beginning or a renewal and carries that hope for renewal from month to month. It is a very dark day—the darkest day of the month—and yet it marks the moment when the darkness begins to retreat and the light appear.

Its celebration commenced when Israel came into the Land, and so the hope then translated to hope for national renewal in the Land. In the days of the kings, the king becomes the figurehead for the nation, and the New Moon celebration becomes the king's holiday.

It is significant that this turning point in First Samuel 20 should happen on this day, when the kingdom hangs in the balance between these two kings.

The New Moon is still observed today in Jewish liturgy. The special readings from the Law and the Prophets include First Samuel 20 for the reminder of a promised covenant of peace. They also include Isaiah 66, which foretells a coming kingdom of peace and righteousness when the great Messianic King will rule on earth and all flesh shall come to worship Him from new moon to new moon.

Thus, the hope for physical renewal and national renewal is tied to the hope of a future kingdom and a future reign of a (Davidic) king. This belief is perpetuated even today in orthodox circles with the pairing of these passages.

16. How does Saul react to David's absence?

The first day David's absence is noted. Meanwhile Jonathan holds his tongue and pretends that nothing is amiss. Saul figures that David hasn't come because he is unclean and lets it pass.

The second day, Saul questions Jonathan about David's continued absence, and Jonathan gives the prearranged excuse that David's brother had commanded David to come home for a yearly feast. David requested leave and Jonathan granted it.

17. Why is Saul angry with Jonathan?

Jonathan uses a loaded word when he relates David's request.

> *"And now, if I have found favor in your eyes, please let me <u>get away</u> and see my brothers."* (20:29, emphasis added)

The phrase "get away" is a translation of the Hebrew word *malat*, which means "to slip away, slip from one's grasp, or escape." Jonathan is pricking his father a little in his choice of words by saying that David requested to escape from Saul's table, and Jonathan granted him the favor. Jonathan drops this loaded word into what should have been a casual conversation, and Saul explodes in fury.

18. What is the thrust of Saul's grievance?

We can see from Saul's words that David's absence is a secondary issue. He doesn't argue whether Jonathan had the authority to do what he did. He doesn't even get angry that David's brother would supersede his own authority as king. What is really eating Saul is Jonathan's loyalty to David instead of himself—the fact that Jonathan would let him escape. Saul curses his son with obscene language for having whored himself to the man who would supplant him as king. Saul insults his son deeply with shaming words.

When David spoke to Jonathan, he didn't bring up the topic of his rivalry for the kingship against Saul, but that is the sole focus of Saul's argument. He reveals to Jonathan that David is Jonathan's rival for the throne. If David remains alive, Jonathan will lose the kingdom. And so Saul orders Jonathan to bring David to him so that he can kill him.

19. How does Jonathan react?

Jonathan asks: *"Why should he be killed? What has he done?"*

Think about those questions. Jonathan doesn't even bat an eye at the bombshell news. He doesn't seem to care about the kingdom, but protests David's innocence. As he did before, he points out that what his father is doing is unjustified and sinful, regardless of what is motivating it. He rebukes his father, but his words can also be taken as a rejection of his father's kingdom. David is more important than the kingdom. This infuriates Saul, and he tries to kill his traitorous son who has shunned his inheritance.

This is all the proof Jonathan needed, and now Jonathan is as angry as his father. He leaves the table and refuses to eat the feast with his father out of his grief. The feast became a fast. David's words back in verse 3 were the truth. Saul had hidden his animosity so that Jonathan would not be grieved, but now that the animosity was revealed, the son was indeed grieved.

20. Why does Jonathan grieve?

His father has just shamed him openly, and yet he doesn't regard his own shame as anything. Instead, he grieves over the shame his father has dealt to David. His world has just imploded. He has lost trust and respect for his father, and now he will have to send away his best friend.

21. Does he grieve over the loss of the kingdom?

No. Why? Because he has made a covenant of peace with the new king. Whatever happens between David and Saul, Jonathan has made the better choice in David. He passed the test in pursuing an eternal crown instead of an earthly one, and yet it was not without cost.

Jonathan Returns to David in the Field (20:35-42)

22. What is the significance of Jonathan giving all his weapons to the lad and sending him back to the city before Jonathan goes to see David?

Jonathan faces David, his rival, unarmed. It is a sign that he has nothing against David. He comes in peace. David returns the honor by bowing himself before the king's son three times.

23. Why does David weep more?

David has been waiting three very dark days for Jonathan to return with the verdict, not knowing what Saul might do to Jonathan or if he would see his friend again. What a bittersweet thing to be proved right in his accusations against Saul and to cause such grief to his best friend. And what bitterness to be parted from such a friend, to face what will become an exile-like wandering. Jonathan has had a night to come to terms with the situation, but this breaks on David with suddenness, and he weeps more. Jonathan leaves him with the reminder of their covenant of peace.

How important is it to leave each other with peace between us, knowing the struggle that we face in the days to come?

APPLY THE PICTURE

David's Model

David is a man who has been unjustly wronged and is seeking understanding and help in the midst of a struggle with another man. He turns to his best friend who is in a tenuous position because that friend is also related to the man who has wronged David.

- **Is it a good strategy to appeal to your friend for support when you are struggling with one of their own family members?**

    As a rule, no. It creates a horrific test of loyalty on your friend's part. How many friends in this position would side with you over family to the point of breaking relations with family? Jonathan is not going to want to believe David, but David needs Jonathan to believe him.

- **So, how does David go about convincing him?**

    Notice the questions he asks: What have I done? What is my sin, that your father seeks my life? First of all, David allows for the possibility that he, David, is to blame. Saul's actions are clear to David, and he knows he isn't to blame, but he doesn't immediately launch into accusations or recriminations, nor does he demand validation from Jonathan. He asks Jonathan to investigate the matter and judge for himself.

    Secondly, he doesn't alienate Jonathan from the father. He reaffirms Saul's love for his son by saying that Saul didn't want to grieve Jonathan with his animosity toward David. David doesn't mince words over the evidence of Saul's actions, only Saul's motivation for hiding them from his son.

    Finally, David keeps the issue focused on the sin and relationship aspect, instead of any physical gain that might be motivating either party. The rivalry for the kingdom doesn't even enter the conversation. David withholds that part of the information.

    When we find ourselves in conflict with another person, and we are hurting and struggling, it is natural to seek an intimate friend for comfort, help, and advice. And it is perfectly natural to want to disclose everything about the situation to try to get some closure or reconciliation. The information we disclose or withhold in a moment like this can influence the direction of conflict and ultimately the resolution. Instead of staying focused on the issue, we can open the proverbial can of worms, and suddenly the issue explodes into multiple issues, and the conversation goes off on tangents without anything being resolved.

When we disclose too much, we can jeopardize our friend by tying them emotionally to us and demanding loyalty in our own self-pity. We can create conflict between our friend and our antagonist where none existed before or is even warranted. You may seek your friend for prayer or insight or intercession or even counseling, but it can come at a cost. I admit I have struggled with this issue of how to seek resolution without compromising friends, and to this day, I don't feel I have struck the right balance that David did.

Jonathan's Model

Jonathan models a couple of things. Let's look at the small picture first. This involves his reaction to the warning David gives him in regards to his intercessor role. David tells him, "Do not take me back to your father again. You tried intercession once, and it didn't work. Let it go."

- **How is that a warning to intercessors?**

    When intercessors become involved in resolving conflict between two parties, especially if they have personal relationships with both sides, a failure to reconcile the issue can feel like a personal failure for the intercessor. The intercessor may want to keep trying to force that reconciliation, but they can do so to the death of the relationship between themselves and the parties in conflict. There comes a point when the intercessor must just let go and let God deal with the issue. To his credit, Jonathan expresses surprise that David would believe that he, Jonathan, would still pursue a reconciliation with his father if evil was determined for David.

The second behavior Jonathan models is in regards to his decision over where his loyalties are. He stands in this very precarious position of having to decide between two kings who pursue kingdoms of two different natures. One king offers an earthly kingdom and all its riches, but it comes at a price. There is never peace and there will never be peace because his father is grasping after something already lost to him. The other king promises a future kingdom of peace that might not be realized in Jonathan's own day. He sees the natures of both men, the way each seeks to keep the crown, and for what reasons. He judges between the two and decides to pursue an eternal crown over the earthly one.

The Choice Between Two Kings

David is a type of Christ, certainly, but I hesitate to cast Saul as Satan, though he is clearly aligned with that master. Perhaps it would be better to consider Saul modeled after an anti-Christ—a type that is opposite of Christ. Let's look at the contrast between Saul and David and then consider them from Jonathan's perspective.

Saul is the current ruler over a rich and glorious earthly kingdom with all the wealth and benefits for his taking. But he is a king who has lost the blessing of an eternal kingship, and as a result, he now has only this current physical kingdom to which he grasps with oppressive force. All of his identity and worth are wrapped up in the physical kingdom, and he pursues power and glory in the earthly realm. He is a man of violence, hate, treachery, lies, vengeance, and rebellion against the God of heaven, and is possessed by a terrifying demonic spirit. He has all the characteristics of a son of Belial.

By contrast, David is a king who has been anointed but has not yet come into his kingdom. A few select people know of it, but the greater congregation does not. He has not been proclaimed king, though many of the people unwittingly give him kingly praise. He cannot be crowned and come into his kingdom until the current king is dethroned.

There is a duality in David's nature. On one hand, he is a nurturing shepherd and a man of peace. He is a man possessed of God's Spirit and brings peace and well-being, where the spirit that possesses the current king brings fear and torment. David is a thinking man who behaves wisely and his words are true, although their truth is unproven at first.

He also has a reputation for being a man of war, but he fights for the vision of the kingdom as God envisioned it—a holy kingdom characterized by righteousness, a knowledge of God, and peace. He fights for God's glory, not his own, and Jonathan believes God will put David's enemies beneath his feet.

David and Saul are the antithesis of one another. Where one is successful, honorable and without sin (in this instance), the other is a failure and dishonorable, whose sin multiplies as he acts on his jealousy and hate. One is superior; the other, inferior.

Jonathan comes to this crossroads in life. He is a man in pursuit of a crown, although he does not realize it at the moment when he has to make this decision to align his loyalty with one king or the other. Jonathan is asked to choose between all that the king of the earthly kingdom has to offer—that which Jonathan sees, understands, and even values—and something much greater, much less tangible, and which may not even be realized in his own lifetime.

Jonathan understands the earthly kingdom, and the loyalty that is demanded of him. His father is family, and he has certain obligations in regards to family loyalty. His father is king and demands loyalty due that station as well. As his father's son, Jonathan himself is royalty, and so his identity, status, and future inheritance are bound up in that familial relationship. His father is wealthy and powerful, but he is also fearful, angry, jealous, treacherous, suspicious of his own family, and possessed at times by a demonic spirit that makes him mentally unstable. There will never be peace in his father's kingdom, and Jonathan knows it.

But is peace more desirable than all the other benefits? That is the question.

Jonathan is a peacemaker at heart, and he aches for peace at this point. He has lived all his life with this violent, grasping father, and peace is more valuable than what his father has to offer. The proverbs tell us that it is better to live in a corner of the housetop with peace than to share a household with a contentious person, and we can certainly see the truth of this in regards to Jonathan's experience.

Jonathan can only imagine what a kingdom under David's authority will entail, but he knows that God has given David success, and he is sure God will put David's enemies under his feet; and most of that belief stems from his understanding of David's character. He sees David as a man after his own heart. A covenant relationship with David offers the potential reward of a kingdom of peace and safety, and even if it isn't realized in his own lifetime, it may be realized in his descendants' lifetime. Jonathan wants an eternal reward. Even before the truth of David's charge against Saul is proven, Jonathan makes that covenant with David. He switches his loyalty, even though it will cost him everything in terms of his relationship with his father, his king, and his earthly inheritance.

When Jonathan learns that the physical kingdom was lost to him—that there was never any hope of it to begin with—then the covenant with the new king becomes that much more significant. He made the right choice over the king with whom to align himself and which kingdom to pursue. Though Jonathan has lost an earthly kingdom, in doing so he has gained a heavenly one.

Jonathan is a man who seeks for the truth until he finds it, and when he finds it, he clings to it. And he does not grieve that loss of an earthly kingdom. And that is the way to pursue the crown.

But what neither he or David know yet is that there is a reward coming for David in the form of an eternal kingship, and so there will be reward on top of reward for Jonathan in that future kingdom if David perseveres.

The contrast between David and Saul is the contrast between Christ and anti-Christ, respectively. Jonathan represents us. He is the picture of every person who has ever been asked to give up an earthly kingdom with its earthly rewards under an oppressive, demonic king, and place their hope in a king-to-be whose kingdom remains as yet a promise of peace and safety and well-being. Our understanding of that future kingdom can only be understood as the outworking of the character of that Messianic King who is a duality of love and power, a shepherd of peace but also a man of war.

Like Jonathan, the first obstacle we must get past is the perception that everything is fine in the earthly kingdom. But Christ confronts us with the truth of his Word and challenges us to pursue the truth of the real nature of the demonic king who reigns over the world. What we know of Christ's character and person may be sufficient for us to enter into that covenant relationship with Him. That is our salvation. And yet there remains a time of testing to see if we will remain loyal to him when we have lost it all in terms of our family relationships or earthly possessions. There is an earthly cost for following Christ, but there is also an eternal gain.

There are right and wrong kings with whom to align yourself.
There are right and wrong crowns to pursue.
There are right and wrong ways and reasons for pursuing them.

Questions for Reflection

- How well do you know the character of the King-to-be? What do you imagine His kingdom will be like?

- Do you take His Word as truth, or do you need proof first?

- How will you recognize the anti-Christ when he comes on the scene in the End Times? What will be some warning signs to look for?

Moving Forward: David in Exile

From this point until the end of First Samuel, David will be on the run from Saul, and it will seem like the king-to-be has lost his kingdom. But that is not the case. God is sending David into a time of exile because he needs training to be a king. Exile is part of David's narrative, but not Saul's. God did not invest Himself in training Saul to be king as He does with David, and that is one of the major contrasts between the two kings.

There is also the endurance test that David must pass. The test is not just about enduring Saul's relentless persecution, although that is the catalyst driving the training lessons. The endurance test is about sticking to one path in pursuing a reward, and that requires single-mindedness—something Saul lacks. Once David learns what are the right and wrong ways and reasons to pursue a crown, then the endurance test becomes a matter of making the right choices consistently over time and in various situations until that wisdom become internalized as part of the king's character. Single-mindedness trained toward justice, righteousness, faithfulness, self-control, and mercy is something David must achieve before he takes Saul's place as king, because with the crown comes the power to pursue any desire under the sun.

INTRODUCTION: FIRST SAMUEL 21-31

The Exile Years

First Samuel 9-20 focused on Saul as king. David took the forefront at his anointing and battle against Goliath, but then subsided into a passive role while Saul's thoughts and emotions were highlighted. Now, in Chapters 21–31, the focus will switch to David, and we will get glimpses of his thoughts and emotions throughout the exile experience.

David's exile spans First Samuel 21–31, but there is a very particular structure to these chapters that I should explain first. The two final chapters (30–31) are set apart as the resolution to the theme of pursuing crowns. The remaining chapters (21–29) are arranged thematically in a chiastic structure around Chapter 25, which is introduced by the oddly placed note about Samuel's death. Chapter 25 is the longest chapter in this selection and a pivotal chapter. Here are the themes that mirror themselves across Chapter 25 (also, see chart on next page):

First Samuel 21: David rejected by the Philistines
   First Samuel 22: Saul kills the priesthood
      First Samuel 23: David escapes a trap through God's wisdom
         First Samuel 24: Saul in David's hands
            First Samuel 25: David and Nabal
         First Samuel 26: Saul in David's hands
      First Samuel 27: David gets into a trap by his own wisdom
   First Samuel 28: Saul seeks a medium
First Samuel 29: David rejected by the Philistines

------------------ CONCLUSION ------------------

   First Samuel 30: David's final battle and reward of the crown
   First Samuel 31: Saul's final battle and loss of the crown

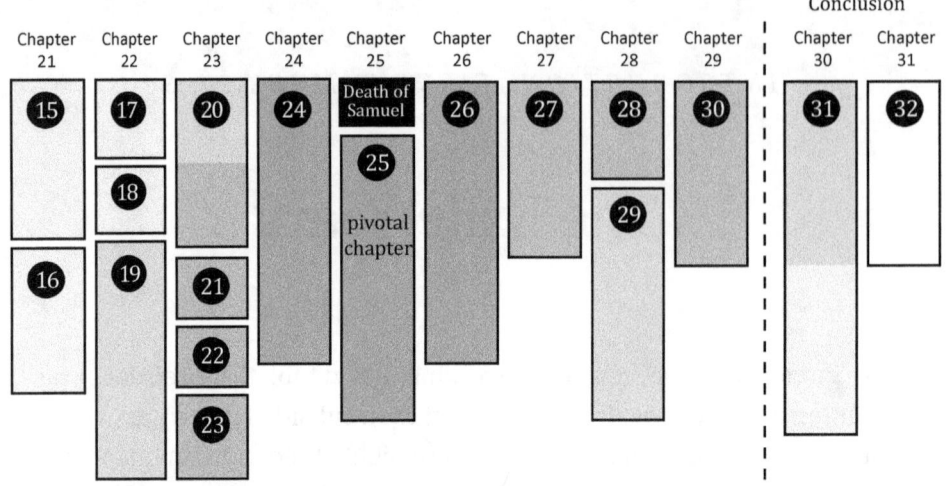

Pictures for Comparison, First Samuel 21–31

15	David Flees to the Tabernacle	First Samuel 21:1-9
16	David Flees to Gath	First Samuel 21:10-15
17	David Flees to the Cave of Adullam	First Samuel 22:1-2
18	David in the Stronghold	First Samuel 22:3-5
19	Saul Murders the Priests of Nob	First Samuel 22:6-23
20	The Battle at Keilah	First Samuel 23:1-13
21	In the Wilderness: The Statement	First Samuel 23:14-15
22	In the Wilderness: The Comforter	First Samuel 23:16-18
23	The Rock of Escape: The Experience	First Samuel 23:19-29
24	David at the Rock of Wild Goats	First Samuel 24:1-22
25	Death of Samuel/David and Nabal	First Samuel 25:1-44
26	David at the Hill of Hachilah	First Samuel 26:1-25
27	David Returns to the Philistines	First Samuel 27:1-12
28	David's Dilemma	First Samuel 28:1-2
29	Saul Seeks the Medium	First Samuel 28:3-25
30	Philistines Reject David	First Samuel 29:1-11
31	David's Final Battle (Reward)	First Samuel 30:1-31
32	Saul's Final Battle (Loss)	First Samuel 31:1-12

Thematic Picture Series

First Samuel 21–31 is broken into 17 pictures (Pictures ⑮ to ㉜). Some chapters have only one picture, while others will have multiple pictures. The narrative structure is tightly interwoven in cascading series and specific picture comparisons, and the author uses various narrative devices to establish the parallels. There are seven main themes in these series. The themes are:

>**Series #1:** David's Descent into Exile (Pictures 15, 16, 17, and 18)
>
>**Series #2:** The Importance of Inquiring of God (Pictures 19 and 20)
>
>**Series #3:** Out of Enemy Hands (Pictures 20, 21, 22, and 23)
>
>**Series #4:** My Enemy in My Hands (Pictures 24, 25, and 26)
>
>**Series #5:** Into Enemy Hands (Pictures 27, 28, and 30)
>
>**Series #6:** The Importance of Inquiring of God (Pictures 29 and 31)
>
>**Series #7:** Final Battles and Rewards (Pictures 31 and 32)

Central to the series is **Series #4** with its theme of vengeance and glorification. Central to that series is the picture of David, Nabal, and Abigail.

Series #3 and #5 have the contrasting theme of being out of enemy hands and into enemy hands (It seems like it should be reversed, doesn't it? Shouldn't it end with David being delivered out of enemy hands?)

Series #2 and #6 have the matching themes of the importance of inquiring of God.

Series #1 and #7 are the opening and closing scenes. In the first, David seems to lose the kingdom only to begin another kingdom of sorts in the Cave of Adullam. In the final pictures, he receives the reward and kingdom when Saul's life is brought to an end.

The chapters are presented in chiastic order. The series themes are presented in chiastic order. Chiastic structures drive many of the individual pictures themselves. For all of the chaos of David's life while he is in exile, there is a grand order and purpose in all of it.

A Note About the Characters

Samuel is mentioned only three times in these chapters. His death is noted once in First Samuel 25:1 and again in 28:1, and then he makes his final appearance when he is summoned from the grave, also in Chapter 28. The one time he does appear, it is only to interact with Saul and not David.

There is one mention of the prophet Gad giving David direction in the beginning while he is in the stronghold, but that is the last mention of a prophet helping David through his exile years. Instead, we see brief interactions with intercessors like Jonathan, Abigail, and the priesthood.

In regards to the priesthood, the lineage of Eli continues with Ahimelech, who dies at Saul's hand in First Samuel 22 after becoming an unwitting party to David's escape, but his son Abiathar escapes Saul and allies himself with David. Abiathar will remain with David for the duration of David's reign.

There are three pictures where the narrative breaks away sharply from David to focus solely on Saul: when Saul kills the priesthood, when he visits the medium, and his death in the final chapter. In addition to Saul, there are three notable villains: Doeg the Edomite, Nabal, and the medium of En Dor. Doeg and the medium coincide with Saul's signature pictures, and Nabal is featured in the pivotal Chapter 25.

LESSON 13: FIRST SAMUEL 21:1–22:5

My Hiding Place

SERIES STRUCTURE

First Samuel 21 opens with David on the run from Saul. He spent three dark nights waiting for Jonathan to discover for himself Saul's deception and true intentions. When the truth was ascertained, David was sent away for his own safety. Now he is left alone, without provisions or protection in what has become enemy territory. He can't go to his king, his men-at-arms, his best friend, or even his family for help. It should not surprise us to see him stumble as the fear takes him.

David's descent is described in a series of three pictures (#15, #16, and #17) with a sudden reversal in the fourth picture (#18). This is a three-and-four literary structure where the first three pictures are of like kind and the fourth sets off a climactic contrast.

In **Picture #15** (21:1-9), David flees to the Tabernacle.

In **Picture #16** (21:10-15), David flees to Gath.

In **Picture #17** (22:1-2), David flees to the Cave of Adullam.

Picture #18 (22:3-5) is the contrasting picture where David comes out of the cave with the right mindset and plan of action.

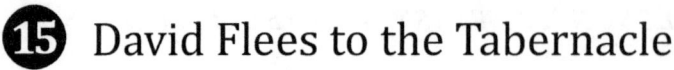 David Flees to the Tabernacle

READ

First Samuel 21:1-9

NARRATIVE STRUCTURE

Picture #15 (21:1-9) records David's first stop at the Tabernacle. It is divided into two sections, which are broken by an oddly placed narrator's comment in verse 7 introducing Doeg the Edomite who is simply there without having any part in the action at this point. In addition to the narrator, there is extensive dialogue between David and the priest. There is no ending narrator's note.

BUILD THE PICTURE

The picture begins with a narrator's comment describing David's movement. He comes to Nob seeking Ahimelech the priest.

1. **What do we know about Ahimelech?**

    Not much, really. He is just Ahimelech the priest who is presiding over the Tabernacle at Nob. There is no mention of his lineage.

2. **What do we know about the Tabernacle at Nob?**

    The location of Nob is not exactly known, but Isaiah 10:32 indicates that it was on a hill across from Jerusalem and within sight of Jerusalem, probably located on the Mount of Olives, east of Jerusalem.

    Here in First Samuel 21, it is the place where the Tabernacle stood. Nothing has been said about the Tabernacle being set up again since the Ark of the Covenant left Shiloh in First Samuel 4, but now it seems that the Tabernacle has been reestablished in its tent with all the furniture in place—except for the Ark. The Ark is still in the house of Abinadab in Kirjath Jearim and will remain in exile there until David brings it to Jerusalem once he is king.

Imagine this moment from Ahimelech's point of view. The commander of the king's army has just shown up at the Tabernacle without any men. David's position and relation to the king demands that at least a servant be in attendance with him, and it scares Ahimelech because this is not normal.

3. **What explanation does David fabricate?**

   I'm on a secret mission... I can't tell you the details... my men are in position... and I need supplies. Now think about this. Would the commander of the army go personally on a supply run? That seems a little odd. Needing food is one thing, but for the commander to come away without a sword is also odd.

   David's words are a deliberate lie. This is in stark contrast to David's truthfulness in the previous chapter when he was talking with Jonathan. David has been exalted very highly in the previous chapters as a man of truth and without deception in contrast to Saul. But now, as David flees for his life, he resorts to very Saul-like behavior.

4. **What bread does the priest give David?**

   He gives him the bread from the showbread table in the Tabernacle that is being removed and replaced with fresh loaves. It's week-old bread, but it is holy from having been in the Tabernacle. Normally, the priests would eat it. Ahimelech offers it to David on condition that "his men" are ritually clean. David can assure him that "his men" are indeed clean, because he has been out in the field for three days waiting for Jonathan's communication.

   So, Ahimelech gives him five loaves of bread.

5. **David and Ahimelech are observed by Doeg the Edomite. What do we know about Doeg?**

   Doeg is a servant of Saul, he is chief of the herdsmen who belonged to Saul, and he is an Edomite. You will remember that Edom is another name for Esau, who was Jacob's brother—the one from whom Jacob stole the father's inheritance and blessing. Now this Edomite witnesses another son of Jacob involved in a deception for the purported purpose of stealing the kingdom away from the king.

The only reason the Edomite is here at all is because he has been detained before the LORD. The text doesn't explain why he has been detained. It seems that the LORD deliberately put the Edomite in position to give him this glimpse of David's interaction with the priest.

Immediately after the narrative mentions Doeg, David makes another request, this time for a weapon—perhaps in reaction to seeing Doeg there. Ahimelech offers him Goliath's sword that was being kept in the Tabernacle.

6. **What does Goliath's sword signify to David?**

It was a reminder of that battle and the overwhelming odds he had faced and overcome with the LORD's strength. It's a trophy sword with a big reputation behind it and easily recognizable. Just having it with him would have been an encouragement but also a statement.

Ahimelech remarks that the sword is hidden behind the ephod. Isn't it curious that, given the choice, David asks for the trophy sword and not the ephod? He wants the weapon, but doesn't ask Ahimelech to inquire of God for him. That is a very Saul-like action.

7. **How do these actions appear to Doeg?**

Let's consider what Doeg witnessed. He doesn't hear the conversation, but he sees the actions. He sees David go to the high priest. He sees the high priest give David bread. He sees the high priest disappear inside the Tabernacle for a few minutes and return with Goliath's sword. He isn't sure what else Ahimelech did in the Tabernacle while he was out of sight, but Doeg imagines he inquired of God on David's behalf. At least, that is what he tells Saul in the next chapter.

16 David Flees to Gath

READ

First Samuel 21:10-15

NARRATIVE STRUCTURE

Picture #16 (21:10-15) marks David's second stop, this time at Gath. The only dialogue in the narrative is the Philistines. Again, there is no ending narrator's note.

BUILD THE PICTURE

The picture begins with a narrator's note that moves David forward to the next stop at Gath in Philistine territory.

8. **Look at the order of information in verse 10. What is driving David's actions?**

    David fled from King Saul to King Achish. He is only looking back at what he is trying to avoid while he is running forward headlong. He is reacting without thinking of the possible problems his actions will create for him.

    Fear is driving David, and he is making uncharacteristically bad choices. But this is what fear does. It robs you of power and sound reasoning. It makes you flail about when discipline and self-control are needed. The picture of David acting like a madman is suitable in this moment.

9. **Why would David go to Achish, the king of Gath?**

    There is an old (non-biblical) proverb that says, "The enemy of your enemy is your friend." That sounds as if it should be true, but it isn't, as shown in the case here. David seeks refuge with Saul's enemy, thinking that Saul would stop at the edge of Philistine territory and not pursue him there.

David is the slayer of Goliath of Gath, the slayer of ten thousands of enemy Philistines, and the vaunted champion of Israel. Even the servants recognize him. And yet he is a pathetic figure when he shows up on Achish's doorstep as a refugee without any servants or army. Only a madman would show up in Gath alone carrying Goliath's sword and expecting refuge from the people he had defeated.

When David realizes he has been recognized, he becomes afraid that he will be captured. That is not an unfounded fear. Pretending to be a madman isn't a bad tactic to get out of a sticky situation, and that is what David does to make the Philistines drive him away. He raves and scratches at the city gate like an animal, and lets his saliva drool down his beard. It is enough to make Achish think he is insane and put him away, and so he escapes from Gath.

David Flees to the Cave of Adullam

READ

First Samuel 22:1-2

NARRATIVE STRUCTURE

In **Picture #17** (22:1-2), David finally comes to a stop in the Cave of Adullam. Here we have the ending narrator's note, indicating the end of the series of three. Here, the final picture is only two verses long and delivered wholly by the narrator. The diminishing number of voices lends a certain quietness to the final scene, which is appropriate.

BUILD THE PICTURE
---

10. Where is the cave of Adullam?

This cave is in the hills above the Elah Valley where David defeated Goliath, in the no-man's land, geographically and politically, between

Israel and the Philistine territory. Here David finds refuge from the Philistines on one side and Saul on the other.

The name Adullam means "justice of the people," which is interesting considering the kind of people who gather to David at this place.

11. Who gathers to David here?

First, his family—his brothers and all of his father's house. With Saul on an obsessive rampage to hunt down David, the rest of his family is in extreme danger.

After his family comes a whole host of misfits—the distressed, the debtors, and those who are discontent or bitter of soul, as it says in the Hebrew. The Hebrew word for "distressed" is almost always in the context of a people under siege and in dire circumstances. They are trapped with no way out and at the end of their resources.

The debtor is the debtor.

Those who were "bitter of soul" is a phrase that crops up in Judges 18:25, where the Danites become bitter of soul over being unable to take their inheritance from the Amorites—the land that the Philistines now hold. The inheritance of the Danites slipped from their grasp, and as a result, they sought an inheritance elsewhere, but they went with bitter souls—with disillusionment and anger and hopelessness over a lost inheritance. Naomi in the book of Ruth expresses the same bitterness of soul when her sons die and her family's lineage is cut off.

This is the ugly side of Saul's kingdom. It is a kingdom where a king is so preoccupied with his own vendetta that he neglects the running of his country and the needs of the people. The people had chosen him as king, but he turned out to be a poor choice, and four hundred of them now seek David.

12. What do they want from David?

Safety, security, an inheritance, justice, or maybe just peace.

The text says that David became captain over them, but the English translation implies a military ranking like a commander. The Hebrew word is *sar*, which has a much broader application. It means prince, ruler, leader, or chieftain. We see the word used in Isaiah 9:6 where one of the noble names given to the promised Messianic king is Sar Shalom, Prince of Peace. This is the hope that David becomes to the people, this prince of peace.

The Psalms of David

I don't want to make this a study of the Psalms, but since several of them are specifically identified with this time in David's life, we might visit them briefly. I have pulled out a selection of verses from each that give us some insight into David's reflection on the episode.

Psalm 34

This psalm opens with *"A Psalm of David when he pretended madness before Abimelech [Achish], who drove him away, and he departed..."* It is a psalm devoted to praise of the LORD and is summarized in the ending verses.

> *"The righteous cry out, and the LORD hears, and delivers them out of all their troubles. The LORD is near to those who have a broken heart, and saves such as have a contrite spirit. Many are the afflictions of the righteous, but the LORD delivers him out of them all. He guards all his bones; not one of them is broken. Evil shall slay the wicked, and those who hate the righteous shall be condemned. The LORD redeems the soul of His servants, and none of those who trust in Him shall be condemned."* —Psalm 34:17-22

Psalm 56

This psalm opens with *"...A Michtam of David when the Philistines captured him in Gath..."* It is a prayer for relief from tormentors.

> *"Be merciful to me, O God, for man would swallow me up; Fighting all day he oppresses me. My enemies would hound me all day, for there are many who fight against me, O Most High. Whenever I am afraid, I will trust in You. In God (I will praise His word), in God I have put my trust; I will not fear. What can flesh do to me?... In God I have put my trust; I will not be afraid. What can man do to me?"* —Psalm 56:1-4, 11

Psalm 57

This psalm opens with *"... A Michtam of David when he fled from Saul into the cave..."* It is a prayer for safety from enemies. Notice David's focus on the power, mercy, and glory of God compared to his enemies.

> *"... Be merciful to me, O God, be merciful to me! For my soul trusts in You; and in the shadow of Your wings I will make my refuge, until these calamities have passed by. I will cry out to God Most High, to God who performs all things for me. He shall send from heaven and save me; He reproaches the one who would swallow me up. Selah. God shall send forth His mercy and His truth. My soul is among lions; I lie among the sons of men who are set on fire, whose teeth are spears and arrows, and their tongue a sharp sword. Be exalted, O God, above the heavens; Let Your glory be above all the earth."* —Psalm 57:1-5

Psalm 142

This is a short but very poignant insight into David's thoughts while he was in the cave.

> *"A Contemplation of David. A Prayer when he was in the cave. I cry out to the LORD with my voice; with my voice to the LORD I make my supplication. I pour out my complaint before Him; I declare before Him my trouble. When my spirit was overwhelmed within me, then You knew my path. In the way in which I walk they have secretly set a snare for me. Look on my right hand and see, for there is no one who acknowledges me; Refuge has failed me; no one cares for my soul. I cried out to You, O LORD: I said, 'You are my refuge, my portion in the land of the living. Attend to my cry, for I am brought very low; deliver me from my persecutors, for they are stronger than I. Bring my soul out of prison, that I may praise Your name; the righteous shall surround me, for You shall deal bountifully with me.'"* - Psalm 142:1-7

This psalm in particular reflects David's conclusion that his deliverance and refuge can only be in the LORD. In general, the psalms reflect a single-mindedness in David's dependence on the LORD, but that single-mindedness only develops after he has exhausted his own wisdom and resources. It is the first step in his training to be king.

18. David in the Stronghold

READ

First Samuel 22:3-5

NARRATIVE STRUCTURE

First Samuel 22:3-5 is Picture #18, David in the stronghold. This fourth picture offsets the first three with a reversal of action. A brief conversation between David and the king of Moab is sandwiched between two narrator's comments, highlighting David's statement that he intended to wait for God's instructions. So we have a mini-chiastic structure (A-B-A).

- (A) *"Then David went from there to Mizpah of Moab, and he said to the king of Moab, 'Please let my father and mother come here with you, ...'"* (22:3a)

- (B) *"'... till I know what God will do for me.'"* (22:3b)

- (A) *"So he brought them before the king of Moab, and they dwelt with him all the time that David was in the stronghold."* (22:4)

The final verse is partly instruction from the prophet Gad and partly narrator's comment that ends the sequence with a departure statement. The fact that David immediately follows the prophet's instruction reinforces his statement that he will be obedient to the LORD's instruction.

BUILD THE PICTURE

13. Why does David take his parents to Moab?

This small breakout of verses explains the situation with David's parents (22:3-4). David's family is in danger, and fugitive life would be too rigorous for elderly parents to endure, so he seeks refuge for his parents by taking them down to Mizpah of Moab, to his grandmother Ruth's people. Moab is technically an enemy in Saul's estimation, but they are not a current threat to Israel, and so Moab presents a temporary refuge.

14. What/where is the stronghold?

After leaving his parents in Moab, David's first, brief stop is at a place called the *metsudah* or "the stronghold." This desert area is rugged and marked with high mountain plateaus that give a commanding view of the area and are relatively impregnable to enemies. A small group can withstand a very large force from this vantage point. But such strongholds can become death traps if the enemy decides to lay siege to it, as history has shown with places like Masada. Strongholds can be deceiving in their appearance of strength.

God tells David through the prophet, Gad, not to trust in that strength. God will be his rock, not this physical stronghold. Do not stay in the stronghold. This picture of God as his rock figures in many of the psalms attributed to David. This lesson made a definite impression on him.

15. What do we know about the prophet Gad?

Well ... he is a prophet, and his name is Gad. He is not given any introduction or genealogy. He is mentioned in Second Samuel 24:11 (cf. First Chronicles 21:9) as being David's prophet. After Samuel dies, Gad, along with Nathan, become the prophets associated with David's reign and his chroniclers (First Chronicles 29:29). He is a minor character who only shows up in David's life at specific moments. In this case, he warns David not to stay in the strongholds but to go to the land of Judah. And David heeds his warning. He leaves the stronghold and seeks refuge in the forest of Hereth. Like the Stronghold, the Forest of Hereth is not a known place, just a general area.

⑮ ⑯ ⑰ Comparison: Three Stages of David's Descent

From the heights of Nob where the Tabernacle stands, David descends first into enemy hands and then into a cave in the ground. What seems to be a low point for the anointed king becomes the start of a sort of kingdom. He is not crowned yet, and he will not be crowned until the current king is ousted, and yet he has followers to whom he is already prince, if not king.

Isn't it curious that David's ascent to the throne should begin with a descent? This is a lot like the narrative's portrayal of the Ark of God's journey in Chapters 5–6. It, too, left the Tabernacle to fall into Philistine hands before finally being sent back to Israel again. The Ark of God will remain in exile in the mountains of Kirjath Jearim, even as David will remain in exile for the remainder of First Samuel. The Ark's exile will not end until David's exile ends, and he brings it back to the Tabernacle in Jerusalem in Second Samuel 6. So there is an interesting association made between David and the Ark of God, beginning here with David's journey.

If Nob's location is on the Mount of Olives, that is significant. The Mount of Olives features heavily in the life of Christ, of whom David is a type.

16. What role did the Mount of Olives play in Christ's narrative?

> It was a place from which Jesus often taught the people. It was a place where the disciples came to inquire of Him and learn His teachings. It was the place where Jesus delivered the Olivet discourse and the explanation of how the kingdom was going to come about, which was not going to be how the people expected.
>
> If the Tabernacle itself was set up at this place, that further reinforces the picture. The Tabernacle, with its coverings of cloth and skins, was the place from which the LORD spoke and instructed His people. Jesus embodied the picture of the Tabernacle, being the Word of God and essence of God hidden within a common human skin and clothes. When He set Himself on the Mount of Olives to teach the people, it was like an echo of this picture of the Tabernacle at Nob.
>
> According to Luke 19, the Mount of Olives is the place where Jesus actually begins His triumphal entry into Jerusalem (Luke 19). The people hailed him as king, while his enemies sought to kill him. Again, the kingdom wasn't going to come about the way they thought.
>
> The Garden of Gethsemane is located at the foot of the Mount of Olives. It is the place where Jesus sought refuge and guidance from the Father in prayer on the eve of His death, and it was also the place where the enemy betrayed Him. Jesus knew exactly whom the enemy would be when the betrayal happens, just as David knew that Doeg would betray him, as we will see in Chapter 22.

Only Luke relates a particular instruction that Jesus gives his disciples as they leave the Passover and head for the Garden of Gethsemane.

> *"And He said to them, 'When I sent you without money bag, knapsack, and sandals, did you lack anything?' So they said, 'Nothing.' Then He said to them, 'But now, he who has a money bag, let him take it, and likewise a knapsack; and he who has no sword, let him sell his garment and buy one.'"* —Luke 22:35-36

Jesus is saying, "This is a turning point, and things are going to be different going forward." Jesus' words echo David's actions in preparing himself with provisions and a sword for flight and fight.

⑮⑯/⑱ Contrast: David's Deceit with His Truthfulness

17. How do David's words and actions now compare to his previous attempts to seek refuge?

David begins to think proactively instead of reactively. He doesn't slip his parents into the country by underhanded or deceptive means. He goes formally to the King of Moab, almost as king to king, and requests asylum for his parents. He knows the extent of Saul's obsession, and it's almost as if he is making the king aware of the potential conflict that might come from his actions. He leaves his parents in Moab while he is in the stronghold, then waits to see what the LORD will have him do next. This time he decides to inquire of God before acting.

The candid nature of his exchange with the King of Moab is a contrast to his previous deception of Ahimelech. With Ahimelech, he chose to lie and deceive to get the help he needed, and he took away the sword instead of seeking the ephod. But this time he asks openly and plainly, and declares his intention of waiting for the LORD's direction.

What changed David's behavior?

He spent some time in the cave of Adullam. He finally quit running and took some time to reflect.

APPLY THE PICTURE

"And everyone who competes for the prize is temperate in all things. Now they do it to obtain a perishable crown, but we for an imperishable crown. Therefore I run thus: not with uncertainty. Thus I fight: not as one who beats the air. But I discipline my body and bring it into subjection, lest, when I have preached to others, I myself should become disqualified." —First Corinthians 9:25-27

David's Model

David's first reaction to a crisis in his life was a flailing moment for him. He fled from person to person seeking the help and refuge he needed with little success. His crisis sent him down the same path as Saul in terms of his behavior. He made hasty decisions and let fear drive him. He resorted to deception and self-defense, which only got him deeper into trouble until he finally sought isolation. That was when the LORD began to bring him the people who could comfort and support him, and he regained his perspective.

Endurance tests are part of pursuing the crown/reward, and one of those endurance tests is how we react in crisis. Our actions and reactions in a crisis reveal a lot about how well we are aligned with God, and we can stumble when troubles break over us unexpectedly.

- **What was David's first knee-jerk response?**

  David sought help first from the priests at the Tabernacle. For us, this might be like seeking help from the church. David shows up at the church under odd circumstances, and he isn't acting normally. The church leader is skeptical and questions him.

- **David isn't truthful over why he is really seeking help. Why does David lie to Ahimelech?**

  Fear of being betrayed, or maybe to protect Ahimelech by giving him a plausible excuse should he be questioned.

- **What would he have told Ahimelech if he had told the truth?**

  I am the new king that Samuel anointed, and now Saul is seeking to kill me, so I am fleeing. I need food and a weapon.

- **What might be the consequences for telling the truth?**

  If he had been upfront with Ahimelech, then it would have been Ahimelech's choice as to where to place his loyalty. Ahimelech might have helped him, or Ahimelech might have refused him provisions, informed on him to Saul, and put his life in jeopardy.

- **Was it right for David to lie in this case?**

  This is one of those difficult moments that we ourselves face in having to discern right from wrong. There are consequences for telling the truth but also consequences for lying. David's lie achieves an immediate goal of securing food and a weapon, but other consequences will follow for the church leadership that he did not anticipate. We will revisit this question once we see how events play out.

Next, David sought help from the opposition. The Philistines contrast to the priesthood the way the carnal world contrasts to God's people.

- **Why turn from God's people to the Philistines for help? What kind of help did David think he would get from them?**

Finally, David sought refuge in a cave.

- **What happened while David was in isolation?**

  He had time to reflect and re-establish his relationship with God. Once he stopped trying to seek the help on his own, God was able to bring people to him who could give him the support he needed. David had to quit doing things by his own understanding and power before God could begin to work.

Questions for Reflection

- What is your first go-to place for help?
- Have you ever asked God to bring people into your life to help you in times of need, or do you rely on your own judgment in seeking help?
- Have you ever lied when asked why you are seeking help? If so, why?

- What do you think would have happened if you had told the truth?

- Why would you seek support from the outside (carnal) world? How might resorting to this option entrap you?

- What are some pros and cons of being isolated in times of crisis?

- When crises happen in your life, do you seek time alone to reflect and pray about them?

- In his psalms, David dwelt heavily on praising God. How does praising God in the midst of crisis help us maintain the right perspective?

LESSON 14: FIRST SAMUEL 22:6–23:13

The Importance of Inquiring of God

SERIES STRUCTURE

In **Picture #19** (22:6-23), the narrative segues abruptly away from David to focus wholly on Saul.

Picture #20 (23:1-13) details David's battle to save the town of Keilah. What happens in this battle is directly linked to Saul's actions in the previous picture, so we will study them together. Picture #20 also shares a theme with the next series, so we will touch on it again in the picture comparisons.

Saul Murders the Priests of Nob

READ

First Samuel 22:6-23

NARRATIVE STRUCTURE

Picture #19 has four sets of dialogue that are arranged in a three-and-four literary structure where the first three dialogues are of like kind and the fourth sets off a climactic contrast. In addition to this, the first three are arranged in a chiastic structure (A-B-A):

1) Saul addresses his servants, Doeg's response (22:6-10)
2) Saul addresses Ahimelech, Ahimelech's response (22:11-16)
3) Saul addresses his servants (again), Doeg's response (22:17-19)
4) Abiathar's report, David's response (22:20-23)

The picture opens with a narrator's comment, but then ends with a final dialogue between David and Abiathar in verses 20-23. The ending dialogue connects **Picture #19** with **Picture #20** thematically.

BUILD THE PICTURE

Saul Addresses His Servants, Doeg's Response (22:6-10)

1. **Where is Saul?**

   The detail about Saul's location is inserted into the text almost like an oddly placed note. The text says that Saul is at Gibeah, sitting under a tamarisk tree at Ramah. Gibeah and Ramah are two different locations, so his placement is a little ambiguous. Since we left Saul at Gibeah in Chapter 20, we will assume he is still there. The verse could read that Saul was at Gibeah, under the tamarisk tree on a *ramah* or high place. Ramah may be the common word and not a proper name in this case. Tamarisk tree is the word *esel* in the Hebrew, which can also mean any large tree or grove of trees, which is more likely since tamarisk trees aren't native to this area.

   The structure of verse 6 is very similar to First Samuel 14:2. Compare:

   > "And Saul was sitting in the outskirts of Gibeah under a pomegranate tree which is in Migron. The people who were with him were about six hundred men." —First Samuel 14:2

   > "... now Saul was staying in Gibeah under a tamarisk tree in Ramah, with his spear in his hand, and all his servants standing about him—" —First Samuel 22:6

   So, Saul is sitting under a tree with his men around him when he should be out doing something productive—just like he was in Chapter 14. It is a very similar picture, and when we find two verses of similar structure like this, it should prompt us to compare the other details of those pictures. We will work through the comparison once we get to the end of this picture.

2. **What are Saul's grievances?**

    a. *"Will the son of Jesse..."*—note that Saul can't even say David's name. It is a demeaning thing not to call a man by his name but refer to him as the son of someone because it demotes him in status. *"Will the son of Jesse secure your inheritance in the land?"* Saul raves at the Benjamites in particular over this. David has become his rival for the throne, but David is from Judah, not Benjamin. David will divide his inheritance among his own kin and give them prominent ranks, not the Benjamites.

    b. His own people have conspired against him and aren't telling him what is going on, namely that: 1) Jonathan had made a covenant with David, and Saul didn't known about it; and 2) Jonathan has stirred up Saul's servant (another derogatory reference to David) against Saul.

    Jonathan's lack of loyalty is an extremely sore point with Saul, since he had been his father's confidant all this time. That's an irony. Saul had kept his son in the dark about his dealings with David, but now the son has done the same back to Saul, and Saul is furious.

    c. Saul says David is lying in wait for him, which is a lie. Saul is the aggressor pursuing David, but self-pity has made him see himself as the victim. Beware of letting the victim mentality take you. It will skew your thinking and get you into sin.

    None of Saul's servants answered him except Doeg the Edomite.

3. **What is Doeg the Edomite's testimony?**

    He saw the son of Jesse talking with Ahimelech, the son of Ahitub. Note that he mimics the same derogatory address that Saul used for David, but gives Ahimelech a higher honor by mentioning his lineage with his name.

    Doeg said that Ahimelech gave David provisions and a sword and inquired of God for him. That last part wasn't true. Doeg made that assumption based only on what he saw and not what he heard.

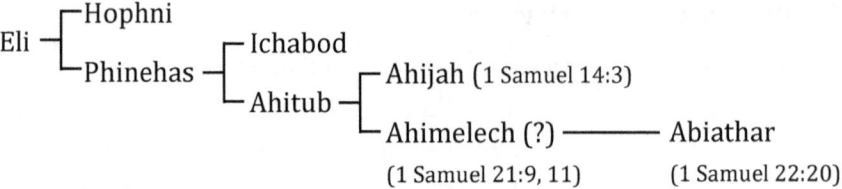

4. What more do we find out about Ahimelech now?

When Ahimelech was mentioned in Chapter 21, he was just called Ahimelech the priest without any more information than that. Now his lineage is mentioned, which connects him with the cursed house of Eli. Being the son of Ahitub makes Ahimelech the great-grandson of Eli.

Back in Chapter 14, we see Ahijah, the son of Ahitub, and now in Chapter 22 we see Ahimelech, the son of Ahitub. The text doesn't tell us what the relationship is between Ahimelech and Ahijah, or how much time has elapsed between the two chapters. Ahimelech is either the brother of Ahijah or they may be the same man whose name has been changed to reinforce the picture of what is happening here in Chapter 22. (Name changes like this aren't unusual. Gideon was alternately called Jerubbaal for picture purposes.)

If the same man's name has been changed to reflect this picture, then let's consider the meanings behind the names:

> **Ahijah** means "brother of God."
> **Ahimelech** means "brother of the king."

The comparison is merely of the names, not of the men. Ahijah was no great example of a man who might be called brother to God, nor was Ahimelech necessarily labeled a brother to the king. But the comparison between the names adds nuance to the narrative in that the difference between them reflects a difference in loyalty. Where one name aligns the priest with God, the other name aligns him with a king who has rejected God. In this scenario, Ahimelech's loyalty to the king is under suspicion.

There are right and wrong kings with whom to align yourself when trying to keep the crown to which you have been anointed. This is part of the endurance test of the royal priesthood.

Saul calls Ahimelech and the priests from Nob to him and accuses them of conspiring with David.

Saul Addresses Ahimelech (22:11-16)

5. What are Saul's charges against Ahimelech?

Ahimelech conspired against him to help David. Saul repeats what Doeg said, then gives Ahimelech's actions a motive—that David should rise against him and lie in wait to take his life.

6. What is Ahimelech's defense against Saul's charges?

Ahimelech declares he is innocent of all these charges, and his defense rests mostly on what he knows of David's character. David was a servant of unimpeachable integrity. He would never do something dishonorable or faithless to his father-in-law. Ahimelech also denies inquiring of God on David's behalf, which is the truth, but Saul doesn't believe it.

Saul Addresses His Servants, Doeg's Response (22:17-19)

7. What is Ahimelech's sin in Saul's eyes?

He demands that Ahimelech and his house be put to death, not for any sin against God, but for what Saul considers treason against himself. He imagines their loyalty is with David because they knew when David fled and didn't tell him. Saul sees enemies in every corner, and the fear is driving his paranoia and anger.

Saul's guards won't lift a hand against the priests, so instead he orders the foreigner, Doeg, to do it, which Doeg does with enthusiasm.

8. Who gets caught in the massacre?

Doeg kills eighty-five priests, but then goes on to cut down the entire city of Nob including all the humans and animals with the edge of the sword. The phrase "edge of the sword" is repeated twice in verse 19 for added emphasis. It was a slaughter.

9. Why didn't the people of Israel intervene to save the priests?

Saul's guards would not raise a finger to kill the priests, but neither would they raise a finger to save them—even when Doeg went on a killing spree. The people intervened once before to stop Saul's madness when he would have killed his own son (Chapter 14), but no one values this priesthood. We have to remember that there is a curse on Eli's house, and the curse is playing out here.

Abiathar's Report, David's Response (22:20-23)

Only one priest escapes the massacre to tell David, and that is Abiathar. This fourth dialogue segues sharply away from Saul and back to David, and provides the transition to the next picture.

10. What is David's response to Abiathar's news?

He knew that Doeg would betray him. He admits that he is the one who caused the deaths and put Abiathar in danger, and so he offers him protection and refuge.

11. Did David's deception of Ahimelech cause the massacre?

No, actually, it didn't. Doeg reported to Saul what he had seen and not heard. David's deception was known only to himself, Ahimelech, and God. The fate of Ahimelech was sealed by just being seen talking with David. And yet, isn't it curious that the minute David begins to engage in deception, God orchestrates events to make it a bad experience?

12. Would it have mattered if David had inquired of the LORD instead of taking the sword?

It might have. Doeg reported that he had, even though it wasn't true, so David might as well have asked direction from God. Even if Saul's actions were determined, God might have offered another solution that would have preserved the lives of the priests, if only by warning them that they were now in jeopardy.

13. Why did God arrange for Doeg to witness David's actions?

Doeg reports on David, but the consequences fall on Ahimelech and not David. We cannot forget that Ahimelech belongs to the cursed house of Eli, and David's actions facilitate an occasion for the LORD to keep His word.

But the LORD's actions facilitate something else. In the past Saul had always had the benefit of having a priest with an ephod for inquiring of God—not that he used it often, and when he did, he often got an answer he didn't want. But now that he has killed Ahimelech and the priests, the one surviving priest, Abiathar, now defects to David with the ephod. God has effectively transferred the communication link with Himself from Saul to David, and now we will see if the new king makes better use of it than Saul, and to what end.

 The Battle of Keilah

READ

First Samuel 23:1-13

NARRATIVE STRUCTURE

Picture #20 begins with dialogue. Third-party informants always introduce the four pictures where David and Saul interact (Pictures #20, #23, #24, and #26).

This picture is divided into three main sections, capped off by the narrator's ending comment in verse 13:

1) David saves Keilah from the Philistines (23:1-6)
2) Saul's plot to capture David (23:7-8)
3) David's escape (23:9-13)

The main structural feature of this picture is the oddly placed comment in verse 6, which sets up the pivotal point in the battle action as well as the contrast between David's approach to the battle and Saul's. Saul loses the communication link to God in the previous picture, and that has consequences in this subsequent battle.

Lesson 14: The Importance of Inquiring of God | 303

BUILD THE PICTURE

David Saves Keilah from the Philistines (23:1-6)

The Philistines are attacking Israel again, this time at Keilah. Saul should be the one dealing with the threat, but he isn't. Instead, he is focused on the manhunt for David. David hears of the Philistine attack and wants to do something about it.

This is the first time David goes into battle independently from Israel's army. He is a lot like Jonathan in that he decides to take on the Philistines with only his own men and without the greater help of Saul's forces.

14. What do we know about the Philistine attack?

> From verse 1, we see that the Philistines have attacked in force, and they are robbing the threshing floors, which would place these events in the summer when the wheat is harvested.

> From verse 5, we know that part of the Philistines' tactics were to drive cattle into the area so that the animals would eat the grain. This is much like the Midianite's tactics that Gideon faced. It was a way of looting the land and leaving the people impoverished.

15. What do we know about Keilah?

> Keilah is in Judah's territory, just south of the cave of Adullam and the Elah Valley where David took down Goliath. This puts it right in the buffer zone between Israel- and the Philistine-held lands. This episode is the only time in the Scripture where this place figures.

> Keilah is a walled city with bars and gates. The name Keilah means "fortress" in the sense of being enclosed, in the same way a stone is enclosed in a sling or a man's hand. The imagery of a stone caught in a sling is reinforced by the repeated references to someone being delivered into someone's hands. It is a similar picture. But a stone is caught in a sling only temporarily, while it waits to be deployed.

> Notice the rhythm of this section. The men speak, then David, then the LORD. The men speak, then David, then the LORD. And then David and his men act.

16. Why note that Abiathar carried away the ephod in verse 6?

This detail seems oddly out of place and unconnected to the immediate narrative—although it does link the narrative back to the previous chapter. But then why not mention it in the previous chapter where it talks about Saul killing all the priests and Abiathar fleeing to David?

Any time a verse seems out of place, it is out of place for a reason. In this case, the author places this information here to create a structural break in the narrative between David's action and Saul's action and gives us a theme for comparing the two. We are comparing David to Saul with a focus on the theme of inquiring of God. When Saul had the priest with the ephod, he rarely used it. David is a stark contrast to Saul in this.

Saul's Plot to Capture David (23:7-8)

Verses 7-8 have a tight chiastic structure. Saul hears the news. Saul interprets the news. Saul acts on the news. Saul's interpretation is the point of the chiasm.

17. How does Saul interpret the news of David's location?

He declares that God has delivered David into his hand. Saul doesn't ask God if this is His doing. He believes it is God's doing simply because it benefits his own agenda.

18. Saul plans to besiege the city. Who else will this affect besides David and his men?

When Saul besieges the city, he won't just besiege David and his men. He will besiege everyone in the city. Keilah's resources have already been severely compromised by the Philistines' raids. They won't be able to hold out long under siege. Saul never thinks about the collateral damage, or, if he does, then he shows little regard for the lives of Keilah's citizens. But then he has no problem wiping out an entire city just to take vengeance on one man, as he demonstrated with Nob. That kind of threat might induce the citizens of Keilah to turn David over, just to save their own lives.

David's Escape (23:9-13)

Note that the rhythm in this section is similar to the beginning, except that we don't have David's men in the dialogue. David asks and the LORD answers. David asks and the LORD answers. Then David and his men act. There is no balking on the part of David's men this time.

The repetition in the text seems belabored, but it is belabored to make a point. Twice David faced a battle, both times in an effort to save Keilah. That is his motivation. Twice he inquired of the LORD, and twice he succeeded by following the LORD's word. The repetition creates a symmetry with the first section, but also an emphasis on the fact that David is pursuing a reward correctly and for the right reason—to save God's people.

Saul, by contrast, only wants to kill David and destroy Keilah. He doesn't inquire of the LORD at all but declares the LORD's intent to his men based on his own interpretation of events, saying "God has delivered him into my hand . . ." But God did not. Saul's effort is thwarted.

19. How do David and his men escape?

> First of all, we should note that David now has six hundred men, instead of four hundred. David and his men rocket out of the gate of Keilah like so many pebbles slung out of a sling. They went wherever they could go, and no one could catch them. It is assumed that they reconvened somewhere, but the effect was that they escaped Saul. It was told to Saul that David had escaped, and he just gave up at that point.

❼/❿❷⓿ Comparison: Saul and David Inquiring of God

Picture #7 is First Samuel 14:1-46, which encompasses Jonathan's scaling the cliffs to battle the Philistines and Saul's rash oath.

Pictures #19 and #20 encompass Saul's loss of the ephod and the battle at Keilah here in First Samuel 22–23. The theme of this lesson has been the importance of communicating with God, and it is also the theme of this comparison.

The author prompts us to compare these pictures by creating parallel elements in the narratives. I will chart out the parallels, and then we will look at the implications that come from the comparison.

7 First Samuel 14	**19 20** First Samuel 22–23
(14:11) The scene begins with the children of Israel hiding in caves and rocky hills for fear of the Philistines.	**(23:3)** David and his men are hiding in a cave in the rocky hills. David's men are afraid to leave the refuge of the cave for fear not just of the Philistines but Saul as well.
(14:1) Jonathan decides to engage the Philistines taking just his bodyguard with him, but without his father's army as backup. **(14:6-12)** Jonathan is known for acting independently of his father's army when fighting the Philistines, and he doesn't hesitate to engage them with only a small contingent of men. Jonathan goes into battle, but he waits for a sign from God that he should go. God gives him the go-ahead.	**(23:1-2, 13)** David hears about the battle and decides to engage the Philistines with only a small contingent of men. This is the first time David has entered into battle independently of Saul and the armies of Israel. David inquires of God, and God gives him the go-ahead.
(14:2) "And Saul was sitting in the outskirts of Gibeah under a pomegranate tree which is in Migron. The people who were with him were about six hundred men."	**(22:6)** "... now Saul was staying in Gibeah under a tamarisk tree in Ramah ..." **(23:13)** "So David and his men, about six hundred ..."
(14:3) "Ahijah the son of Ahitub, Ichabod's brother, the son of Phinehas, the son of Eli, the LORD's priest in Shiloh, was wearing an ephod ..."	**(23:6)** "Now it happened, when Abiathar the son of Ahimelech fled to David at Keilah, that he went down with an ephod in his hand."

In both cases, Saul is sitting at home while Jonathan and David are out fighting battles, and he only finds out about it after the battles are underway.

Both David and Saul have six hundred men with them and a priest with an ephod. Previously, David only had four hundred men with him in the cave of Adullam, but now the number has increased to 600. That is a new detail that was added to show that David and Saul are equals in this comparison.

Chapter 14 doesn't give us Saul's dialogue with his servants that we have in Chapter 22, nor does it have a parallel to Saul killing the priesthood. That episode was included to show how the ephod transferred to David. The similarities in the pictures pick up again when Saul hears that the battle with the Philistines is underway. Now we come to our comparison of how David and Saul conduct themselves in battle in regards to inquiring of the LORD. That is our theme.

⑦ First Samuel 14	⑲⑳ First Samuel 22–23
Saul inquires of God twice in the course of battle.	David inquires of God twice in the course of battle.
(14:18-20) The first time Saul inquires of God is in the battle with the Philistines. Saul started to inquire of God but stopped.	**(23:2-5)** The first time David inquires of God is in the battle with the Philistines. David inquired of the LORD, and the LORD gave him the go-ahead. David's men balked, so David inquired again, and the LORD gave the go-ahead again.

- **Why didn't Saul follow through with inquiring of God?**
  Because of urgency. The battle was pressing, and he was lagging behind when he should have been leading. It was urgent that he get onto the battlefield.

- **Was it really all that urgent that he get to the battlefield?**
  No. God and Jonathan had it covered.

- **Did David allow himself to be driven by a sense of urgency?**
  No.

- **Was David swayed by his men's resistance to going into battle?**
  No.

In both scenarios, Saul has besieged his own people.

⑦ First Samuel 14	⑲⑳ First Samuel 22–23
(14:24) The people have been forced to go without food until Saul has avenged himself on his enemies. Saul had, in essence, laid the people under siege by denying them food.	**(23:8)** Saul proposes to lay the people of Keilah under siege until he avenges himself on his enemy, David. Keilah is already beleaguered after the Philistine raid. They will not be able to endure a siege, but Saul doesn't care.
(14:36-37) The second time Saul inquired of God was when he wanted to continue the battle with the Philistines.	**(23:9-11)** The second time David inquired of God was when Saul wanted to continue the battle with him at Keilah.
(14:41-42) The focus of the battle turned at this point from Saul fighting the Philistines to an internal battle where Saul is hunting one of his own. When Saul inquired of God the second time, it was to seek a determination of fate of his people, with the intent to kill.	**(23:7-13)** After the narrative describes the battle with the Philistines, the focus suddenly turns to an internal battle where Saul is hunting David. When David inquired of God the second time, it was also to seek a determination of the fate of his people, but his intent is to save.
The Urim and Thummim were almost Jonathan's undoing, for they placed him at his father's mercy. It is the people who had to rescue Jonathan.	Instead of putting David at Saul's mercy, the Urim and Thummim saved him from both Saul and the people of Keilah who would betray him.
(14:46) *"Then Saul returned from pursuing the Philistines, and the Philistines went to their own place."*	**(23:13)** *"... Then it was told Saul that David had escaped from Keilah; so he halted the expedition."*

- **What is Saul's order of inquiry?**

    He proposed his intention to the people first, and then he asked God. And God did not answer.

- **What is David's order of inquiry?**

  In both cases, David inquires of God first. When his men balk, he inquires of God again, but he doesn't let their fear sway him from what God has said.

- **Why didn't God answer Saul? (Consider James 1:5-8.)**

- **Was Saul swayed by God's resistance to his continuing the fight?**

  Actually, no, he wasn't. He was bent on continuing the battle, but because he had asked the LORD in front of everyone, he was forced to stop until he got the go-ahead from God. Then he decided to force the issue and find out why God wasn't speaking to him.

- **Why didn't the people stand up for David like they did for Jonathan?**

  Because of what Saul did at Nob. Back in Chapter 14, the people did not fear to stand up to Saul; but when we compare the two accounts, it is the intervening detail in Chapter 22 of Saul killing the priests of Nob that changed the dynamic. The people of Keilah are now afraid of Saul.

  Saul always allowed himself to be swayed by the people for fear of losing their support.

- **Did David's decision to follow God's directions lose him the support of his men?**

  No.

- **Did David's decision to follow God's direction keep him from getting trapped?**

  Yes!

APPLY THE PICTURE

David versus Saul

In this passage, we are given two obvious examples of how to fight a good fight. David and Saul are pursuing two different rewards, and they have different reasons and ways of pursuing those rewards. I've been working out the models for you so far. Why don't you try answering the questions this time?

- **What are the rewards?**
- **What are the reasons?**
- **What are the ways they go about it?**

The Importance of Communication with God

Saul interpreted what he considered to be a fortuitous turn of events to be God's will, and he let that conviction drive his actions. Do we ever do that? When things are going our way and we are presented with a sudden opportunity that seems good to us, do we just chalk it up to God's will or do we actually take time to ask Him if it is His will?

What is the benefit of inquiring of the LORD?

Keilah was a stronghold and a tough place to tackle. It was a death trap without any means of escape except through the same gate where you entered—which could be barred against you at any moment—and yet there were people caught in that place that desperately needed help. For men who were already in a vulnerable position (as most Christians around the world are these days), to try to save those people caught in a stronghold overrun by the enemy seemed an impossible mission. There was so much at stake when it came to their own safety, and yet the LORD sent them in there. **It was a test of faith, first, to ask Him for direction, and, second, to act on that direction.**

But think about this: If God could send a man to the grave and bring him back up again, then getting you in and out of a bind like this really isn't so hard, is it?

There's a scary side to inquiring of the LORD, because He might send you into those kinds of places. But there is a wonderful side as well, because the same God who sends you there gives you the strength to accomplish the mission and doesn't abandon you there. And the advantage you have in the battle may not be superior tactics or having a superior army, so much as having the right timing. The right timing can give a single, unarmed man the advantage over an army of thousands with superior training and resources. But timing is something that is really in the LORD's hands.

Knowing which fight to fight, knowing when to fight and when to stop fighting, and disciplining yourself to go when the LORD says go and stop when He says stop—these are all part of fighting a good fight.

Other Battle Do's and Don'ts

In the picture comparison, two kings with exactly the same resources model a crisis for us. The key to their success or failure rested on their use of their communication link to God, but there were also some other subtle dos and don'ts that they give us.

- Do not let yourself be driven to decisions based solely on urgency.
- If God says go, don't be swayed by other people's fear or resistance.
- Do ask God if this is a battle you should be fighting. (Sometimes it isn't.)
- Don't ask people first and then seek God's opinion, or vice versa. That is being double-minded.
- Maintain your focus on God's agenda, even when you are under pressure.

Questions for Reflection

- Are we being hunted as David was? (First Peter 5:6-9)
- How do you deal with crises in your life?
- How do you know if the battle is one you should be fighting?

LESSON 15: FIRST SAMUEL 23:14-29

Out of Enemy Hands

SERIES STRUCTURE

First Samuel 23:1-13 was Picture #20 and detailed David's battle to save the town of Keilah. While this picture was linked to the one preceding it with the theme of inquiring of God, it also goes with the next three pictures in First Samuel 23 that have the common theme of God saving David out of enemy hands. Here is a rundown of the series:

> **Picture #20** (23:1-13) was an **experience of deliverance.** David and his men were trapped at Keilah and faced betrayal, but David inquired of the LORD and took the LORD's warning. Thus, David and his men escaped from Saul at Keilah.
>
> **Picture #21** (23:14-15) makes **the statement** that God did not deliver David into Saul's hands.
>
> **Picture #22** (23:16-18) presents **the comforter,** Jonathan, who assures David that God will not deliver him into Saul's hand and that David's place in the kingdom is secure.
>
> **Picture #23** (23:19-29) is another **experience of deliverance** as God actively delivers David from Saul's hand, just as He did in Picture #20 in the battle of Keilah, but this time there are a few differences that we will examine.

Pictures #21, #22, and the second half of #23 have tight chiastic structures that draw them into closer relationship with each other structurally. We will work through each one individually, then look at the series overall.

21 In the Wilderness: The Statement

READ

First Samuel 23:14-15

NARRATIVE STRUCTURE

Picture #21 has so few verses and they are so tightly structured that I will just copy them here to show you the chiastic structure.

- (A) *"And David stayed in strongholds in the wilderness, and remained in the mountains <u>in the Wilderness of Ziph</u>..."*
- (B) *"<u>Saul sought him</u> every day..."*
- **(C) *"... but God did not deliver him into his hand."***
- (B) *"So David saw that <u>Saul had come out to seek his life</u>..."*
- (A) *"And David was <u>in the Wilderness of Ziph</u> in a forest."*

The statement is at the crux of the structure.

BUILD THE PICTURE

1. Where is David?

The opening statement says that David is in the mountain strongholds of the Wilderness of Ziph. The ending statement adds that he has hidden himself in a forest. The Wilderness of Ziph is associated with the town of Ziph just below Hebron. It is in the hill country that rises up from the desert wilderness called the Jeshimon, which is next to the Dead Sea.

The statement is delivered from the narrator's point of view alone, as an outsider observing another person's life from a distance. We are given the who, what, and where, but not the when. It doesn't say how long this episode goes on.

But, sandwiched as it is between the Battle of Keilah and the deliverance at the Rock of Escape, the statement that God did not deliver David into Saul's hands is both a comment on what God had done already and what He would continue to do. The deliverance to come is as assured as the deliverance already granted.

APPLY THE PICTURE

When you are in the trenches of life as David is, knowing that a man like Saul is hunting you every day, day in and day out, and there doesn't seem to be an end in sight, does it feel like God is doing anything?

Here in America, we don't live with persecution the way that Christians in other countries do. I have never faced persecution from Muslims or other religions who are antagonistic to our faith, so I cannot speak to that level of experience—yet.

But persecution happens in other venues as well, and a little closer to home. Imagine what it would be like to have, let's say, an antagonistic boss, co-worker, or client. The person doesn't like you. Maybe they want you removed from their realm. They are always on your case about something, and they wait for opportunities for you to slip up and then they land on you. It's not a situation you can get out of. Making peace with this person is not an option. So you live day-to-day with this feeling of being hunted and harassed. And when you get to the end of the day, and it has been another day when you have somehow managed to keep out of trouble, you breathe a sigh of relief for the moment and try not to think about tomorrow.

- **Does it feel like God is doing anything in your situation?**

We often recognize what God has done for us when something unusual happens, but in the day-to-day living when nothing really good or bad happens, it can be a little more difficult to see Him at work and give Him credit for our deliverance. But then we don't see the close calls that could have gone very wrong. We don't see all the schemes our antagonist is planning to catch us out over something, and how God frustrates that effort.

David is in a forest. When you are in the woods, you can lose a sense of direction, vision, and perspective—you can't see the forest for the trees. But when you crest that hill and look back at what you have come through, then you see God's hand in it.

This is a way that God works in our lives that can only be seen over time, and it is only experienced by those who endure. **Living day-to-day under persecution is the endurance test of a king in pursuit of a crown. It takes time and patience and perseverance.**

And it is good to give God thanks even for days when nothing really good nor really bad happens.

> ## Questions for Reflection
>
> - How is life for you right now—good, bad, or just so-so?
> - How often do you talk to God on the so-so days? What do you pray for?
> - Does it feel like God is doing anything in your life day-to-day?
> - How would you like to feel more engaged with God?

In the Wilderness: The Comforter

READ

First Samuel 23:16-18

NARRATIVE STRUCTURE

Picture #22 is also arranged in a tight chiastic structure.

- (A) "Then <u>Jonathan, Saul's son, arose</u> and went to <u>David in the woods</u>..."
- (B) "... and <u>strengthened his hand in God</u>."
- (C) "And he said to him, 'Do not fear, for the hand of Saul my father shall not find you. You shall be king over Israel, and I shall be next to you. Even my father Saul knows that.'"
- (B) "So the two of them <u>made a covenant before the LORD</u>."
- (A) "And <u>David stayed in the woods</u>, and <u>Jonathan went to his own house</u>."

316 | Lesson 15: Out of Enemy Hands

BUILD THE PICTURE

This section also begins and ends with a repeated note to David's location. He is in the woods—that connects this section to the previous section. This time Jonathan joins him to give him some encouragement.

This is the second chiasm (ABA). It begins with Jonathan going to David in the woods and ends with Jonathan leaving David in the woods. Then there are the parallel comments that Jonathan strengthened David's hand in God and made a covenant between them before God. The focus of the chiasm is on Jonathan's dialogue.

2. **What risk does Jonathan take to see David?**

   The Wilderness of Ziph covers an extensive area deep in the Judean desert. It is a significant distance from Jonathan's home in Gibeah, if that is where Jonathan was. Saul had sent out troops to comb the area for David daily, but I doubt if he would have put his son into any of the search parties, knowing Jonathan's loyalty to David. The irony is that while Saul is flailing about the countryside, Jonathan knows exactly where David is.

   So Jonathan is operating on his own under the suspicious eye of his father and without an excuse for being in the area at all, and yet he makes this risky trip for the sole purpose of encouraging David.

3. **How does Jonathan encourage David?**

   He tells him: 1) My father will not find you; 2) you will be king over Israel; and 3) I shall be next to you.

   He says these things using imperfect verbs, meaning these things have happened in the past and they will continue to happen.

   - As surely as Saul has not found you until now, he will continue not to find you.
   - As surely as you were anointed to be king in the past, you will continue to be king.
   - As surely as I have been with you in the past and supported and suffered with you, I will continue to be with you in the future.

4. **How could Jonathan be so sure of these things?**

   Jonathan is like the narrator. He has been witnessing all that has happened to David and God's faithfulness to David over time. Based on the evidence of what he has seen, he is convinced of these truths, and the conviction strengthens his own faith and allows him to strengthen David. He gives David the bird's-eye view at a time when David is in the woods.

   Such encouragement is most effective if the encourager identifies with the victim.

5. **How does Jonathan identify with David?**

   As we studied in Lesson 10, there is a sameness of heart between David and Jonathan. Both are men of war who desire peace. Both understand their place before God. They brought God into their battles and gave Him glory for their successes, unlike Saul who took the glory for himself. And both have suffered persecution by Saul. Twice Saul tried to kill his own son, and Saul resents Jonathan for his loyalty to David.

APPLY THE PICTURE

Jonathan's Model

Encouragement like Jonathan's can be helpful, or not.

To be reminded of the kingdom that we are ultimately pursuing can strengthen us and help us to focus on the true reward and not just our current circumstances. It can help us reset our perspective in regards to which crown we are pursuing—an eternal crown of peace or just immediate relief in the temporal kingdom.

But the relief can be so very needed, and the reward can seem so very far from us in times like this. And if we consider that we might live a lifetime of persecution and die in pursuit of that vision of a reward, then the hope can lose a lot of its luster. It can be very hard to accept encouragement to continue on, particularly if our encourager seems removed from an understanding of our situation.

As much as Jonathan identified with David, his circumstances were vastly different from David's at this point in time. Jonathan lived like royalty while David was a fugitive hiding in caves. Jonathan's day-to-day needs were well-met while David suffered want. He offered no solution to David's current situation, but only talked about the future reward that David would receive if he pressed on. He came into David's life for a fleeting moment to deliver this encouragement, then went back home to a relatively easier life and left David struggling in the wilderness.

Jonathan was completely removed from where David was physically, experientially, and even emotionally, but he identified with him as a co-heir in a future kingdom, and he was fighting his own battle with the same adversary, just in a different way. It was on this basis alone that he sought David out just to give him some encouragement.

Encouragers can be like this.

So, imagine you are David. You are the one in dire circumstances, alone, and feeling like an emotional wreck. One day a fellow believer seeks you out—maybe in person, or with an email, or phone call, or just a handwritten note—with what seems like a trite word of encouragement to press on for the kingdom and the reward. They aren't in your same circumstances. They aren't going to relieve your current physical suffering or offer a solution to your problems. They identify with you solely on the basis of a shared faith and hope, and their faith and hope are stronger than yours at the moment.

- **Is their encouragement comforting?**
- **How do you define comfort?**

Now imagine you are Jonathan. You are the one trying to give comfort to a person whose circumstances you have difficulty identifying with. Here is an example. Our church missions team once shared this newsletter report from a missionary in Pakistan:

> *"This week, D— from Pakistan was sharing about the seeming current strategy that Muslims are following in his country in order to tempt 'Christians' to convert to Islam. He shared that in Pakistan, the Muslims have the power, control, and wealth within the country. To be a Christian in Pakistan means persecution in many forms. From being*

> *prevented from buying food and drawing water in certain locations to outright physical attacks, martyrdom, and everything in between. D— shared that the desire for 'wealth' and relief (from the persecution), lately, has been too strong of a temptation for many, and they are leaving 'Christianity.' One of the most difficult examples of this for him is when a wealthy Muslim family finds a beautiful Christian girl they want for their son. They will offer a large sum of money to the Christian family in exchange for them to give their daughter in marriage for their son. D— said that the temptation to receive such wealth has proven to be too tempting for many families."*

Seeking relief from persecution is a big motivation to abandon the eternal reward. So how do we encourage a family who is under this kind of persecution to resist the temptation? Of what do they need to be reminded? The missions team suggested this:

> *"A person's view and version of Christianity has to move away from being a mere religion to being a real relationship with the Almighty Creator of the Universe, Who loves them with a love that surpasses all knowledge, and Who has promised them an eternal hope and inheritance in heaven that He is preserving with His own divine power. This true version of Christianity is not only worth being persecuted for, but it's worth dying for."*

Isaiah 40 challenges us with the same questions. God says "Comfort, comfort my people!" but when the voice in the wilderness asks Him how, He says, "Tell them their lives are like the grass." Is it comforting being told that our lives are fleeting and mortal? No. But then God goes on to give this glorious picture of His own strength and wisdom and faithfulness and eternality, and He leaves us with the question of where we seek comfort. Is it about our comfort in the temporal world that is here and gone like grass, or the comfort we will find in the eternal realm?

Isaiah 49-50 builds on this same theme. Israel declares that the LORD has forsaken her, and God returns with a two-fold reassurance along the same lines as our passages today. First, He offers a verbal statement of His future deliverance after the time of persecution is over (Isaiah 49:14-26), then sends a Comforter who identifies with Israel's suffering (Isaiah 50:4-11) and can say with assurance that the LORD will deliver her, even as Jonathan said to David.

Interesting how this picture of comfort is presented here with Jonathan and David at the beginning of the time of the kings with David in exile, and again in Isaiah at the end of the time of the kings with Israel facing exile as a nation.

> ## Questions for Reflection
>
> - Where do you seek comfort, distraction, or escape when you feel oppressed?
>
> - Has there ever been a time in your life when you refused to be comforted because of weariness or despair? If so, why?
>
> - Have you ever tried to offer comfort, but your comfort was refused? If so, why was it refused?

23 The Rock of Escape: The Experience

READ

First Samuel 23:16-18

NARRATIVE STRUCTURE

We've had the statement. We've had the comforter. Now we come to the actual experience of deliverance in **Picture #23**. There are two sections to this episode:

1) David's betrayal by the Ziphites to Saul (23:19-24).
2) David's rescue from Saul's subsequent pursuit (23:24-29).

In the second half, David's rescue is arranged in a chiastic structure that highlights the message that Saul receives to draw him away from what is a sure capture of David. This is the third and final chiasm in this series.

Where the first two pictures were somewhat passive statements of God preserving His king, the third is an active example. The passive and active examples are offset by the betrayal account.

BUILD THE PICTURE
---

6. **Who are the Ziphites?**

    The Wilderness of Ziph is attached to the town of Ziph located just below Hebron in the territory of Judah. Ziph is about 25 miles away from Gibeah where Saul is. The Ziphites are of the tribe of Judah and David's own kinsmen, but they propose to betray him to Saul. According to Psalm 54, which David wrote about this particular incident, the Ziphites are described as fearing Saul and not God.

    The word Ziphite comes from the word *ziph,* which means "battlement," but its root word, *zepheth*, means "pitch," that black, tar-like substance. *Zepheth* is used in two contrasting pictures in Scripture. The first is when Moses' mother hid him in the reeds, in a basket lined with *zepheth*. So it is associated with that picture of a temporary dwelling place that has been shored up (like a battlement) in which God's leader is preserved. But in Isaiah 34:9, the text uses it in context of a day of judgment against the nations when streams will be turned to pitch (*zepheth)* and the land shall become burning pitch (*zepheth)*. Thus, the place that was once a defensive battlement and haven becomes a "hot zone" from which people will desire to flee. For David, the Wilderness of Ziph has become just such a place, thanks to the Ziphites' betrayal.

    The Ziphites know the area very well, and they give Saul a very detailed description of where David is in the Wilderness of Ziph. He is in the strongholds in the woods in the hill of Hachilah, which is south of and facing Jeshimon (the barren waste that stretches toward the Dead Sea).

7. **How does Saul react?**

    First, he blesses them. Why? For having compassion on him. Saul is expressing satisfaction at being pitied. How pathetic does that sound? Saul is hunting David mercilessly and yet he bemoans the lack of compassion the people have for him, Saul.

Then, Saul sends the Ziphites out as spies to seek out all of David's hiding spots. He calls David shrewd and crafty to tarnish his reputation. If the Ziphites can deliver good intel, then Saul will go with them. We should note that there is no mention of reward for the Ziphites' help, unless they count not having their city put to the sword like Nob.

So that is the end of the first section. We have the betrayal. The narrative now segues abruptly to David.

8. **Where are David and his men now?**

Word came to David from someone somewhere that Saul had been told of his location, so David leaves the Wilderness of Ziph and moves ten miles south to the Wilderness of Maon. But then that is reported to Saul as well. The Wilderness of Maon is mentioned three times in the narrator's opening report to emphasize the targeted pursuit. Saul is closing in.

9. **So why did David run to Maon?**

Maon means "dwelling place," but it is most often used in reference to God's dwelling place or habitation, whether in heaven, in His Tabernacle, or in Jerusalem. To David, Maon is a refuge associated with God's presence and protection, and he seeks a mountain stronghold there. He writes about his *maon* in Psalm 71:

> *"In You, O LORD, I put my trust; Let me never be put to shame. Deliver me in Your righteousness, and cause me to escape; incline Your ear to me, and save me. Be my strong refuge **[maon]**, to which I may resort continually; You have given the commandment to save me, for You are my rock and my fortress. Deliver me, O my God, out of the hand of the wicked, out of the hand of the unrighteous and cruel man. For You are my hope, O Lord GOD; You are my trust from my youth."* —Psalm 71:1-5

But the physical rock in the Wilderness of Maon becomes a trap. While David and his men take refuge on one side of the mountain, Saul is on the other side. Saul simply divides his army and encircles the rock in a siege-like fashion. Even if David and his men fled from the rock, they would be caught. It's a done deal unless God intervenes.

10. What causes Saul to call off?

A message is delivered by an unnamed messenger about a vague Philistine threat. Does it seem odd that at the moment when capture is assured, Saul would call off so abruptly? It makes you wonder what exactly the Philistines were doing that overrode Saul's obsessive pursuit of David. The text doesn't tell us, but it must have served Saul's interest to let David go.

All that God's deliverance required was a simple message delivered at just the right moment. The sheer simplicity of it is remarkable, but it demonstrates God's power and sovereignty over the situation, and how easily He is able to deliver his king. What seems like an impossible situation isn't so impossible. And it was really a matter of timing. Time is in God's hands.

The account ends with the narrator's comment that David went to the strongholds of En Gedi which is located right on the Dead Sea. En Gedi is the only real oasis in the area because of the fresh water springs and waterfalls sourced from the canyons in that region. En Gedi means "spring of the young goat" and it is a place known for wild goats and ibexes.

⓴/㉓ Picture Comparison: God's Deliverance

This is the second time David has been trapped by Saul in Chapter 23.

11. What is the difference between the two situations?

When David was at Keilah and heard that Saul plotted against him, he didn't immediately run. He stopped and inquired of God. Then he decided what to do with God's warning and ran. It was told to Saul that he had escaped, and Saul called off the expedition.

This time, David is trapped at Maon, and the author doesn't relate any effort on David's part to inquire of God. A diverting message comes to Saul, but it isn't because David has escaped this time. Even so, Saul calls off the pursuit.

Sometimes God gives a warning and then human reasoning takes over from there, but this time human reasoning played no part. It wasn't a matter of David having to make a decision over what to do or how to save himself and his men. God deliberately took the decision-making out of his hands.

Of the two pictures, this is the stronger experience of God's deliverance, and this rock in the Wilderness of Maon becomes a monument to God's deliverance. The NKJV renders the name Rock of Escape, but in the Hebrew, it is more closely translated as the Rock of Separation or the Rock of Divisions, since it was at this point that Saul and David were separated by God's intervention. The physical rock itself was not an escape. It would have become a snare for David and his men. God is David's true *maon*.

Speaking of monuments . . . This isn't the only monument in this area. Just a little ways off in Carmel stands the monument that Saul set up for himself after defeating King Agag and the Amalekites. That monument is now the reminder of Saul's faithlessness and that he has lost the kingdom. Compare that to God's great monument hill that testifies of His faithfulness and promise to establish his true king. God's monument eclipses Saul's by a majestic degree.

After David's initial headlong run from Saul that ends with him alone in a cave, we now see another headlong run that gets him cornered and cut off on top of a mountain. Unlike the situation at Keilah, David doesn't inquire of God before beginning his somewhat panicked run to Maon, and while the end deliverance is a testament to God's glory, we should consider how it might have turned out differently if David had held his ground. This same scenario will come up again, and David will take a different action, but that comparison is for a future lesson.

APPLY THE PICTURE

Exile is a rich training ground for kingship, and it is good to stop periodically and review the progress of the lessons.

In the cave of Adullam, David is brought to a time of reflection on the predicament in which he finds himself. He didn't ask for the anointing as king or for the glory people had heaped upon him, and he certainly didn't intend to make an enemy of the king he did his best to serve. It would be very easy to slip into self-pity as Saul did, but David is a man with a different heart. Saul sat himself down under a tree in a sulk, but David waited for the LORD's direction and launched into battle again as soon as he got the go-ahead.

The first lesson produced a single-mindedness in David, theoretically. He understood in his mind who God was and what relationship he needed to have with God as he pursued the crown. He needed to trust God and not be fearful of enemies. He needed to inquire of God. He needed to rest in God's faithfulness and believe that when he cried out to God, God would hear him. David knew all that, theoretically. But what about practically?

There is a world of difference in knowing something in your mind and having the actual experience of it. That is why the second stage of David's training required some day-to-day living with persecution. There were days when life was neither good nor bad—it could have been better, but also a lot worse—and while David may not have felt God was actively with him through all that, He was. But notice how David's resolve degrades over time. He comes out of the cave, regroups, and begins strong at Keilah. He inquires of the LORD and steps out boldly. The enemy threatens, and David cries out to the LORD again, then acts on the LORD's instruction. So far so good. But then time passes, and the constant pressure begins to work on David. God is with him, but it doesn't feel like it. He needs a comforter to remind him of the reward he is pursuing and that it is not just for himself but for others as well. Then there is another crisis moment, but this time David doesn't inquire of God before acting. He has the priest and ephod available, but he doesn't use them. He runs from Saul, just like he did initially.

This is the endurance test of a king. David knows the LORD is with him, and the knowledge carries him for a while, but just having that knowledge doesn't replace the need for experience and continued communication. When the communication begins to dwindle, David's decisions become less and less wise. The trend is only seen over time and often when crisis moments strike. Then the degree of falling away becomes evident. God rescues David at the Rock of Escape to His glory, but the instances of David inquiring of God before acting will lapse for a while in David's life, and we will see the impact of that on his pursuit of the crown.

Pursuing a crown is a practical activity. We can have a passive knowledge of who God is and what our relationship with Him should be, but if we are going to progress toward the goal of that reward, that knowledge needs to be experienced practically, and keeping the communication link from degrading becomes vitally important.

> ## Questions for Reflection
>
> - What do you know about God?
>
> - What do you know of God's power from past experience? Has He been faithful to you in the past?
>
> - If you give your situation over to Him, do you believe He has the power to deal with it?
>
> - If He has the power to deal with your circumstances, do you trust Him to deal with it? Are you willing to let go of your own control and empowerment and give Him control?
>
> - Do you trust Him enough to be at peace with His handling of the situation?
>
> - What else do you know about God that you have seen working out in a practical way in your life over time?
>
> - Has God ever delivered you from a bad situation like He did with David at Maon? If so, how did that affect your relationship with Him?

LESSON 16: FIRST SAMUEL 24:1–26:25

My Enemy in My Hands

SERIES STRUCTURE

We now begin a new series with a new theme. Instead of delivering David out of enemy hands, God is going to deliver his enemies into his hands. We will see how David handles the power. Here is a rundown of the series:

Picture #24 (24:1–25:1) finds David and his men hiding in a cave at the Rock of Wild Goats when Saul comes into the cave alone. David cuts off a corner of Saul's robe while Saul is otherwise engaged.

Picture #25 (25:2-44) is the account of David and Nabal, which is the pivotal chapter in David's exile account. The structure is presented in an extensive chiasm introduced by an oddly placed note about Samuel's death.

Picture #26 (26:1-25) finds David and his men back at the Hill of Hachilah where he sneaks up on Saul by night and takes his spear and water jug. The picture opens with the Ziphites informing on David's whereabouts with almost the same words as in Chapter 23:19. David reacts to the news differently this time, and we will compare that. Also the structure of Chapter 26 parallels Chapter 24 very closely, yet with some important differences that show a lesson learned in David's life.

The narrative structures for the individual pictures are extensive, so I will flesh them out as we come to them.

㉔ David at the Rock of Wild Goats

READ

First Samuel 24:1-22

NARRATIVE STRUCTURE

Picture #24 has four sections and is structured around two conversations:

1) Opening dialogue that sets the scene (24:1-2)
2) David's conversation with his men (24:3-7)
3) David's confrontation with Saul (24:8-22)
    a) David's charge (24:8-15)
    b) Saul's initial address (24:16)
    c) Saul's penitent response (24:17-19)
    d) Saul's acknowledgment of David (24:20-21)
4) Narrator's note of departure (24:22)

This picture will compare to Picture #26 in structure and content, but some of the elements will be rearranged. We will compare them.

BUILD THE PICTURE

Saul has come back from fighting the Philistines and has picked up David's trail again based on a tip from another unnamed betrayer. He takes three thousand men to En Gedi and begins to comb the Rocks of the Wild Goats for David and his men.

David's Conversation with his Men (24:3-7)

1. **Where does the conversation take place?**

   This first conversation takes place in the cave. Somewhere along the road, Saul decides he needs to "attend to his needs," which is a very polite way of saying he needed to relieve himself, and so he ducks into a cave that was being used as a shelter for sheep and offers a little privacy. Apparently, the cave is deep enough and big enough to hide

David and his men. It is dark inside, so Saul can't see into the depths of the cave, but David and his men can see Saul silhouetted in the light. Saul's attention is focused elsewhere, and he doesn't hear this conversation between David and his men.

2. **What do David's men encourage him to do?**

   To do to Saul as it seems good to David. They tell him that this moment was the fulfillment of God's promise to David to deliver his enemy into his hands.

   Of course, they mean for David to kill Saul, but their statement leaves plenty of wiggle room for additional ways of satisfying David's desire for vindication and vengeance. Vengeance can go far beyond simply killing an enemy.

3. **Did God ever say that to David?**

   No, actually He didn't. He never promised to deliver Saul into David's hands and give David carte blanche to do with Saul as he desired.

4. **Why would the men say that?**

   Because opportunities like this don't just happen. It is a miraculous thing to have Saul dropped right into their laps like this. They are interpreting the circumstances as God giving His go-ahead.

5. **What's the problem with that thinking?**

   The circumstances may be divinely orchestrated, but that does not mean that they are a sign from God giving you permission to pursue your desires. Sometimes they are a test.

   Didn't Saul say something similar to this when he thought he had David caught at Keilah?

   > *"So Saul said, 'God has delivered him into my hand, for he has shut himself in by entering a town that has gates and bars.'"* (23:7)

   On what was Saul basing that statement? The circumstances fit his own agenda; therefore the opportunity must be from God. Was Saul right? No. Is it right what David's men are saying now? No. But their words tempt David to follow Saul's model.

6. **What does David do?**

    He doesn't kill Saul, but he sneaks up on him and cuts a corner of his robe off. But why do that at all? If he wasn't going to kill Saul and relieve the persecution, why take any action at all?

7. **What does this act do for David?**

    It's his little coup on Saul. It's a little trophy that he takes as proof that he could have killed Saul but he didn't. It tells us that the desire is in David to take vengeance against Saul. He has that craving for vindication, and the temptation to take that piece of robe as proof of his coup on Saul was something he decided to act on.

    Taking a scrap of cloth off someone isn't the same as killing him. It's an innocent act, right?

    Consider the order of the conversation:

    > (24:4a) **David's men:** *"This is the day of which the LORD said to you, 'Behold, I will deliver your enemy into your hand, that you may do to him as it seems good to you.'..."*

    > (24:4b-5) **David's actions:** *"...And David arose and secretly cut off a corner of Saul's robe. Now it happened afterward that David's heart troubled him because he had cut Saul's robe."*

    > (24:6-7a) **David's response to his men:** *"...And he said to his men, 'The LORD forbid that I should do this thing to my master, the LORD's anointed, to stretch out my hand against him, seeing he is the anointed of the LORD.' So David restrained his servants with these words, and did not allow them to rise against Saul."*

    If David had rebuked his men first, and then cut off the robe, then that would imply that killing Saul was wrong, but taking the trophy was okay. But that isn't the order. David's rebuke of his men includes a rebuke of his own actions.

8. **Why does David's heart trouble him? What is significant about cutting cloth like this?**

    Whether you cut a man down or merely cut off part of his clothing, the physical cutting is symbolic of cutting off the relationship with the man. Acts of cutting are part of covenant making, but also covenant breaking. We already saw an example of this when Saul tore a piece off of Samuel's robe. Samuel told him that the LORD had torn the kingdom from him that day.

Another example of this is the Jewish practice of cutting the strings on a man's prayer shawl when he dies. Those strings are a reminder of his obligation to keep the Mosaic Covenant, and cutting them signifies that in death, the man has been released from the requirements of that covenant. You can cut a covenant, or you can be cut off from the covenant. Cloth-cutting is symbolic of this.

When David considers the import of what he has done after the fact, his heart troubles him.

9. **How does David see himself in relationship to Saul?**

Note that when David speaks of Saul, he doesn't call him Saul, or even the king. He refers to him once as master, and then twice as the LORD's anointed.

A man who is in pursuit of a crown should respect the authority of the crown, regardless of the man who wears it. It is in David's own best interest as a future king to demand respect for the king's rank and authority. The key to doing that is to see the man not as a leader elected by the people, but a leader installed at God's will and for God's purpose. His respect for the crown transcends the man and becomes a respect for God's sovereignty.

10. **What is the effect of David's statement on his men?**

It has a restraining effect on David's men.

Questions for Reflection

- How do you talk about the masters in your life?

- Whether they are good or bad, do you respect their authority as being God-given, or do you see them only as masters/leaders chosen by men to be challenged or taken down?

- How you speak about them has an effect on those who listen to you. What message should you be conveying to others?

- How is David's model in line with New Testament teaching? (Consider First Timothy 5–6, First Peter 2–3.)

- Just because David has respect for the authority of the king, does that mean he sits silently and doesn't make an effort to defend himself against the king's persecution?

   Of course not. But let's consider how he did that.

David's Confrontation with Saul (24:8-22)

11. How does David confront this authority in his life who is persecuting him?

He begins with showing respect in how he addresses Saul (my lord the king!) and in his body language. He bows his head and prostrates himself in verse 8. David even calls Saul "my father" in verse 11. All of that communicates his relationship to Saul.

He pleads his case. First he points out that Saul is listening to people who are not telling him the truth. Letting other people drive his actions has been a problem for Saul throughout his reign, but isn't it interesting that David himself listened to his own men in this case, and it caused him to sin. The outworking of his sin wasn't on a level of committing murder like Saul's was, but the fact that his heart troubled him indicated it was a sin for him.

Even so, he makes a point that Saul is listening to lies, and then shows Saul the evidence of it.

He holds up the robe as evidence and brings his charge against Saul. That piece of robe is proof that David is innocent. He did not take Saul's life when he could have—even when he was urged to, as Saul is being urged by his men. David understands the desire to take vengeance on a very personal level. But then he explains to Saul why he didn't give in to the urgings. It is because he respected Saul as the LORD's anointed king and his own master.

David says, *"... I have not sinned against you, yet you hunt my life to take it."* Saul would shed blood without cause purely for the sake of vengeance. David's magnanimity is a stark contrast to Saul's jealous grasping of the kingdom.

David gives the judgment over to the LORD. There are two inclusios in this section.

The first inclusio (24:12-15) is framed by the phrase *"Let the LORD judge between you and me"* and forms the theme of David's summary statement. Saul may be king, but there is a greater King who is also the great Judge who judges between kings.

The second inclusio (24:12-13) is nested within the first and is bookended by the phrase *"But my hand shall not be against you."* This draws our attention to the target statement that is the proverb in verse 13a: *"Wickedness proceeds from the wicked."* The proverb creates **the first contrast** between Saul's and David's actions with the implication that their actions reflect their character. David is reiterating that Saul is the wicked one, but he isn't going to fight Saul's wickedness. The LORD will deal with him.

A second contrast between David and Saul follows in verse 14 with the statement, *"After whom has the king of Israel come out? Whom do you pursue? A dead dog? A flea?"* He exalts Saul as a king and casts himself as something of no regard—a dead dog or a flea. According to Jewish sources, such expressions of submissiveness and humility were customary in the ancient Near East, but it has a point to it. What Saul is doing does not befit a king.

The bookend of the first inclusio is verse 15 where David gives his grievance over to the LORD and lets the LORD plead his case to Saul. Verse 15 ends with a reversal of David's first statement in verse 10.

> *"your eyes have seen that the LORD delivered you today into my hand ... But my eye spared you ..."* (24:10)

> *"Therefore let the LORD be judge ... and deliver me out of your hand."* (24:15)

Having made the right decision to spare Saul, David asks the LORD to reward him in turn by delivering him from Saul's hand now. He doesn't appeal to Saul for this. He appeals to the LORD. *"The LORD avenge me . . . the LORD see and plead my case . . ."*

12. What is Saul's reaction?

First there is the initial address (24:16), then the penitent response (24:17-19), and finally the acknowledgment (24: 20-21).

He begins by addressing David *"Is this your voice, my son David?"* Calling David his son is a response to David addressing him as father in verse 11. So he begins with an acknowledgment of relationship. And then Saul weeps.

13. Why does Saul weep?

Imagine the scene through Saul's eyes. The man who would be king stands before him holding a torn piece of robe. It is the image of himself before Samuel that day when he lost the kingdom. Do you remember how that went in Chapter 15?

⑨/㉔ Picture Comparison: The Torn Cloth

In Chapter 15 (**Picture #9**) Samuel had just rebuked Saul for not killing King Agag of the Amalekites, saying, *"For rebellion is as the sin of witchcraft, and stubbornness is as iniquity and idolatry."* Then Saul tore off a piece of Samuel's robe, and Samuel told him that the kingdom would be torn from him in the same way. He had broken the covenant with the LORD, and the LORD in turn had broken covenant with him. Then he abased himself to Samuel, begging for the mercy of not being humiliated in the people's eyes, and so Samuel granted him that dignity.

Here in Chapter 24 (**Picture #24**), David stands before Saul with a torn cloth in hand, and he is leveling an echo of Samuel's charges against Saul, saying that wickedness proceeds from the wicked. It is like a flashback to that moment with Samuel, and Saul reacts in much the same way. Just as he abased himself before Samuel, admitting his guilt and begging for a last honor, he does the same with David. We have the penitent response when Saul declares that David has been more righteous than himself in rewarding evil with good. Reward is mentioned three times.

14. What reward does Saul ask the LORD to give David in verse 19?

The word for reward is the Hebrew word, *shalam*, and is akin to the word *shalom*. *Shalam* means to be in a covenant of peace, and to be at peace, but also to be complete and sound. It involves the return of something that has been taken from you that injured you or put you at a loss. *Shalam* then is the peace that comes with having that lost thing restored or recompensed to you so that you are healed and whole and at peace again.

15. How does Saul finally acknowledge David?

"Now I know indeed that you shall surely be king." Saul acknowledges David as the king who holds the cloth and to whom the kingdom will be given. He understands the significance of that cut cloth—and that the new king has the right to cut off his lineage forever and destroy his name in his father's house. He begs a last honor that his descendants not be cut off in the kingdom. He asks not to be humiliated, and David grants him that dignity.

16. How does David respond?

David grants him that dignity, just as Samuel did in Picture #9. Humiliation is a big part of vengeance. It's about taking back a dignity that was taken from you, but often it is a reward that we can be tempted to take back for ourselves instead of letting God restore our dignity. David grants Saul some dignity.

Even so, the momentary truce is not enough for David to trust Saul. As they leave each other, they go their separate ways, just as Samuel and Saul did in Picture #9.

APPLY THE PICTURE

The last four pictures from Chapter 23 showed God's deliverance of David when he was at the mercy of Saul. This time, by contrast, David faces the king from whom he will one day rightly take the throne (if he will wait for

God's timing), but he is given a chance to deliver himself by his own hand, put his enemy under his feet, and take the kingdom. This is a temptation and a test.

- **Why is taking the kingdom by your own effort the wrong way to gain a kingdom?**

Think of Christ and His temptations. We have seen this picture comparison before, but it crops up again here. Satan showed Jesus all the kingdoms of the world in their glory and tempted Him to take them. The kingdom was already His by the Father's determination, but the Father had a greater purpose in deferring that reward. Satan offered Jesus a way to fast track things and played to Jesus' human desire to forgo the suffering and take the kingdom by His own will and timing. All He had to do was switch allegiance.

It is not enough to pursue the right reward. It has to be pursued the right way. Vindication, validation, and the restoration of dignity are all valid rewards, but they will slip from your grasp if you take them by your own power and will instead of letting God reward you.

If we are in pursuit of a crown, we will have antagonists like Saul in life. There is the test of how we live from day to day with them, how we temper our behavior if they are masters over us, and finally, how we deal with them when given the opportunity to retaliate.

Taking vengeance is the key issue in this picture, and expands on the topic of humiliation on which we touched with the Chapter 15 parallel. How we deal with our enemies when they fall into our hand is one of the biggest tests we face in pursuing our reward.

Vengeance goes beyond justice. Justice has a prescribed punishment for an offense. You deliver the punishment, receive the compensation, and then the issue is settled. Vengeance is about inflicting injury, harm, or humiliation of like kind as it has been inflicted on you—and often to a greater degree, just to make a point. Vengeance is about showing your power over another person for your own pleasure and glorification. It is an act of domination used to re-establish one's reputation and authority when someone challenges it. It falls into the category of lusts of the flesh and the pride of life.

Saul has modeled vengeance for us. Taking vengeance for himself and for the wrong reasons was one of Saul's greatest failures as king. God had given him the crown but then took it from him for this reason, and yet he tried to keep it by force and by dealing out punishment and retribution against those he considered his enemies, both real and imagined. And now David is given the opportunity and the encouragement not just to end Saul's persecution but to take his own vengeance—to do to Saul as seemed good to him.

The Scenario

So, imagine that you have a Saul in your life. This is a person who is antagonistic to you without reason and beyond reasoning with. They hound and harass you daily. They persecute you. They lie and trash your reputation. They seek every advantage over you and wield their power with punitive force every chance they get.

In regards to living with them day to day ...

There will be losses on your side. The losses may include the loss of physical benefits. You may endure physical and verbal abuse or harassment. More often you will suffer the loss of intangible things like dignity, justice, a good reputation, security, love, and peace. These are things that have to be returned to you for you to feel whole again—to have that reward of *shalam*.

- **If you have lost these to your Saul in life, what would it take to have that wholeness returned to you? Is that something you can do for yourself?**

- **Did David taking that piece of Saul's robe restore what Saul had taken from him?**

In regards to retaliation ...

Our antagonists can slip up on occasion or get themselves into trouble or a vulnerable position. Maybe it was the imprudent email, text message, or Facebook comment that they didn't mean for us to see. Maybe it was a conversation overheard in the bathroom, or a receipt for something that they were trying to hide. Maybe it was proof of their harassment or prejudice against you. Maybe you caught them in an embarrassing situation or a lie. It's one of those moments where you can point the finger and say AH HA! All your friends see it, and they are telling you to go for it. You have every right; your antagonist deserves it. *And* it will get your antagonist off your back. So, do you go for the jugular? Of course, we aren't talking about a literal kill, but there are many ways to twist the knife that can ruin a person socially, emotionally, or psychologically.

- **When you have your antagonist at your mercy, what do you do?**

David had Saul dead to rights there in the cave, and while he was magnanimous to Saul and didn't go in for the kill, per se, he did take a trophy. He took something that he could hold onto and bring out at a later time to show Saul and remind him that he had been caught.

We can take trophies like this. We can hold on to that damaging bit of intel. It doesn't have to be physical; we can just keep it in our minds. And we keep it as our little proof of having gotten the upper hand over our antagonist—of being the righteous one. These kinds of trophies can be a way of achieving our own vindication and validation. They can be something that we comfort ourselves with, something we gloat over privately, and maybe if our antagonist hassles us too much one day, something we bring out as our little proof to remind them of how magnanimous we have been to them.

- **Is there sin in that?**
- **Have you ever had a person hold something like that over you?**
- **Do you do that to others?**

Knowledge is power, and the temptation to use that power to abuse your abuser can be potent. David didn't need to take that trophy. Simply following Saul out of the cave and accosting him would have been proof enough of the dangerous position in which Saul had placed himself.

David almost went down a wrong path in dealing with his antagonist, but he self-corrected and did what was right. He had a legitimate case against Saul, and he made his case and did not stoop to humiliating Saul once he had the acknowledgment of guilt.

While the breaking of a person may be necessary, humiliation should never be part of it. It may give you personal satisfaction to deal with them as they have dealt with you or even go beyond, but it will never gain their respect or restore peace to the relationship.

If you are a king in pursuit of a crown as David is, then peace must be the goal. **Read Romans 12:9-21** for Paul's discussion on this.

The Death of Samuel (25:1)

First Samuel 25:1 is an oddly placed note. Technically, it falls at the beginning of Chapter 25, and yet it has no particular bearing on the immediate context. It does, however, provide a cap to this picture in Chapter 24 with a corresponding parallel to the comparison picture. I've charted the comparisons below. Notice how the corresponding pictures have been tracking one another.

❼ Chapter 14:1-46	⓵⓴ Chapter 22:6–23:13
❾ Chapter 15:1-35	㉔ Chapter 24:1–25:1
(15:27-28) Saul tears a piece from Samuel's robe	(24:4) David tears a piece from Saul's robe
(15:30) Saul repents to Samuel *"Then he said, 'I have sinned; yet honor me now, please, before the elders of my people and before Israel, and return with me, that I may worship the LORD your God.'"*	(24:17-21) Saul repents to David *"Therefore swear now to me by the LORD that you will not cut off my descendants after me, and that you will not destroy my name from my father's house."*
(15:31) *"So Samuel turned back..."* (he granted Saul the request)	(24:22) *"So David swore to Saul..."* (he granted Saul the request)
(15:34) *"Then Samuel went to Ramah, and Saul went up to his house at Gibeah of Saul."*	(24:22) *"...And Saul went home, but David and his men went up to the stronghold."*
(15:35) *"And Samuel went no more to see Saul until the day of his death..."*	(25:1) *"Then Samuel died..."*

The comparison between Saul and David now break off as Chapter 25 segues abruptly to David's interaction with a couple, Nabal and Abigail, who are entirely removed from his issues with Saul and yet still part of this lesson in his life.

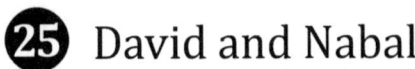 David and Nabal

---
READ

First Samuel 25:1-44

NARRATIVE STRUCTURE

First Samuel 25 stands out for a few reasons. It is the longest chapter in this body of chapters we are comparing (Chapters 21-31). First Samuel 25 opens with a pivotal narrator's comment, which is appropriate since the entire chapter itself is a pivotal chapter in regards to its place within the greater structure of chapters.

All of the external structure brings the focus to bear on Chapter 25. The internal structure continues that focus in its chiastic arrangement. Excluding the oddly placed narrator's note in verse 1, it is broken into seven main sections arranged in chiastic order:

Section 1: **Narrator comment:** Nabal and his wife Abigail (25:2-3)

Section 2: **Conversation 1:** David, his men, and Nabal (25:4-13)
This section is arranged in four elements (1-2-3-4)

Section 3: **Action:** Abigail prepares a gift for David (25:14-20)
This section is arranged in four elements (A-B-C-D)

Section 4: **Conversation 2:** David and Abigail (25:21-35)
This section is the chiastic turning point, arranged in three elements (E-F-E)

Section 5: **Reaction:** God prepares a reward for David (25:36-39a)
This section is arranged in four elements (D-C-B-A) in reverse order of Section 3.

Section 6: **Conversation 3:** David, his men, and Abigail (25:39b-42)
This section is arranged in four elements (1-2-3-4).

Section 7: **Narrator comment:** David and his wife Abigail (25:43-44)

The verses in Conversations #1 and #3 parallel each other (1-2-3-4), as if events are being replayed to end with an opposite result.

The verses in the Action, Conversation #2, and Reaction flow together in a chiastic structure (A-B-C-D-E-F-E-D-C-B-A) with the focus (F) being on Abigail's dialogue. Her grace-filled dialogue becomes the central focus of the picture, the chapter, and the greater body of First Samuel 21-29.

We are going to read all the way through First Samuel 25 once to get the full picture, and then we will begin to work back through it section by section.

BUILD THE PICTURE

The Death of Samuel, First Samuel 25:1

As previously noted, Chapter 25 opens with a narrator's comment, but it is one of those single, oddly placed verses that seems to have no bearing on the narrative action before or after it, except that it completes the previous picture comparisons made between Chapters 24 and 15. It sets us up for the action in Chapter 28, but the information could have as easily been given there as here. In the immediate context, it doesn't seem relevant.

17. What is the purpose of the narrator's comment here in verse 1?

In general, when you have an oddly placed narrator's comment, its main purpose is to provide a pivot point for a comparison/contrast between what happened in the preceding picture and the coming picture, and gives us a focus on a particular theme that links them.

In **Picture #24,** David chose not to avenge himself against Saul; in **Picture #25,** David sets out to avenge himself on Nabal. So, there is the repeated theme of vengeance and glorification surrounding this oddly placed first verse; however, you won't see the theme of glorification unless you consider the odd name of the place to which David now retreats noted within the verse. This is why an investigation of the who, what, when, where, etc., becomes vital. The text says that David goes to the Wilderness of Paran, except he isn't in the Wilderness of Paran when he engages Nabal. He is in the Wilderness of Maon.

18. Why does the text say David goes to the Wilderness of Paran?

We should ask: What picture do we think of when we read "the Wilderness of Paran"?

The Wilderness of Paran was featured back in the book of Numbers. It was where the children of Israel spent a good deal of time wandering after they came out of Egypt—and after they failed to enter the Promised Land when God told them to go. They lost faith in God and disobeyed, and as a result, that generation of Israel did not come into their inheritance in the kingdom.

But this Paran is far south of where the narrative of Chapter 25 takes place. David and his men are still in the general vicinity of Maon, Carmel, and Ziph—all the places David has been wandering around for the past several chapters. These places are David's version of exile and wilderness wandering; they are his figurative "Wilderness of Paran."

Sometimes it's not where the place is located that is important; sometimes it's the meaning of the name. The meanings of names are part of the narrative picture, so we should look at what the name Paran means. Paran means "a place of caverns," which is a suitable description of where David and his men have taken refuge. But the root word for Paran is *pa'ar*, which means "to glorify, beautify, or adorn"—to embellish, the way a tree is embellished and beautified with leaves, or a person is embellished and beautified with boasting or praise. When applied to people, it can be applied to self-glorification or the glorification of someone else, like God.

Just like the nation of Israel in their wilderness wandering, David has come to his own Wilderness of Paran that will be a place where either he or God is glorified by his actions. Israel failed to give God glory and ended up wandering another forty years, only to die in that wilderness. As we go through the account of David, Nabal, and Abigail, we will look at how this issue of who gets the glory works out.

So, the oddly placed narrator's comment now provides us with a theme of glorification in its use of the name, Paran.

APPLY THE PICTURE

How does glorification relate to theme of vengeance?

Glorification is the motive for vengeance. Vengeance is a way of glorifying yourself by inflicting punishment or retribution for an injury or wrong—particularly an injury to one's reputation. It's an act of domination in taking back what is due to you, plus a little more for good measure and to ram home the message of who is greater.

- **Is vengeance a reward you pursue for yourself, or is this a reward God gives to you?**

- **Do you lift yourself up and avenge yourself against your antagonist when you do good to them but receive evil in return, or do you let God avenge and glorify you?**

- **Are you seeking glory for the building up of yourself and your kingdom, or God and God's kingdom?**

- **And who gets the praise when all is said and done?**

This brings us back to the pursuit of crowns. There are right and wrong rewards to pursue and right and wrong reasons to pursue them. Vengeance is not the reward you should be pursuing, because when you do it, it is for self-glorification. That is the wrong reason. This was Saul's great failing that lost him the kingdom, just as that first generation of Israel lost their kingdom in the Wilderness of Paran. Will it be David's failing as well? This is the key focus and theme for this chapter.

BUILD THE PICTURE

Section 1: Nabal and His Wife Abigail (25:2-3)

The picture begins with a narrator's comment introducing our characters.

19. What do we know about Nabal?

He is very great, not because he is of upright moral character, but because he has achieved a reputation in the world's eyes as a wealthy business man with exceedingly large flocks of sheep and goats. He lives in Maon but his business and possessions are in Carmel (Carmel means fruitful field or garden-land). The author paints a picture of someone likened to a king in a small kingdom enjoying an exceeding abundance of prosperity and blessing. He is given quite the build-up. After telling you all that about him, the author then announces that his name is Nabal—which means fool. The contrast is very rich. Nabal is a very great fool.

The name Nabal, comes from the common word nabal which means "fool or foolish." There are five kinds of fool in the Scripture, and they range from those who are simply naive, to those who are arrogantly ignorant, to those who are deliberately perverse and evil. Nabal is at the evil end of the scale. Here are some examples of how the word is used in Scripture:

"They were sons of fools [nabal], Yes, sons of vile men; They were scourged from the land." —Job 30:8

"To the Chief Musician. A Psalm of David. The fool [nabal] has said in his heart, 'There is no God.' They are corrupt, they have done abominable works, there is none who does good." —Psalm 14:1

"For three things the earth is perturbed, Yes, for four it cannot bear up: For a servant when he reigns, a fool [nabal] when he is filled with food..." —Proverbs 30:21-22

"The foolish [nabal] person will no longer be called generous, nor the miser said to be bountiful; For the foolish person will speak foolishness, and his heart will work iniquity: To practice ungodliness, to utter error against the LORD, to keep the hungry unsatisfied, and he will cause the drink of the thirsty to fail." —Isaiah 32:5-6

Nabals in general are vile, corrupt, miserly, evil, perturbing, and impious. They deny there is a God. There is a particular end reserved for the *nabal*, which we understand from its root word *nabel*. Nabel means "to wither, fade, and fall away," like a dead leaf on a tree.

> *"Blessed is the man who walks not in the counsel of the ungodly, nor stands in the path of sinners, nor sits in the seat of the scornful; but his delight is in the law of the LORD, and in His law he meditates day and night. He shall be like a tree planted by the rivers of water, that brings forth its fruit in its season, whose leaf also shall not wither* **[nabel]***; and whatever he does shall prosper. The ungodly are not so, but are like the chaff which the wind drives away. Therefore the ungodly shall not stand in the judgment, nor sinners in the congregation of the righteous. For the LORD knows the way of the righteous, but the way of the ungodly shall perish."* —Psalm 1:1-6

> *"A Psalm of David. Do not fret because of evildoers, nor be envious of the workers of iniquity. For they shall soon be cut down like the grass, and wither* **[nabel]** *as the green herb. Trust in the LORD, and do good; Dwell in the land, and feed on His faithfulness. Delight yourself also in the LORD, and He shall give you the desires of your heart. Commit your way to the LORD, trust also in Him, and He shall bring it to pass. He shall bring forth your righteousness as the light, and your justice as the noonday. Rest in the LORD, and wait patiently for Him; do not fret because of him who prospers in his way, because of the man who brings wicked schemes to pass. Cease from anger, and forsake wrath; Do not fret—it only causes harm. For evildoers shall be cut off; but those who wait on the LORD, they shall inherit the earth."* —Psalm 37:1-9

> *"If you have been foolish* **[nabel]** *in exalting yourself, or if you have devised evil, put your hand on your mouth. For as the churning of milk produces butter, and wringing the nose produces blood, so the forcing of wrath produces strife."* - Proverbs 30:32-33

The last verse reflects and reinforces our theme of glorification.

Nabal has a wife named Abigail. The name Abigail means "my father is joy." She is the daughter of joy and rejoicing. The text tells us she is beautiful and of good understanding (Hebrew: *sakal*: intelligent, sensible, wise, discreet).

Abigail is a second contrast to Nabal, who is now described as churlish and evil in his doings. Churlish means to be hard, cruel, severe, and obstinate. Again, the contrast is rich. Nabal and his wife are opposites.

Finally we get this little detail tacked on at the end: Nabal is of the house of Caleb.

20. What does the house of Caleb add to the picture of Nabal?

Caleb's family is an old, honorable family in Israel—or at least, they were at one time. Caleb and Joshua were among that first generation of Israel who wandered in the wilderness for forty years, but they survived the wandering and came into the kingdom because they believed and glorified God when the rest of their generation did not. Caleb and his family were among the first to claim their inheritance in the kingdom and were given this territory that takes in Hebron, Ziph, Carmel, and Maon. We already know that the Ziphites eagerly betrayed David once (and they will do so again). Nabal is related to the Ziphites, who are also of the house of Caleb and loyal to Saul.

The more renown men in Caleb's family have reputations as aggressive characters. The name Caleb actually means dog or having a dog-like character in being aggressive and forceful, like a hunting dog straining at its master's leash to be released after a prey. That isn't a bad thing if God is the master and the caleb is in pursuit of a promised inheritance in the LORD's kingdom. It only becomes a bad thing when the caleb becomes instead a celeb, a feral dog who acknowledges no master and is running aggressively around the countryside in pursuit of an inheritance of his own making in his own little kingdom.

There are right and wrong kingdoms to pursue, and right and wrong ways to pursue them. This imagery of the caleb and celeb will return when we get to Nabal's response to David's men.

Section 2: David, the Young Men, and Nabal (25:4-13)

David hears that Nabal is shearing his sheep in Carmel.

21. What is significant about Carmel?

Carmel is where Saul set up that monument for himself after he defeated the Amalekites but failed to kill King Agag. It still stands in Carmel, now as a monument to a king who lost a crown and a kingdom because of self-glorification and disobedience. There is a warning in that.

22. What is significant about sheep-shearing?

Sheep-shearing is an event that happens in the summer time usually around the time when the early grain harvests happen. It is a time when the profit is reckoned for the wool, the shearers and shepherds are given their wages for their work (plus a bonus if they had a generous master), and everyone celebrates as if it were a little festival holiday.

23. Why does David send his young men to Nabal?

He is looking for a share in the reward that Nabal is reaping because David's men protected Nabal's shepherds. They had worked for Nabal's good and expected to share in that good.

24. Did Nabal ask David and his men to do this?

No, this was something David and his men did voluntarily, out of compassion for Nabal's shepherds. David had been a shepherd himself and knew the dangers shepherds faced, and extended his protection to them.

25. Knowing what we know of Nabal's character, do you think Nabal cared about the welfare of his shepherds?

I don't think so. He is a ruthless businessman who is only focused on his riches, but brutal, miserly, and unreasonable to deal with. The shepherds were undoubtedly thankful for David's protection, but from Nabal's perspective, David could as easily be a panhandler who washed his windshield without asking and then demanded money for it. Nabal didn't ask for the help or want the help, so why should he pay for the service?

26. How does David instruct his young men to approach Nabal?

1) Begin with a threefold offering of shalom—peace to the man, peace to his house, peace on all that he has (his kingdom).

2) Explain how they helped Nabal's shepherds by protecting them and the flocks (*Ask the shepherds. They will tell you.*)

3) Make the request. Please grant us favor by giving us a share of your profit.

27. What was Nabal's reply?

> *"Who is David, and who is the son of Jesse? There are many servants nowadays who break away each one from his master. Shall I then take my bread and my water and my meat that I have killed for my shearers, and give it to men when I do not know where they are from?"* (25:10-11)

"Who is David?" That is a scornful and contemptuous reply. "And who is the son of Jesse?" is also scornful. When you refer to a person by a subservient relationship and not by their name, it is demeaning. Nabal clearly knows who David is. Who in Israel doesn't know who David is? David is somebody, but Nabal treats him as if he was a nobody.

Interesting how the names of the father's houses crop up like this. Nabal was introduced as a descendant of Caleb, and now we have mention of the son of Jesse, so a comparison is suggested. Let's consider the ancestor's names, beginning with the name Caleb.

Caleb

The name Caleb, which is spelled without vowel in the original Hebrew, and, depending on the context and which vowels are added, the name can mean dog-like in two different senses:

> **Caleb** (with an "a") is an aggressive hunting dog that is under the will and restraint of a master.

> **Celeb** (with an "e") is also an aggressive dog, but one who does not acknowledge his master—one who has slipped its leash and has become a vicious, predatory mongrel dog that runs wild. A celeb is also a euphemism for a male cult prostitute.

Nabal says, *"There are many servants nowadays who break away each one from his master."* That is a subtle dig at David for being a servant who has broken away from his master—like a *celeb*, a mongrel dog who has slipped his leash and is running about the hillside scavenging food—in comparison to himself who is of the house of *caleb*.

Jesse (Yissiy)

The name Jesse (Yissiy) is difficult to translate. It is the along the lines of the word "something" as opposed to "nothing." Its root word *yis* is used Proverbs 8:21 where it says: *"That I may cause those that love me to inherit **yis**."* In other words, they will inherit 'this', but what is 'this'? It is something of substance, a reward of some kind, but you have to read the rest of the passage to see how 'this' is defined. Jesse (Yissiy) is "this one" or "someone" but who?

By the world's standards, Nabal is "someone." He is a great man. He has much prosperity compared to David, the son of Yissiy, who has—what? A hand-out begged from a rich man? David asks that whatever comes to Nabal's hand be shared with his servants, but what is that? Who is this David? Is he the son of "someone"? In Nabal's estimation, David is the son of nobody.

28. What is David's reaction?

Everyone get your swords. We are taking him down. The girding on of swords is mention three times, which emphasizes David's intent to use force.

29. What is driving David into this fight with Nabal?

There are two factors, I think. There is the injustice of what Nabal is doing, and then there is blow to David's ego over the personal dig.

We cannot forget that David is the anointed king-to-be. He isn't some panhandler that has come to Nabal seeking a handout. He has only asked for a modest gift, not as a king but simply as a co-laborer. It is not an unreasonable request on a feast day. Hospitality rules on feast days require a certain extension of generosity, especially if the harvest has been rich.

A worker is worthy of his wage. David has a very strong conviction when it comes to sharing prosperity with others. No one's effort or participation is overlooked on the reckoning day when the reward is handed out. He has cared for and protected the poor shepherds as he would himself, and he has looked out for the rich man's interests as well. He is a man who is generous to a fault, but now he has run up against a fool who is inhospitable and unreasonable to a fault.

Nabal wouldn't have the prosperity he enjoys without David's men protecting him, and yet Nabal treats them like panhandlers and thugs who are demanding a hand-out rather than workers who have earned a wage for their effort. Nabal has returned evil for the good that David has done him.

So, David is justified in dealing out some retribution, right?

It is tempting to want to validate him from a justice aspect, but when he straps on that sword, is he just going out to recoup his wage, or is he out to get something more? If a generous offering was laid before him at this point, would he be satisfied with it and return to camp, or is bloodshed the only thing that will appease him now? It isn't just about the wage anymore. It's about his reputation.

Since we are talking about rewards, here is another thought. Until now, David has pursued a reward of peace and prosperity for his righteousness and faithfulness to God, but now he is pursuing a reward for his works—and he is asking for it from the world and not from God. Somewhere along the road, David has gotten sidetracked into pursuing the reward from the wrong person and for the wrong reason. And he gets rebuked by a fool for his foolish expectations.

APPLY THE PICTURE

David's Model

Nothing gets you sidetracked from the LORD's mission and the LORD's reward like a fool. And a fool can get you into the kind of battle in which you should never engage. But we get into these battles because, let's face it, it is absolutely humiliating to have a fool make a fool out of us and force us to concede to their unreasonableness and unfairness. We can identify with David's situation. We have all run into fools in life, and we have to respond to them with some wisdom.

So here is another bit of wisdom given to us from the Proverbs:

> *"Do not answer a fool according to his folly [foolishness], lest you also be like him. Answer a fool according to his folly, lest he be wise in his own eyes."* —Proverbs 26:4-5

This is the paradox of wisdom. Does a wise person answer a fool or not?

If David answers Nabal, then he will be just as harsh and brutal and arrogant as Nabal—and we can see that he was well on his way toward that end. But if he doesn't answer him, then Nabal will think himself wise in his own eyes in humiliating the king-to-be and might lead others to do the same, because people are watching. Nabal's own servant was watching and reported what he saw back to Abigail.

- **Will answering back have any effect on the fool?** Not this kind of fool. The *nabal* is beyond reasoning with.

- **Will it do any good for those who are watching and would be tempted to follow the *nabal's* example?** Maybe. Those who are simply naive might learn from seeing the consequence of the *nabal's* punishment—if it is a punishment and not just an act of petty revenge for a hurt ego.

- **Do you retaliate for your own glory and reputation or God's glory?** That is the bottom line. Is it truly a matter of justice or is it self-glorification?

- **What effect did David's decision to answer this fool have on him?**

    Pursuing a reward for good works from the world, and not God, sent David down a path of frustration, anger over being victimized, vengeance, and murder not just of Nabal but a lot of innocent people who would have supported him. It would have left him with regret and a troubled conscience for his sin. It would have alienated him from God, but also the people he would one day rule over. Saul pursued the same reward, and we can see where it took him. It does the same with us.

- **If there are negative effects, then how do you avoid them?**

    If David had offered protection to Nabal's shepherds as a good work to be seen by the Lord and let it go at that, he would never have started down this path with Nabal. As it works out, he is now in a fight that a commander in the LORD's service has no business engaging in.

In Second Timothy 2, Paul instructs Timothy to keep his perspective when dealing with a divisive and foolish world, and to consider whether or not the fight is worth fighting and why. **Read Second Timothy 2.**

A Note About the Reward for Works . . .

Our salvation and place in the kingdom is not based on works, but there is a reward for works (both good and bad). This is why we don't equate the reward to salvation. Salvation is by grace alone by faith alone in Christ alone, and not by works, lest any man should boast. Salvation is not earned, but rewards for works are. But the LORD promises repeatedly to reward both the righteous and the wicked for their deeds.

> *"For the Son of Man will come in the glory of His Father with His angels, and then He will reward each according to his works."* —Matthew 16:27

> *"And behold, I am coming quickly, and My reward is with Me, to give to every one according to his work."* —Revelation 22:12

The reward for works is spoken of in several places in the New Testament. Matthew 6 (Sermon on the Mount) speaks of the reward for good works:

> *"Take heed that you do not do your charitable deeds before men, to be seen by them. Otherwise you have no reward from your Father in heaven. Therefore, when you do a charitable deed, do not sound a trumpet before you as the hypocrites do in the synagogues and in the streets, that they may have glory from men. Assuredly, I say to you, they have their reward. But when you do a charitable deed, do not let your left hand know what your right hand is doing, that your charitable deed may be in secret; and your Father who sees in secret will Himself reward you openly."* —Matthew 6:1-4

> *"Do not lay up for yourselves treasures on earth, where moth and rust destroy and where thieves break in and steal; but lay up for yourselves treasures in heaven, where neither moth nor rust destroys and where*

thieves do not break in and steal. For where your treasure is, there your heart will be also." —Matthew 6:19–21

Luke 6 speaks of the reward for loving an enemy:

"But I say to you who hear: Love your enemies, do good to those who hate you, bless those who curse you, and pray for those who spitefully use you. To him who strikes you on the one cheek, offer the other also. And from him who takes away your cloak, do not withhold your tunic either. Give to everyone who asks of you. And from him who takes away your goods do not ask them back . . ." —Luke 6:27–30

"And if you lend to those from whom you hope to receive back, what credit is that to you? For even sinners lend to sinners to receive as much back. But love your enemies, do good, and lend, hoping for nothing in return; and your reward will be great, and you will be sons of the Most High. For He is kind to the unthankful and evil. Therefore be merciful, just as your Father also is merciful." —Luke 6:34-36

Paul also exhorts us:

"And whatever you do, do it heartily, as to the Lord and not to men, knowing that from the Lord you will receive the reward of the inheritance; for you serve the Lord Christ. But he who does wrong will be repaid for what he has done, and there is no partiality."
—Colossians 3:23–25

If we go to the unrighteous world expecting a reward for our righteousness, we will rarely receive anything for it, because the world's idea of reward will be according to the world's values and not God's. This world is not where our reward and validation lies, and that is one of the lessons we learn in pursuing our crown.

BUILD THE PICTURE

Section 3: Abigail Prepares a Gift (25:14-20)

30. What news does the young man bring to Abigail?

He gives Abigail a good report of David, a bad report of Nabal, and then tells Abigail what David plans to do. Harm is planned not just for Nabal, but for all of Nabal's household—that includes his wife, children, and servants. David is getting ready to wipe out everyone for one man's offense—just like Saul did with Nob and was going to do with Keilah.

When the servant says it is impossible to speak to Nabal, that implies that he tried to tell Nabal about the help David gave him, but Nabal would not listen, so now he is appealing to Abigail.

31. How does the servant describe Nabal?

Different Bible version render the servant's description of Nabal differently: scoundrel, ill-tempered, a wicked man, a worthless man. The phrase in the Hebrew is "a son of Belial." The children of Belial crop up a number of times in First Samuel.

- In First Samuel 1, Hannah rebukes Eli for having thought her a daughter of Belial for being drunk, whereas Eli's own sons are called the sons of Belial for their licentiousness and their deliberate scorning of the LORD and His sacrifices.

- In First Samuel 30, the term describes those of David's men who refuse to share the spoil of battle with their fellow servants. David comes down very hard on his men for this.

- In First Samuel 10:27, some unnamed children of Belial denied Saul's rulership over them, just like Nabal now denies David. Here's a picture comparison . . .

In First Samuel 10:27 (Picture #2), Saul had been proclaimed king, but not yet crowned. And there was a group of rebellious men referred to as sons of Belial who said "How can this man save us?" They despised him and brought him no presents. But Saul held his peace and didn't answer back. After he had proven himself in battle, these same men were brought back to him, and the people cried out that they should be put to death for not acknowledging the anointed king-to-be. Saul has not been a man known for his magnanimity to his enemies, but, in that first instance, he was. He refused to have them killed, despite their earlier rebuke.

As the new anointed king-to-be, David experiences the same

treatment at the hands of Nabal, whom the shepherd calls a son of Belial. Does David hold his peace? No, he doesn't. For a man known for his magnanimity toward his enemies, he has no patience with Nabal. He takes issue with Nabal over not giving him a gift befitting a magnanimous king, and goes on the warpath. He ordered Nabal and all his house killed. So, where Saul acted righteously, David takes the opposite tact and acts unrighteously. Isn't that a flip? And doesn't that make him look foolish, that his actions should be more churlish than even a bad example like Saul.

32. How do you go about making peace with an offended king when he has purposed in his heart to kill you?

That is something David has been grappling with himself. Funny how he now ends up in Saul's shoes. Just as Jonathan reasoned with Saul over killing David, the LORD now sends Abigail to reason with David over killing Nabal.

Abigail prepares a magnificent feast as a peace offering. This is the reward David had sought from Nabal and been denied, so Abigail now offers it in Nabal's place, and it is kingly. She sends the offering first, and then follows after the servants to meet David personally.

But she does not tell her husband.

33. Why didn't Abigail tell Nabal?

Nabal is unreasonable, cruel, evil, and he has already said no. He doesn't want David and his men to be given anything. He would most certainly have stopped her if he had known what she was planning. What will be his reaction when he finds out what she has done after the fact?

This is the dilemma David has created by seeking vengeance and not justice. Justice would have dealt with Nabal alone, but now he has embroiled Abigail in this dilemma. On one hand, she has an angry king coming to kill her and her household if she doesn't stop him. On the other hand, she is being forced to disobey her husband. If she succeeds in dissuading David from killing everyone, she still has a brutal husband to face back at home who will probably kill her when he finds out. There is the consequence to herself if she succeeds, but the consequence for her entire household if she fails. But she is going to lose, regardless.

What an awful decision to have to make. Sin does this. It creates problems to which there are no good solutions, and the decision over what to do now requires one person to sacrifice herself to save the rest. And that is what Abigail does. It's very noble.

Abigail knows with surety what the outcome will be in dealing with her unreasonable husband. David seems compassionate—at least that is how the young shepherd described him. Maybe she has a chance in appealing to David. She certainly has nothing more to lose.

And so she goes to intercept David at the hill.

Section 4: David and Abigail (25:21-35)

34. What are David's thoughts at this point?

The author gives us a very transparent glimpse of what David is thinking as he comes upon Abigail. He is brooding, and he is whipping himself up into a fury over having been victimized in such a brutish fashion. *"Surely in vain I have protected all that this fellow has in the wilderness."* Surely in vain . . . What about the shepherds he protected? Did they count for nothing?

David had offered the protection with the expectation of a reward—a wage for his good deed. He doesn't get his reward and now he regrets the good he has done.

We knew from the shepherd's report that David is coming to kill not just Nabal, but all the men in his employ. We now see it in David's own words. Notice he phrases this as an oath, but it is a rash oath like the ones that Saul usually makes. This is David's frame of mind when Abigail intercepts him and brings him the reward feast.

But now Abigail is faced with another task: She must convince an angry king bent on vengeance that what he is doing is morally wrong before God. This intercession is a lot like what Jonathan tried (unsuccessfully) to do with his father Saul on several occasions, and it never worked. Abigail doesn't even have the benefit of an intimate relationship with David that Jonathan had with his father. So how does she go about it?

35. What does Abigail do to turn David's wrath and dissuade him?

  a. She humbles herself before David and gives him the respect due him. The text belabors her action: *"she fell on her face . . . bowed to the ground . . . fell at his feet . . ."* From this posture of humility she speaks to him. She calls him lord but refers to herself as his maidservant. (25:23-24)

  b. She admits there has been an iniquity done, but she asks that the consequences fall on her. She does not diminish Nabal's offense—she points out that he is aptly named a fool—but she takes the iniquity upon herself for not being more vigilant. If she had only known they were coming, she could have intercepted David's young men and prevented the offense.

  c. She begins, very tactfully, to advise David of the sin he is about to commit which he will regret.

36. How does Abigail build her case?

  a. *"Now therefore, my lord, as the LORD lives and as your soul lives, since the LORD has held you back from coming to bloodshed and avenging yourself . . ."* (25:26a)

  She reminds David of his relationship with the LORD. The LORD is restraining him, which implies that the only reason that he is living is because the living God holds his life in His hand. This is not about her trying to convince David to abandon this fight. The LORD is the one who orchestrated this intervention. She is the intercessor, but she is only the instrument.

  She begins (and ends) her argument with the statement that David is getting ready to shed innocent blood for one man's offense and avenge himself by his own hand. Automatically we think of Saul because this is typical behavior for Saul. Saul nearly killed his own people with a rash oath while pursuing vengeance on the Philistines (Chapter 14). Saul killed the priests of Nob to avenge himself on David (Chapter 22). Saul would have killed the people of Keilah to avenge himself on David (Chapter 23).

The whole reason David is a fugitive at the moment is because of a man seeking his own vengeance to the point of murdering innocent people. While Nabal may not be innocent, Nabal's shepherds and the rest of his house were.

b. *"... let your enemies and those who seek harm for my lord be as Nabal."* (25:26b)

May all of David's enemies be so dishonored and treated with contempt as one would a *nabal* and may they *nabel*, that is, languish and wither like leaves and fall away. When I read this statement, I think of David's own words when he said to Saul *"After whom has the king of Israel come out? Whom do you pursue? A dead dog? A flea?"* (24:14) Why would a king of Israel waste his time dealing with fools who offer him no gifts?

c. *"And now this present which your maidservant has brought to my lord, let it be given to the young men who follow my lord. Please forgive the trespass of your maidservant."* (25:27-28a)

She presents herself as Nabal's representative by offering the reward for David's services that Nabal should have offered, and then as substitute for Nabal's trespass. She abases herself before him and asks forgiveness for a much lighter offense of not being vigilant enough. Thus, the gift is something of a trespass offering to turn away wrath.

d. *"For the LORD will certainly make for my lord an enduring house, because my lord fights the battles of the LORD."* (25:28)

She reminds David of what reward he is pursuing, from whom David will receive that reward, which battles he is meant fight and what his motivation should be. The LORD's promise to him hinges on David staying on track and not getting himself entangled in battles with fools. He has been tasked with a greater battle, a greater vision, and a greater reward than the paltry food she has placed before him.

e. *"Yet a man has risen to pursue you and seek your life, but the life of my lord shall be bound in the bundle of the living with the LORD your God; and the lives of your enemies He shall sling out, as from the pocket of a sling."* (25:29)

To make her point, she now alludes to David's situation with Saul.

When Nabal alluded to David's relationship with Saul, but it was to condemn David for being the rebellious dog who did not acknowledging his master. Abigail's allusion to Saul is also an implied condemnation of David but for a different reason. She holds Saul up as an illustration of what David is doing.

Saul is the one who is pursuing David and seeking his life, but God is the one preserving David. But now David has risen to seek another man's life after Saul's example. We know from Saul's example that the glory and satisfaction that David gains from this will be short-lived, and it is not the way to establish peace in his kingdom.

Abigail then presents two rewards: To be held in the LORD's hand or to be slung away from Him like a stone flung from a sling. (Interesting that she uses the same stone-in-a-sling imagery that we noted back in narrative about Keilah. It is imagery that would resonate with David as a shepherd.) These are the ultimate rewards that David should be considering. Is he God's friend or God's enemy? This isn't about David and Nabal. This is about David and God.

Note: To be "bound in the bundle of the living" is a metaphor for having a long life, but in post-biblical times, the "bundle of life" came to signify eternal life in the next world, and therefore the expression is found on many Jewish tombstones with this reference to First Samuel 25:29. Interesting that this Jewish idea of having eternal life would be tied back to David and this choice of reward.

f. *"And it shall come to pass, when the LORD has done for my lord according to all the good that He has spoken concerning you, and has appointed you ruler over Israel, that this will be no grief to you, nor offense of heart to my lord, either that you have shed blood without cause, or that my lord has avenged himself."* (25:30-31a)

Abigail reminds David of the crown he is pursuing. She reaffirms that she believes the LORD will keep His word concerning David and make him a *nageed*, (ruler or commander), but will he be a commander who lives with grief and regret over the consequences of his commands?

The last time that word *nageed* was used, it was when Samuel told Saul his kingdom would not continue:

> "But now your kingdom shall not continue. The LORD has sought for Himself a man after His own heart, and the LORD has commanded him to be commander **[nageed]** over His people, because you have not kept what the LORD commanded you." — First Samuel 13:14

A commander is only worthy of his command so long as he is obedient to God's commands. David is at the same crossroad where Saul had been, and he is heading down the same path. If he continues on this path, it will bring him to grief, just as it did Saul. Again, Abigail reiterates the opening statement of David shedding innocent blood and avenging himself. David's conscience already troubled him once when he cut the corner of Saul's robe. The actions he is preparing to take now would reap even greater regret and troubled conscience.

Is recouping his reward and the temporal pleasure of venting his wrath on Nabal worth the eternal reward of living with regret and a troubled conscience? Whatever glory he gained from it would be short-lived.

g. "But when the LORD has dealt well with my lord, then remember your maidservant." (25:31b)

David asked Nabal to remember him when Nabal reaped the reward that David had secured for him, and Nabal refused him. Now Abigail asks David to remember her when all the good that the LORD has secured for him comes to pass. Will he be as stingy with his own prosperity? Not David.

37. What is David's response to Abigail's tactful rebuke?

Bless the LORD, who sent you ... Bless your good advice ... Bless you ... Abigail has made God's point, and her argument was sufficient to turn David back. He lavishes a three-fold blessing on her, much like the three-fold offering of peace that he initially offered Nabal. He takes the gift, and sends her away in peace and with his respect.

What made David a man after God's own heart is not that David was a perfect man. David was just as guilty of the same sinful desires that drove Saul to sin. But what made him different is that David was sensitive to his own sin and his relationship with God, he heeded warnings, and he corrected his behaviors when he was confronted with his sin. He was capable of a change of heart where Saul and Nabal weren't.

Did Abigail go away in peace? Where her relationship with David was concerned, yes. But consequences were waiting for her at home as a result of what she did for David. She would probably suffer the wrath of an unreasonable, brutal husband when Nabal found out that she had gone behind his back and undermined his authority by doing something that he didn't want done. This is the cost that must be weighed: whether to keep temporary peace with her husband or make a lasting peace with David. She chose the right king with which to align herself, but it wasn't without cost.

APPLY THE PICTURE

Abigail's Model

Abigail turned back wrath with a soft answer, and yet her soft answer had some teeth to it.

- **Abigail reminds David of his relationship with the LORD**, which is something precious to David.

- **She doesn't make the argument a battle of wills between herself and David, or even Nabal and David, but between the LORD and David.** The LORD is the one restraining David by sending him this warning. The LORD is the one holding David's life in His hand, even as He holds Saul's and Nabal's lives. The LORD will judge them as either His friend or enemy.

- **She doesn't downplay Nabal's offense.** She knows all too well what it is like to deal with a fool. **Even so, she admits her own lack of vigilance and asks forgiveness.** It seems like a trifling confession, but it really isn't. If you know of a potential danger (like having an unpredictable animal in the house) and you are not vigilant when people come into the realm of that animal, you bear some responsibility for a lack of vigilance if something bad happens.

When approaching a person to deal with sin in their lives, you have to begin by acknowledging your own failing in the situation. Humility levels the playing field, and it can turn their heart toward you so that they will then listen to your advice.

- **She addresses the justice issue.** I think you have to address the issue of injustice because that is the point that victims often use to justify their taking vengeance. But they need to understand that there is more to be gained in letting the LORD deal with the injustice.

- **Suffering humiliation can be a stumbling block in a person's life. How did Abigail remove that stumbling block for David?**

    In addition to humbling herself, Abigail offered David the tangible gift he was due, but more importantly, she addressed the intangible losses he has suffered by granting him respect. She reminded David of the LORD's promise to make him an enduring house. But that promise hinged on him fighting for God's glory and not his own.

That is a pretty good model for an intercessor to follow. She also models for us Second Timothy 2:24-26; Colossians 4:2, 5-6; First Thessalonians 5:12-15; and Romans 12:9-21.

> *"And a servant of the Lord must not quarrel but be gentle to all, able to teach, patient, in humility correcting those who are in opposition, if God perhaps will grant them repentance, so that they may know the truth, and that they may come to their senses and escape the snare of the devil, having been taken captive by him to do his will."*
> —Second Timothy 2:24-26

> *"Continue earnestly in prayer, being vigilant in it with thanksgiving; . . . Walk in wisdom toward those who are outside, redeeming the time. Let your speech always be with grace, seasoned with salt, that you may know how you ought to answer each one."* —Colossians 4:2, 5-6

"And we urge you, brethren, to recognize those who labor among you, and are over you in the Lord and admonish you, and to esteem them very highly in love for their work's sake. Be at peace among yourselves. Now we exhort you, brethren, warn those who are unruly, comfort the fainthearted, uphold the weak, be patient with all. See that no one renders evil for evil to anyone, but always pursue what is good both for yourselves and for all." —First Thessalonians 5:12-15

"Let love be without hypocrisy. Abhor what is evil. Cling to what is good. Be kindly affectionate to one another with brotherly love, in honor giving preference to one another; not lagging in diligence, fervent in spirit, serving the Lord; rejoicing in hope, patient in tribulation, continuing steadfastly in prayer; distributing to the needs of the saints, given to hospitality. Bless those who persecute you; bless and do not curse. Rejoice with those who rejoice, and weep with those who weep. Be of the same mind toward one another. Do not set your mind on high things, but associate with the humble. Do not be wise in your own opinion. Repay no one evil for evil. Have regard for good things in the sight of all men. If it is possible, as much as depends on you, live peaceably with all men. Beloved, do not avenge yourselves, but rather give place to wrath; for it is written, 'Vengeance is Mine, I will repay,' says the Lord. Therefore 'If your enemy is hungry, feed him; If he is thirsty, give him a drink; for in so doing you will heap coals of fire on his head.' Do not be overcome by evil, but overcome evil with good."
—Romans 12:9-21

BUILD THE PICTURE

Section 5: God Prepares a Reward for David (25:36-39a)

38. What did Abigail find when she got home?

Nabal is holding a feast in his house, like the feast of a king, and he is roaring drunk and in high spirits. Meanwhile, the real king has retreated back into his exile in the hills to share a much more meager meal with his men. The author purposely makes the comparison between kings to heighten the offense and foolishness of Nabal's behavior.

If Nabal is unreasonable when he is in his right mind, he is even less so when drunk. Abigail decides to wait until the next morning to inform him of the danger that his life was in the night before. I wonder how she felt facing him the next morning?

39. What happened to Nabal?

His heart died within him. We can reason that maybe he had a heart attack and became paralyzed, but in the Hebrew, the heart has a broader picture. It is that thing which is in the midst of a man. It is the inner place where inclinations and resolutions form and where a man determines the action he will take. It is the seat of appetites, emotions, conscience, and moral character. It is connected with the mind as a place of memory, reflection, and thinking, e.g. *"Mary pondered these things in her heart."* All that died within Nabal, and he became like stone.

The LORD left him in that condition of spiritual death for ten days, and then struck him so that he died physically. Ten is one of the numbers representing completion and testimony. In the book of Genesis, the phrase "God said" appears ten times which is testimony to His creative power. It represents the fullness of the law, in the giving of the ten commandments. It represents completeness of order, but also the fullness of judgment, as seen in the ten plagues on Egypt or the ten days between the Feast of Trumpets and the Day of Atonement when Israel's judgment for sin is rendered. The fullness of judgment is being visited on Nabal here.

40. How does David react to the news of Nabal's death?

First, he blesses the LORD. He gives God the glory for having kept him from sin and taking glory for himself. God lifted the reproach—shame and humiliation—that David had received at Nabal's hand. David's desire for vengeance was never about the wages he was denied. The issue was really about the humiliation he had suffered. David's validation and vindication had to come from the LORD for him to feel truly released. And he admits his own sin. What he was planning to do was evil.

Then, he remembers Abigail.

Section 6: David, the Young Men, and Abigail (24:39b-42)

41. David sends his men out with a message again, just as he did with Nabal. How does Abigail's response compare?

This section mirrors the earlier section of David, the young men, and Nabal, almost like a do-over, except this time the young men go to Abigail at Carmel instead of Nabal. And this time David's request is awarded as Abigail graciously agrees to become his wife. She presents herself humbly and yet there is a regal quality about her as she rides in state with her attendants to meet David.

The structure of Section 6 parallels Section 2. Let's compare them:

(24:4-8) "And David sent" a proposal to Nabal
(24:39) "And David sent . . ." a proposal to Abigail.
(In Section 2, the dialogue is paired with David. In Section 6, the dialogue is paired with the servants.)

(24:9) "So when David's young men came, they spoke to Nabal according to all these words in the name of David, and waited."
(24:40) "When the servants of David had come to Abigail at Carmel, they spoke to her saying, 'David sent us to you . . .'"

(24:10-11) Nabal's answer: He rejects David request.
(24:41) Abigail's answer: She accepts David's request.

(24:12) David's men returned empty-handed.
(24:42) David's men returned with Abigail.

42. Why would the author go to such lengths to create these parallels?

He deliberately makes parallels to focus us on the pictures we need to compare, and to consider the two picture and understand the good by its comparison with the bad. It isn't always an obvious line, as we will see when we get to the next chapter.

The point is to reinforce the importance of Abigail's intervention. Without that intervention, events would have taken a devastating turn for David and for Abigail and all of Nabal's household. A wise word offered at a timely moment reaps tremendous results.

This reward is as much for Abigail as it is for David. David will be king, and yet he now extends the status of royalty to Abigail for her faithfulness to him.

Section 7: David and His Wives (24:43-44)

The closing narrator's note mirrors the opening verses by introducing wives. Where Abigail is introduced as Nabal's wife at the beginning, now she is David's wife. And in addition to Abigail, David takes Ahinoam the Jezreelitess. Altogether, David has three wives so far, and yet his first wife, Michal, is not with him.

The last time we saw Michal was in First Samuel 19 when she helped David escape from Saul after Saul had sent men to watch David's house. She deceived Saul's deputies, and Saul realized her deception too late, but the text didn't tell us what became of her after David fled.

Now we find out that Saul had done something wicked by giving Michal to a man named Paltiel, the son of Laish, who was from Gallim. She will not be restored to David until Second Samuel 3.

APPLY THE PICTURE

Nabal's Model

Nabal models very well the warning against the rich fool whose life was required of him in a night because he laid up treasure for himself but was not rich toward God (Luke 12:16-21). The parable is very apt.

The Young Men's Model (Sections 2 and 6)

Young men are minor characters in the narrative and are featured three times. First, David sends ten of his young men out with a message to bear witness of him and what he has done for Nabal. Next, another young man goes to Abigail and bears witness of how David and his men have impacted his own life. Finally David's young men are sent out with a final message—a marriage proposal—for Abigail.

Their only action in the narrative is to obey the king and deliver a message.

When David first sent his ten men out, his gives them this message:

> *"David sent ten young men; and David said to the young men, 'Go up to Carmel, go to Nabal, and greet him in my name. And thus you shall say to him who lives in prosperity: "Peace be to you, peace to your house, and peace to all that you have!"'* —First Samuel 25:5-6

It reminded me of what Jesus said when he sent out the twelve apostles in Matthew 10.

> *"These twelve Jesus sent out and commanded them, saying: 'Do not go into the way of the Gentiles, and do not enter a city of the Samaritans. But go rather to the lost sheep of the house of Israel. And as you go, preach, saying, "The kingdom of heaven is at hand." Heal the sick, cleanse the lepers, raise the dead, cast out demons. Freely you have received, freely give. Provide neither gold nor silver nor copper in your money belts, nor bag for your journey, nor two tunics, nor sandals, nor staffs; for a worker is worthy of his food. Now whatever city or town you enter, inquire who in it is worthy, and stay there till you go out. And when you go into a household, greet it. If the household is worthy, let your peace come upon it. But if it is not worthy, let your peace return to you. And whoever will not receive you nor hear your words, when you depart from that house or city, shake off the dust from your feet. Assuredly, I say to you, it will be more tolerable for the land of Sodom and Gomorrah in the day of judgment than for that city!"* —Matthew 10:5-15

Jesus then goes on to speak to them about the persecutions that are coming—how brother would deliver brother unto death and his believers will be hated for His name sake. But the passage in Matthew ends with the promise of a reward for those who receive the apostles.

> *"He who receives you receives Me, and he who receives Me receives Him who sent Me. He who receives a prophet in the name of a prophet shall receive a prophet's reward. And he who receives a righteous man in the name of a righteous man shall receive a righteous man's reward. And whoever gives one of these little ones only a cup of cold water in the name of a disciple, assuredly, I say to you, he shall by no means lose his reward."* —Matthew 10:40-42

In a way, we are the young men and the apostles. When we are sent out into the world with the message of peace that Christ has given us, we will meet Nabals and Abigails. They represent the two opposing responses to the King.

- **Who, then, are the Nabals?**

    The Nabals are the worldly-wise fools who set themselves up in their own little kingdoms like kings. They are the somebodies, and everyone else are the nobodies. They judge us by who we are in their kingdom without recognizing the greater King we serve. They don't receive us or the message of peace that we bring in Christ's name. They will scoff at our King, revile us, and refuse to acknowledge our effort toward their peace. Jesus tells us, "Shake them off and move on. This is not your battle. God will deal with this. Just let it go."

- **Who, then, are the Abigails?**

    The Abigails of this world are the ones who hear and accept the message of peace (and the marriage proposal) and become partakers of the reward with us. We bring them with us as brides when we return to the King.

David's Model: Returning evil for evil

The theme of returning evil for evil is a major focus in David's grievance against Nabal, as it says in First Thessalonians 5:15:

> "See that no one renders evil for evil to anyone, but always pursue what is good both for yourselves and for all."—First Thessalonians 5:15

But there are a couple other places in the New Testament where this issue is mentioned, and I want to flesh out the details of those.

Peter also mentions returning evil for evil in First Peter 3. Remember, when we were in First Samuel 24, we read First Peter 2 talking about submission to masters. Now in First Samuel 25, we are continuing on track with First Peter 3–4, this time in submitting to one another and suffering for Christ.

> *"Finally, all of you be of one mind, having compassion for one another; love as brothers, be tenderhearted, be courteous; not returning evil for evil or reviling for reviling, but on the contrary blessing, knowing that you were called to this, that you may inherit a blessing."* —First Peter 3:8-9

Returning evil for evil gets you one kind of reward, and it is about us taking our satisfaction from one another. But we are called to seek satisfaction of a different sort and from a different source. Peter then goes on to quote Psalm 34:12-16:

> *"For 'he who would love life and see good days, let him refrain his tongue from evil, and his lips from speaking deceit. Let him turn away from evil and do good; let him seek peace and pursue it. For the eyes of the Lord are on the righteous, and his ears are open to their prayers; but the face of the Lord is against those who do evil.'"* —First Peter 3:10-12

We previously studied Psalm 34 because it is prefaced by this time of exile in David's life. It was his reflection after falling into Philistine hands, and he had to pretend madness to escape (how humiliating). He had sought to lengthen his own life by his own effort and improve his own lot in life (kind of like what he does here with Nabal), but his effort was thwarted and he ended up looking like an idiot (just as he does now with Nabal). His effort took him farther and farther from the peace he desired. Peace was supposed to be the end goal and the reward, but returning evil for evil or reviling for reviling never brings peace. Peter then goes on:

> *"And who is he who will harm you if you become followers of what is good? But even if you should suffer for righteousness' sake, you are blessed. 'And do not be afraid of their threats, nor be troubled.' But sanctify the Lord God in your hearts, and always be ready to give a defense to everyone who asks you a reason for the hope that is in you, with meekness and fear; having a good conscience, that when they defame you as evildoers, those who revile your good conduct in Christ may be ashamed. For it is better, if it is the will of God, to suffer for doing good than for doing evil."* —First Peter 3:8–17

Which is better—to suffer at the hands of the world for having done a good deed in conscience to God, or to suffer at the hand of God for having strayed into sin in avenging yourself?

> *"For we have spent enough of our past lifetime in doing the will of the Gentiles—when we walked in lewdness, lusts, drunkenness, revelries, drinking parties, and abominable idolatries. In regard to these, they think it strange that you do not run with them in the same flood of dissipation, speaking evil of you. They will give an account to Him who is ready to judge the living and the dead . . . If you are reproached for the name of Christ, blessed are you, for the Spirit of glory and of God rests upon you. On their part He is blasphemed, but on your part He is glorified. But let none of you suffer as a murderer, a thief, an evildoer, or as a busybody in other people's matters. Yet if anyone suffers as a Christian, let him not be ashamed, but let him glorify God in this matter. For the time has come for judgment to begin at the house of God; and if it begins with us first, what will be the end of those who do not obey the gospel of God?"* —First Peter 4:3-5, 14–17

We have to be discerning in how we look at the source of our suffering, because sometimes we bring it on ourselves. David suffered rebuke for his good works and righteousness, but only because he went looking to the world for a reward for that act. He did the right thing for the wrong reward and suffered for it. If he had done his charitable deed solely out of conscience toward God, he would have avoided Nabal's abuse. If he had followed through with his intent to murder, then he would have compounded his suffering by incurring God's wrath as an evildoer on top of Nabal's abuse.

We, too, can suffer the world's abuse when we look for a worldly reward for our spiritual righteousness. We can do good, but for the wrong reasons, and that can cause some of our suffering. This is downfall of the prosperity cults, where they believe that if you give and do good works, then you will receive a worldly form of prosperity in return.

If we become trespassers by choosing to take our own vengeance, then we will suffer God's wrath and not His reward. Not all suffering is going to reap a blessing from God.

In Romans 12, Paul echoes Peter's words:

> *"Beloved, do not avenge yourselves, but rather give place to wrath; for it is written, 'Vengeance is Mine, I will repay,' says the Lord. Therefore 'If your enemy is hungry, feed him; If he is thirsty, give him a drink; For in*

so doing you will heap coals of fire on his head.' Do not be overcome by evil, but overcome evil with good." —Romans 12:19–21

In Romans 12, Paul quotes Deuteronomy 32:35 and Proverbs 25:21-22. That's an interesting pairing and significant when applied to this picture.

- **Why is it the LORD's right to avenge, and what was gained by letting God deal with Nabal instead David?**

  David reflects on the *nabal* in Psalm 53, which begins with the statement *"The fool [nabal] has said in his heart, 'There is no God.'"* This is an important point to remember. When we are confronted with a *nabal* it is not our reputation that is on the line but God's. God is the one who chose David and anointed him as His king, so a slap in the face to God's anointed is a slap in the face to God Himself. Similarly, God is the one who chose us, so when we are faced with someone who treats us like a nobody, they are treating God as a nobody as well. Thus, it is God's right to avenge Himself on the *nabals* of this world, and in doing so He avenges us as well.

  One of the prerequisites for kingship is obedience to commands. If you can't obey commands, you won't be given the right to command. God states in the Law that taking vengeance is an act reserved for Him and Him alone. Another prerequisite is not taking God's glory for yourself. It is to God's glory that He be given the right to avenge His servants, and He does it justly and thoroughly as we see with Nabal; David's vengeance would have strayed beyond justice and brought him under judgment.

  When you take vengeance yourself, you are treading into God's territory. It is the hardest thing in the world not to react to the *nabals* of this world, but there is a reward for you if you restrain yourself. Even more than that, there is a reward for you if you go to the opposite extreme as Abigail did and show mercy and kindness. The LORD certainly rewarded Abigail.

  It is a tough lesson I myself have had to learn, but I will tell you, the times that I have let God deal with my *nabal*, the vindication I received was beyond anything I could have achieved myself. It is thrilling to have that answer from God. The consequences for my *nabal* were so perfectly fitting and thoroughly accomplished that I knew—*I knew*—it was from God.

But be careful how you respond to the LORD's vengeance on your behalf, because if you take glory for yourself by gloating, there will be consequences for you as well.

Proverbs 24 reminds us:

> *"Do not rejoice when your enemy falls, and do not let your heart be glad when he stumbles; lest the LORD see it, and it displease Him, and He turn away His wrath from him. Do not fret because of evildoers, nor be envious of the wicked; For there will be no prospect for the evil man; The lamp of the wicked will be put out. My son, fear the LORD and the king; Do not associate with those given to change; for their calamity will rise suddenly, and who knows the ruin those two can bring?"* —Proverbs 24:17-22

Abigail's Model: Vigilance

Abigail's confession brings up the topic of being vigilant, which will carry into the next picture in Chapter 26. Being vigilant is something we are called to do, and there are a number of New Testament passages that apply what Abigail, David, and Nabal picture for us.

> *"But take heed to yourselves, lest your hearts be weighed down with carousing, drunkenness, and cares of this life, and that Day come on you unexpectedly. For it will come as a snare on all those who dwell on the face of the whole earth. Watch therefore, and pray always that you may be counted worthy to escape all these things that will come to pass, and to stand before the Son of Man."* —Luke 21:34-36

> *"For you yourselves know perfectly that the day of the Lord so comes as a thief in the night. For when they say, 'Peace and safety!' then sudden destruction comes upon them, as labor pains upon a pregnant woman. And they shall not escape. But you, brethren, are not in darkness, so that this Day should overtake you as a thief. You are all sons of light and sons of the day. We are not of the night nor of darkness. Therefore let us not sleep, as others do, but let us watch and be sober. For those who*

sleep, sleep at night, and those who get drunk are drunk at night. But let us who are of the day be sober, putting on the breastplate of faith and love, and as a helmet the hope of salvation. For God did not appoint us to wrath, but to obtain salvation through our Lord Jesus Christ," —First Thessalonians 5:2-9

Sifting out the fine points . . .

Sections 3, 4, and 5 of the narrative are arranged in a grand chiastic structure that focuses on Abigail's dialogue (F). I want to look briefly at the various parallels that are being made as the chiastic structure stacks up, because there are more points to consider when we compare the parallels.

(A) Verses 14-17 compared to verse 39. The opening and closing verses of the chiasm reflect our theme of glorification.

- **Who is receiving the praise initially?**

    Initially, Nabal's servant offers a praise of David to Abigail. Then the good that David did turns to evil as he sets out to take glory for himself by killing Nabal and a household of innocent people out of vengeance for Nabal's offense.

- **Who gets the praise in the end?**

    In the end, God's servant, David, offers a praise of God for keeping him from the evil he had planned and for lifting his reproach by avenging David on Nabal.

So, we see the reversal. David set out to take vengeance himself but then turned and let the LORD handle the situation.

(B) Verses 18 compared to verse 37-38. The first is about Abigail preparing the feast. The second set is Nabal's death. These two elements don't seem to have any connection to each other except that they are paired together in the chiastic structure as a mirror of one another, so there must be a thought that connects them—and there is.

- **What reward/gift is being offered to David initially by Abigail?**

    In the initial instance, we see Abigail preparing a feast for David and his men. It is the reward that he should have received as wages for the work that he had done for Nabal. It is a reward based on works.

- **What reward/gift is being offered to David in the end by God?**

    Mirroring Abigail's gift is God taking Nabal's life to avenge David. That, too, is a reward. It is a reward for obedience. David set out to take the reward that was his due but his actions would have led to sin. David heeded Abigail's warning and turned back from sin, and God rewarded him for it.

    The LORD took Nabal's life, not as a reward for what David had done—his works—but for what he *hadn't* done. If David had continued pursuing the reward he had set his sights on, his works would have lost him the reward from the LORD. The LORD rewarded David's decision not to take his own vengeance but to let the LORD Himself take away David's reproach.

    There was a reward for that decision to let go of the personal offense and the injustice and leave it in the LORD's hands. So, we have a comparison of two rewards—one based on works and one based on faith that is similar to the rewards we discussed with Hannah and Peninnah in First Samuel 1–2. The theme now carries from the comparison of those women to the king and the fool, and it is in keeping with the greater theme of how we pursue glorification and validation.

- **Which was more validating—the reward for works or obedience?**

    The reward for obedience. Not only did David receive what was his due, he walked away vindicated and with a clear conscience. A clear conscience before God is a reward of eternal value.

(C) Verse 19 compared to verse 36b. Here we see the repeated comment that Abigail tells her husband nothing about her dealings with David. She tells him nothing when she leaves, and she tells him nothing when she returns that night (because he is drunk), but then she tells him everything in the morning. Again, there is a very purposeful use of phrasing to connect these two steps in the chiastic structure:

> *"But she did not tell her husband Nabal . . . therefore she told him nothing, little or much, until morning light."* (25:19, 36)

(D) Verse 20 compared to verse 36a. At first we see Abigail leave Nabal's house to intercept David with the feast she had prepared for him; afterward she returns to Nabal's house to find him feasting on a feast he made for himself.

(E) Verses 21-22 compared to verse 32-35. This element we see David's initial thoughts and then his drastic reversal and change of heart after Abigail talks to him. It is like night and day. These two pictures are paired with repeated phrases: *"if I leave one male of all who belong to him by morning light . . . by morning light no males would have been left to Nabal."* Even the order of the wording is reversed.

(F) Verses 23-31. These are Abigail's pivotal dialogue.

The narrative of David, Nabal and Abigail touches on so many themes. There are the themes of not repaying evil for evil or seeking vengeance, not getting caught up in fights over words, being a focused on the true battle, and being a worker worthy of our wage. This story makes a good pairing with these New Testament teachings.

I think the overall thrust of this account is knowing what reward you seek and the king from whom you seek validation for your works. It is better to pursue a reward for obedience than to pursue a wage for good deeds. But then I also look at Abigail's pivotal role, and I recognize the vital importance of the role an intercessor plays in averting a person's headlong run in seeking revenge on an enemy. That, too, is worthy of reflection.

26 David at the Hill of Hachilah

READ

First Samuel 26:1-25

NARRATIVE STRUCTURE

This is our last picture in the series on taking vengeance, and now we are going to see what lessons David has learned from past experience.

Picture #26 has five sections and is structured around three conversations:

1) Opening dialogue that sets the scene (26:1-4)
2) David's conversation with his men (26:5-12)
3) David's conversation with Abner (26:13-16)
4) David's confrontation with Saul (26:17-25a)
5) Narrator's note of departure (26:25b)

This picture will compare to Picture #24 in structure and content, but there are some differences. David's conversation with Abner is an addition. Also, David's conversation with Saul has all the same elements of the initial address, penitent response, and acknowledgment, but Saul initiates the conversation this time instead of David, and David's responses are interspersed with Saul's statements.

BUILD THE PICTURE

Opening Dialogue (26:1-4)

> "Now the Ziphites came to Saul at Gibeah, saying, 'Is David not hiding in the hill of Hachilah, opposite Jeshimon?'" (26:1)

43. The Ziphites are familiar enemies. When did we last find them in the text?

> "Then the Ziphites came up to Saul at Gibeah, saying, 'Is David not hiding with us in strongholds in the woods, in the hill of Hachilah, which is on the south of Jeshimon?'" (23:19, Picture #23)

44. What happened in Picture 23?

God delivered David from Saul at the Rock of Escape. The Ziphites reported on David to Saul. Saul sent the Ziphites out as spies to find David's hiding places, and it was reported to David. David fled from the Wilderness of Ziph to the Wilderness of Maon, but then he was trapped on one of the stronghold rocks. David would have been caught except that the LORD intervenes by sending Saul a message that the Philistines were invading.

So, we are returning to the same place we had been before, but David is in a new place in regards to the kingship lessons he is learning. Picture #23 showed him wholly dependent on God in those early pictures where it is really God carrying him through some lessons. But now the lessons have taken a new dimension.

45. If events were following the same pattern, what would David do once he had verified that Saul was coming after him?

He would flee.

Conversation 1: David with His Men (26:5-12)

46. What does he do this time?

This time David doesn't run. David goes on the offense, and he sends spies out to locate Saul's encampment (that is what Saul had done to David previously) and to pinpoint exactly where Saul is. Saul is ensconced in the middle of the camp with all of his army encircling him so that no one can come at him from any direction without someone being alerted.

47. The text seems to belabor that Saul lay within the camp. Why repeat that part of the picture in verse 5b?

Let's map out the verses, breaking them at the repeated phrases.

(A) "So David arose and came to the place <u>where Saul had encamped</u>."
(B) "And David saw the place <u>where Saul lay</u>, . . ."
(C) ". . . and Abner the son of Ner, the commander of his army."
(B) "<u>Now Saul lay</u> within the camp, . . ."
(A) ". . . with the <u>people encamped all around him</u>.

By repeating the information, the author creates a mirroring effect that brings us to a focus not so much on Saul as on Abner, the commander of his army. Abner is the one detail not repeated. Therefore, he is the pivotal focus.

48. David proposes to go down to Saul in the camp. Why?

We don't really know. He has sworn not to raise his hand against Saul, so he is not bent of vengeance, right?

49. Why do his men think he wants to go down to Saul in the camp?

To kill him in the dark while the camp is asleep.

50. Who does David ask to go with him?

Ahimelech the Hittite (Ahimelech means "brother of the king; Hittite comes from the word for "the fear") and Abishai the son of Zeruiah (David's sister). Abishai is David's nephew and the brother of Joab. Abishai means "my father is a reward."

Of the two men, Abishai is the one who seeks the reward and volunteers.

51. What reward does Abishai ask David for?

To let him kill Saul—to take Saul's own spear and kill him with it.

52. How does David respond?

First, he rebukes Abishai, saying,

> *"Do not destroy him; for who can stretch out his hand against the LORD's anointed, and be guiltless? . . . As the LORD lives, the LORD shall strike him, or his day shall come to die, or he shall go out to battle and perish. The LORD forbid that I should stretch out my hand against the LORD's anointed. But please, take now the spear and the jug of water that are by his head, and let us go." (26:9–11)*

53. Why take the spear and water jug?

Like the robe in the previous picture, these things are also symbolic. The spear is a symbol of Saul's kingship (like a scepter), and the water jug a symbol of life because, without water in the wilderness, a man will die. So, David has figuratively taken the kingship and Saul's life from him.

54. When did we last see David having a conversation like this with his men?

Back in the cave at En Gedi when David took a piece of Saul's robe. We paid careful attention to the order in which things happened. It was apparent from his own fit of conscience that David's rebuke was as much for himself as his men. We see almost the same wording in the rebuke now, but the rebuke is given at a different place in the order. David rebukes Abishai, and then takes the spear and water jug without a pricking of conscience.

55. Why was it wrong to cut the robe in the first instance but okay to take the spear and water jug this time? What is the difference?

The cutting of the robe was a trophy for David. It was for his own glorification. Did he take the spear and water jug as a trophy, or did he have another purpose? (It is a trophy—a proof of a coup—but against whom?) He had another purpose, and we see his purpose in who he addresses first. He addresses Abner.

Conversation 2: David and Abner (26:13-16)

56. Where do David and Abishai go?

The details are very specific. He went over to the other side (to an opposing hill) and stood on top of the hill. The narrative emphasizes the great distance—but not too far to be heard.

57. Who does David call out to?

To Abner, specifically, and to the army—not to Saul. That, too, is a departure from what he did last time. Last time, when he came out of the cave holding that piece of Saul's robe in his hand, he immediately cried out *"My lord, the king!"* but this time, he says nothing to Saul but addresses Abner instead.

58. What charge does he bring against Abner and the camp?

Not being vigilant. Abner is the son of Ner, whose name means "light or lamp." Thus, Abner is the son of "the light" or son of "the lamp." As the one entrusted to keep the watch fires burning, Abner failed to guard against the enemy. He lay down thinking that he had peace and safety, and David came like the thief in the night.

Abner makes an interesting counter-point to Abigail, who confessed to not being vigilant. Abigail missed seeing David's men in the day, but she made up for her lack of vigilance by intercepting David and his men that night when David came to kill Nabal and his household.

Abigail protected her husband from his own folly, but Abner has not protected his own king from his folly.

If Abigail had not been vigilant that night, she would have died—and deserved to die because she would have known of the danger and done nothing to stop it. David now tells Abner he deserves to die for not having guarded his master.

What good is a lamp if it is put out when it is most needed?

59. Why did Abner let down his guard?

Because he did not see David as a threat. David wouldn't tackle an army of three thousand men with only his small band of six hundred and was undoubtedly on the run as he had been before. Abner went to sleep that night in relative peace and safety (and the LORD saw to it that he slept quite soundly).

60. Why make this a lesson for Abner and not Saul?

- If Abner is like Abigail, then who is Saul like? Nabal.
- Is there any point in trying to teach a man like Nabal a lesson? No. He won't ever change.
- Is there hope that Abner is more teachable? If he is like Abigail, yes.

61. What has David learned about fighting with fools?

Do not engage the fool. There is no point. God will deal with them Himself. David says as much to Abishai. But don't assume that everyone who is in the fool's house or his army are fools like he is. Speak to those who are watching and following the fool's example, so that maybe those who are teachable will come to their senses and see the truth, because the fool has convinced them that there is nothing to fear or guard against.

However, the fool of a king does not remain silent while David is rebuking Abner.

Conversation 3: David and Saul (26:17-25a)

David and Saul's conversation will run along the same lines as it did in Chapter 24, except Saul will initiate it, and David's responses are interspersed. Let's work through the dialogue.

[Saul's Greeting] *"Then Saul knew David's voice, and said, 'Is that your voice, my son David?'"* (26:17a)

[David's Answer] *". . .'It is my voice, my lord, O king.' And he said, 'Why does my lord thus pursue his servant? For what have I done, or what evil is in my hand? Now therefore, please, let my lord the king hear the words of his servant: If the LORD has stirred you up against me, let Him accept an offering. But if it is the children of men, may they be cursed before the LORD, for they have driven me out this day from sharing in the inheritance of the LORD, saying, "Go, serve other gods." So now, do not let my blood fall to the earth before the face of the LORD. For the king of Israel has come out to seek a flea, as when one hunts a partridge in the mountains.'"* (26:17b-20)

62. Who initiates the conversation?

Saul. Saul is the king, and yet David has pointedly not addressed him or even acknowledged him. David did not intend to engage the fool. Saul can't see David in the darkness, but he can hear him. Note: he calls him "son."

63. What tone does David take with Saul?

David answers civilly, but does not reciprocate by calling Saul his father this time like he did last time (24:11). Saul is lord and king but not father. Where his words had been pleading in Chapter 24, his questions now are somewhat rhetorical—he asks them but doesn't wait for an answer.

David rebukes the king's actions but doesn't curse the king. Instead, he curses the men who have stirred up Saul against him because they are, in effect, driving him from Israel to serve a foreign master who worships idols.

64. Is David saying that he is leaving Israel?

It seems so. It sounds like David is saying he is giving up. Saul doesn't need to kill him because he is leaving. If Saul continues seeking David, it will be purely for sport and not befitting a king. David would end the conversation here, but Saul keeps it going.

[Saul's Penitent Response] *"I have sinned. Return, my son David. For I will harm you no more, because my life was precious in your eyes this day. Indeed I have played the fool [sakal] and erred [shaga] exceedingly."* (26:21)

[David's Answer] *"And David answered and said, 'Here is the king's spear. Let one of the young men come over and get it. May the LORD repay every man for his righteousness and his faithfulness; for the LORD delivered you into my hand today, but I would not stretch out my hand against the LORD's anointed. And indeed, as your life was valued much this day in my eyes, so let my life be valued much in the eyes of the LORD, and let Him deliver me out of all tribulation.'"* (26:22-24)

Saul says he has played the fool. The Hebrew word used for "fool" is *sakal*. *Sakal* means "foolish," but is sounds exactly like the word for "wise" which is how Abigail was described in 25:3 where is said she was of good understanding. Foolishness can easily be mistaken as wisdom, and it is a fool who considers himself wise in his own eyes.

The Hebrew word for "err" is *shaga*, meaning to go astray (morally, ignorantly—to reel drunkenly). Funny, how Saul's words echo that picture of drunken Nabal.

65. How does David respond to the penitent words?

He ignores Saul's invitation and his promise because it is just so much foolishness. Saul has said all these things before and gone back on every word of it. Instead, David makes a strong statement. Come, get your spear, and face the judgment from God for your actions. David isn't seeking a reward from Saul for his righteous act. He is seeking his validation and vindication from God this time. (Lesson learned!)

Notice that his words change slightly from what he had previously said in Chapter 24:

> *"Therefore let the LORD be judge, and judge between you and me, and see and plead my case, and deliver **[shaphat]** me out of your hand."* (24:15)

> *". . . and let Him deliver **[natsal]** me out of all tribulation **[tsarah]**."* (26:24)

In Chapter 24, the word "deliver" was the word *shaphat* which means to deliver by rendering a judgment for a plaintiff. It has the sense of justice playing out, which reinforces the picture there. But here, the word for "deliver" is *natsal*. *Natsal* means delivered in the sense of being "snatched away" or "plucked up"—to be rescued unexpectedly.

The Hebrew word for "tribulation" or "troubles" is the word *tsarah* which means distresses or troubles, but it can also refer to a rival. In First Samuel 1:6, Peninnah is called Hannah's *tsarah*, her tormentor. David asks that the LORD vindicate him and rescue him from his rival and tormentor. The picture is a little different.

[Saul's Acknowledgment] *"...'May you be blessed, my son David! You shall both do great things and also still prevail.'"* (26:25)

[David's Answer] Nothing.

Note: These are the last words Saul will say to David, and it is ironic that he calls David his son and leaves him with a blessing. The Hebrew words emphasize that David will achieve great success.

66. What did David do this time when faced with a fool?
- He didn't engage him initially. He gave a warning instead to those who might be teachable.
- When the fool tried to engage him, he was civil and respectful of Saul's authority, but was not drawn in by Saul calling him "son."
- He addressed the foolish behavior openly.
- He pricks Saul's conscience over his relationship with God, and then he pricks Saul's own sense of dignity in reminding him that his actions are unfitting for a king. (David learned that from Abigail.)
- He isn't swayed by Saul's empty promises nor does he accept Saul invitation to return. He will waste no more time on Saul.

David's Departure (25:25b)

David does a whole lot of things right in this episode, but he does one thing very wrong, and that is in where he goes from here. Throughout all these pictures, the author has been very attentive in telling us exactly where David goes next. "He escaped to the cave of Adullam . . . he went to the forest of Hereth . . . he remained in the mountains of the Wilderness of Ziph . . . he went to the strongholds of En Gedi . . ." But here, the author leaves us with this vague statement: "So David went on his way . . ." His way to where? It leaves us hanging a little bit.

APPLY THE PICTURE

David's Model in Dealing with Fools

In a nutshell, David models some good ways for dealing with a fool.

- Don't let them draw you into an argument.
- Don't try to reason with them.
- Speak the truth to them, but your words should be more for the sake of those who are listening and watching the exchange.
- Do not be fooled by penitent statements and false flattery. Remember where your validation and reward are.
- Be merciful to them as the LORD is merciful to them. The LORD's vengeance will be enough.
- Then walk away.

David and Abner: The Prophetic Model

> *"For you yourselves know perfectly that the day of the Lord so comes as a thief in the night. For when they say, 'Peace and safety!' then sudden destruction comes upon them, as labor pains upon a pregnant woman. And they shall not escape. But you, brethren, are not in darkness, so that this Day should overtake you as a thief. You are all sons of light and sons of the day. We are not of the night nor of darkness. Therefore let us not sleep, as others do, but let us watch and be sober. For those who sleep, sleep at night, and those who get drunk are drunk at night. But let us who are of the day be sober, putting on the breastplate of faith and love, and as a helmet the hope of salvation. For God did not appoint us to*

wrath, but to obtain salvation through our Lord Jesus Christ"
—First Thessalonians 5:2-9

The Day of the LORD comes like a thief in the night, and those who are sons of light (like Abner) are exhorted to be vigilant and wait for the day of the LORD's vengeance. We are not appointed to suffer God's wrath but to obtain salvation, and, with it, deliverance from the tribulation to come. In the narrative, David uses these words *natsal* and *tsarah* that mean to be "snatched away or rescued unexpectedly from tribulation."

67. What do these words add to the prophetic picture?

They speak to the Rapture—being snatched away so that we escape the wrath and tribulation that is about to fall. The equivalent Greek word for *natsal* is *harpazo* which also means "caught up" as it says in First Thessalonians 4:16-17:

> *"For the Lord Himself will descend from heaven with a shout, with the voice of an archangel, and with the trumpet of God. And the dead in Christ will rise first. Then we who are alive and remain shall be caught up **[harpazo]** together with them in the clouds to meet the Lord in the air. And thus we shall always be with the Lord."*
> —First Thessalonians 4:16-17

68. What tribulation is David being saved from?

When David asked the LORD to deliver him from Saul's hand, it was fairly clear what he meant. But when David speaks of being delivered from tribulation, that's a little vague. It doesn't give us much indication of what the source or nature of the tribulation will be. It's like this big umbrella term that can mean deliverance from a rival, a tormentor, or from distress or troubles. But it does give you the sense that a bigger conflict is on the horizon, even if it isn't clearly seen yet.

There is a battle coming between Israel and the Philistines that will be staged in the Jezreel Valley, and it will be a day of reckoning and reward for Saul and David, respectively. We will see how that plays out in the next couple of chapters.

There is a battle coming in the prophetic picture as well. It is the Battle of Armageddon, when the world's armies are called to the

Jezreel Valley to wage war against Israel. But that battle will be the last thing to come before Christ returns to take his throne.

In his second letter to the Thessalonians, Paul goes on to describe the Day when God's final judgment and glory will be brought to bear not just on those who do not know God but on those who do not obey the gospel of our Lord Jesus Christ (First Thessalonians 1:6-7). But the Day will not arrive until after the great falling away has come and the man of lawlessness has been revealed.

> *"And for this reason God will send them strong delusion, that they should believe the lie, that they all may be condemned who did not believe the truth but had pleasure in unrighteousness."*
> —Second Thessalonians 2:11–12

When I read that, I think of the deep sleep that the LORD placed on Abner and all of Saul's camp because they believed the lie, thinking that they were safe from danger and judgment. David's wake-up call presented them with the truth of their situation and the exhortation to be vigilant.

Paul goes on to exhorts those of us who are of the Day and of the light to guard against idleness—sleep— and that if a man will not work, neither shall he eat. Interesting how our current culture is plagued with this sudden lethargy of people who refuse to work and still expect to be fed. At the same time, crime and lawlessness have hit a new height for our nation (I write this relative to the year 2023.) This is a sign of the times. The days of deep sleep are already beginning because the people have fallen for the lie—the belief that there will be no judgment or reckoning for their lawlessness. I don't know what it is like in the rest of the world, but that is where we are right now in America. The stage is being set for the man of lawlessness to come upon the scene. We as believers are to work in quietness and eat our own bread, and to withdraw from those who walk in a disorderly fashion (Second Thessalonians 3:6-12). Do not be one of those who sleep.

㉔ ㉕ ㉖ Series Comparison: Vengeance and Glorification

Back in Chapter 23, we were given a series of pictures of God delivering David from his enemies. We had the statement that God delivered David from his enemies on a daily basis (23:14). We had Jonathan's reassurance that strengthened David's hand in God (23:16) and renewed the promise in his mind. And then we saw the physical experience of being delivered when David and his men miraculously escaped from the Rock of Escape by divine intervention (23:19-29).

The message has been rammed home for David that God is his rock, his refuge, his deliverer, and his rewarder. It is necessary for David to depend on God when he is powerless, but what happens when God puts him in a position of power? Will David continue to let God glorify him or will he use the power God has given him to take glory with his own hand and at a cost to his relationship with God, like Saul did?

When we are pursuing the reward, our worthiness will be tested in how we treat our enemies when we are given power over them.

In these three chapters, David is tested over this issue of vengeance and self-glorification.

Picture #24 (First Samuel 24) was Test #1, when David had Saul at his mercy in the cave. He cut the corner of Saul's robe and it caused him a troubled conscience for having raised his hand to God's anointed king. We talked about motivations for taking trophies and the need to respect authority, even the authority of a harsh master.

Picture #25 (First Samuel 25) was Test #2, where David had to deal with a fool who returned him evil for good. The dynamic changed a little because this time David wasn't dealing with a king who was above him, but a fool who was beneath him (although the fool would argue that). Two things were wrong with David's actions in Nabal's case:

1) He sought a reward from the wrong king.
2) He was looking for a reward for his works. That was the wrong reason for pursuing the reward.

God has been providing for David's needs all this time. When David approaches Nabal, it isn't really about having needs met. This is about wanting a reward for doing a good deed. But instead of seeking God's validation and reward, he goes to Nabal, who is a king by the earthly standard of riches, but he is a fool by spiritual standards.

David goes looking for a reward of riches from the world on the basis of his works. He meets with a fool who pokes fun at him the way the people of the world do, doesn't respect his authority, and sends his men away empty-handed. And that makes David mad. David is a man who holds generosity as a noble quality, and he doesn't take a very high view of those who refuse to share. This isn't the last time this issue will come up in David's life. Fortunately, he has an intercessor who restores his perspective and gets him back on track.

Picture #26 (First Samuel 26) was Test #3. This is another case of Saul being at David's mercy, and we see how David's behavior changes from the first time when he cut Saul's robe in Chapter 24. He has come back to the same place in his physical journey, but he is not in the same place he once was in his spiritual journey. He has learned a thing or two.

So far, the issue of self-glorification and taking vengeance have been at the forefront of First Samuel 24–26, but there have been several and minor lessons that have come out of the narratives as well, which included:

- Submitting to oppressors when they are authorities and harsh masters. First Peter 2 speaks on that topic.
- Taking trophies which was really a way of taking glory for ourselves.
- Answering a fool (or not), and not getting entangled in the affairs of this world when we are commissioned as soldiers to fight the LORD's battles (Second Timothy 2:3-5)
- Not rising to the bait in those "I'm a somebody, you're a nobody" challenges (Second Timothy 2:19)
- Esteeming those who labor, including our intercessors who turn us from sin (First Thessalonians 5:12-15)
- Not returning evil for evil (First Thessalonians 5:15)
- Counting the cost when choosing to make a lasting peace with the Davidic king and gain a place in his kingdom instead of making a temporary peace with a worldly master to keep a place in a kingdom already lost to us (Matthew 16:24-27)
- Correcting each other with humility (Second Timothy 2:24-26)

- Speaking with grace, seasoned with salt (Colossians 4)
- Being vigilant

A Side Thought . . .

I think it's curious how, in the midst of struggling with Saul, the narrative takes a break to focus on another equally foolish man, and yet not one with whom David has so much emotional baggage. If Chapter 25 had been another case of Jonathan trying to intercede between David and Saul, David would have rejected the lesson, but this time it was Abigail and Nabal, two people seemingly unrelated to his difficulty with Saul, and he was receptive to the lesson. I think sometimes when we are struggling for a long time with one person, as David was with Saul, it wearies and hardens us to where we aren't receptive to the LORD's lesson. To get us past the emotional block, God may continue the lesson, but switch up the people and circumstances.

David may have been receptive to the lesson, but even so, you get a sense of his frayed emotional state as he blows the incident with Nabal way out of proportion. This is the endurance test of a king, and he is reaching the end of his rope.

LESSON 17: FIRST SAMUEL 27:1-28:2, 29:1-11

Into Enemy Hands

SERIES STRUCTURE

In this series, David decides of his own accord to return to the Philistines in an effort to escape Saul. That didn't work very well the last time he tried it in Chapter 21 (Picture #2). Each picture in the series gets David deeper into bondage to the Philistine prince, Achish, up to the point when he is suddenly rejected by the Philistine lords and sent away. The end result is the same as in Picture #2, but God has a purpose in sending David back to Ziklag.

David's time with the Philistines is detailed in **Pictures #27, #28**, and **#30**, spanning First Samuel 27–29, but the series is interrupted by **Picture #29** in the second half of Samuel 28 as the focus segues suddenly to Saul and the medium of En Dor. I think this departure from the linear picture order is intentional to set up the last four pictures in a particular order beginning and ending with Saul as he loses the kingdom. For this lesson, we will skip Picture #29 to focus on David among the Philistines.

In this series, I want to look carefully at how David copes with balancing conflicting agendas, and then consider if what he is modeling for us is the right or wrong way to go about pursuing a crown. I admit that I am at odds with his model. He goes to the Philistines for the wrong reason, but when we see Achish's response to him at the end of Chapter 29, we find that David somehow manages to do something that we ourselves are called to do—to live blamelessly and at peace in a Philistine world (as seen through Achish's perspective) without losing a sense of identity or mission as children of God.

The question is: David accomplished that goal, but did he pursue that goal the right way?

I found my applications changing from incident to incident and becoming muddled because David's behavior seems at odds with New

Testament teachings at times. For this reason, we will work through all the pictures, and then at the end I will give a series summary of what David has said and done, and we will sort out what we should or shouldn't do from David's model.

27 David Returns to the Philistines

READ

First Samuel 27:1-12

NARRATIVE STRUCTURE

Picture #27 atypically opens and ends with dialogue. The opening dialogue is David speaking within his heart. The ending dialogue signals a continuation to the next picture.

The narrative is divided in two sections:

1) David goes to dwell with the Philistines (27:1-6)
2) David deceives Achish (27:7-12)

BUILD THE PICTURE

1. **Why does David decide to return to the Philistines now?**

    I think he is tired. He has been running and running and dealing with fools left and right, and he is just tired. He's hit the wall, and he just wants to be out of Saul's reach.

    This isn't the first time David has made this decision. Why did he go to the Philistines last time, and how did that work out?

2/27 Picture Comparison: David Goes to Gath

Last time David wasn't running to the Philistines so much as he was running away from Saul. His whole focus was on getting away from Saul when he should have been thinking about the danger he was putting himself in. Just because you have an enemy in common does not mean that the enemy of your enemy is your friend.

David showed up at Achish's doorstep in Gath, alone and carrying Goliath's sword, and was immediately recognized as the great hero who the women of Israel had lauded as "the king of the land" for having slain his ten thousands. All of a sudden David woke up to the danger he was in, and he deceived his enemy by playing the fool to discredit himself so that Achish threw him out. And then he ended up in the cave of Adullam, doing some serious self-reflection. So, that didn't end so well.

Here in **Picture #27**, he makes this statement in his heart: *"Now I shall perish someday by the hand of Saul..."* It is the same reason for his initial actions, but the fact that he is saying this now carries some serious implications. David isn't in the same place in his spiritual walk with the LORD as he was initially. He has been through a lot of lessons with the LORD, and yet his words now call into doubt everything he believes about the LORD's promises and faithfulness to him. Why would he believe this after everything he has been through?

Let's consider his journey so far . . .

Pictures #15, #16, #17, and #18

David started out running blindly. At the Tabernacle at Nob, he ran to the priests for help and resorted to using deception to meet his immediate needs. Given the choice between Goliath's sword and inquiring of the LORD with the ephod, he chose the sword and fled for Philistine territory. If he had inquired of God while he was at the Tabernacle, he might not have gone to Gath. He is driven from Gath to the cave of Adullam, where he came to his senses and began his journey with the LORD again very strongly as we saw in the Psalms.

Pictures #20, #21, #22, and #23

In the battle of Keilah, David inquired of the LORD with the ephod, and then acted on the LORD's word and escaped from Saul. All the time he was in the wilderness strongholds and forests of the Wilderness of Ziph, God kept Saul at bay. We discussed how difficult it is when you are in the woods—in the middle of trials and harassments—to see God's hand working at those times, and sometimes you need encouragement from someone. In David's case, God sent Jonathan to remind David of the vision and promises. David fled from the Wilderness of Ziph, only to get caught on the rock in the Wilderness of Maon, but God delivered him at the Rock of Escape without him having to make any decision over what to do. Saul got the message and just left.

God carried David through those early days of Saul's pursuit, but maybe from where David was hiding in those woods, it didn't seem like it. God delivered David from Saul's hand at the Rock of Escape, but maybe it didn't seem like it. The narrator tells us about the message Saul received, but from where David and his men were standing, one minute Saul's army were all around them, and the next they were gone without explanation. What just happened? We see God working very clearly from the narrator's point of view, but maybe it wasn't so clear for David. Then God moves on to testing David by putting his enemies in his power.

Pictures #24, #25, and #26

David had three opportunities to take vengeance. At the cave of En Gedi, he was tempted by his men to kill Saul because they interpreted the fortuitous turn of events as God's will—which it wasn't. But it begged the question of how you know when God is working and when He isn't, especially when He isn't speaking directly to you.

At the confrontation with Nabal at Carmel, David pursued the wrong reward for the wrong reason, and while God didn't speak to him directly, He sent Abigail to intercept David. David self-corrected.

Then David returned to face Saul at the Hill of Hachilah, where he was put through the same test again to see if he had learned the lesson; and while he passed the test in not taking vengeance, his words to Saul implied that he was leaving, which he was.

Now we get this glimpse of his thoughts. He is back to square one believing that Saul is going to kill him if he stays in Israel, and he is running back to the Philistines again. Why would he believe this after everything he has been through? It begs the question: **Did David ever believe God's promises to preserve him and make him king?**

Perhaps we should consider when was the last time David inquired of

God. The last time was at the battle of Keilah back in Picture #20. Ever since then, David has been running on his knowledge of God and the promises, but never actually communicating with God. Do you think that has anything to do with his crisis of heart at this moment?

APPLY THE PICTURE

Why does a person who has been strong in the faith for so long suddenly decamp to the world?

We can drift into the habit of living the Christian life and making those day-to-day decisions but never really engage God or talk to Him through our struggles. When our communication ties to God begin to weaken or fall into disuse, we may be able to maintain the right path for a while, but eventually we will wear down under the onslaught of the enemy. This is why vigilance is necessary—not just being aware of what is going on around us, but also of what is going on inside us.

There is a singular difference between David and us, and that is that David was promised a physical crown in a physical kingdom *in his lifetime.* The crown that we pursue is a crown in a kingdom that might not be realized in our lifetime. We wait for the day of the LORD's vengeance, but we also accept the fact that that day may not come for many generations yet—which means that the world's persecution and harassment and constant temptation will remain at work in this body, and it is not something we will escape in this life, however much we desire it—and we will desire it.

And so an apathy and tiredness can set in, particularly after a time of testing. We may pass the test that the LORD puts before us because we know in our minds what is the right thing to do, but the journey ceases to be a rewarding experience and so the heart goes out of it.

There are stumbling blocks that we run into along the journey, and the first is where we seek comfort or escape in times of oppression. Do we seek a fleeting form of comfort from this world, or do we seek refuge in the power and faithfulness of an eternal God?

This is the endurance test of a king. If we are pursuing that reward of royalty, we are going to come to this place at some point in our journey.

BUILD THE PICTURE

2. **What is different this time when David goes to Achish? Why does Achish accept him?**

   Last time David arrived in Gath, he was alone, and a fugitive with a big reputation for having conquered the Philistine's champion Goliath. He was even carrying Goliath's sword. Now he has an army of six hundred men, all of whom are against Saul. They show up in Gath en masse and with their families with them. First Chronicles goes hand in hand with First Samuel and gives us more of the picture of this fighting force David is commanding at this time.

   > "Now these were the men who came to David at Ziklag while he was still a fugitive from Saul the son of Kish; and they were among the mighty men, helpers in the war, armed with bows, using both the right hand and the left in hurling stones and shooting arrows with the bow. They were of Benjamin, Saul's brethren . . . Some Gadites joined David at the stronghold in the wilderness, mighty men of valor, men trained for battle, who could handle shield and spear, whose faces were like the faces of lions, and were as swift as gazelles on the mountains . . . Then some of the sons of Benjamin and Judah came to David at the stronghold . . . And some from Manasseh defected to David when he was going with the Philistines to battle against Saul . . . And they helped David against the bands of raiders, for they were all mighty men of valor, and they were captains in the army. For at that time they came to David day by day to help him, until it was a great army, like the army of God." —First Chronicles 12:1–2, 8, 16, 19, 21–22

3. **What else do we learn about Achish?**

   There is a small detail added this time when the narrative speaks of Achish. In Chapter 21, he had simply been referred to as Achish the king of Gath, but now he is called Achish, the son of Maoch, the king of Gath. Why add the detail "son of Maoch"?

   The meaning of Achish's name is unknown, but Maoch means "oppression," from the verb *ma'ak* meaning "to be pressed or squeezed." Gath is the word for winepress. Achish is the son of oppression, king of the winepress.

David has tried to get away from Saul's pressure and squeezing only to put himself into an even more high-pressure situation by seeking refuge in the winepress of the oppressor. Out of the frying pan, into the fire. Now he must find a way to live in an idolatrous place in the enemy's presence without losing his identity as a man of Israel and God's anointed king. He stays in Gath just long enough to establish the fact that he has decamped from Israel and to get Saul off his back, but then he begins to negotiate with Achish to give him a place in some country town, away from the royal city.

4. **Why does he need to get out of the royal city?**

    David is going to have to tread a very fine line in life if he is going to remain true to God and to his calling while he is living with the Philistines, and his actions can't bear too much scrutiny. To be in the royal city, right under the king's nose, is a very dangerous place to try to live this compromised lifestyle.

    Notice how he phrases his request to Achish. He abases himself as Achish's servant. He is unworthy to dwell in the king's royal city with him. Just give him a town in the country somewhere.

5. **Where does David end up?**

    Achish gives him Ziklag in the southern desert. Ziklag means "winding," which is appropriate because David is going to have to walk a winding road of coping and compromise in order to find some peace in this place. Interesting, that this place should belong to the kings of Judah from now on.

6. **How long does he stay?**

    He stays there for one full year and four months. He manages to live this compromised lifestyle and maintain a relative peace with the enemy for a while. This is what happens. When a child of God takes this path, they often experience a deceptive lull—a false peace where nothing good but nothing bad happens—and it makes them think that they can actually do this.

7. **What is David's strategy?**

    He goes out to war in Israel's territory—that would include southern

Judah, the territory of the Jerahmeelites and Kenites—but he doesn't war against Israel. Instead, he takes down all of Israel's enemies living in those areas. Those would be the Geshurites and Girzites and Amalekites. So, David is managing to maintain his role as commander of Israel fighting God's wars, while appearing to be waging war for Philistine interests.

8. **On what does the success of his deception depend?**

    It depends on no one bringing the truth of what he is doing to Achish's attention. For this reason he leaves no survivors when he attacks. All he brings back to Achish is the spoil—the sheep, oxen, donkeys, camels, and apparel—as proof of his raids.

9. **To what conclusion does Achish come when David brings back the spoil?**

    He believes the deception. He is deluded into thinking that David has burnt his bridges with Israel, and Israel wouldn't have him back even if he wanted to go. So, Achish figures he has now become master over David forever.

10. **Is Achish master over David?**

    He is, and yet he isn't. David has made himself a vassal to Achish, but notice that David is the one calling the shots and directing the work of his men in how they battle and with whom they battle. David still has some autonomy to make those decisions, and therefore he can pursue God's agenda without compromising himself with his Philistine master.

    This strategy works only because David is hiding his actions from Achish. He is deceiving Achish, and the peace will only last until Achish assumes command over David and his men in terms of who they will fight. That will cause a conflict of agendas and then David will have to declare with which master his loyalties lie—with Achish or with God.

11. **What is Achish's agenda that he expects David to pursue?**

    He wants the Philistines to rule over Israel, and that includes conquering not just Israel but all the Canaanite inhabitants as well. He wants power, glory, and earthly riches.

12. What is God's agenda?

He wants David to remove the Canaanite inhabitants (including the Philistines) and rule over Israel under Him. God doesn't need the earthly riches, but He accepts glory and tribute from His people as His due.

13. How does David walk the line?

David has identified the one goal that Achish and God agree on—removing the Canaanite inhabitants—and David pursues that wholeheartedly. Then David gives the spoil to Achish, which increases Achish's wealth and glory as well as David's own reputation in Achish's eyes.

He pursues whatever goals of the earthly master he can without compromising himself with God, and he lives in a way that brings no shame on either master. But he uses deception to keep Achish from knowing that he is pursuing the LORD's agenda, which causes problems when Achish expects him to join a fight he should not be in. That is going to cause conflict of another sort.

 David's Dilemma

READ

First Samuel 28:1-2

NARRATIVE STRUCTURE

Picture #28 has only one short dialogue between Achish and David and ends with dialogue. The ending dialogue signals a continuation to the next picture which would be Picture #29, except this picture switches abruptly away from a focus on David to what is going on with Saul. We have to skip to Picture #30 to find the final picture in this series.

BUILD THE PICTURE

14. What does Achish ask David to do?

He asks him to go to war against Saul.

15. What issues does this raise for David?

This means he will be killing his own people, and he will have to do it openly and thoroughly—as thoroughly as he has been taking down Israel's enemies so far. That's a problem for a man who is going to be king over these people someday and will expect their support and loyalty. Also, he will have to raise his hand against God's anointed king, which is something he has sworn before his men he would not do, and told them not to do, either.

Achish isn't the only one watching him. David's men are watching as well. Twice he has backed away from murdering Saul and rebuked his own men for suggesting such a thing. He has stated repeatedly that he will not lift his hand against his master, the LORD's anointed. He told Abishai, *"As the LORD lives, the LORD shall strike him, or his day shall come to die, or he shall go out to battle and perish."* (26:10) So, here is the battle in which Saul is destined to perish, but will it be David's hand in that battle that strikes the blow?

What an incredible twist on the vengeance issue. David is being given the opportunity to go after Saul and Abner and all of Saul's army that has been pursuing him all this time. And he doesn't just have a band of six hundred men with him. This time he has the full weight of the Philistine army with him. This isn't just his men urging him to kill Saul in a dark cave somewhere when no one else is watching. This is the King of Gath pressuring him to take a front line role in a war that will end Saul's reign and open the way for David to become king.

Just because the opportunity and the motivation is there, should you act on it? What is the down side?

David stands to lose a lot in allowing himself and his men to be inducted into the Philistine ranks. It will compromise his relationship with God, with his men, and with the people he will be king over, and it will leave him with some regrets. And it will not even get him the reward of the crown that he is pursuing. Why?

16. Will the Philistines let him become Israel's king once Saul is dead?

No. Achish has every intention of keeping David as his bodyguard forever. So, if the Philistines win and Saul is defeated, David will be left with only a small contingent of men with which to fight for his freedom from the Philistines. Out of the frying pan, into the fire.

17. What if David says no to Achish at this point?

He has to think about the consequences that will fall on his family and his men's families if he comes out as being loyal to Israel. They are vulnerable. One of his first acts when he came out of the cave at Adullam was to seek refuge for his family before he began to engage Saul. He doesn't have time to do that now, plus it would look suspicious if Ziklag suddenly became deserted overnight.

18. What do David's words to Achish suggest about what he is thinking?

David replies, *"Surely you know what your servant can do."* It's a brag—a little self-glorifying. He lets his reputation speak for him, but he confesses nothing in the way of loyalty to one king or another. He *can* do it, but *will* he do it? It's a wishy-washy statement meant to hide his true reaction.

Consider the position David is in right now. He has gotten himself a bit entrenched in the situation, and there really isn't any good way out of it. But just because there doesn't seem to be a way out at this moment, doesn't mean that a solution might not present itself if he lets events unfold a little farther. He was caught on that rock with Saul's army surrounding him, and then they just went away and the battle didn't even happen. Just because man determines a course of action doesn't mean it always happens that way. So, what if he just waits and sees how things play out?

Or how about this . . . maybe, in his heart, David wants to be at this battle. Maybe he wants to see Saul taken down—not by his own hand, but by the Philistines. Maybe he wants to glory a little in seeing Saul get his due when the LORD's vengeance plays out—to gloat over Saul. David's vague reply deliberately leaves his actions and motives open to wide interpretation.

19. How does Achish interpret David's remark?

He figures David is loyal to him—so loyal that he feels safe in making David his bodyguard. Note the change in pronouns from what Achish previously said and what he says now:

> (27:12) "... _he_ will be my servant forever."
> (28:2) "I will make _you_ one of my chief guardians forever."

Achish's word in 27:12 are delivered in the third person as if he is saying this to himself or someone else. This time, Achish is declaring his intent openly to David to which David doesn't respond. The picture ends abruptly with Achish's words, suggesting that this isn't the end of the story, but the narrative switches abruptly back to Saul. We will pick up the rest of the story in Picture #30 in Chapter 30.

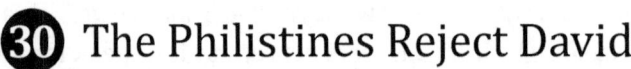 The Philistines Reject David

---
READ

First Samuel 29:1-11

NARRATIVE STRUCTURE

Picture #30 begins and ends with a narrator note, and is structured around two Philistine conversations.

1) Narrator note (29:1-2)
2) Princes of the Philistines and Achish (29:3-5)
3) Achish and David (29:6-10)
4) Narrator note (29:11)

BUILD THE PICTURE

20. Where does the action take place?

The Philistines are going to war with Israel. Saul and his army are already encamped in the Jezreel Valley, but the Philistines are gathering together at Aphek as a staging place.

> *"And the lords [seren] of the Philistines passed in review by hundreds and by thousands, but David and his men passed in review at the rear with Achish."* —First Samuel 29:2

While Achish may be king of Gath, he himself is subject to the consensus of the Seren, a term for the ruling body that consisted of five Philistine lords. The Seren figure heavily in Judges and First Samuel but aren't referred to after that, which suggests that this consolidated alliance was broken up in the days of David's reign. Elsewhere in the text they are referred to as *sar* or princes.

21. Why don't the princes want Achish to bring David into the battle?

They think David will turn on them in battle as an adversary (Hebrew: *satan*) and kill them in order to get back into Saul's good graces. I think it is funny that David reminds Achish of his reputation (*"You know what your servant can do!"*) and yet it doesn't occur to Achish that David might actually be a danger to himself. Achish even persists in saying, *"I have found no fault in him."* And yet the princes see David's reputation in a much different light.

Knowing what we know about Saul and David's history, do you think David is trying to get back into Saul's good graces at this point? That's laughable.

22. Would David kill the Philistine princes for another reason?

Maybe, if he decided it was part of the LORD's agenda.

23. What is Achish's assessment of David's service to him?

"As the LORD lives..." is an oath that is repeated often in the Old Testament, but it is only used by the people of Israel, except for this one instance. Achish is the only heathen ever to invoke this oath as

an acknowledgment of the LORD, and he does it in praise of David's good works (as he sees them). We know that David hasn't been doing what Achish thought he was doing, but even so, David has managed to conduct himself in a way that compels his heathen master to acknowledge God to an extent. Achish says, *"... you have been upright ... good in my sight ... I have not found evil in you ..."* David hasn't done anything to harm Achish and has, in fact, been an asset to him. Achish's appreciation is completely opposite to Nabal's scorn for David rendering the same services. There's an interesting comparison.

So David has accomplished the goal of conducting himself in service to a master in such a way that when the master sees his good works, not only is David glorified, but God is glorified as well. He has done something right.

Even so, the Philistine lords force Achish to send David and his men back to Ziklag. You would think that David would breathe a sigh of relief for having dodged a fight that he should never have entered and without alienating Achish in the process. But then he says:

> *"But what have I done? And to this day what have you found in your servant as long as I have been with you, that I may not go and fight against the enemies of my lord the king?"* (29:8)

24. Why would David argue to stay in this battle?

This is a discordant note. David is being released from a task that would put him at odds with God's agenda and make him go back on his words to his men. He also made an oath to Saul not to cut off his descendants, so there is a possible conflict if David should run into Saul's sons in battle. In word, David is aligning himself with Achish against Israel in desiring to *"fight against the enemies of my lord the king."*

Is David truly counting Israel as his enemy? Is he being loyal in word only with the intent to deceive, or has he truly pitched himself in allegiance and service to the Philistines? It's hard to say.

APPLY THE PICTURE

Let's begin with a high-level overview of David's words and actions in this series, the apply those to ourselves.

Series Summary: David in Enemy Hands

David's Motivation:

> "And David said in his heart, 'Now I shall perish someday by the hand of Saul. There is nothing better for me than that I should speedily escape to the land of the Philistines; and Saul will despair of me, to seek me anymore in any part of Israel. So I shall escape out of his hand.'" (27:1)

David's Challenge:

> To live in a Philistine world serving a foreign master whose agenda conflicts with God's, and yet continue to pursue a crown as king of Israel and serve the LORD's mission in the process.

David's Strategy:

> "And David and his men went up and raided the Geshurites, the Girzites, and the Amalekites. For those nations were the inhabitants of the land from of old, as you go to Shur, even as far as the land of Egypt. Whenever David attacked the land, he left neither man nor woman alive, but took away the sheep, the oxen, the donkeys, the camels, and the apparel, and returned and came to Achish." (27:7-9)

> "... And Achish said to David, 'You assuredly know that you will go out with me to battle, you and your men.' So David said to Achish, 'Surely you know what your servant can do...'" (28:1-2)

The Foreign Master's Assessment of David:

> "Surely, as the LORD lives, you have been upright, and your going out and your coming in with me in the army is good in my sight. For to this day I have not found evil in you since the day of your coming to me." (29:6)

David receives praise from the foreign master for his loyalty and good works in that master's service. He is sent home in peace and not asked to compromise himself in battle against Israel.

The Question of David's Loyalty:

> *"So David said to Achish, 'But what have I done? And to this day what have you found in your servant as long as I have been with you, that I may not go and fight against the enemies of my lord the king?'"* (29:8)

Now let's look at the parallels in our own lives.

Our Motivation

After coming through an extensive time of testing, David stumbled over a lack of faith in God's promises and faithfulness to him, and he reverted to doing what was right in his own eyes. He made a conscious choice to decamp to the Philistines—the heathen world. It was a point of stumbling for him.

There are those of us who also decamp for this reason. It is a wrong choice because it reflects a lack of faith in God's power, His love, and the reward that He has reserved for us if we persevere.

But the rest of us as believers end up among the Philistines because of our faithfulness. God sends us out into the Philistine world under the Great Commission as warriors for the faith. What David did for questionable reasons is something that we do intentionally.

There are right and wrong reasons for seeking a place in the carnal, unbelieving world.

Our Challenge

Regardless of how David came to be in this situation, he is now in this situation, and he has become a picture of a man living in a lifestyle to which we ourselves can relate. We are children of God living in a world of Philistines with a particular mission that we are pursuing. This will have some consequences.

If we have decamped into unfaithfulness for a time, we will begin to align ourselves with the world, place ourselves under a new master, and begin to pursue the world's values and goals. We may think we can make a life for ourselves in the world and live on our own terms, and maybe we are given that luxury for a while. Maybe we experience the lull and slip into that sleep of delusion. But the peace will be fleeting, because at some point we will be asked to take a stand and declare our loyalty for one king or another—for God with His values and agenda or for a worldly master with his opposing values and agenda. We might find ways to defer taking that stand for a while, as David did, but eventually it will happen, and sometimes the choice ends up being made for us.

If we have decamped to the world as an act of faithfulness to our commission, then we, too, must find a way to be in this world but not of it—to find a way to live at peace with the world around us and serve an earthly master without compromising our identity, values, and relationship with God. We, too, face the same conflict of having to juggle the agendas of a spiritual master (God) and physical masters whose demands may put us in conflict with our convictions.

Peter exhorts us:

> *"Beloved, I beg you as sojourners and pilgrims, abstain from fleshly lusts which war against the soul, having your conduct honorable among the Gentiles, that when they speak against you as evildoers, they may, by your good works which they observe, glorify God in the day of visitation."* —First Peter 2:11–12

Our Strategy

When we look at David's actions, we can see that he is still aligned with God's mission. He found a common goal between what God expects of him and what Achish expects of him, and he pursues that. Achish is quite happy with the work David has been doing, even though he doesn't know the whole of it. But then events begin to spiral out of David's control, and his path is not so clear. He becomes pressed over his loyalty to Achish, and he fails to take a stand one way or another, choosing instead to give the wishy-washy answer: "Surely you know what your servant can do."

Do we do this when the world presses us? I think we do. We can end up in a situation where we are caught between God's agenda and the world's agenda, and then the world comes to us, expecting our loyalty, and they want us to do something that conflicts with God's agenda. And no matter what course of action we decide on, we know it will end badly for someone. So what do we do? Do we decide not to commit to anything but just let events play out a little longer with the hope of a solution presenting itself? Maybe we think the issue will resolve itself before we have to get involved.

There are right and wrong ways to live among the Philistines and serve those masters, but there is a line you cannot cross without compromising your loyalty to your spiritual Master.

David is engaging in a very subtle form of deception to achieve an immediate goal while avoiding confrontation, and this isn't the first time he has resorted to this strategy. In First Samuel 21, he fabricated a story for Ahimelech the priest in order to get some bread and a sword. And we questioned why he would lie. Certainly, he may not have gotten the help he needed from Ahimelech had he told the truth, but was Ahimelech his only recourse? Was God powerless to provide for His king? That, too, was an act of faithlessness and stumbling.

But what would David have told Ahimelech if he had told the truth? What would he say to Achish now? I will not fight against Israel or raise my hand to Saul? That wouldn't have gone over well. And what consequences would there have been? There are consequences for lying but also consequences for telling the truth. The consequences are even more serious now with Achish. Now David is not just responsible for himself alone, but for six hundred men and their families who are relying on his leadership.

David has the reputation of being a truthful, upright man, but his use of deception runs counter to a godly character. He doesn't exactly lie. He just doesn't tell the whole truth, and he is hiding his actions by leaving no witnesses because he fears Achish's reaction.

David may be pursuing God's mission, but is the way he goes about it something we should model?

I don't think so. God doesn't like deceivers, and if we are engaged in the Great Commission, the goal is not to hide what we are doing. He calls us to bear witness of Himself and to leave witnesses of our work on His behalf.

> *"You are the light of the world. A city that is set on a hill cannot be hidden. Nor do they light a lamp and put it under a basket, but on a lampstand, and it gives light to all who are in the house. Let your light so shine before men, that they may see your good works and glorify your Father in heaven."* —Matthew 5:14–16

But didn't David's actions accomplish this? Didn't he receive praise from Achish for his good works and for being an upright man without sin or evil in him? Yes, but then the world judges by what they see and according to their own values. Achish saw only what David showed him. God sees deeper.

How open are we to be about our actions in the world?

Jesus said:

> *"Behold, I send you out as sheep in the midst of wolves. Therefore be wise as serpents and harmless as doves. But beware of men, for they will deliver you up to councils and scourge you in their synagogues. You will be brought before governors and kings for My sake, as a testimony to them and to the Gentiles. But when they deliver you up, do not worry about how or what you should speak. For it will be given to you in that hour what you should speak; for it is not you who speak, but the Spirit of your Father who speaks in you. Now brother will deliver up brother to death, and a father his child; and children will rise up against parents and cause them to be put to death. And you will be hated by all for My name's sake. But he who endures to the end will be saved . . .*
>
> *"Whatever I tell you in the dark, speak in the light; and what you hear in the ear, preach on the housetops. And do not fear those who kill the body but cannot kill the soul. But rather fear Him who is able to destroy both soul and body in hell. Are not two sparrows sold for a copper coin? And not one of them falls to the ground apart from your Father's will. But the very hairs of your head are all numbered. Do not fear therefore; you are of more value than many sparrows. Therefore whoever confesses Me before men, him I will also confess before My Father who is in heaven. But whoever denies Me before men, him I will also deny before My Father who is in heaven . . .*
>
> *"And he who does not take his cross and follow after Me is not worthy of*

> *Me. He who finds his life will lose it, and he who loses his life for My sake will find it."* —Matthew 10:16-22, 27-33, 38-39

We can try to live in this world and avoid confrontation by hiding the fact that we are Christians and pursuing God's agenda under the radar. We can exist on the fringes and maintain an image that fits the world's perception of a "good" person without having to actually declare ourselves. And that may work—it may work really well. It may work so well that we actually convince the heathens around us that we are just like them and will go along with whatever they propose to do.

Have you ever found yourself among company where someone suggested doing something that you, in your heart, didn't feel right about doing? But before you could decide how to react, events suddenly spun out of control and you found yourself swept along with them into doing what you didn't want to do? How far do you go in letting them think you are on board with their values and their mission before you push back?

Be wary of joining causes. When tides change in the affairs of this world, opportunities can present themselves, and a reward can be gained in allowing yourself to be carried along in the flood of events. Being carried along like that can produce a motivation—a feeling of being compelled to do something, for better or worse. But what happens when you let yourself be carried along like this is that you can lose a sense of identity and, with it, a sense of personal accountability, choice, and self-control. Those are not in line with godly behavior.

David's deceptive actions may have achieved the immediate goal, but look at how they entrenched him deeper and deeper into a compromising situation. At each phase, Achish assumes more and more control over David, and David has to let him. The only other option is to take a stand. So, how do you strike a balance?

How do we serve a worldly master and still accomplish God's agenda?

A worker must work for his wage and his food, and we end up serving masters in this world to this immediate type of goal. It is a luxury to serve a master who is a believer, but even if we work for an unbeliever, we are to grant them an honor as our master.

> *"Let as many bondservants as are under the yoke count their own*

masters worthy of all honor, so that the name of God and His doctrine may not be blasphemed. And those who have believing masters, let them not despise them because they are brethren, but rather serve them because those who are benefited are believers and beloved. Teach and exhort these things." —First Timothy 6:1–2

Paul speaks to our motivation and understanding of where our reward and validation lie. We do not seek those things from the earthly master (the master according to the flesh) but the heavenly one. We learned that from David's experience with Nabal.

"Bondservants, be obedient to those who are your masters according to the flesh, with fear and trembling, in sincerity of heart, as to Christ; not with eyeservice, as men-pleasers, but as bondservants of Christ, doing the will of God from the heart, with goodwill doing service, as to the Lord, and not to men, knowing that whatever good anyone does, he will receive the same from the Lord, whether he is a slave or free."
—Ephesians 6:5–8

"Bondservants, obey in all things your masters according to the flesh, not with eyeservice, as men-pleasers, but in sincerity of heart, fearing God. And whatever you do, do it heartily, as to the Lord and not to men, knowing that from the Lord you will receive the reward of the inheritance; for you serve the Lord Christ. But he who does wrong will be repaid for what he has done, and there is no partiality."
—Colossians 3:22–25

"Servants, be submissive to your masters with all fear, not only to the good and gentle, but also to the harsh. For this is commendable, if because of conscience toward God one endures grief, suffering wrongfully. For what credit is it if, when you are beaten for your faults, you take it patiently? But when you do good and suffer, if you take it patiently, this is commendable before God. For to this you were called, because Christ also suffered for us, leaving us an example, that you should follow His steps: 'Who committed no sin, nor was deceit found in His mouth'; who, when He was reviled, did not revile in return; when He suffered, He did not threaten, but committed Himself to Him who judges righteously; who Himself bore our sins in His own body on the tree, that

we, having died to sins, might live for righteousness - by whose stripes you were healed." —First Peter 2:18-24

Abigail is another good model for this. She was a faithful wife to her faithless and harsh husband. She looked after his interests, even when he didn't deserve it. In going to David with that gift, she went against her husband's wishes and would have incurred Nabal's wrath, but she did it to save his life as well as her own. She would have been made to suffer wrongly, but the Lord rewarded her instead.

The Issue of Loyalty to Masters (Spiritual and Physical)

David's argument over why he should not be sent from the battle calls into question just how far his loyalties have gone toward serving Achish.

Serving unbelieving masters does not always create conflict with our service to the Lord or even living out our faith, but we have to walk a fine line in one aspect—how deeply we allow ourselves to become yoked with them. When I say yoked, I am talking about having a relationship in which we share an equal authority level with them that then gives them power over us to force us off a righteous path or to implicate or obligate us in their sin. This is why Paul says:

> "Do not be unequally yoked together with unbelievers. For what fellowship has righteousness with lawlessness? And what communion has light with darkness? And what accord has Christ with Belial? Or what part has a believer with an unbeliever?"
> —Second Corinthians 6:14-15

It is one thing to work for a master where you still have the autonomy to walk away from them, but it is another thing to give them power over you and to decide what direction the work will go. David has been doing some work for Achish, and David's strategy for serving this master has worked pretty well, so long as he was the one deciding where to raid and what enemies he would tackle. But then he ran into a dilemma when Achish told him to raise his hand against Saul. You will inevitably end up in this dilemma at some point when you fall into partnership with the world. For this reason, I would not recommend being yoked in marriage or even in business.

There is a right and wrong king with whom to align yourself when pursuing a crown, and a right and wrong way to pursue a crown. And there are fights in which you should and shouldn't engage.

Questions for Reflection

- How open are you about your faith when you go out into the world?

- Is there anyone in your life whom you would rather not know that you are a Christian? If so, why?

- In what areas of your life do earthly masters hold sway?

- Have you ever had an employer or authority of some sort ask you to do something unethical? If so, how did you react?

- If taking a stand for your convictions means losing your job or resources for needful things (like housing, food, water, medicine), would you cling to your convictions or let them go?

- Do you feel entrenched in a compromising situation? How did you get into that position?

- Have you ever found yourself in a fight you shouldn't have been in? How did it happen?

- Sometimes you can get into a fight because one party or another demands your loyalty. How do you sort out the loyalty issue?

This path for David began with his becoming weary in the throes of the endurance test of faith. His communication with God had broken down and his decision to go to the Philistines seemed out of character for a godly man. It could easily lead us to question if he ever believed the promises in the first place.

- Do we make that judgment of Christians—that because they decamped to the world they were never really believers to begin with?

- Is their decamping a reflection on their salvation status?

LESSON 18: FIRST SAMUEL 28:3-25, 30:1–31:12

The King's Reward

SERIES STRUCTURE

In the last lesson, we followed David's interaction with the Philistines through First Samuel 27, 28, and 29, but we skipped the picture of Saul and the medium of En Dor in the second half of Chapter 28 (Picture #29) for a couple of reasons. First, the focus shifted rather jarringly away from David to Saul and disrupted the narrative flow. I wanted to stay focused on David's actions to get the applications from them. Secondly, Picture #29 is out of chronological order but with reason.

The Timeline Issue of Chapters 28, 29, and 30

To understand the discrepancy in the timeline, let's look at how the narrative builds, starting in **Picture #28** at the beginning of Chapter 28.

> **(28:1)** *"Now it happened in those days that the Philistines gathered their armies together for war, to fight with Israel."*

This then blends into **Picture #29**, with the battle shaping up in the Jezreel Valley.

> **(28:4)** *"Then the Philistines gathered together, and came and encamped at Shunem. So Saul gathered all Israel together, and they encamped at Gilboa."*

Picture #29 leaves us on the eve of battle with Saul inquiring of Samuel through the medium; however, **Picture #30** takes a step back.

> **(29:1)** *"Then the Philistines gathered together all their armies at Aphek, and the Israelites encamped by a fountain which is in Jezreel."*

Saul may be at Gilboa, but here the Philistines have only reached the staging point at Aphek, half way between Philistine lands in the south and

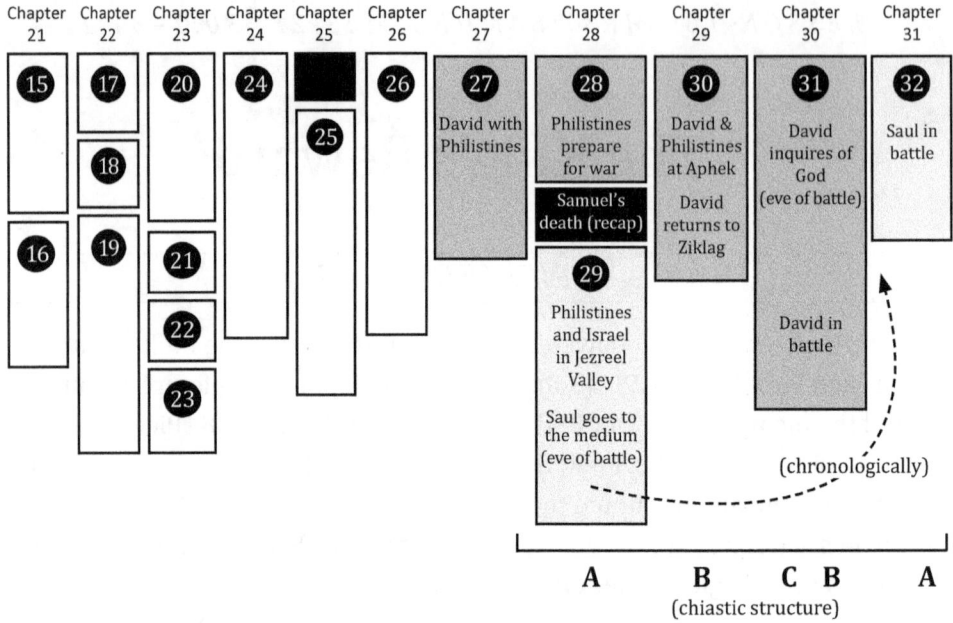

the Jezreel Valley to the north. The focus now turns to David. From this staging point, David and the Philistines part ways, and David and his men return to Ziklag.

(29:11) *"So David and his men rose early to depart in the morning, to return to the land of the Philistines. And the Philistines went up to Jezreel."*

(30:1) *"Now it happened, when David and his men came to Ziklag, on the third day..."*

It takes David and his men three days to get back to Ziklag. During the same time period, the Philistines are traveling in the opposite direction to the Jezreel battlefield where Saul is.

Picture #31 puts us back at the eve of battle again, only this time with David inquiring of God.

You would think the author would have put the account of Saul and the medium (Picture #29) after David gets to Ziklag (Picture #31) so that the eve-of-battle accounts are in chronological order, but he doesn't. Instead, the author puts them out of chronological order to create the chiastic structure (A-B-C-B-A) to keep the focus on David inquiring of God. That is

418 | Lesson 18: The King's Reward

the pivotal moment. The recap of Samuel's death at the start of the chiasm acts as a marker to set off these chapters as a series.

This is the chiastic structure:

> **(A) Picture #29:** Saul seeks the medium at En Dor and inquires of Samuel.
>
> **(B) Picture #30:** David returns to Ziklag and finds it destroyed.
>
> **(C) Picture #31:** David calls for the ephod and inquires of God.
>
> **(B) Picture #31:** David goes into battle and gains the reward.
>
> **(A) Picture #32:** Saul goes into battle and loses his kingdom and life.

The chiasm begins and ends with Saul, bringing his narrative to an end, but switches abruptly in the middle to focus on the pivotal moment when David inquires of God. This is the right way to pursue the reward and gain the crown.

㉙ Saul and the Medium of En Dor

READ

First Samuel 28:3-25

NARRATIVE STRUCTURE

Picture #29 (28:3-25) opens with an oddly placed comment recalling Samuel's death. Then we have the opening comment setting the scene, followed by three conversations, and a closing comment, all arranged in chiastic order:

- (A) Setting the scene (28:4-7)
- (B) Conversation 1: Saul addresses the Medium (28:8-14b)
- **(C) Conversation 2: Samuel addresses Saul (28:14c-20)**
- (B) Conversation 3: The Medium addresses Saul (28:21-25a)
- (A) Narrator's Departure Comment (28:25b)

Conversations 1 and 3 both begin and end with a narrator note, but Conversation 2 begins and ends with Samuel's dialogue, just like the picture in Chapter 12 (Picture #4). We will compare those pictures.

BUILD THE PICTURE

Samuel's Death, Revisited (28:3)

The opening verse is an oddly placed note, and almost a repeat of First Samuel 25:1 . . .

> "Then Samuel died; and the Israelites gathered together and lamented for him, and buried him at his home in Ramah . . ." (25:1)

> "Now Samuel had died, and all Israel had lamented for him and buried him in Ramah, in his own city. And Saul had put the mediums and the spiritists out of the land." (28:3)

1. **Why add the note about Samuel's death?**

   First, it is a way of reintroducing the character of Samuel who has been out of the scene since his death, but it also prompts us to remember Saul's history with Samuel. Back in Picture #9, Saul tore the robe from Samuel's mantle and Samuel told him then that he would lose the kingdom. Fast forward to Picture #24, and we see David standing outside the cave, holding that scrap of cloth from Saul's robe, and Saul gets a flashback to himself holding Samuel's robe. He knows at this point that David will be his successor. This event in Picture #24 is end-capped with a note about Samuel's death.

   Now we see the same note about Samuel's death at the beginning of Picture #29 as the theme then picks up again. Saul asks the medium to bring up Samuel, and Samuel again predicts that Saul will have the kingdom torn from him, and when. This is Saul's third and final reminder. Events play out from here just as Samuel predicts.

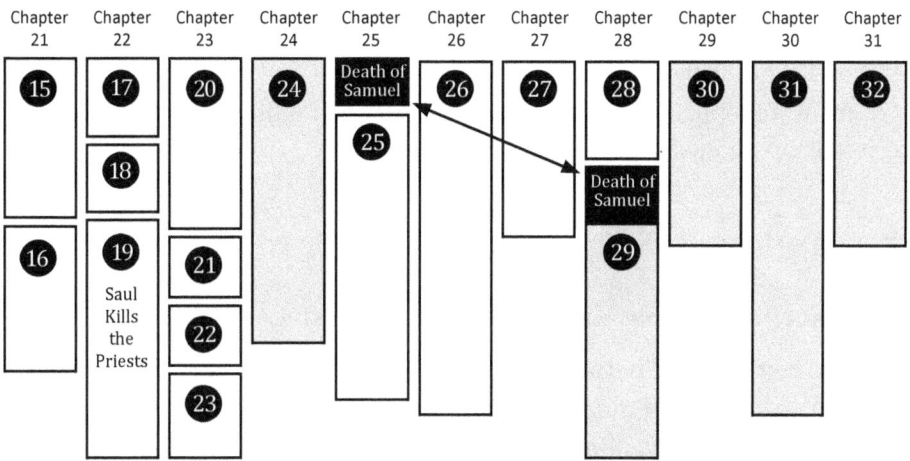

We should remember a few more details about those two incidents. The first happened when Saul returned from war with King Agag and the spoil, and Samuel rebuked him, saying, *"For rebellion is as the sin of witchcraft, and stubbornness is as iniquity and idolatry"* (15:23). Then, at En Gedi, David leveled similar charges against him in saying, *"Wickedness proceeds from the wicked"* (25:13). We are now going to see that picture of Saul at its fullest.

Lesson 18: The King's Reward | 421

2. **Why note that Saul put the mediums and spiritists out of the land?**

   That bit of information sets us up for the appearance of the medium in the narrative to come, but it's a jarring note. At some point Saul had purged the land of this wicked element, but, in typical Saul-like fashion, he obeyed the Law in part but not wholeheartedly. The Law says:

   > "A man or a woman who is a medium, or who has familiar spirits, shall surely be put to death; they shall stone them with stones. Their blood shall be upon them." —Leviticus 20:27

   > "There shall not be found among you anyone who makes his son or his daughter pass through the fire, or one who practices witchcraft, or a soothsayer, or one who interprets omens, or a sorcerer, or one who conjures spells, or a medium, or a spiritist, or one who calls up the dead." —Deuteronomy 18:10–11

   It also reminds us of David's remark that Saul and his men had driven him from Israel to a heathen people who didn't worship God (26:19). Now Saul's own actions have driven him to seek something just as bad, if not worse. (I think it's a bit ironic that Saul would seek advice from someone whom he had put out of the kingdom when he himself will be put out of the kingdom shortly.)

Setting the Scene (28:4-7)

3. **What do we know about the battle being staged?**

   It is being waged in the Jezreel Valley. The Philistine forces camped at a place called Shunem. Shunem means "a place of rest," but in the plural form. They didn't just sit down in the place. They sit-sit down. They establish themselves there.

   Saul has settled Israel's army at Gilboa. Gilboa means "a swelling heap." You get a sense of something mounding up upon itself, but there is a little darker tone to it when you dig deeper into the meaning of that name.

   Gilboa is a combination of two root words: *gal* and *ba'a*.

   Gal means a "heap, spring (of water), a wave or billow"; hence the translation—fountain. But when you look at the contexts where this word is used in Scripture, it is associated with rolling a heap of stones together in a mound (either for making a covenant or covering a dead body) or reducing something to a mound of stones by bringing it to ruin. It is also associated with the LORD rising up in strength or judgment against a people, like the rolling or churning of overflowing waters. Rather a grim picture.

Similarly, *Ba'a* means "to swell or gush over," but in a slightly different sense. Figuratively, it means to boil up inside—to desire something earnestly and rise up to seek it or inquire after it.

The very name Gilboa has these dark undertones of judgment, death, ruin, and an internal up-welling of emotion that causes a man to rise up and seek advice. So, you see the picture. Saul is sitting at Gilboa looking at the Philistines, and fear swells up in him and pushes him to seek out a solution. I think this is similar to what happened to David when he decided to decamp to the Philistines. He had this moment of up-welling fear or despair that pushed him over the edge to seek a solution. David relied on his own judgment, whereas Saul will seek it from another source, but it was a misstep for both.

We previously compared the meanings of the names, Saul and David, desire and love, but we should look a little deeper into Saul's name because it adds more to the picture. The name Saul means "desired" in the sense of being requested, with an emphasis on the act of requesting. His name derives from the verb *sa'al,* which describes the act of asking, begging, seeking, or inquiring after something desired. He is the king that Israel had desired and for whom they had asked, but the man himself now lives up to his name as his desire to keep his kingdom drives him to the extremity of inquiring of a medium. But she isn't the first person he seeks with his request.

4. **Of whom does Saul inquire first?**

   Surprisingly, he inquires of God, but God isn't talking to him. Not by dreams, or by Urim, or by the prophets. It is interesting that the Urim is mentioned, because it immediately makes us remember that Saul once killed the priests at Nob and lost his access to God through the ephod and Urim. Back in Chapter 23, the text belabored how Abiathar took the ephod with him to David, and then David began to use it.

From what I have researched, there was only ever supposed to be one Urim and Thummim, and they were held by the high priest of the day who would technically be Abiathar at this point. It is not clear from the text if Saul didn't have access to them or if he had constructed another set that the LORD refused to recognize. Regardless, Saul isn't getting an answer from God by any means. So, he seeks out the medium at En Dor.

5. **What do we know about the medium of En Dor?**

    This unnamed medium is living across the valley by another fountain located about four miles beyond Mount Tabor.

    En or Ein means "eye" or fountain. Fountains are likened to eyes in that they weep water or tears. Dor, in general, means "generations," but it can also mean the place of habitation where all generations end up eventually. It is figurative of the grave, as described in Psalm 49:16-20 (see also Isaiah 38:12).

    > "Do not be afraid when one becomes rich, when the glory of his house is increased; For when he dies he shall carry nothing away; His glory shall not descend after him. Though while he lives he blesses himself (for men will praise you when you do well for yourself), he shall go to the generation **[dor]** of his fathers; they shall never see light. A man who is in honor, yet does not understand, is like the beasts that perish." —Psalm 49:16–20

    The place where this woman stays has these undertones of being a graveyard and place of weeping. This is, appropriately, where Saul ends his quest.

Conversation 1: Saul Addresses the Medium

6. **How does Saul approach the medium at En Dor?**

    He disguises (Hebrew: *haphas*) himself and puts on other clothes (Hebrew: *beged*). Let's look at the Hebrew words being used here.

    Haphas means "to search out or be searched for"—like playing a game of hide and seek. The medium herself is in hiding, as she herself admits. Saul has found her, but he hides himself beneath his *beged* so that she doesn't discover who he is.

Beged is clothing, but clothing with a particular character. It is often described as the clothing that goes on "beneath the sheet" or outerwear. "Beneath the sheet" suggests something purposely hidden and, therefore, it is figurative of something treacherous or deceitful, and that is what *beged's* root word, *bagad*, means. It means "to be treacherous, deceitful, or unfaithful," or to transgress in this manner. Saul has clothed himself in this character.

7. **Why would Saul ask for Samuel?**

   That is a curious thing, given their history. Not that he has many options, but *Samuel?* He and Samuel had never done anything but clash over Saul's not being obedient to instruction. Repeatedly Samuel has instructed him with what God wants him to do, and Saul repeatedly refuses to follow the instruction. Historically, Saul has not been the one to seek out Samuel to ask him what to do. More often than not, Samuel has had to go after him. But this time Saul is the one seeking Samuel as a last recourse.

   It is foolishness for Saul to say to the medium, *"As the LORD lives, no punishment shall come upon you for this thing."* Of course, there is going to be punishment, for both of them. Saul is using deceiving words as well as appearances to get her to do what he wants.

8. **What is the medium's reaction when she sees Samuel?**

   She cries out because she now recognizes Saul for who he is. She didn't make the connection at first when Saul asked her to bring up Samuel for him, but something happened in the process that revealed Saul to her, and now she realizes she has been deceived.

   Apparently, only the medium sees Samuel. Saul doesn't (28:13). She describes Samuel as an old man covered in a mantle. The author belabors this revealing moment. Saul perceives that it was Samuel, and he abases himself. He bows with his face to the ground. Funny, but this is how he ended up last time he and Samuel met. When David sought refuge with Samuel and the prophets as he was being pursued by Saul, Saul followed him, only to end up prophesying with his face to the ground in front of Samuel.

Conversation 2: Samuel Addresses Saul (28:14c-20)

9. How does Samuel feel about being called up?

Very, very grouchy. He asks, *"Why have you disturbed [ragaz] me?" Ragaz* means "to quiver or agitate with violent emotion, especially fear or anger." I think it is probably anger in Samuel's case.

10. What is Saul's excuse?

In typical Saul-like fashion, he begins to blither. "I'm distressed . . . The Philistines are fighting with me . . . God isn't talking to me . . . I need you to tell me what I should do."

11. Why did Saul think Samuel would be able to tell him anything?

Saul usually sought advice in the human realm instead of the spiritual realm, but now that his human enemies have become more powerful and are threatening to overrun him, he turns to the spiritual realm for direction. It is absurd for him to think he has the power to command those spiritual forces the way he does his human minions—to summon Samuel and bend him to his will. This is the height of arrogance. It just goes to show that Saul never really grasped God's sovereignty over him. It is also absurd to think the dead can see the future.

Samuel points out that it is useless when God, who is King of heaven and earth, has become your enemy. God is the one orchestrating these events. When Samuel reiterates the prophecy, this time he adds some details. The judgment doesn't just fall on Saul. It falls on Saul's sons and Israel as well. Their impending judgment (28:19) is delivered in an inclusio bookended with the statement that the LORD Himself will deliver Israel into the hands of the Philistines.

> A) "Moreover the LORD will also <u>deliver Israel with you into the hand of the Philistines</u> . . ."
>
> B) ". . . And tomorrow you and your sons will be with me . . .
>
> A) "The LORD will also <u>deliver the army of Israel into the hand of the Philistines</u>." (28:19)

The word "deliver" means to give as a gift. God is gifting them to the Philistines, which is a statement of His sovereignty and command over their lives.

❹/㉙ Picture Comparison: Israel and Saul's Indictments

Conversations 1 and 3 between Saul and the medium both follow the standard structure of beginning and ending with a narrator's comment, but Conversation 2 begins and ends with Samuel's dialogue, just as the indictment of Israel did in Picture #4 (Chapter 12). The structure is atypical and comparative, and links these pictures thematically.

Back in Chapter 12, Samuel warned the people of the consequences of choosing this king when he coronated Saul before the people:

> *"If you fear the LORD and serve Him and obey His voice, and do not rebel against the commandment of the LORD, then both you and the king who reigns over you will continue following the LORD your God* [meaning all will be well and good]. *However, if you do not obey the voice of the LORD, but rebel against the commandment of the LORD, then the hand of the LORD will be against you, as it was against your fathers."*
> —First Samuel 12:14–15

Now in Samuel's address to Saul, we see that the king's disobedience will bring Israel down with him. The fate of Israel is bound up in her king, and Israel is not guiltless before the LORD. The nation has come to a day of reckoning along with Saul for having chosen the wrong king with whom to align itself, and he has become a stumbling block and snare for it. The fine details of the narrative structure highlight this connection.

12. What is Saul's response?

He says nothing, but pitches himself full length on the ground in fear.

Judgment has been determined for him and Israel, and I wonder if, in desperation, he might not have considered his options at this point. He could simply flee from his enemies and avoid the battle, but that wouldn't look good in the eyes of the people. He could admit that the fault was his alone and ask God to spare the people's lives, but then he has never been that generous to his family or people. Or he could go into battle, and die the hero in people's eyes and take them with him.

Interestingly, David comes under a similar judgment at the final scene of Second Samuel, and it makes a good comparison picture to this scene. Unlike Saul, God gives David choices: a punishment on the land for seven years, on himself as he flees from his enemies for three months, or a plague on the people for three days. His decision makes an interesting comparison to Saul's here, but that is for the next study.

Saul sought power from the spiritual realm and has been denied it, and now even his physical power can't sustain him because he has been fasting. The author belabors that he hasn't eaten all day or all night.

Conversation 3: The Medium Addresses Saul (28:21-25a)

The narrative began with Saul addressing the medium. Now the medium addresses Saul (a chiastic reversal). She calls herself his maidservant and makes him a feast—almost like Abigail did with David. But where Abigail was honorable, this woman is detestable in the eyes of the LORD.

Again Saul is swayed by the urgings of servants and the medium to lift himself up. He rises and eats and strengthens himself again. Funny, that the author would belabor that point. This is a small point of comparison between Saul and David in that David will strengthen himself in the LORD on the eve of his own battle. But I am getting ahead of the narrative.

Narrator's End Comment (28:25b)

In the opening scene, the narrator remarked, "... they came to the woman by night." (28:8a) Now we have a note of departure, capping off the chiastic structure: "... Then they rose and went away that night." (28:25b)

APPLY THE PICTURE

Saul's Model: What Should I Do?

Throughout his history as king, Saul did not inquire of God as a rule, and when he did, God didn't answer him because 1) he asked for the wrong thing; 2) he asked the wrong way; and 3) he asked for the wrong reason. Here, on the eve of his final battle, he tries to hold on to a kingdom already lost to him. He has already purposed in his heart to fight this battle, and, in defiance of God's silence, he seeks advice from a dead prophet through a detestable medium. His question to Samuel is, "What shall I do?" The question has already been answered, but Saul has not wanted to believe it. He knows what he did wrong and has no intention of changing his ways, so the end destined for him remains unchanged. Yet he still asks the question as if hoping to get a different answer.

Have you ever had people come to you as Saul did to Samuel and ask, "What should I do?" You have only to look at the history of their behavior to know that any advice you might give is pointless. They have lived their lives in pursuit of the wrong things that took them farther and farther away from God's will and blessing, and even when those behaviors get them into trouble and the fear takes them, they still have no intention of giving up those self-destructive pursuits. When they ask you, "What should I do?" they aren't asking how to get their lives right with God or even for His instruction. What they are really asking is for an immediate solution to their current dilemma to avoid the consequences; and if you won't tell them, then they will go to the next person, and next, until they get the answer they want.

That is the stubbornness and the flailing of the double-minded man who is destined to lose a crown and a kingdom.

Being Single-Minded or Just Plain Stubborn

It takes perseverance and single-mindedness to pursue a crown. That is what carries us through the endurance test. But stubborn perseverance alone will not achieve the crown. We have to pursue the right crown, in the right way, and for the right reason, namely, for God's glory and not our own. You can be equally single-minded in pursuing the wrong reward for the wrong reasons and in the wrong way, as Saul was, and end up losing it all.

When Saul ran into difficulties, he mulishly tried to force solutions to his problems, especially when he received the silent treatment from God. As king, he had the right to demand an answer from those over whom he had authority, but he had no right to demand an answer from God or even Samuel. Instead of submitting to God's silence and accepting his fate, he went on the offense in search of an answer and became an even greater offender in the process.

Responding to the Silence of God

Have you ever found yourself in a dilemma and asked the LORD the question, "What should I do?" Of course, you have. All Christians have. And like all of us, sometimes you get an immediate answer, sometimes a delayed answer; but then sometimes, silence.

How do we deal with the silence of God? Is the silence in itself an answer, or is it just a cue to begin seeking and knocking on various doors in search of an answer?

That is a question I have pondered at length. Having an Urim and Thummim would be pretty handy at times, or even a prophet, but as the text shows, God didn't always answer these ways, even when they were available. I have asked God a multitude of questions over the years and never once heard His voice speak from the whirlwind or thunder; a few times, I have heard the echo of a still, small voice in my ear. There have been a number of times when God answered a specific question through an unsolicited person or circumstance, but I have had to wait for those. Ask and wait is the time-honored method of getting an answer, but when time is of the essence (or so it seems to me), I find myself resorting to seeking and knocking in a somewhat flailing manner. Sometimes I simply plunge ahead, hoping that the LORD will stop me at some point if He doesn't want me going down that path. I'll give you an example from my own life . . .

As I was preparing my previous study on the book of Judges, I found myself getting into some very deep topics of sin and brokenness, far beyond my own experience, and I began to worry how people who had actually experienced these things might take my observations. A sudden fear took me that I might be doing more harm than good with my applications of the lessons, and I confessed as much to the LORD. Mind you, I didn't actually ask Him if I should just continue as I was doing. I had so convinced myself that I was unqualified to do the study that I began to cast about for advice from people I knew who had counseling backgrounds or had been through certain experiences. I must have applied to at least five or six people and received about a thimbleful of help, which was no help at all, really. This went on for months until, finally, I reached the point of frustration where I sat down to reflect. (I always do this last, it seems.) What I discovered was that I hadn't learned much from the very study I was teaching.

You see, in the book of Judges there is this one judge named Shamgar who killed six hundred Philistines with an ox-goad. It is the shortest narrative in the book—all of one verse—but the whole lesson Shamgar teaches is that we just need to step out in faith for God's glory and in obedience to His will, do the best we can with what we have, and it will be enough. And I had to laugh at myself. It was as simple as that. I didn't need a counseling degree or a panel of experts to do that Bible study. All I needed was God working through the text with me, and wherever that ox-goad connected would be God's decision. The realization gave me a certain peace, and then I was able to move forward again. Please, don't get me wrong. I still felt as if I was flailing at times as I worked through the study, but in the end, it turned out to be one of my better efforts.

The goal may be the right goal and pursued for the right reason, but perhaps not always pursued in a God-glorifying way. It was more glorifying to God that I work through the study with Him alone than give credit in the end to a panel of human "experts."

It's difficult dealing with the silence of God, and more often than not, we can try to force an answer or get God to react by acting first. Maybe finding His answer *is* a matter of seeking and knocking, but before we plunge into action, I think it would be wise to test and see whether the question we are asking is a question we *should* be asking.

Questions for Reflection

Think of a time when you asked God "What should I do?" and He remained silent.

- What dilemma you were facing?

- If you sought human advice, to whom did you turn first?

- If the advice didn't help, to whom did you turn next?

- Did you spend any time reflecting on whether you were 1) pursuing the right goal, 2) pursuing it the right way, or 3) pursuing it for the right reason?

> The next time you start to ask God "What should I do?" spend a little time reflecting on what it is you are asking for.
>
> - What greater goal am I pursuing by asking for this?
>   - » Is this request aligned with God's values and commands?
>   - » What has God already set as my roles or pursuits in life?
>   - » Will this benefit God's kingdom or my own?
> - Why am I asking for this? What is motivating the request?
>   - » Is my request to avoid some consequences to previous decisions? If so, how did I get into this situation?
>   - » Is my request just to get out of difficult circumstances? (Am I running away from something or running toward something?)
>   - » Is my current difficulty serving a greater purpose? What is God trying to teach me in these circumstances?
>   - » Is getting out of the difficulty for my comfort alone? (Comfort is a perishable crown.) Who else will be affected, for better or worse?
> - Have I already decided my course of action? Am I just looking for validation, or do I actually want God's direction? Will I cease striving if He says no?
> - What glory will God receive from granting my request?

⑮⑯⑰ / ㉙ Picture Comparison

If we look back at the beginning of David's exile years, we find him running in fear from place to place, seeking a means of deliverance from Saul. He goes to the priest at the Tabernacle, but instead of inquiring of God with the ephod, he asks for the sword instead. Then, like a fool, he seeks refuge with the outside enemy and is driven away as a fool. Finally he ends up at the Cave of Adullam where he does some serious self-reflecting as his army and family are gathered to him.

Saul, by comparison, is also running in fear at this point. He got no answer from the Urim (or from dreams or prophets). He then goes to a medium, who is as much an outsider as the Philistines, and is made to look like a fool. His next stop will be the grave, and he will die in the company of his army and family.

David righted his thinking, strengthened himself in God, and as a result, rose from that cave with the reward of a kingdom in his future. Saul will not see the same reward.

 David Returns to Ziklag

---
READ

First Samuel 30:1-31

NARRATIVE STRUCTURE

Picture #31 (30:1-31) begins on the eve of battle. Saul is facing his battle in the Jezreel Valley and seeking Samuel for advice via a medium. David has now returned to Ziklag and is facing a crisis and battle of his own. Like Saul, he will inquire of God, but unlike Saul, God will answer him. So we are returning to the theme of inquiring of God that we first explored at the opening of David's exile years.

Picture #31 is structured as follows:

1) Narrator's opening comment (30:1-5)
2) David inquires of God (30:6-10)
3) David sets a captive free (30:11-16)
4) The battle (30:17-20)
5) David rebukes the sons of Belial (30:21-25)
6) David shares the reward (30:26-31)

BUILD THE PICTURE

Narrator Comment (30:1-5)

13. What have David and his men lost?

The text belabors the burning of Ziklag, but more intensely, the loss of family—the loss of wives, sons, daughters, and even servants.

Let's think about this. David has been leading these men for a long time now. Four hundred of them came to him at the Cave of Adullam as men who had lost everything. *"And everyone who was in distress, everyone who was in debt, and everyone who was discontented gathered to him. So he became captain over them . . ."* (22:2)

They came to him as people who had been disenfranchised from their inheritance by Saul with the hope of regaining that inheritance. The four hundred quickly grew to six hundred, and they took wives for themselves and had families. It was the beginning of David's kingdom.

These men had pitched their hope upon David. Many had been with him all the days he ran from Saul. They had been with him when he made errors in judgment and put them in jeopardy, even when he would have gone to battle with Philistines against Saul. They had remained faithful through all of that because David was where the kingdom and the inheritance lay.

Now, all is lost. All that they had in terms of a place to stay is burnt. Their families are gone. Those children who were the embodiment of the father's hope for a continued lineage in the coming kingdom are gone. Even their standing among the Philistines is in jeopardy.

David is the leader. He made the decision to defect to the Philistines without asking God the wisdom of such a move. It had worked out well for a while, but now everything is lost, and all the distress and sense of hopelessness and loss returns to these men.

David Inquires of God (30:6-10)

14. How did David respond?

Fear of Saul had driven David to the Philistines, and he had lost family to the Amalekites as well. His own people have become *marah*—that is, bitter, grieved, contentious, rebellious—and they want to stone him. Where do you turn for comfort or strength or advice?

David was distressed. He was *yasar*, which means to be hemmed in or cramped, or besieged on all sides. Sometimes, when you get into that situation, the only place to look for help is up. The text says David strengthened himself in the LORD his God and called for the ephod (unlike Saul who fasted until he was without strength and sought a medium for help).

15. When was the last time David called for the ephod?

Way back in Chapter 23 at the Battle of Keilah. Saul had heard that David had become hemmed in while fighting at Keilah and came out to capture him while he was still in the walled city. David didn't ask the LORD for deliverance as much as an understanding of the situation so that he could then decide how to act, and God gave him the necessary information.

Now David asks for something similar.

> "So David inquired of the LORD, saying, 'Shall I pursue this troop? Shall I overtake them?' And He answered him, 'Pursue, for you shall surely overtake them and without fail recover all.'" (30:8)

Why would David ask that question? Why wouldn't he immediately set out after the Amalekites to take back his family and livestock? He has a huge army at his disposal. Why wouldn't he seek vengeance?

To David's credit, he has learned something about seeking vengeance and he hesitates before going after the Amalekites. He asks the LORD and waits for the LORD's permission to pursue the enemy. He passed that test, and God rewards him for it. David gets the go-ahead with a blessing.

David and six hundred men now head for the desert after the Amalekites. On the way, they come to this place called the Brook

Besor, where David is forced to leave two hundred of his men because they are weary. Keep in mind: they have been on a three-day march to Aphek with the Philistines, and another three-day march back. After a week of being on their feet, they get home to find a crisis waiting for them and another pitched battle in the offing. I imagine some of them were fatigued. Two hundred stay at the brook. The other four hundred cross over with David for the battle.

16. What do we know about the Brook Besor?

It is one of the few streams feeding the desert area as it flows toward the Mediterranean Sea. This is the only time this brook is mentioned in the Bible.

The name Besor means "cheerful or joyful" in the sense of bringing good news or refreshment. It comes from the root word *basar*, meaning "to bear good news or glad tidings." It is found in these verses, which add to the picture of what will transpire here:

> *"How beautiful upon the mountains are the feet of him who brings good news **[basar]**, who proclaims peace, who brings glad tidings **[basar]** of good things, who proclaims salvation, who says to Zion, 'Your God reigns!'"* —Isaiah 52:7

> *"The Spirit of the Lord GOD is upon Me, because the LORD has anointed Me to preach good tidings **[basar]** to the poor; He has sent Me to heal the brokenhearted, to proclaim liberty to the captives, and the opening of the prison to those who are bound; to proclaim the acceptable year of the LORD, and the day of vengeance of our God; to comfort all who mourn"* —Isaiah 61:1-2

17. What kind of good news might come in this situation?

Maybe the defeat of the Amalekites and return of the king with the spoils of war. Maybe the release of captives and deliverance of the men's families. Maybe the day of vengeance and death of Saul? Remember that even as David is waging his war with the Amalekites, Saul is waging war with the Philistines, and it won't end well. But would that be good news for David? David's men would say yes. It would mean an end of the persecution at the very least. And yet, when David hears of Saul's death, he doesn't take it as good news.

> *"But David answered Rechab and Baanah his brother, the sons of Rimmon the Beerothite, and said to them, 'As the LORD lives, who has redeemed my life from all adversity, when someone told me, saying, "Look, Saul is dead," thinking to have brought good news **[basar]**, I arrested him and had him executed in Ziklag—the one who thought I would give him a reward for his news."*—Second Samuel 4:9-10

Isn't that a curious insight into David's thinking, that he would not want his worst enemy killed under such circumstances? Do you ever feel pity on your adversaries like that?

David Sets a Captive Free (30:11-16)

18. What do we know about the Egyptian?

He is the slave of an Amalekite who fell sick and was left behind to die after the Amalekite raid three days before. He has been without food and water all this time. He has information about the raid and can also tell David where the enemy is camped.

19. Where were David and his men three days before?

They were being sent home by the Philistines. This is one of those moments whre you appreciate God's orchestration of things. When David spoke previously to Achish, he had argued over being sent home. He wanted to continue the fight in the Jezreel Valley, but he had no idea of what was happening back at home. He was being called home to save his people, and this Egyptian slave as well.

What random person might you run into three days from now and what kind of impact might you make on their life?

20. What information did the Egyptian give about the raid?

He said the Amalekites had invaded the southern area of the Cherethites, who are described as being on the seacoast of Philistia (Zephaniah 2:5) and in the neighboring territory, which belonged to the house of Caleb in Judah's territory. Ziklag was caught between the coast and Judah's territory, and so was sacked when the Amalekites swept through.

The Philistine Cherethites are later mentioned as becoming a group of mercenary soldiers serving as King David's bodyguard and into the days of Solomon. Cherethite means "executioner" or "life guardsman." (Funny how Achish had intended to make David his bodyguard for life, but instead David will take the Philistines as his body guard. A neat reversal.)

21. What is the Egyptian's condition for helping David?

That David would not kill him or surrender him to the old master again. David must have agreed because the young man then took them to the Amalekite camp.

The Battle (30:17-20)

22. What do we know about the battle?

For all the build-up, there isn't much detail about the battle itself. It lasted one day. David killed all of the Amalekites (except for four hundred young men on camels who escaped) and recovered everything that they had taken from Ziklag, plus the livestock that the Amalekites had captured from other places. All this became David's spoil. In the NKJV, verse 20 is worded as if David himself declared these things as his spoil, but in the Hebrew, the pronouns seem to indicate that the troops who drove the herds were the ones who declared it as David's spoil, not David himself. The NASB has a better translation:

> "So David had captured all the sheep and the cattle which the people drove ahead of the other livestock, and they [the troops] said, 'This is David's plunder.'" —First Samuel 30:20 NASB

So, this jubilant affirmation is a reversal of the men's previous bitterness toward David. But notice how the focus is more on the recovered items and the spoil than the battle.

❾/㉛ Picture Comparison: Fighting Amalekites

David wasn't the only one who fought the Amalekites. Saul was originally tasked with wiping them out in Chapter 15, and his failure to kill King Agag is what led to him losing the kingdom. If he had done a more thorough job, David and his men wouldn't have suffered this loss.

The big issue for Saul in that incident was disobedience, but also self-glorification. The LORD had told him to utterly wipe out the Amalekites, but instead, he and his men kept the best of the spoil for themselves, and Saul paraded it through Judah's territory for his own glorification. And let's not forget that he set up a monument to himself as a way of rubbing in the fact that he had gotten rid of Judah's enemies when they couldn't manage it.

Now we see David being glorified for the battle and his men taking all the spoil from the Amalekites, but without condemnation. What is the difference? Why was what Saul did wrong, but what David did, okay? Is self-glorification an issue here? Actually it is, but the problem is not with David as it was with Saul. It is with some of David's men.

David Rebukes the Men of Belial (30:21-25)

23. What do we know of the men of Belial (30:22)?

In verse 22, the English versions describe this group of men among David's warriors as "wicked and worthless men" ... "evil troublemakers" ... "wicked and base fellows." The phrase in the original Hebrew is "men of Belial." We have seen several examples in First Samuel of people who are called sons/men/women of Belial in the examples of Eli's sons, Nabal, and the rebels who refused to acknowledge Saul as king and gave him no gifts. In general, they are greedy, brutal, and unreasonable.

Are you surprised to find them among David's mighty men? I was. They always seemed so heroic to me.

24. What issue do the men of Belial raise?

They refuse to share the spoil with the two hundred men who were left at the Brook Besor. They feel that only the men who fought the battle deserved to take the spoil, and that those who were left behind should only receive their families back.

Every man in David's company lost not just their family but all their possessions as well. What the men of Belial are proposing is not just to keep the enemy's spoil, but to despoil their own brethren as well—almost as if they are taking their brothers' goods as their wage for having fought the battle for them. In reality, it is simply an act of covetousness.

These men of Belial did not acknowledge God, nor did they see the spoil as a gift being granted to them by God. They thought they had earned it for themselves by their own power and prowess. They valued the material wealth, but did not value their co-laborers or see themselves as one body working toward a goal.

25. What was David's rebuke for these men?

David reminds them that whatever they have been given has been given by God. It is the LORD who had preserved them and delivered the enemy into their hands. Otherwise they would have been defeated.

Then David makes the rule that all who played a part in the endeavor should have their share of the reward. This is the first ordinance David makes as king over his kingdom.

I think David's heart attitude over taking the spoil is what separates him from Saul in their comparison. Saul was a man of Belial at heart.

David Shares the Spoil (30:26-31)

26. Why would David send spoil to the elders?

All the places listed in verses 27-31 are within the wilderness area that David and his men used to patrol between Beersheba and Hebron.

Did these people have a part in the battle? Maybe, maybe not. Maybe some had supported him, or maybe he was just sending them gifts to encourage their support when he became king. His generosity is unparalleled, and it glorifies the LORD and not himself.

APPLY THE PICTURE

David and the Men at Besor: The Prophetic Picture

"The Spirit of the Lord GOD is upon Me, because the LORD has anointed Me to preach good tidings to the poor; He has sent Me to heal the brokenhearted, to proclaim liberty to the captives, and the opening of the prison to those who are bound; to proclaim the acceptable year of the LORD, and the day of vengeance of our God; to comfort all who mourn" —Isaiah 61:1-2

David models the Isaiah 61 passage in a literal, physical way. He brought good tidings to the men who had lost all, comforted those who mourned, and healed the brokenhearted. He proclaimed liberty to a captive, freed those who were imprisoned, and wreaked the LORD's vengeance on Israel's perpetual enemies, the Amalekites.

- **Did Christ model this in His first coming or second (or both)?**

    This is the same passage that Jesus read in the synagogue (Luke 4), the one which He said was fulfilled in their hearing that day. But was His first coming to fulfill this picture in a literal, physical way as David had done and as the people expected? No, not in the physical sense. It was to release captives on a spiritual level, and restore the spiritual relationship with God so that they could then enter the kingdom.

    When those men came to Ziklag on the third day and found the place deserted and their hope gone, they immediately fell into mourning and disillusionment, even to the point of rejecting the king they had placed their hope in.

    I imagine the disciples who found that empty tomb felt the same way.

    But then Jesus reappeared and promised them that while He was leaving for a while, He would come back for them and bring them into His kingdom and the reward. And they took hope from that and continued in that hope as they labored as stewards over the ministry He had placed in their keeping, all the while waiting for the good news of His return.

    I imagine the men left behind at the Brook Besor felt the same way.

David also models the Isaiah 62 passage in a literal, physical way.

> "Indeed the LORD has proclaimed to the end of the world: 'Say to the daughter of Zion, "Surely your salvation is coming; behold, His reward is with Him, and His work before Him."'" —Isaiah 62:11

David is the victorious king who returned to take his throne. He brought with him the reward but also a judgment of the men's works. That is a picture of Christ in His second coming when He will fulfill that picture literally, to which the book of Revelation refers.

> "And behold, I am coming quickly, and My reward is with Me, to give to every one according to his work." —Revelation 22:12

David is the victorious king who returned to take his throne. He brought with him the reward but also a judgment of the men's works. That is a picture of Christ in His second coming when He will fulfill that picture literally.

It is interesting that in our scenario, as the king returns with the spoil to share among his men, the issue of a reward for works would arise between the men waiting at Besor and the men of Belial.

The Men of Belial: Covetousness and Being One Body

Until now, David's men had been working together as one army—one body. They were aligned under one king, pursuing the same reward for the same reasons and in the same way (we thought). But now we find a small group of men among them contesting the right to the reward, and contention and division have sprung up within the group. Covetousness is driving the men of Belial to deny their brothers not just the enemy spoil but what actually belongs to them.

They are faithful to David, but are they aligned with David's values? No. Can we be faithful to Christ and yet not aligned with His values? Yes.

They pursued the king's reward, but did they go about it the right way and for the right reason? No. Can we do the same thing? Yes. We can do it covetously.

- **What is covetousness?**

    When we are in pursuit of the crown, we can run forward while looking back and get ourselves into trouble. This is how David ended up in Philistine lands. He was reactively running away from Saul instead of proactively running toward the goal God had given him.

But we can also get into trouble when we run the race looking from side to side, imagining our co-laborers as our competition for the reward. Paul speaks of running a race to win an individual crown, but we forget that we are part of one spiritual body, all striving for that goal, and we do not compete with one another but help one another toward that shared goal.

When we look from side to side, we begin to compare our performance with others. This is how the body of Christ can come to be treated as a sort of kingdom to be divided and awarded based on merit, which it is not. Ministries can be coveted. Status in the church can be coveted. We can begin to rank one laborer's sacrifice against another and place a value on each other's contribution, which is not our right to judge. It is the King's right to judge. Paul reminds us:

> *"But now I have written to you not to keep company with anyone named a brother, who is sexually immoral, or covetous, or an idolater, or a reviler, or a drunkard, or an extortioner—not even to eat with such a person."* —First Corinthians 5:11

> *"But fornication and all uncleanness or covetousness, let it not even be named among you, as is fitting for saints ... For this you know, that no fornicator, unclean person, nor covetous man, who is an idolater, has any inheritance in the kingdom of Christ and God."* —Ephesians 5:3, 5

> *"Therefore put to death your members which are on the earth: fornication, uncleanness, passion, evil desire, and covetousness, which is idolatry."* —Colossians 3:5

- **Why is covetousness a form of idolatry?**

Because it reveals a shift in our focus away from eternal values and onto physical ones. Jesus said:

> *"...Take heed and beware of covetousness, for one's life does not consist in the abundance of the things he possesses."* - Luke 12:15

> "Let your conduct be without covetousness; be content with such things as you have. For He Himself has said, 'I will never leave you nor forsake you.'" - Hebrews 13:5

Think about that last statement in Hebrews.

- **Why is Christ's promise never to leave us or forsake us a help in battling covetousness?**

    Covetousness stems from a desire for more of what others have, and it drives us to grasp for more than what we need and hoard it. When we covet, it is an act of faithlessness. It communicates our doubt in the LORD's ability to determine what our needs are and to meet them. It also communicates an attitude that what He has given us is not sufficient or of value.

    The first command is to be content with what He provides. The second is to rest on the promise of His eternal presence and care. If He left us, our source for needful things would be gone. If He forsakes (abandons, neglects) us, then it would be up to us to meet our own needs as we see them. But He will not leave us, nor will He forsake us in regards to our needful things or in the promised reward. Our hope of the reward is as sure as the hope of the men at the Brook Besor.

    Paul exhorts the Corinthian church over sharing gifts with co-laborers:

    > "Therefore I thought it necessary to exhort the brethren to go to you ahead of time, and prepare your generous gift beforehand, which you had previously promised, that it may be ready as a matter of generosity and not as a grudging obligation **[pleonexia]**." —Second Corinthians 9:5 Pleonexia means "greedy desire, covetousness."

- **Why is a gift given grudgingly a reflection of covetousness?**

    When we give grudgingly, it is because we are being asked to give up something we believe we have earned and, therefore, own. But these things are not ours. They belong to the King and have been granted to us for a time, but ultimately they are for use toward His purposes.

    The men of Belial felt they had earned the reward and belittled their co-laborers' work as not being worthy in comparison to those who had battled on the front lines. David reminded them that God is the one who gave them the increase of their efforts, and he validated the men at Besor for doing what they could with what strength they had. So Paul reminds us of the same thing.

> *"So then neither he who plants is anything, nor he who waters, but God who gives the increase. Now he who plants and he who waters are one, and each one will receive his own reward according to his own labor."* —First Corinthians 3:7–8

> *"But God has chosen the foolish things of the world to put to shame the wise, and God has chosen the weak things of the world to put to shame the things which are mighty . . . that no flesh should glory in His presence."*—First Corinthians 1:27–29

We are taught how we are to value one another's effort in pursuing our crowns and how we should see our responsibility toward one another in that joint effort so that we do not follow the model of the men of Belial. Other passages on this include First Thessalonians 5:12-15, Hebrews 12:12-15, Romans 12:3-8, First Corinthians 12:20-27.

⓯ ⓱ ⓲ ⓴ / ㉗ ㉘ ㉚ ㉛ Picture Comparison

There is a tremendous symmetry between the opening events of David's exile and the closing events here, in addition to the shared theme of inquiring of God. Let's compare them:

Pictures #16, 17, 18, 20	Pictures #27, 28, 30, 31
(21:10-15) David flees to Gath to escape Saul but is rejected by the Philistines.	**(27:1-28:2, 29:1-11)** David flees to Gath for the same reason but is rejected in the end by the Philistines.
(22:1-2) David faces his crisis of faith at the Cave of Adullam. He is surrounded by his men who are in distress over their loss of inheritance.	**(30:3-6)** David faces another crisis of faith at Ziklag. He is surrounded by his men who are in distress over their loss of family and inheritance.

(22:3-5) David strengthens himself in the LORD (implied in his declaration to wait on the LORD's direction).	**(30:6)** David strengthens himself in the LORD.
(23:1-4) David calls for the ephod and asks the LORD if he should go into battle at Keilah.	**(30:7-8)** David calls for the ephod and asks the LORD if he should go into battle with the Amalekites.
(23:5-13) David goes to battle with the Philistines, delivers the people, and escapes from Saul.	**(30:9-31)** David goes to battle against the Amalekites, and delivers the people (and avoids a fight with Saul in the process).

A tremendous number of practical lessons separate these two episodes in David's life, and while he gained wisdom from those lessons, in the end, the victory hinged on his act of inquiring of God. His decision to decamp to the Philistines was a misstep in both instances, and the scene at Ziklag has the distinct echo of the Cave of Adullam about it as a low point in David's career so far. But what impresses me most is how David rights himself. His determination to strengthen himself in the LORD and wait for the LORD's direction was part of a lesson learned.

The flow of David's account is interrupted in both cases by the accounts of Saul's outrageous behavior, which only heightens the contrast between them. Despite his fear and despair, David's actions appear purposeful and decisive; Saul's reaction, by contrast, is impulsive, impatient, and rash.

32 The Death of Saul

READ

First Samuel 31:1-13

NARRATIVE STRUCTURE

Picture #32 (31:1-13) now switches to Saul's battle. The narrative is divided into two main parts. The first part has a tight chiastic structure that brings the focus down to his death in verse 4. The second section provides a contrast between the Philistines' dishonor of Saul and Saul's final honoring by the men of Jabesh Gilead:

1) The death of Saul (31:1-7)
    (A) The Philistines fought against Israel.
    (B) The men of Israel fled and fell slain on Mount Gilboa.
    (C) The Philistines killed Saul's sons.
    (D) Saul falls in battle.
    (E) Saul asks his armor bearer for mercy but receives none.
    (D) Saul takes his own life.
    (C) Saul, his sons, and armor bearer all died. (repeated statement)
    (B) The army of Israel fled. (repeated statement)
    (A) Therefore all of Israel fled, and the Philistines took all.
2) Saul's final honor (31:8-13)

BUILD THE PICTURE

The Death of Saul (31:1-7)

Unlike David's battle, there is tremendous detail about Saul's death on the battlefield (that's a reversal from their first battles where Saul's battle was given one verse to David's thirteen). The chiastic structure gives you a sense of the totality of the defeat as the battle progresses by stages from the routing and death of Israel's forces overall to the death of Saul's family and finally to the death of Saul himself. The progression from national to

Lesson 18: The King's Reward | 447

family to individual levels of experience is typical of the author's writing style and communicates the all-encompassing consequences of the action.

The chiastic structure brings us to a focus on Saul's plea to his armor bearer to kill him, but his armor bearer refused to do it because he is afraid. I think it is ironic that in this final scene, Saul must appeal to a servant. Throughout his narrative, servants have always been the ones to bolster Saul with help and advice, but now, the servant refuses to help him on account of fear. Fear has pursued Saul, and now it has been the death of him.

Saul was a man who repeatedly took glory from God, and, in the end, the Glory departed from him and left him to his own demise, just as it had with Eli. **Taking glory from God is a sure way to lose a crown and a kingdom.**

27. Where is Abner?

After David's warning to be vigilant in protecting his king, Abner is notably absent when Saul is under attack. Abner survives the battle when all the rest of Saul's family dies. Isn't that curious?

Saul's Final Honor (31:8-13)

The Philistines' brutality in verses 8-10 is contrasted to the compassion of the men of Jabesh Gilead in verses 11-13.

28. What details does the author give about Saul's inglorious death?

- The Philistines cut off his head (as David did with Goliath's).
- They stripped off his armor and put it as a trophy in the temple of the Ashtoreths (like the sword of Goliath being kept in the Tabernacle). The Ashtoreth cult was a prosperity cult that celebrated the gain of riches and wealth. That's an ironic picture. All his life, Saul pursued the reward of earthly riches over the eternal ones, and now in his death, his armor—that symbol of his strength—is on display in the house of those who worship material wealth.
- They published (*basar*-ed, sent the good news) throughout their temples and territory.
- They fastened his body to the walls of Beth Shan. Beth Shan means "house of ease or peacefulness." Again, ironic for a man who didn't value peace in the least.

29. Why would the men of Jabesh Gilead do this honor for Saul and his family?

As we noted in Lesson 6, there is a familial connection between Jabesh Gilead and Saul's hometown of Gibeah. But more than that, Saul's first war as king of Israel was to save the people of Jabesh Gilead from Nahash, king of the Ammonites, who was threatening to bring them into bondage. It was the only stellar moment in all of Saul's career as king, and it earned him the loyalty of the men of Jabesh Gilead, who now honor him by retrieving his body.

APPLY THE PICTURE

When Saul left the medium of En Dor, he knew he was going to die that day. If you knew you were going to die today, you spend your last day battling Philistines?

Why did Saul go to battle when he knew what the outcome would be? Why not avoid it? Why not spend your last day on your own pleasure? Why not seek oblivion your own way? *Why go to battle?*

I think Saul did it for the honor it would give him in the people's eyes. What would the people have said if he hadn't gone to war? That he was afraid of the Philistines? David had never been afraid of the Philistines. (Oof, there's a dig. I couldn't resist.)

Seeking honor has been Saul's motivation all along. It was why he asked Samuel to turn back with him to worship God in front of the people after he had torn Samuel's cloak. Even when he knew all was lost, he sought a way to preserve a facade of honor and respectability in front of the people. Perhaps he thought he could achieve a form of immortality in being remembered by people as a war hero. People can seek immortality this way. It was why, when he saw his own torn cloak in David's hand, he made David swear not to destroy his name from his father's house or cut off his descendants after him, and why he set up the monument to himself at Carmel. His only hope was in being remembered.

To die honorably in battle against an enemy threat is laudable. It is a sacrifice that many men have made throughout time, and we honor them for it, as we should—as the men of Jabesh Gilead attempted to do. God turns the hearts of kings for His own purposes and sends them into these battles that they often fight to their own hurt, and He gives them armies with which to fight. And yet how tragic the death toll and shallow the honor when a king's only motive in war is to take his own glory without acknowledging the King to whom he owes his crown.

To obey is better than sacrifice. Saul's reward would have been so much greater and long-lived if he had just obeyed God and given Him the honor instead of making his own life a tragic sacrifice in pursuit of his own glory. That isn't to say that obedience to God always ends well for us. It can require the sacrifice of our lives, but the reality is that life in our temporal, earthly bodies is a perishable thing to grasp after. **Being remembered by people is a perishable reward.**

God always dealt Saul a tit for tat when it came to the issue of honor. Even here, God granted him his wish for immortality with a divine tweak. So long as the Word of God endures, the name of Saul will be remembered—not as being a good and glorious king, but for his rebellion, dishonor, and failures. The thoughts and schemes he sought to hide are written plainly for all to read, and his reputation will forever live in David's shadow. I imagine such a phenomenal loss of face would occasion much wailing and gnashing of teeth for eternity.

Questions for Reflection

If you knew you were going to die tomorrow and stand before God to have your works assessed for the reward, how would you judge your own effort?

- How have you acknowledged God's sovereignty over your life?
- What courses of action have you taken in life that began with asking God first if you should?
    - » Were you just asking Him for the go-ahead over something you had already purposed to do, or did you wait for an answer?
    - » Did you ever put your plans aside when the answer was silence?
- What kind of legacy do you want to leave behind?

Conclusion

The narrative of David's life continues on through Second Samuel, but the break between First and Second Samuel at Saul's death is a good stopping point in terms of both narrative and theme. It happens roughly at the halfway mark in David's life, and brings a natural transition from David's exile years into the beginning of his official reign. There are a number of loose ends to tie up, namely, the establishing of the David's monarchy, the return of the Ark from its exile, and the wrap up of several character accounts such as Abner and Michal. The picture comparison between Saul and David is by no means complete. First Samuel ends with David having been through kingship training, but he has not yet been given the kingship and the power that comes with it. How will he apply the lessons he has learned in his exile years? How will he deal with his enemies when he has power over them? How will he rule when Saul is taken out of the picture and the pressure is off? Will he remain true to the great King, and be granted the eternal kingship that Saul lost? And then there is the issue of David's men, who came through the exile years with him. They had the same experiences that he had, but did they learn the lessons and apply them?

The story is not over, but the break here at Saul's death brings a natural conclusion to the theme of rewards that has been building through the book of First Samuel. Let's revisit our starting premises and discuss some take-aways from the character models of the brides, priests, and kings.

There are right and wrong kings with whom to align ourselves.

God is always King of the Kingdom. That unchanging truth was established by Hannah in her prayer, in the take-down of the house of Eli, in the mighty works God performed while His Ark was in Philistine hands, and in His removal of Saul from the throne.

Conflict arises when people do not acknowledge and align themselves with the heavenly King. We saw that particularly in Saul. Not only did he come into conflict with God, but all of his earthly relationships deteriorated into conflict as well, including his relationships with his family, his advisor Samuel, and the nation as a whole. Continual, systemic conflict in any social dynamic can be a sign of either a leader whose life is not aligned with God or a people not aligned with God in spite of godly leadership. Wrong attitudes toward authority are usually at the crux of the conflict.

When earthly rulers come on the scene, they can set up a rivalry between themselves and God because they will often define their kingdom (or whatever their realm of authority is) by earthly riches instead of heavenly ones and pursue self-aggrandizing goals. The earthly ruler then presents a difficulty for God's people who are faced with a choice over whether to align their loyalties with God the King or the ruler, who is antagonistically opposed to God and pursuing his own agenda. That was certainly the case for Israel with Saul, but we, too, struggle with this even today.

On one hand, Paul exhorts us:

> *"Let every soul be subject to the governing authorities. For there is no authority except from God, and the authorities that exist are appointed by God. Therefore whoever resists the authority resists the ordinance of God, and those who resist will bring judgment on themselves."*
> —Romans 13:1-2

On the other hand, those same governing authorities can demand that we align ourselves with their worldviews and values that deny God's kingship and undermine His goals, or face persecution for it. So, the ruler's rebellion against God now puts us in conflict with them. Sometimes we can walk that fine line like David did when he lived among the Philistines and served Achish, but that only works for a time. No matter how hard we seek to keep the peace, conflict will find us in the end because there is a line we cannot cross. We may have to take a stand and declare our loyalties at considerable personal loss in this life, just as Jonathan did, but we will have gained a more eternal reward if we stay aligned with God and His anointed King. Jonathan provided a a good example of this in that he did his father's bidding at times, but at other times, he let his loyalties to David drive him and, on occasion, defied his father and faced the king's wrath. He pursued an overall set of goals that aligned with God, but how he reacted in different circumstances varied. What dictated his actions was his understanding of the reward he was pursuing, and the king under which he needed to align himself to gain that reward.

There is a line we cannot cross, but knowing where that line is depends upon our understanding of what kingdom and crown we are pursuing, and how they are defined.

There are right and wrong crowns to pursue.

There is a perishable, earthly crown and an imperishable, heavenly crown. The earthly crown is a tangible one that fixates on earthly riches, material gains, and the satisfaction of carnal lusts, including the lust for intangible things like power, prestige, validation in men's eyes, and influence—things that glorify the man or woman. The earthly crown is temporal and fleeting. Its benefits will not carry into the heavenly kingdom to come. Hophni, Phinehas, Eli, and Saul were all men who pursued earthly crowns, and when they died, they left that crown behind.

By contrast, the imperishable heavenly crown is not based on earthly things, but heavenly qualities such as peace, righteousness, justice, faithfulness, and well-being for all the people. These are the qualities that the King values and on which He builds His kingdom, and if we wish to rule with Him in that kingdom, we must align ourselves with the King's vision and values.

There are right and wrong ways to pursue the crown.

Pursuing the heavenly crown is not about glorifying ourselves but the King who grants us the right to reign with Him. This requires an attitude contrary to the character of people who are only concerned with glorifying themselves as they pursue earthly crowns. Penninah counted her worth by her earthly children, but Hannah glorified God by giving her one son back to the Him for His service and the building up of the His legacy, not her own. A pursuit of justice is a God-glorifying thing, but it cannot stray into vengeance and humiliation, which are self-glorifying, as David learned with Saul and Nabal. Power and authority are given by God, but when people try to take power for themselves and lift themselves up, they must resort to violence, treachery, lies, and oppression to do so. People in pursuit of earthly crowns will rob themselves, their families, and their people of peace and well-being, and fear will take over. We saw that with Saul. To achieve the heavenly crown, it takes self-control, patience, and perseverance to bring our carnal nature into submission even as we push back the influence of the external carnal culture around you. By contrast, those in pursuit of the earthly crown will flail and be tossed about, pursuing what is right in their own eyes, according to their own lusts. We saw that modeled by Eli's family.

Paul exhorts us:

> "And everyone who competes for the prize is temperate in all things. Now they do it to obtain a perishable crown, but we for an imperishable crown. Therefore I run thus: not with uncertainty. Thus I fight: not as one who beats the air. But I discipline my body and bring it into subjection, lest, when I have preached to others, I myself should become disqualified." —First Corinthians 9:25-27

There are right and wrong reasons for pursuing a crown.

Again, you do not pursue the heavenly crown for your own glory or gain, but for God's; nor do you treat the LORD's kingdom like an earthly kingdom to be fought over and coveted like earthly people pursuing an earthly kingdom and reward. The King shares the reward with whomever He chooses. David had to take some of his men to task when they return from the final battle because they would not share the reward with their colaborers. They pursued the right reward, but for the wrong reason.

You do not pursue the heavenly crown out of fear of losing your citizenship in the kingdom. Paul tells Timothy:

> "This is a faithful saying: For if we died with Him, we shall also live with Him. If we endure, we shall also reign with Him. If we deny Him, He also will deny us. If we are faithless, He remains faithful; He cannot deny Himself." —Second Timothy 2:11-13

If we died with Him . . . Obviously we haven't literally died, but as believers we confess a belief in Jesus' death as payment for our sins and His resurrection by which we are granted eternal life. We identify with that death and resurrection, and so we are granted citizenship in the kingdom for that reason.

If we endure, we shall also reign with Him. Now that is another level of experience. Enduring speaks to having been tested over time and learned a few lessons. The right to reign requires more training and a deeper internalization of the King's vision and values. But a loss of the right to reign doesn't mean a loss of citizenship. They are two separate conditions.

Finally, we should not give up a pursuit of the heavenly crown out of fear or worry over earthly needs. In Matthew 6:33, Jesus says:

> *"But seek first the kingdom of God and His righteousness, and all these things shall be added to you."* —Matthew 6:33

He is speaking of the needful earthly things that can cause people to abandon their pursuit of the kingdom. We might consider His statement a bit skeptically in light of the want we see among God's people living under persecution in many parts of the world. To be in pursuit of the heavenly kingdom does not mean you will not suffer want in this life. Quite the opposite. But if you study pictures of the kingdom of heaven, particularly in the Old Testament, you find that it is rich, not just in peace and justice and righteousness, but in jewels and food and all manner of abundance, far beyond earthly standards. Seek first the righteousness, and these things shall be added to you—when you come into *that* kingdom. The key is to remain focused on what is in the kingdom beyond and not be derailed in your pursuit of that kingdom by the conditions you experience in this life, which are fleeting. This world is perishing. What you gain in this world will only be counted as loss in the next, so do not cling to it. Do not be consumed with worry over it. Do not even be concerned for your own life. The persecution you are enduring may seem unending, but it will end.

If there is one take-away that I want you to gain from this book, it would be the cementing in your mind of what reward you are pursuing. Many people have heard the teaching of the kingdom, and yet it has failed to take root or produce fruit in them, as Jesus observed in the Parable of the Sower:

> *"When anyone hears the word of the kingdom, and does not understand it, then the wicked one comes and snatches away what was sown in his heart. This is he who received seed by the wayside. But he who received the seed* [the word of the kingdom] *on stony places, this is he who hears the word and immediately receives it with joy; yet he has no root in himself, but endures only for a while. For when tribulation or persecution arises because of the word, immediately he stumbles. Now he who received seed among the thorns is he who hears the word, and the cares of this world and the deceitfulness of riches choke the word, and he becomes unfruitful. But he who received seed on the good ground is he who hears the word and understands it, who indeed bears fruit and*

produces: some a hundredfold, some sixty, some thirty."
—Matthew 13:19-23

How deeply rooted are you in your pursuit of a crown in the heavenly kingdom? Enough to fight for it? Enough to endure some persecution for it? Is it a lifelong pursuit, or more like a New Year's resolution? How deeply entrenched are you in your pursuits of an earthly reward? Life gets thorny when you get in too deep. Maybe it's time for some reflection.

Questions for Reflection

- How are you giving God glory in your life?
- What are you pursuing in life?
- How are you pursuing it?
- Why are you pursuing it?

www.ingramcontent.com/pod-product-compliance
Lightning Source LLC
Chambersburg PA
CBHW060417010526
44118CB00017B/2251